ACTIVE LEARNING STRATEGIES IN HIGHER EDUCATION: TEACHING FOR LEADERSHIP, INNOVATION, AND CREATIVITY

ACTIVE LEARNING STRATEGIES IN HIGHER EDUCATION: TEACHING FOR LEADERSHIP, INNOVATION, AND CREATIVITY

EDITED BY

ANASTASIA MISSEYANNI
Deree – The American College of Greece, Athens, Greece

MILTIADIS D. LYTRAS
Deree – The American College of Greece, Athens, Greece

PARASKEVI PAPADOPOULOU
Deree – The American College of Greece, Athens, Greece

CHRISTINA MAROULI
Deree – The American College of Greece, Athens, Greece

United Kingdom – North America – Japan – India – Malaysia – China

Emerald Publishing Limited
Howard House, Wagon Lane, Bingley BD16 1WA, UK

First edition 2018

British Library Cataloguing in Publication Data
A catalogue record for this book is available from the British Library

ISBN: 978-1-78714-488-0 (Print)
ISBN: 978-1-78714-487-3 (Online)
ISBN: 978-1-78714-944-1 (Epub)
ISBN: 978-1-78754-937-1 (Paperback)

ISOQAR certified
Management System,
awarded to Emerald
for adherence to
Environmental
standard
ISO 14001:2004.

Certificate Number 1985
ISO 14001

INVESTOR IN PEOPLE

Contents

SECTION III: A VISION FOR HUMANITY THROUGH HIGHER EDUCATION

About the Authors

Cristina Alcaide-Muñoz is a PhD Student in the Business Administration Department at the Public University of Navarre, Spain. She holds a research grant in the Department of Business Administration (Public University of Navarre) to develop the line of research based on operations management, focusing on high-performance manufacturing organizations. Her research encompasses operations management, particularly, quality management and strategic planning. Moreover, she teaches operations management and human resources management at the Public University of Navarre.

César Augusto R. Bastos is a PhD Student in Information Systems at the Federal University of the State of Rio de Janeiro (UNIRIO), Brazil. He has experience in education, focusing on educational technology, and more specifically on the following subjects: Teaching-Using computers, Robotics, and Physics. He attained his Bachelor in Licenciatura em Física from the Universidade Federal do Rio de Janeiro (1988) and Master in Computer Science from the Universidade Federal do Rio de Janeiro (2005), Brazil.

Azril Bacal Roij has a long higher educational career in Perú, México, Sweden, and Spain. He was Humanities Endowment Scholar at Otterbein College (1995), and Visiting Lecturer at UCLA (1996). He is currently affiliated with the Sociology Department, taught a course on Dorothy Lee at the Anthropology Department, Uppsala University. He teaches peace education/culture of peace at "Centro Internacional de Prospectiva y Altos Estudios" (CIPAE), Puebla, México. He held academic administrative posts in Perú and México. His work covers various fields, and he has authored books, chapters, and journal articles on: ethnicity, citizenship, national identity, higher education, peace education, rural development, and intercultural dialogue.

María Graciela Badilla-Quintana is Assistant Professor and Associate Researcher at CIEDE-UCSC, Universidad Católica de la Santísima Concepción, Chile. She is a Journalist, Licentiate in Social Communication, Teacher of Primary Education, Master in Education, and PhD in Pedagogical Investigation. Currently, she is Director of the Doctoral in Education program, and Editor-in-Chief of the *REXE Journal*.

Her research focuses on ICT integration on Educational Innovation and includes immersive virtual worlds and gamification. Between 2016 and 2018 she is Visiting Researcher (postdoc) in the Laboratory for Embodied Cognition and Embodied Games at Arizona State University, USA thanks to Becas Chile scholarship.

Wendy Barber holds a BPHE, BEd, Med, and a PhD from the University of Toronto. She is Assistant Professor in the Faculty of Education at the University of Ontario Institute of Technology in Oshawa, Canada and has also been a program director in that faculty. Her research interests are: Health and Physical Education, wearable technologies for fitness and well-being, as well as working in the Education Informatics Lab (EILab.ca) developing leading edge frameworks for Fully Online Learning Communities. She is a passionate advocate for teacher education, and she currently teaches in both graduate and undergraduate programs.

Marcelo Careaga Butter is Associate Professor and Associate Researcher at CIEDE-UCSC, Universidad Católica de la Santísima Concepción, Chile. He is Professor of History and Geography, Master in Education (in curriculum specialty) and has a PhD in Philosophy and Educational Sciences. Currently, he is Head of the Educational Computer and Knowledge Management Unit. His research focuses on Cybernetic Curriculum, Knowledge Management and Virtual Epistemology, and Integration of ICT in educational and intercultural contexts. Currently, he is a postdoctoral fellow in the final phase related to ICT and Knowledge Management in intercultural contexts at the University of Bristol, UK.

Zbyněk Filipi has a Master's Degree in Pedagogy, specialized in Computer Science, and a Doctorate in Pedagogy. He works at the Department of Computer Science and Educational Technology at the Faculty of Education at the University of West Bohemia in Pilsen, Czech Republic, which provides training for pre-service teachers, focused on computer science. He lectures on didactics and digital literacy. He is the author and co-author of articles focused on ICT in education. He has gained a wide range of experience in implementing projects for the professional development of teachers.

Inés González-González is a Professor in the Business Administration Department of the Public University of Navarre, Spain. She has a PhD in Business Administration – Accounting and Finances – from the University of Valladolid, and Executive MBA for the European School

Business of Madrid, both in Spain. She has worked as a Manager at several companies linked to Public Administration, and has worked as a Strategy Consultant. She has written more than 40 papers in prestigious international journals, having presented communications in national and international Congresses, and is directing doctoral research theses. She was Senior Researcher at i2TIC. Award in Education and Emerging Technology, 2017 awarded by The Financial Studies Center (CFS).

Ana Isabel Jimenez-Zarco is Associate Professor in the Business and Economic Studies of the Open University of Catalonia, Spain. She was Senior Researcher at i2TIC. She has PhD in Economics and Business from the University of Castilla La Mancha and Postgraduate in Building Models in Ecology and Natural Resource Management from the Polytechnic University of Catalonia. Both universities are in Spain. She was Evaluator at the European Union Program "Marie Sklodowska-Curie Actions Innovative Training Networks." She is an author of over 70 national and international publications. Award in Education and Emerging Technology, 2017 awarded by The Financial Studies Center (CFS).

Gretchen Kreahling McKay received a BA in Art at Colby College, USA, and her MA and PhD in the History of Art from the University of Virginia, USA. Currently, she is Professor of Art History and Chair of the Department of Art and Art History at McDaniel College, USA, and a speaker and consultant on active learning in the higher education classroom. She was the recipient of the 2015 Ira G. Zepp Distinguished Teaching Award at McDaniel College. She is also the Faculty Mentor to the McDaniel College Green Terror football team.

Miltiadis D. Lytras is Research Professor of Information Systems at Deree – The American College of Greece, with a research focus on semantic web, knowledge management, and e-learning, with more than 100 publications. He has authored/(co-)edited more than 45 special issues in international journals and 42 books. He has served as the (Co) Editor-in-Chief of 8 international journals (e.g., *International Journal on Semantic Web and Information Systems, International Journal of Knowledge Society Research, International Journal of Knowledge and Learning, International Journal of Technology Enhanced Learning*).

Christina Marouli is Assistant Professor of Environmental Studies at Deree – The American College of Greece. She has a long career as Educator in diverse contexts and as Consultant on environmental issues, while she has worked for years in non-governmental organizations for women and children. She has founded and directed the Center of Excellence for Sustainability at the American College of Greece. She has been a recipient of a Fulbright scholarship for research on multicultural environmental education and has significant experience in experiential and active learning as well as in collaborative teaching and learning practices.

Anastasia Misseyanni is Associate Professor of Environmental Studies at Deree − The American College of Greece. She has research experience in the fields of Biochemistry and Molecular Biology. Her present research interests focus on innovative teaching and learning strategies in higher education and science pedagogy, with emphasis on active learning; also on Mediterranean biodiversity, green roofs, and sustainability in higher education. She has developed and taught many undergraduate natural science and environmental studies courses. She is coordinator of the Deree Environmental Studies program and serves as Head of the Department of Science and Mathematics at Deree − The American College of Greece.

Ronney Moreira de Castro graduated in Systems Analysis from the Higher Education Center of Juiz de Fora, Brazil. He is a Specialist in Computer Science as well as an MSc, both from the Federal University of Viçosa, Brazil, and a PhD Student in Information Systems at the Federal University of the State of Rio de Janeiro (UNIRIO), Brazil. He is currently Professor and Coordinator of the Bachelor of Information Systems at Granbery Methodist College, Brazil. He has experience in Computer Science, with emphasis on Software Engineering and Web projects. His research is currently focused on the area of computer education, more specifically on Active Learning.

Daniel Moscovici is Associate Professor of Environmental Studies & Sustainability at Stockton University, USA. He has completed a PhD in Environmental Planning & MS in Environmental Studies at the University of Pennsylvania, USA, and an MBA at Villanova University, USA. His main areas of interest include natural resource management, environmental pedagogy, regional planning, and land conservation.

William (Bill) Muirhead is the founding Associate Provost at UOIT. He completed a PhD at the University of Alberta, Canada, in the area of online and distance education. An active researcher, he has attracted and participated in more than $8m of funding. He is the recipient of numerous awards including those from the Government of Alberta,

Canadian Association for Distance Education, Association for Media in Education, Industry Canada, and from UOIT for Excellence in Leading Teams. He has conducted research on aspects of online education, learning technology infrastructure development, and digital literacy in health-related fields.

Paraskevi Papadopoulou is Professor of Biology at Deree – The American College of Greece. Her research interests are focused in the fields of Structural Biology/Molecular Biophysics and Bioinformatics. She contributed to the development of genetic testing protocols for rare genetic diseases. Her current research engagement is on Mediterranean biodiversity and green roofs, in addition to higher education research and innovative ways of teaching and learning in STEM disciplines and big data analytics in Bioinformatics and Healthcare. She has served as Head of the Department of Science, Technology and Mathematics at Deree – The American College of Greece for 6 years.

Maria Cristina Pfeiffer Fernandes graduated in Engenharia Elétrica from Pontifícia Universidade Católica do Rio de Janeiro (1977), Brazil is Master in Production Engineering from Universidade Federal do Rio de Janeiro (1984), and has a PhD in Production Engineering from Universidade Federal do Rio de Janeiro (1989), Brazil. She has experience in education, with a focus on the following subjects: distance learning, collaborative learning, web-based learning environment, web, and education.

Linda Pospisilova is a University Teacher of Specific and Academic English in Bachelor, Master, and Doctoral programs of the Faculty of Chemical Technology, University of Pardubice, Czech Republic, with years of experience in eLearning and ePortfolio areas. She researches ePortfolio, student autonomy, and goal setting in language learning and deals with LMS Moodle course management, methodology, and administration. She is also a part of the Czech Padagogy Wheel translation team, an author of several online courses which have been awarded EUNIS prizes, and a Mahara system administrator.

Eva Rimbau-Gilabert is a Human Resources Lecturer at the Economics and Business Faculty of the Universitat Oberta de Catalunya (Open University of Catalonia, UOC, Spain) and a member of the Digital Business Research Group (DigiBiz). Since 2004, she has taught at the UOC in the areas of human resource management, change management, and corporate social responsibility. She is also a member of the UOC's Academic Committee for the Doctoral Programme in

Information and Knowledge Society. She has served as Academic Director of several programs: the Bachelor's Degree in Labour Sciences, the Master's Degree in Work Safety, and the Graduate Studies of Business and Economics.

Lorayne Robertson is Associate Professor in the Faculty of Education at the University of Ontario Institute of Technology in Ontario, Canada. She specializes in online course design, program design, and quality assurance. Other research interests include investigations of the student experience and instructor role in polysynchronous online environments, with a particular focus on digital technologies and assistive technologies at the point of instruction in applied settings such as schools, colleges, and higher education. She is a former school principal, district superintendent, and education officer in Ontario, earning her doctorate at the University of Toronto, Canada.

Lucie Rohlíková has focused on higher education, distance education, and the use of technologies in education since 1998, and has been publishing her work on higher education continuously since then. She has gathered extensive practical experience in the use of blended learning for the training of academic staff, and has implemented several projects with a specific focus on training pre-service teachers and new faculty members. Since 2010, she has popularized mobile technologies enhanced learning, and she leads the Czech Pedagogy Wheel Team.

Sean W. M. Siqueira is Associate Professor at the Federal University of the State of Rio de Janeiro (UNIRIO), Brazil. He is Editor-in-Chief of the *RBIE: Brazilian Journal on Computers in Education*. He is the founder and coordinator of the Semantics and Learning research group and is a member of the special committees on Computers and Education (CEIE) and on Information Systems (CESI), both from the Brazilian Computer Society (SBC). His research interests are knowledge representation, web science (including social and semantic web), and advanced technologies for teaching and learning.

Eileen Sepúlveda-Valenzuela is an English Teacher from Universidad Católica de la Santísima Concepción, Chile. She has a Master in Technology and Knowledge Management in Education. She is a second year PhD Student at the University of Bristol, UK, thanks to Becas Chile scholarship. She has researched on the use of digital technology in education and has worked as research assistant for Universidad Católica de la Santísima Concepción. Currently, she is researching about intercultural dialogue in Chilean higher education.

Peter J. Shaw is Associate Professor at the University of Southampton, UK, specializing in interdisciplinary environmental science. He has a diverse background, holding degrees in Physics, Environmental and Ecological Sciences, and Biology. His interests in education encompass pollution, freshwater and marine science, resource and waste management, and contemporary environmental issues. He is a long-standing executive member of the UK's Committee of Heads of Environmental Sciences through which he has been involved with developing Professional Body accreditation of Environmental Science degrees.

Susan Stetson-Tiligadas has a PhD in Education with a specialization in Instructional Design for Online Learning. She has been teaching at Deree – The American College of Greece since 2006 in the English for Academic Purposes program and more recently in the MA TESOL program. She also helped develop the Online Faculty Training program and co-facilitates this program at the college. As an instructional designer, she has worked with subject-matter experts in Psychology, TESOL, Music, and Writing. Her research interests include motivational instructional strategies, instructional design theories, learner-centered instruction, and online professional development.

Emma Witt is Assistant Professor of Environmental Studies at Stockton University, a position she has held since September 2014. She completed a PhD in soil science at the University of Kentucky and an MS at the University of Minnesota. Her main areas of interest include implementing a range of active learning techniques in the classroom and field, as well as researching hydrologic responses to disturbance.

Preface

Undoubtedly, higher education is in an era of transition. The quest for fast integration of knowledge into innovative services and products, capable of promoting a socially inclusive sustainability vision for our societies, challenges the design of academic programs as well as the priorities of higher education top administrators and policy officers.

At the same time, the young generation is more and more attached to the use of technology in their daily lives; they have transformed into technology advocates, with various side effects — mainly their motivation not to use the monolithic, static learning content that is promoted in the traditional learning paradigm for decades.

In another context, the archetypal vision and mission of the academic learning process, especially as it relates to the cultivation of active citizens, personalities with critical thinking and creativity, aiming to contribute to better societies, is also being reconsidered.

What should be the vision for the learning strategies in higher education of our century? Which are the determinants of a learning philosophy promoting knowledge dissemination, the development of skills and competencies, and the ethos and social responsibility of students? Which is a viable and sustainable model for the integration of the numerous learning technologies that appear every few years and are promoted as panacea for any learning insufficiency? How can we facilitate a collaborative, distributed culture of mutual understanding, respect, and cross-fertilization between peers, disciplines, institutions all over the world? Is there a way in our turbulent times to cultivate peace-making processes and long-term sustainable — i.e., simultaneously environmentally friendly, socially just, and economically viable — interactions between nations, religions, and cultures based on shared values incorporated in modern educational systems? Which is, at the end of the day, the best contribution of education to the well-being and happiness of all the stakeholders involved?

With such big questions, our book is a rather humble effort to reposition the focus of our scientific teaching and learning community to the basics. In our opinion, active learning is not a simple didactic approach in a complex world. We define active learning as a holistic philosophy for a humanistic vision in higher education, where individuals, groups, institutions, and nations contribute to a global transformation in balance with nature and with respect toward nature as well. Active learning is a transformative process that brings together knowledge artifacts, learning contexts, humans, and social problems as well as challenges for the present and future of our societies. The ultimate contribution of active learning is an innovative way of thinking, where reality and truth are not a case of black and white, where teaching and learning are an exploratory journey to the wealth of knowledge and different realities, and, finally, where nothing is taken for granted but the provision of a fruitful learning context, full of interactions, that can reveal to everyone his or her own path to inner achievement and fulfillment.

Active learning in our approach is a new way of understanding the dialogue between the accumulated knowledge, the inner inquiry of each person for personal development, and the social exploration for securing a better world for all. Active learning is about balancing personal motivation for self-fulfillment with group capacities for high impact contributions in business, culture, education, and every domain of human activity.

Active learning is a holistic approach. It is transparent in any aspect of higher education and has direct implications and prerequisites for administration, faculty, government, and various stakeholders. The resources required for active learning implementation should be investments with great return in terms of social value, sustainability, and development.

Active learning, furthermore, is about linking human minds and souls in a creative spiral of knowledge transformation and skills development at individual, group, and institutional level. It is hard to accept this in the context of a technocratic society where the specialization and the focus on core disciplines is something like an axiom.

Active learning is about interdisciplinary integration and intersection. This is an additional challenge for higher education. Without a systematic process of launching interdisciplinary programs and curricula, there will always be a critical lack of creativity and impact. It is time to link innovation with active learning strategies that interact with many disciplines at the same time. This will bring back the focus of education to the object of the matter. The learner is not an abstract concept. It is a complex entity with a personality, a psychological background, and cognitive capacities, developing within a certain social context. It is a real challenge for our times to reconsider the motivation we should prompt in the young generation. If the motivation is strictly related to narrow economic models of return on investment or employability terms, our society will always be in lack of responsive actions to address the big social challenges of our times.

Our *Active Learning Strategies in Higher Education* is in fact a journey. At the end of its reading, researchers, academics, policy makers, and students will realize that this is just the beginning. This is because active learning requires a personal vision: the vision of an out-of-the-box education – to consider your learning process as a constructive process that brings you together with other people from all over the world. Active learning is about modifying your context, from the micro-world of your personal beliefs and understandings to a whole universe of magnificent human contributions.

We do believe that our times are the most suitable for such a humanistic shift in the design and delivery of programs in higher education. Global collaboration for the big challenges of our times, such as the preservation of our planet, poverty, socially inclusive and just development, smart and sustainable cities, mutual respect, and generation of new knowledge for providing sustainable solutions to social problems, is the vision for the active learning philosophy we propose. At the end of the day, it is about bringing more light into our souls. We do believe that we all deserve it. Let us imagine and work for a better world for all, for us – now and the next generations – and for all living beings. Learning can always make the difference, as it decreases ignorance which feeds our problems, can mobilize emotions, and can motivate our action.

Our next planned edition goes a step further. It provides practical guidelines for active learning that can lead to social transformation.

People can always make it! Margaret Mead – a renowned anthropologist – said "Never doubt that a small group of thoughtful, committed citizens can change the world. Indeed, it is the only thing that ever has." We do believe in the capacity of the global community of creative minds and caring individuals to use active learning for the development of a new culture that will lead to more sustainable societies.

Acknowledgments

We are grateful to the great scholars and academics who contributed to this edition.

Introduction

Anastasia Misseyanni, Miltiadis D. Lytras,
Paraskevi Papadopoulou and Christina Marouli

In the 21st century knowledge society, higher education (HE) is experiencing a multidimensional transition. Shifting from the traditional, lecture-focused classroom setting to more learner-centered environments, integration of knowledge from different disciplines, interdisciplinary collaborations, use of information and communication technologies (ICTs) to enhance learning, globalization, and internationalization of HE, as well as emphasis on sustainability are some of the elements of this transition. Innovation and creativity are key drivers of change. HE is a significant tool for developing well-informed and knowledgeable citizens, well prepared to face the international job market; it also plays an important role in developing socially responsible and creative individuals, ready to address contemporary global challenges; these roles need to be strengthened and reconceived today.

With this book, we attempt to explore active learning strategies used in HE; strategies that promote leadership, innovation, and creativity. Active learning is a term used by educators to describe a more "learner-centered" approach to teaching. It involves students "doing" things and reflecting on what they are doing. Active learning practices may range from simple methods such as interactive lectures and class discussion to case study analysis, role-playing, experiential learning, peer teaching, and flipped lessons. Active learning may involve problem-based, visual-based, collaborative, project-based, or game-based learning. The editors' long teaching experience in natural sciences and information technology has led to an initial focus on strategies used in Science,

Active Learning Strategies in Higher Education: Teaching for Leadership,
Innovation, and Creativity, 1–13
Copyright © 2018 by Emerald Publishing Limited
All rights of reproduction in any form reserved
ISBN: 978-1-78714-488-0

Technology, Engineering, and Mathematics (STEM) disciplines; the book has been enriched, however, with chapters describing learning experiences from other disciplines as well. The challenge of having to deliver large volumes of information while escaping from the traditional lecture approach and trying to promote deeper learning by stimulating student engagement, motivation, and confidence is addressed. Active learning empowers learners, as it helps them develop more responsibility, participate in the construction of knowledge, and challenge mainstream thinking and opinions. And this is an essential step in the development of informed, socially responsible, and creative individuals.

The use of ICTs in promoting an active learning environment is also explored in this book. Emerging technologies and applications for Science, Technology, Engineering, Arts, and Mathematics (STEAM) Education and other disciplines have received growing attention in recent years from various perspectives. A key strategic shift in the focus of educational strategies is evident, from content-oriented approaches to a collaborative, dynamic, media-enriched evolving paradigm. It seems that we are at a crossroad where the traditional classroom-based model of education has to be critically enriched with technology-enabled, value-added components. Active learning, enhanced and supported by the use of ICTs, is a key element leading toward the new model in HE.

The overall scope and main objective of the book is to expose the reader to the latest developments in active learning strategies used in HE, to provide good examples of such strategies, and to inspire teaching for leadership, innovation, and creativity. The book also aims to serve as a reference edition as well as a guide for teachers, professionals, and researchers; it can also be used as a teaching material at undergraduate and/or graduate level in the relevant domain.

The book is divided into three main sections. The first section is more theoretical and includes two chapters that elaborate on the epistemology of Active Learning and its unique contribution to HE. Steps in designing active learning experiences based on different learning theories are also outlined.

In the second section, the authors' teaching experiences in undergraduate and graduate courses are presented in the form of "stories." Eleven different case studies, which explore different active learning approaches used in STEAM and other disciplines, are presented. This section starts with a more general chapter on "stories" from STEM disciplines and continues with two chapters relevant to the environmental studies field, with emphasis on formative assessment and fieldwork as ways to increase learning and promote student engagement. A chapter on how to engage non-history students in an art history course provides an example of active learning in Arts/Humanities. Seven chapters in the second section include case studies that explore the use of ICTs in promoting active learning. Two of these chapters discuss online learning; one of them also emphasizes collaborative learning. Two chapters on technology-enhanced learning for pre-service teachers, a chapter on active learning in an Information Systems course, a chapter on the use of ICTs in an Accounting course, and a chapter on the use of digital portfolios are also included. The overall aim of this section is to identify and communicate innovative teaching and learning strategies, discuss challenges faced, and provide a guide for future studies on increasing learning effectiveness in different disciplines. It also aims to provide examples of how ICTs can improve the learner's experience and to show how new, advanced learning designs and educational models can expand the frontiers in applied learning technologies toward smart learning and a knowledge society vision.

In the last section, a new vision for HE is presented. A debate paper on the pedagogical legacies of Dorothy Lee and Paulo Freire and a chapter on a new vision for HE based on lessons from Education for the Environment and Sustainability are included. This section provides insights for strategic policy making in HE, as well as a guide for teaching and learning that is fit for contemporary societies that need cultural and social transformations to effectively face significant environmental, social, and economic challenges.

The editors of this book aim to promote a humanistic vision in universities and colleges, linking education to sustainable development,[1] prosperity, and socially cohesive and caring communities. They suggest that HE − and all education − today should be appropriately designed for individual change, empowerment, integration, and social transformation. As authors and editors of this book, we believe it is a unique value proposition for HE.

---

[1]In this book, we use sustainable development to underline the need for a balanced and harmonious relationship between human societies and the environment, an integrated approach to environment − society − economy and culture. Sustainable development and sustainability imply an integrated and deeply ethical approach, looking forward to the future, as was discussed in the document "Our Common Future" prepared by the United Nations World Commission on Environment and Development, 1987.

As stated above, the target audience of this book are educators and researchers, undergraduate and graduate students in the area of teaching and learning in HE. The book can also serve as a guide for educators and researchers; it can provide insights into pedagogies of engagement and give lessons and ideas for teaching and learning in specific fields. It may become a start for exchanging ideas and promoting research on the scholarship of teaching in HE.

A more detailed summary of the content of the chapters based on the chapter abstracts is presented below.

Chapter 1 concerns itself primarily with questions of how students in HE studies can best acquire, apply, create, and share knowledge. It examines the epistemological claims of the supporters and detractors of active learning while simultaneously exploring the nascence and development of some of the major understandings that presently underpin an epistemology of active learning. While the focus of earlier works may have been on changes that HE instructors should make to improve student understanding of key STEM concepts, this chapter addresses changes in the roles of both students and instructors as the co-creators of active learning environments and learning communities. A particular focus is given to the significance of metacognition as a critical skill that enables students to assess their own learning and also critically assess sources of information. The chapter includes a framework that indicates trends toward high-impact active learning skills for students in STEM HE and the research which theorizes and supports these new instructional imperatives.

Chapter 2 outlines the potential steps to take in designing active learning experiences based on several theories underlying the learning process. The chapter examines theories of learning and instruction including information processing, schema acquisition, and cognitive load theory. An explanation of how these theories support problem-centered learning as well as a rationale for the need to help learners develop domain-general, flexible problem-solving skills that will transfer to future needs and contexts is presented. The second half of the chapter focuses on designing active learning experiences based on: the selection of real-world problems as the foundation for learning, activating prior knowledge, demonstration of the process or concept, multiple opportunities for practice with relevant scaffolding, and the chance to integrate that knowledge into the learners' own context. Examples of assessments, strategies, and activities to foster active, problem-centered learning drawn from the literature are also provided.

Chapter 3 discusses the active learning strategies used in STEM disciplines and analyzes the potential of active learning to redefine the value proposition in academic institutions. After providing the theoretical underpinnings of active learning as an evolving practice, an attempt is made to connect it with different learning theories and present an integrative model in which institutional strategies, learning strategy, and ICTs work synergistically toward the development of knowledge and skills. In this chapter, the authors present the results of a survey examining "stories" of active learning from the STEM disciplines, identifying good teaching practices and discussing challenges and lessons learnt. The key idea is that active engagement and participation of students is based on faculty commitments and inspiration and mentoring by faculty. The authors finally present a stage model for the implementation of active learning practices in HE. Emphasis is placed on a new vision for HE, based on systematic planning, implementation and evaluation of active learning methods used, collaboration, engagement with society and industry, innovation and sustainability, for a better world for all.

Chapter 4 is a case study from the environmental science field. It focuses on a specific first-year course (module) offered at the University of Southampton, UK. "Environmental Science: Concepts and Communication" aids students in their journey into Environmental Science by preparing them to face the challenges of university study and beyond. It thus engages students in independent learning and provides them with opportunities to develop and enhance the skills necessary to do so. Formative and student-led activities and tasks are considered important tools to achieve this aim. This chapter provides an overview of selected formative and student-led activities with focus on methods and approaches, values and benefits, and the practicalities of delivery. Three assessments are reviewed: a practice essay, a communication exercise, and a practice presentation. The intended benefits and value of these assessments are (1) engagement with environmental issues and topics, and (2) development and enhancement of study skills. The value of such work is only realized, however, with student engagement. Delivering this module has demonstrated that formative elements are most effective when orientated to tutor group activities. Motivation for engagement appears most effective when the visibility − or absence − of students' work is brought to the foreground though working in small groups. There is added value in that the collation and sharing of feedback within a small group permits students to learn not only from their own work but also from the work of others.

Chapter 5 focuses on field-based education for environmental studies which has been a foundational principle for the Environmental Studies program at Stockton University, and began in 1971. Located within the 445,000-hectare Pinelands National Reserve, on an 800-hectare campus near Atlantic City, New Jersey, USA, two professors in the program discuss their rationale and experiences teaching students about the environment within the environment. Expounding on the interdisciplinary literature of field-based learning, the authors present four unique case studies including local and regional experiences, as well as student learning abroad. The first case proposes that learning outdoors might be beneficial for students with learning disabilities. This is exemplified during a one-week field study to the 2.4-million-hectare Adirondack Park & Preserve. The second instance reveals the benefits of working with local towns and environments; acting as consultants in a multidisciplinary capstone experience. Next, the authors show how on campus data collection and hypothesis formulation help students to learn about environmental design and statistical analysis. Finally, an international trip to the Caribbean opens the minds of students through a service learning project. While on campus, in town, across the United States or at an international destination, learning in the field gives students the opportunity to expand their knowledge through field-based active learning strategies.

Chapter 6 explores issues of quality teaching, learning, and assessment in HE courses from the perspective of teaching fully online (polysynchronous) courses in undergraduate and graduate programs in education at a technology university in Ontario, Canada. Online courses offer unique opportunities to capitalize on students' and professors' digital capabilities gained in out-of-school learning and apply them to an in-school, technology-enabled learning environment. The critical and reflective arguments in this chapter are informed by theories of online learning and research on active learning pedagogies. Digital technologies have opened new spaces for HE which should be dedicated to creating high-quality learning environments and high-quality assessment. Moving a course online does not guarantee that students will be able to meet the course outcomes more readily, or that they will necessarily understand key concepts more easily than previously in the physically co-present course environments. All students in HE need opportunities to seek, critique, and construct knowledge together and then transfer newly-acquired skills from their coursework to the worlds of work, service, and life. The emergence of new online learning spaces helps us to re-examine present higher education pedagogies in very deliberate ways to continue, to maintain, or to improve the quality of student learning in HE. In this chapter, active learning in fully online learning spaces is the broad theme through which teaching, learning, and assessment strategies are re-considered. The key elements of the authors' theoretical framework for active learning include (1) deliberate pedagogies to establish the online classroom environment; (2) student ownership of learning activities; and (3) high-quality assessment strategies.

Chapter 7 describes and analyzes the result of an active, co-operative learning design adopted in "Change Management," an elective course in the University of Catalunya, Spain, which is a fully online university. The chapter describes the context and the foundation that supports the learning design, outlines the learning activities and their evolution, and presents the results of a student survey to assess the effectiveness of the design in reaching its main goals. The results of the survey suggest that students perceived this design as enhancing their teamwork competence, while being interesting and motivating, and useful to learn the course's content. Therefore, the desired goals were attained and the design was kept, with minor changes, in subsequent editions of the course. In addition, students without prior teamwork experience valued collaborative activities more than students who had previously worked in teams in other subjects of their degrees. In contrast, no differences were found for individual learning activities. This suggests that the design can be useful in introductory courses where students are asked for the first time to learn in virtual teams.

Chapter 8 is a case study from Humanities and Arts. It presents how an instructor in a Roman Art class at a US University managed to engage five football players; it provides an account of how she tried to engage the class as a whole. The author discusses the commitment she made to making each class period one in which an active learning technique was used, often paired with some lecture, sometimes not, to engage students and help them learn about Roman Art and Architecture. She discusses the type of assignments she thought would work, based on research and her own observation, as well as the results of a focus group held with the football players a year later. Football players tend to be kinetic learners and thus were chosen as the follow-up to see how the active learning techniques in this class met objectives. Specifically, this chapter discusses the inclusion of a Reacting to the Past game, a research project on "Daily Life in Ancient Rome," case studies where students had to create an artifact (a list, a floor plan, a propaganda program, etc.) in response to a prompt, and presentations on different methodologies of interpreting an image from a Pompeiian tavern.

Chapter 9 presents innovative approaches to active learning that were introduced into the teaching of pre-service teachers at the Faculty of Education of University of West Bohemia, Pilsen, in the Czech Republic. Over the last three years, the Technology Enhanced Learning course has seen substantial innovations in both the content and use of teaching strategies designed to prepare the students for their professional lives. The whole update of the course was implemented using the results of action research — all individual changes were rigorously tracked and analyzed. Besides practical activities with tablets and smartphones, during which students familiarize themselves with various types of applications and reflect on their use in teaching, the course was extended by the use of practical aids for the efficient inclusion of mobile technologies for teaching — the Czech version of Allan Carrington's Padagogy Wheel. During the teaching, students work with internet applications and cloud services. Teaching is complemented with communication on the Facebook social network. A close link to professional life is achieved through workshops, which in-service teachers from elementary and high schools provide to pre-service teachers. A significant part of the teaching consists of co-operative projects between pre-service teachers and pupils of elementary schools. The innovative approach to active teaching in the Technology Enhanced Learning course is apparent even during the exam. In the course of the exam, students process, present, and defend a lesson plan for the implementation of an activity using digital technologies.

Chapter 10 examines how to apply effective teaching and learning strategies as an essential component in understanding the complexity of human groups, especially in educational contexts. To look for the relationship between the contributions that people make, it is critical to understand the singularities of cultures when developing innovations and to foster leadership in education. This chapter presents an experience developed in HE in Chile, focused on the ability of pre-service teachers to enhance the development of individual talents as an active teaching and learning strategy that aims to create a society made up of integrally developed people in educational contexts. In addition, the authors make reference to the use of virtual learning environments as a vehicle to connect students between physical and virtual boundaries. This strategy is based on the Talent Management Model which was implemented in intercultural primary schools by professors and pre-service teachers from the south of Chile. The virtuality dimension promoted the detection of individual traits of students and contributed to the development of a cultural identity. Additionally, it offered theoretical and practical knowledge that implied an innovation in the training of future teachers.

Chapter 11 examines how the use of active learning techniques can significantly improve the teaching–learning process in Information Systems courses, since the content is explored in a more interactive, participative, and relaxed way. Although expositive classes are still broadly used in Brazil, in this chapter the authors present some active learning techniques as well as experiences of their application in Information Systems K-12, undergraduate and graduate courses in Brazil. As a result, the authors have noticed learning has been more effective and students have been motivated by the use of these active learning techniques. Although used in the context of Information System courses, the techniques could be adapted to other scenarios.

Chapter 12 presents a case study from the field of Accounting. Even though students increasingly demand the integration of the varied technologies and mobile devices in the learning environment, educational systems of the public universities continue to be traditional. In this chapter, a teaching innovation for first-year university students using the Socrative app is presented. The authors of this chapter investigate how the university can combine ICT with traditional methodologies of learning, in order to increase student interest in the subject and awakening students' passion and vocation for the accounting area.

Chapter 13 makes reference to a constant growth in digital portfolio use in tertiary education in the recent years. Portfolios are used by educational institutions for assessment, as a showcase of both student and institution work, and with an increasing trend also as a tool for higher employability of graduates and support of lifelong learning. This chapter introduces concepts of portfolio, digital portfolio, language portfolio, autonomy, and self-assessment. It approaches both positivist and constructivist paradigms of digital portfolio and presents examples of ePortfolio implementation at the University of Pardubice, Czech Republic. Selected examples of good practice with respect to autonomous learning, experiential learning, and international cooperation are also given.

Chapter 14 can be described as a debate paper in which the author reintroduces the anthropological and pedagogical insights of Dorothy Lee and Paulo Freire in the ongoing debate on active learning and HE. These insights refer in the case of Dorothy Lee, on "valuing the self" of the student, and additionally on learning (values) from "remote

cultures," and last but not least on the meaning of freedom and autonomy in the teaching/learning process. The author points a few selected
lessons and contributions from Freire: (1) the socio-cultural anchor of
freedom and autonomy, (2) the view of education as a tool for raising-
awareness, critical thinking, inspiration, hope, empowerment, cultural
action, and social transformation, and (3) the view on citizenship education. The author discusses in this regard, the significant role assigned by
Dorothy Lee and Paulo Freire to the neglected notions of dialogue,
freedom, culture, self, autonomy, and structure. Lastly, the author
argues in favor of reincorporating the pedagogical insights of Dorothy
Lee and Paulo Freire in the curricula and structure of HE, and also
reminds those concerned with upholding democracy that these formative values and concepts were acknowledged in the early conception and
development of active learning.

Chapter 15 presents a new vision for HE based on lessons from
Education for the Environment and Sustainability. Environmental Education (EE) and its descendant Education for Sustainability (EFS) or
Education for Sustainable Development, by definition, propose and
adopt active learning and experiential methods, as they seek to prepare
people that will work for a healthy environment and better societies.
And this is where the difference lies between EE/EFS and the generic
active learning approaches. EE or EFS are committed active learning
approaches; they have an explicit goal to work for social — environmental change. The transition from learners to active learners is addressed
by active learning, which however assumes that active learners will also
become responsible and active citizens. EE and EFS have however demonstrated that this is not an obvious development. After a discussion of
the main characteristics of EE/EFS, this chapter explores what facilitates the transition from active learners to active citizens, based on lessons from EE and EFS. Finally, it reflects on the implications of these
lessons for HE and a new vision for HE in contemporary societies and
a brief guide for educators and Higher Educational managers are
proposed. The authors propose the following typology of educational
purposes — i.e. individual change, empowerment, integration, or social
transformation — and corresponding instructional methods and tools.
Higher education institutions and instructors (or academics) should be
clear about the purpose of the educational praxis and instructors should
choose the pedagogical methods and tools that match the selected
purpose(s) in order to facilitate the transition from active learners to
active and responsible citizens.

This book presents best practices for effective active learning and teaching in HE. It includes case studies of active learning approaches adopted at universities in different countries and continents and in different disciplines. It presents best cases of technology-driven learning innovation, as well as insights on HE for sustainable societies. It is a book that highlights the importance of collaborative knowledge sharing, exploration, and creation, involving active engagement of both students and instructor − and even the local community − all as actors of the same play. It emphasizes an integrated pedagogical approach that uses engaging and collaborative learning methods, problem solving, technology-driven learning innovation, collaboration with the community, and other teaching strategies, within the explicit context of a new civic ethic (e.g., personal issues are social problems).

The insights gained in this book could be further enriched with more studies on the effectiveness of different active learning methods. It would be interesting to explore what active learning methods effectively stimulate not only creative thinking but also lead to change in values and behaviors. A systematic study of student performance in classes where active learning is used, as well as a more thorough analysis of teachers' conceptions of effective teaching and an exploration of students' attitudes on the effectiveness of learning methods − also in terms of behavioral change − could provide further insights into how transformative learning can be achieved.

This edition is the first part of a sequence of books already planned. The main goal of this series is to explore active learning pedagogy and methods within the present social context and challenges, as well as the "keys" that can make active learning empowering and transformative, leading to more humane, caring, and sustainable societies.

The objective of this first book, *Active Learning Strategies in Higher Education: Teaching for Leadership, Innovation and Creativity*, which you currently hold in your hands, was to explore active learning practices internationally and introduce our Active Learning Philosophy. We do believe that the variety of chapters and the adopted teaching and learning strategies that have been communicated in the three sections of the book summarize the main aspects of this philosophy: innovation and integration; creativity and collaboration; and leadership and social action. The understanding of the philosophical underpinnings of active learning theory and the challenges of our times, and their integration in HE practices can cultivate an exploratory, collaborative, empowering, and transformative active learning philosophy that can lead to sustainable societies. The role of technologies is also introduced without entering into details.

The next book will concentrate on transformative learning. An indicative title is *From Active Learning to Transformative Learning: Moving Beyond Boundaries and Disciplines*. In this edition, the focus of our discussion will be on a detailed sophisticated methodological framework for the design of transformative active learning programs, with a focus on HE. The greatest challenge is related to the fragmented nature of knowledge and organization in HE institutions. Contemporary social and environmental challenges require integrated approaches and the liquidation of boundaries – between humans and the environment, me and the "other," disciplines, the university and the community. Our unique value proposition is that Transformative Active Learning will be one of the most significant enablers of this innovative, out-of-the-box, technology-enabled education and thinking. For this reason, in the chapters of this edited book, we will present best practices of Transformative Learning; interdisciplinary – multidisciplinary practices in STEAM.

We do hope that our readers will value the individual contributions in each chapter and will also be able to be carriers of our active learning vision. In simple words, our effort will be successful if we find more advocates for active and transformative learning and its adoption in universities and colleges, so that HE:

- Promotes individual contributions and seeks for social humanistic visions for the learning process.
- Acknowledges the value of each individual knowledge artifact but recognizes and supports its integration with knowledge elements from different disciplines.
- Promotes the development of personal values, skills, and competencies but also connects it with a socially beneficial context for their exploitations.
- Compensates group efforts in learning content interaction and explorations and builds connections between universities and communities, different cultures, civilizations, and religions.
- Promotes creativity, imagination, and emotional depth of students along with knowledge acquisition and development – all as equally important and complementary.
- Constructs a dialectic, not authoritarian, communication channel between faculty and students.

- Informs HE administration about the non-countable benefits of active learning at institutional level.
- Promotes employability with advanced ethos and enhances personalities of individuals.
- Cultivates a participatory culture in academia at all levels.
- Makes learning an intellectual process contributing to a vision for a better world for all, designed for active citizens with increased responsibility.
- Makes HE more relevant for a socially inclusive sustainable development.
- Builds bridges between individuals, groups, institutions, and nations.
- Envisions a socially beneficial and effective use of resources in Academia, Industry, and Society.

SECTION I
ACTIVE LEARNING IN HIGHER EDUCATION: A THEORETICAL BACKGROUND

Chapter 1

Toward an Epistemology of Active Learning in Higher Education and Its Promise

Lorayne Robertson

Abstract

This chapter concerns itself primarily with questions of how students in higher education studies can best acquire, apply, create, and share knowledge. Over the past several decades, multiple forms of active learning have been proposed in order to increase student engagement and deepen their understanding. This chapter, accordingly, examines the epistemological claims of the supporters and detractors of active learning while simultaneously exploring the nascence and development of some of the major understandings which presently underpin an epistemology of active learning. While the focus of earlier works may have been on changes that higher education instructors should make to improve student understanding of key STEM concepts, this chapter addresses changes in the roles of both students and instructors as the co-creators of active learning environments and learning communities. A particular focus is given to the significance of metacognition as a critical skill that enables students to assess their own learning and also critically assess sources of information. The chapter includes a framework which indicates trends toward high-impact active learning skills for

Active Learning Strategies in Higher Education: Teaching for Leadership,
Innovation, and Creativity, 17–44
Copyright © 2018 by Emerald Publishing Limited
All rights of reproduction in any form reserved
ISBN: 978-1-78714-488-0

students in STEM higher education and the research which theorizes and supports these new instructional imperatives.

Keywords: Active learning; metacognition; authentic learning; problem-based learning; project-based learning; authentic assessment

Introduction

The Oxford online dictionary informs readers that *epistemology* is derived from the Greek word "to know how to do." An epistemology is a *theory of knowledge* which is designed to explain the different ways in which one can acquire knowledge or competence. A key epistemological question for those teaching higher education might initially be, "How do higher education students come to know something?" but in the more complicated current era of Web 2.0, the Internet of Things, and increasing expectations of higher education graduates from the world of work, the question becomes "How do higher education students BEST come to know something?" We could see this as an imperative, because the future will be impacted by how students in higher education courses across the globe gain competence in their chosen fields and disciplines. The future will also be impacted by how today's students apply their knowledge in order to solve problems; how they communicate, reason, argue, justify, and confirm or refute their assumptions and hypotheses; and then how they draw conclusions, and mobilize and share their knowledge.

As instructors in higher education, our teaching is grounded in our conceptions (and our assumptions and theories) of how people learn. We must, however, be ever mindful that, for most of our students, the academy will not be their career destination. Our students will move into the world of service and the world of work where they will need to know how to function well. The world of work our students will inhabit is continually changing and demanding new skills. This begs the question of how our epistemological assumptions align with these new global imperatives and changing contexts. Are we preparing our students optimally for their career choices? How best can students in higher education acquire the requisite knowledge, skills, and values to function with dexterity in new global knowledge economies? These are questions that move us beyond concerns of efficiency and effectiveness to consider how higher learning can best model ways of *coming to know* or ways of *theorizing learning* in order to build capacity in the next generation of global knowledge workers.

When the epistemology is that of *active learning*, the questions about knowledge become much more strategic and targeted. What understandings constitute the key aspects of an epistemology of active learning? Are there explanations that encompass the full grasp of active learning and its potential in higher education? Where and how did this theory originate? In which pedagogical paradigm(s) does active learning claim its roots? What are the key elements that need to be uncovered and understood in order to grasp the full scope of active learning's claims? In other words, beneath the surface, what are active learning's epistemological assumptions? These questions help us to understand the origins of the active learning paradigm and the reasons why this shift in approach is gaining acceptance and currency.

Next, we need to review the evidence-based claims made about active learning, particularly those claims that have been made in the fields of STEM and STEAM. What is the scope and breadth of active learning's claims about teaching and learning in STEM higher education? Who has made these claims, and in what contexts are the claims made? We also want to understand whether or not this is a passing phenomenon or if the concept of active learning has been shown to have staying power. How significant is active learning's reach in higher education today? What is the extent and capacity of active learning's promise to meet new imperatives to act and think globally? How responsible and responsive is the theory of active learning toward solutions to long-standing social and scientific problems, such as global warming? All of these questions need to be explored in some depth to detail the scope of an epistemology of active learning.

There are also practical questions to be considered, such as how an epistemology of active learning can inform teaching, learning, and assessment in higher education in the digital era. What are the actualized (not theorized) forms of active learning in practice? What does active learning *look like* across higher education disciplines and courses? In which contexts or disciplines has active learning come to be understood in more meaningful ways? If active learning is desirable, then how does one acquire knowledge about active learning, gain competence, and then evaluate active learning approaches in higher education disciplines? How do instructors and students make sense of active learning experiences epistemologically and under what circumstances? How does a theory of active learning apply when the courses are offered online in a range of multi-synchronous settings?

Other considerations include an examination of the reasons why active learning may not be adopted. What are the epistemological assumptions of active learning's detractors? Into which contexts or disciplines in higher education is an epistemology of active learning less integrated and what are the sources of this reasoned skepticism? All of these questions are designed to help to apply an epistemology of active learning to the broader contexts within higher education practice.

Beyond the practical, there are even deeper questions to unravel about active learning. An epistemology of active learning seeks to identify the claims that have been made about active learning and distinguish between evidence, beliefs, and opinions. On what basis do active learning supporters claim its connection to deeper learning, for example? Similarly, how have the connections between active learning and student engagement been theorized or researched? An epistemology of active learning should encourage readers to become engaged beyond simply seeking information about active learning and how it is realized in practice. If you, the reader, join in to the epistemological journey on active learning in this chapter, you will come to better understand active learning's origins, the claims of its supporters (and detractors), and working through the chapter, you should reach some reasoned conclusions about active learning. This is the essence of the epistemological journey of this chapter.

What Is Driving the Shift to Active Learning?

Active learning has been defined by Prince (2004) as any type of instructional method which engages students in their learning process and requires meaningful (relevant, authentic) learning activities as well as requiring students to think about what they are doing (metacognition). This implies that students will eschew roles as passive recipients of information, and instead contribute actively in classes. In defining the active learning methods that are most relevant for engineering education, Prince selects three: collaborative, co-operative, and problem-based learning and concludes that empirical research supporting active learning is "extensive" (p. 3). Within the context of engineering education, he finds that instructors may demonstrate different levels of acceptance and understanding of active learning. While it is common for engineering students to participate in active learning through tutorials or assignments, how active learning can be realized in the lecture or higher learning classroom still requires some explanation. Nonetheless, Prince's (2004) review of the research provides measured support for active learning practices in higher education.

Active learning includes the engagement of the student at a new level of awareness of their own learning, or metacognition, which is defined by Flavell (1979) as *a means of cognitive monitoring*. He outlines the elements of metacognition as follows: metacognitive knowledge (one's beliefs about one's learning capacity); metacognitive experiences or conscious recognition of understanding or misunderstanding; learning goals; and the actions or learning strategies that help one learn. Flavell recognizes that the students should be active participants in the monitoring of their own learning. He also theorizes that metacognition and self-regulation can be taught and should include the scrutiny of information which he describes as: a more conscious awareness of the source of a message, the quality of its appeal, and the related consequences of attending to inputs from different sources (Flavell, 1979). In essence, Flavell was advocating an early form of critical literacy skills, now more requisite than ever due to the proliferation of online information sources.

It is not theory and research results alone which are driving a continual shift toward more active learning in higher education but also new educational imperatives. One of these imperatives is a predicted *skills gap* – or the prediction that there will be insufficient talent to meet the global demands for employment in the decades ahead. Olson (2015) reports that the global market will experience a shortfall of 40 million skilled college graduates, a shortage of 95 million workers in the advanced economies, and a shortfall of 45 million secondary and vocational school graduates in the developing world through the year 2020 and beyond. While Olson does not place the full responsibility for addressing this shortage on education, he finds that many students who pursue 4-year degrees without vocational training or education *outside of the STEM subjects* will be "ill-equipped" for teamwork and knowledge work (Olson, 2015).

A second type of skills gap is more of a perception gap, as reported recently by Cukier (2016), who compares how students graduating from one Canadian university rate their skills with how their employers rate those same skills. The results indicate that the students did not have accurate perceptions of their skills compared to the level of skills expected by their employers. For example, while the students rated themselves above 90% in communication proficiency, their employers saw them as less than 50% proficient. Similar ratings were seen with gaps related to how the students saw their ability to learn on the job (as 93% proficient) versus how employers rated their ability to learn on the job (as 53% proficient). Employers also reported that less than 25% of recently-hired graduates had the required proficiency in digital tools and in ethics (Cukier, 2016). These findings underscore a need for students to be able to gain an accurate assessment of their own goals, skills, and ability to learn while they are in school. Prince (2004) finds that in order for students to more accurately assess their inter-personal skills related to what work requires, they need opportunities to practice these skills in classrooms that employ active learning in project or problem-based learning scenarios, and they need opportunities to assess their own and their group's collaborative skills using metacognition.

Emergent awareness of these skills is leading instructors to reconsider which learning aptitudes take priority in the 21st century. For example, in an era where there are multiple perspectives on every issue, and multiple claims of *truth*, how do students wrestle with moral and ethical implications in a landscape with many disparate claims? One example is the ethical and moral considerations behind releasing government information in leaks that inform citizens but may weaken organizations. Fuchs (2011) applies a Foucauldian discourse analysis to discuss how counter-surveillance activities such as WikiLeaks invite the discussion and interrogation of surveillance as a form of control, and how it can be used also as a mechanism of emancipation. In an increasingly complex world, students will need to learn how to consider and debate these types of ethical complexities.

The world of work requires skills of communication and collaboration. Early studies in the area of group learning were initiated by D. Johnson, R. Johnson, Holubec, and Roy (1984) who describe this as *co-operative learning*. They defined the concept of *positive inter-dependence*, which is the perception that one group member does not succeed unless the others in the group succeed through sharing resources and mutual support (D. Johnson & R. Johnson, 2009). This concept is echoed by others such as Steiner and Posch's (2006) description of *mutual self-responsible learning* in sustainable development studies.

A third imperative driving the need to shift the paradigm toward more active forms of learning has been the (repeated) identification of skills needed to work in the knowledge economy. Trilling and Fadel

(2009) report that the following skills will be required of graduates in the 21st century:

1) *Learning and innovation skills*: critical thinking, problem solving, communication, collaboration, creativity, and innovation.
2) *Digital literacy skills*: information literacy, media literacy, and information and communication technologies (ICT) literacy.
3) *Career and life skills*: flexibility, adaptability, initiative, self-direction, social and cross-cultural interaction, productivity, accountability, leadership, and responsibility (p. xxvi).

Pellegrino (2006) reports similar findings about the needs of the future workforce based on research conducted on behalf of an American economic think tank. Not only will skills of "adaptive expertise" (p. 2) be required of a skilled workforce, but this type of adaptive learning needs to be *modeled by the instructors* who are preparing the workforce. Pellegrino cites some shortcomings in the present education system — which he believes can be remedied through *principles of learning*. The first principle is that education must become more personalized, recognizing that individual learners approach new learning with pre-existing beliefs and perceptions that they acquire through their life experiences. Educators need to more closely understand what students know and then help them to construct new learning. Pellegrino sees that the present reliance on standardized assessments in the United States may not be providing the kind of information instructors need to understand students' misconceptions.

Second, Pellegrino argues that students need assistance to organize knowledge using models and conceptual frameworks to help with information retrieval. This is at the heart of helping students develop deeper understanding; they need to see relationships and patterns and recognize cognitive dissonance in order to gain meaning from what they are learning. He forecasts that very powerful information technologies will be as ubiquitous in education as they are in people's out-of-school lives, and that these new technologies will exponentially and fundamentally change communication and education practices (Pellegrino, 2006).

In views which are reminiscent of Flavell (1979), Pellegrino's third principle encourages more metacognition. Students need opportunities to verbalize their thinking and make it visible. Methods of inquiry can be taught, including methods to help students activate their prior learning, and these inquiry methods should be taught across courses and disciplines. These methods include problem and project-based learning where students are challenged to think deeply about their knowledge and then apply it. For this to happen, educators need to develop repertoires of diverse instructional approaches to support the development of complex learning skills in students (Pellegrino, 2006).

Bransford, Vye, and Bateman (2002), in a landmark review of decades of research on cognition, proposed the How People Learn framework as a theoretical tool to guide the design of learning and to analyze the quality of the learning experience. The framework has four lenses, indicating that high-quality classrooms are learner-centered, knowledge-centered, and assessment-centered, and take place within a community of learners. Their work was key in acknowledging a collective community responsibility for learning outcomes (Bransford et al., 2002).

According to Dede (2008), a shift in epistemology occurred with the advent of Web 2.0, redefining higher education through the multiple ways that Web 2.0 epistemologies contrast with more traditional, classical studies. For example, Wikipedia is redefining who is an expert by constructing knowledge through the collaborations of anonymous volunteers and the exchange of different viewpoints. Students now require significant new skills to help them understand how to determine an expert view on a subject (Dede, 2008). Technology has the potential to assist with many new learning imperatives, including opening education to online learning so that it is more accessible to more people (Garrison, Anderson, & Archer, 2001; Jacobsen & Lock, 2004; Pellegrino, 2006).

Technology has continued to change rapidly even while many of the present higher education instructors have been in their roles. This is requiring continuous shifts in learning how to help students learn using their digital skills. As Jacobsen and Lock (2014) state, "An important job for all educators is to enable learners *to author using the media of their time*" (italics added). Speaking in the context of teacher preparation programs, Jacobsen and Lock find that teachers in training need to be able to respond to the emerging technologies that they will face as their future students become more technologically adept. This advice for preservice teachers can also apply to instructors in higher education.

Another significant reality shift for higher education has been referred to as the *massification* of higher education (Hornsby & Osman, 2014). This global trend is positioned as a benefit to society as it builds health and security for the people of the world through education. As a result of this trend, more students who might not have been able to attend higher education in the past are now enrolling. In studying this phenomenon, Hornsby and Osman remind us that in order for a much more diverse group of students to be successful, shifts in multiple areas are required; these include the design of the curriculum, the design of the classroom environment, the instructional techniques, and the assessment methods. All of these key aspects of higher education influence student learning and engagement (Hornsby & Osman, 2014).

In summary, then, these examples of imperatives for education in the 21st century all point to a need to transform education to make certain that schooling in general, and higher education in particular, becomes more personalized and tailored to individual student learning. In order for this to happen, instructors in higher education will, realistically, need to build larger repertoires of teaching and learning approaches in order to tailor education to adult learners. While this could imply that the program and the instructor need to change the most, the reality is that student roles must similarly transform. Students will need to build skills of self-assessment, self-awareness, and metacognition in order to understand how they learn best, and how they can work collaboratively to prepare for work and for life. They need to become participants in the design of their learning and co-creators of the learning communities in their classrooms. The shift from teacher-centered learning to student-centered learning has implications for everyone involved in the higher education enterprise.

Changing Pedagogical Paradigms

One of the central contrasting paradigms which has been employed to empower students to take more responsibility for their learning is the conceptual model comparing teacher-centered to student-centered learning. Some of the original philosophical underpinnings and advocacy for more student-centered learning originated with Freire's (1970) explication and criticism of the "banking model" of education (p. 72). In the banking model, students are positioned as passive receptacles to be filled with knowledge; instead, students should be active in constructing knowledge. This paradigm shift includes a critical stance toward a *one-size-fits-all* type of education where a single source of messaging (the lecture or the text) delivers the same message in the same way to all students, and the students expect the instructor to prepare, organize, and present the learning. How the message or the information was delivered was the responsibility of the instructor; how the information was received, retained, and reported was considered to be the responsibility of the student. This model is presently under significant scrutiny and revision.

Freire viewed the banking model as a form of oppression because it placed the teacher in a position of power over the students and their learning. In the banking model, the teacher's knowledge was privileged and there were privileges around *voice* – the teacher was the speaker and the students were listeners. Choices such as the sources of information (textbook, lectures) and assignment modalities were also made for the student by the teacher. In this mode of learning, Freire viewed the students as objects in the learning process rather than the subjects of the learning, or as persons (1970). While Freire's theory may not have had immediate uptake in STEM, discussions about the need for students to engage more deeply in their learning in various STEM disciplines have come to similar conclusions about the need for change (Biggs, 1999; G. Catalano & K. Catalano, 1999; Wieman, 2007).

Biggs (1999), in writing about "*What the student does,*" focuses on the ways that higher education instruction should change in four simple steps:

1. Ensuring that students see what the objectives are, what the learning plan is, and how the objectives match the assessment tasks;
2. Working so that students are motivated by the course, program, or instruction;
3. Making the classroom safe so that students feel free to focus on tasks (without unscheduled tests, for example); and
4. Ensuring that students can work collaboratively and dialogue with peers (Biggs, 1999). It is noteworthy that Biggs views the paradigm shift as the responsibility of the instructor without acknowledging that students need to change their roles, also. This overall approach is changing.

Wieman (2007) outlines his concerns with student retention of knowledge and understanding of concepts in physics courses. His work with university physics students began initially in the United States, then continued in Canada through several decades. Though he and colleagues prepared well and professionally for the traditional lecture format, evidence of student learning outcomes and skills development were less than optimal. He noticed first that students who experienced success in the classroom were *clueless* about how to begin to solve research projects, but, after a few years of research, were *transformed* as learners (Wieman, 2007, p. 10). As a result, Wieman began to research and amass evidence with respect to student learning in physics lectures, finding that student retention of information after traditional (lecture) instruction was 10% after 15 minutes. While the gain in conceptual understanding from lectures was measured at 30%, he found, surprisingly, that students regrettably gained more novice-like beliefs after a year of physics instruction (rather than building expert beliefs). The consistency of his findings led him to conclude that, "The traditional lecture is simply not successful in helping most students achieve mastery of fundamental concepts. Pedagogical approaches involving more interactive engagement of students show consistently higher gains on the FCI [Force Concepts Inventory] and similar tests" (Wieman, 2007, p. 11).

Using research that he initiated with his colleagues, Wieman began to unravel the puzzle, looking to cognitive science on how people learn. He found that expert professors have a mental structure to organize their learning and know how to check new information with prior learning, and science instructors need to encourage students to organize and apply the information of the discipline in similar ways. People learn by adding to their prior learning and making sense of the new information. In order for this to happen, effective teaching needs *to engage students in thinking deeply about a topic at an appropriate level, and then monitoring their understanding.* Students, in turn, need to become engaged in this process in order to be successful. This is, in essence, Wieman's epistemological outlook on teaching and learning in physics (Wieman, 2007).

Without using the term *constructivism,* Wieman's findings about physics instruction match the assumptions of constructivism; that students build meaning through active engagement with the material and with guidance to build on their prior learning at an appropriate and attainable level. Similarly, G. Catalano and K. Catalano (1999), in a discussion about student-centered learning in engineering education, note that the view of the *instructor as the center of the learning process* is outdated. They identify the new roles for engineering instructors as follows:

— *Modeling the thinking and processing skills*: this includes modeling how to make sense of an issue or problem;
— *Knowing where students should be cognitively*: strategies here include employing the range of Bloom's (1956) taxonomy to develop the outcomes of the course, and sharing with students how higher-order thinking is required for solving problems;
— *Developing questions to facilitate student growth:* questions should range from recall to more complex questions which require interpretation and prediction;

- *Using visual tools to show connections*: suggesting that instructors use mind maps or graphic organizers to categorize learning or to show relationships and connections;
- *Providing group-learning settings*: encouraging students to solve problems in groups;
- *Using mental models*: employing analogies and metaphors as models to frame learning and debates, and encouraging students to create metaphors; and
- *Providing lower-risk mechanisms for student input*: asking students to explain their thinking using low-stakes mechanisms such as comment sheets and informal quizzes (G. Catalano & K. Catalano, 1999).

Although many student-centered activities have been attempted and documented in the 18 years since these suggestions were provided, discussions have not been clear about the changing roles of both the instructors and the students. I would argue that it is not the role of the instructor alone to determine students' prior learning and cognitive strengths. Students need to be aware of their own backgrounds and experiences and come to class prepared to discuss their perceptions and assumptions in order to build new understandings. While the instructors can model mind maps and cognitive maps for students, the students need to construct models and concept maps for themselves and for the benefit of other learners. Students will also need to build their own skills and capacity toward understanding how learning happens, including their own learning. Added to that, they will need to know how to apply their learning in authentic contexts that mimic or are situated in real-world problems.

Jourdan, Haberland, and Deis (2004) argue that there is a clear shift toward *the student as the person most accountable for whether or not learning happens* in the digital era. They state,

> Higher education is becoming what it has always surreptitiously been through the ages: the internal metamorphism by the learners themselves, brought about by their own agency through a number of educational resources, including interaction with faculty, content of the educational process, and the institutional environment...Students are in a sense the producers of their own education and are ultimately responsible for their own development and outcomes. (p. 24)

Trilling and Fadel (2009), however, theorize that the shift toward less teacher-centered learning and more student-centered learning alone will be *insufficient* for the complex learning of the decades ahead. Students will need some direct instruction but they should not rely on this; students need to learn how to exchange knowledge. Students will develop sources for their learning outside the academy because learning outside-of-school is becoming part of everyday life in a global, digital community. While some teacher-directed skills will be needed in the decades ahead, the scale will tip toward focusing education to build on what students already know, and what they need to learn. Future learning will be more personalized, student-centered, and targeted (Trilling & Fadel, 2009).

To build on this conclusion, I would argue that in order for student learning to become more personalized and targeted, students will need to build skills of self-awareness and learner capacity; come to see themselves as the designers of their learning contexts and learning environments; build their understanding of the concept that meaning is negotiated and constructed; and participate actively to build the capacity of the learning communities who will support them in meeting their learning goals.

Designed Instruction or Situated Cognition?

It has been argued for some time that a higher education instructor's perspective on how to design effective instruction should be based on learning theory, and a deep understanding of that theory must be undertaken in order to design instruction effectively (Bednar, Cunningham, Duffy, & Perry, 1992). According to Bednar et al., teaching and learning theories emerge from and reflect different epistemological assumptions which collectively form the basis for the theory. The field of instructional design, for example, which has informed understandings of teaching in higher education, initially relied heavily on behaviorist learning theory and cognitive science. This can be seen through elements of instructional design, such as the focus on effective sequencing of behavioral learning outcomes and the search for efficient designs of the learning environments. According to Bednar and her colleagues, the reliance on mapping knowledge or outcomes and measuring them objectively falls under the school of thought called "objectivism" (p. 20). One does not have to look far to see elements of objectivism reflected today in course and program maps and structured and sequenced learning outcomes. The missing element in designing a course for students in their absence is the student. Instructors need to seek ways to encourage students to set their own learning goals and measure progress within the context of the overall learning objectives of the course or program.

Bednar et al. offer a comparison between instruction based on the objectivist paradigm and the constructivist paradigm. In a constructivist approach, learning is an active process of developing meaning based on experience. The constructivist view is that knowledge is learned best within contexts, such as a real-life (authentic) contexts rather than learning facts in isolation. Students see learning as more relevant if they can see its connection to other problems and other knowledge, which in turn builds complexity. This building of relevance, authenticity, and complexity is referred to as *situated cognition* (Bednar et al., 1992; Lave & Wenger, 1998; Lombardi, 2007). Authenticity can be built into course design through means such as problem-based learning (Barrows & Tamblyn, 1980; Savin-Baden, 2007) and case studies (Gottschlich, 2000; Zuelke & Willerman, 1995) and discussion case studies (Gill, 2011), for example.

In a very similar vein, Lombardi (2007) describes the types of tasks or problems that constitute more authentic types of learning and defines design elements that need to be present, regardless of the subject matter:

- Learning tasks should have real-world relevance and mimic real problems of practice;
- Tasks are often complex, interdisciplinary, and not well-defined;
- Problems are open to multiple approaches and theoretical perspectives; and
- Learning should be complex, requiring reflection, metacognition, and continuous assessment and feedback (Lombardi, 2007).

Savin-Baden (2007) identifies the same elements in problem-based learning (PBL), and here the responsibility is on the students to undertake a series of steps to clarify definitions, define the problem, generate solutions, and report their findings. The role of the instructor in PBL becomes more of a facilitator who not only can help students to focus, but also provides lectures or tutorials as required. She emphasizes, however, that PBL is an approach which is characterized by flexibility as it can be implemented in various ways (Savin-Baden, 2007).

Other aspects of constructivist learning theory in the literature promote situating the learning within the proximal range of the student's experience and knowledge. Vygotsky (1978) refers to this as the zone of proximal development (ZPD) or the difference between what the student can do unaided versus with support. In other words, the degree of complexity of the problem to be solved should be within the student's reach or within their reach with support (Bednar et al., 1992; Vygotsky, 1978). The role of the teacher changes in a constructivist environment to become more of a coach who models the process of learning, and someone who can also organize and monitor learning. Dewey, who argued that science learning should focus on both knowledge and process, said that teachers should help students learn methods of science inquiry from a young age, and develop these methods throughout schooling (Dewey, 1910).

Students should be encouraged to see that there are multiple perspectives; that problems are seen differently from different vantage points; and that they need to grasp and integrate these alternate views. This process is enhanced through the use of collaborative work groups. In addition, students who construct knowledge for themselves or within their peer group need to understand the processes of thinking, learning, inquiry, and collaboration. The development of these processes should be enhanced through reflection and metacognition.

Research Claims about Active Learning

In this section, selected evidence-based studies related to STEM fields and active learning show that active learning has been researched in STEM classrooms, and the evidence points generally in one direction: there are small but measurable gains shown in multiple studies (Haak, HilleRisLambers, Pitre, & Freeman, 2011; Koohang, Paliszkiewicz, Goluchowski, & Nord, 2016; Smith et al., 2009; Smith, Wood, Krauter, & Knight, 2011; Walker, Cotner, Baepler, & Decker, 2008).

Smith et al. (2009) sought evidence about whether peer discussion improved student performance on in-class concept questions in undergraduate biology lectures. Students responded to biology questions using clickers, but had consistently more correct responses when working in groups. Smith et al. investigated whether students were just leaning on the students most likely to have the right answer or if there were gains made from discussing the responses in groups and examining the clicker histogram. They found that peer discussion can be helpful for developing group understanding of biology concepts even when no one in the group knows the correct answer (Smith et al., 2009). Later studies found that students in the novice and middle range learning groups benefited most from peer discussion plus instructor explanation (Smith et al., 2011) which harkens back to earlier discussions in this chapter about key elements of PBL.

Haak and colleagues claim that the introduction of active learning and culturally responsive teaching have had a "profound effect" on the achievement gap in biology courses (2011, p. 1214). They tackled the issue of the performance and retention of undergraduate biology students from diverse backgrounds in their research and found that a very structured course design combined with active learning reduces the achievement gap. In their case, the active learning in the undergraduate biology class consisted of weekly practice with data analysis, problem-solving, and other higher-order cognitive skills (Haak et al., 2011).

Koohang and colleagues (2016) set out to determine whether or not the stages of guiding learners to become active learners, initiating knowledge construction, and building student ownership of the learning would lead to greater student engagement with the learning material in information technology classes. They found that this was the case: grounding student learning in real-world experiences and using higher-order thinking skills increased student engagement. Similarly, G. Catalano and K. Catalano (1999) found that when they compared the performance of students in student-centered vs. teacher-centered courses in thermodynamics, the students from the student-centered classes showed better progress on standardized tests.

Walker and colleagues (2008), in teaching an introductory Biology class, encountered some of the issues that others have documented with large-class sizes, such as low attendance, low and uneven student engagement, lack of student preparedness, and poor student learning outcomes. As a group, the instructors decided to focus on key understandings rather than "covering" the entire curriculum (p. 362). They broke the class of 500 students into two groups, but changed key elements of the instruction in order to integrate active learning (Table 1).

Walker et al.'s analysis of the distribution of the final grades revealed that students who were lowest in the grade distribution appeared to benefit most from the active learning (Group B in Table 1). What was more surprising was that, in the traditional section, 11 of 240 students had a final grade below 40%; in the active learning section, just one student had a low grade and this student had dropped the course. Students in the traditional section showed higher confidence at the end of the first term, but there were no significant differences in confidence at the end of the full term. Interestingly, the student evaluations for the instructors

Table 1. Different Class Structure for Two Introductory Biology
Classes.

Group A: Traditional	Group B: Active
Lecture	Extremely shortened mini-lectures
Unannounced quizzes	Quizzes
	Wide variety of structured, ungraded, group activities
	A few graded homework assignments
Multiple choice exams	Multiple choice exams

Source: Developed from Walker et al. (2008).

were "significantly and substantially higher" (p. 364) in the traditional
than the active section, which was confirmed in the qualitative data.
Students did not warm up to the change in focus from the teacher-
centered classroom environment to the student-centered one. This
occurred despite the fact that the instructors and TA team were the
same for both courses. This finding hints that students can resist active
learning and may need time and support to make the change from more
passive learning. The overall assessment of the students from the qualitative (focus group) findings was an expressed desire for blending the
traditional and active learning formats. In reflecting on the outcomes
from this experiment, the Biology instructors had to wrestle with
"uncoverage," meaning that, in the active learning class, they were not
able *to cover* all of the content. They found that some of the content
could be covered outside of class as assigned readings. They also found
that attendance was significantly improved in the active section, reflecting more accountability for attendance in active learning than in the
traditional lecture class. As professors they see a gradual evolution from
the whole class lecture to the inclusion of more engaging practices
(Walker et al., 2008).

Wieman (2007) investigates instruction in physics classes in higher
education and suggests the following strategies for STEM instructors:

— Attend to the cognitive load for students using images and explicit
organization;
— Address beliefs such as why a topic is worth learning and its real-
world relevance;

- Consistently monitor student thinking and homework and provide regular feedback. Make assessments as authentic as possible. Create rigorous means to measure the actual outcomes of higher education instruction;
- Use technology for simulations and to provide opportunities for students to see the lecture material and ask questions online in advance of class to build engagement;
- Organize the learning for the lecture around 7–10 key concepts. Use personal-response systems such as clickers to capture students' understandings (and misconceptions) in a somewhat anonymous way. Use small consensus groups to focus on and discuss responses and come to new understandings (Wieman, 2007).

The topic of the lecture (and the form that it should take) continues to be center stage in discussions about higher education, and this crosses disciplines. One possible framework for reconsidering the lecture is to continue to develop the field of large-class pedagogy, which includes taking a critical look at the benefits and constraints of the large-class lecture. It must be acknowledged that, while there is still great interest in what people have to say (consider, for instance, the uptake on TED talks), there has always been the possibility of a gap between a broadcast of interesting information and how it is processed by the individual learners. As Summerlee (2013) points out, while the lecture is effective for broadcasting information, research indicates that students are challenged to maintain their interest through an hour-long lecture and that lectures promote more superficial levels of learning. He also argues that there are increasing numbers of students in universities who have difficulties processing information and therefore will require more personalized instruction because of this. While these are sufficient reasons to reconsider how the lecture needs to be reshaped for the present generation of students, there is resistance to changing the model of the lecture because it is the forum that academics use to share their ideas and their research. Summerlee notes that, although the evidence of the inefficiency of the large-class lecture has been present since the 1980s, there has been insufficient recognition of this and a lack of change in the academy. He concludes that the weight of the evidence connecting lectures to effective learning means that universities should rethink their approaches to teaching and learning (Summerlee, 2013).

There is also support for more interdisciplinary STEM activities such as sustainable development (e.g., R. Lozano, Lukman, F. Lozano, Huisingh, & Lambrechts, 2013; Steiner & Posch, 2006). For example,

Williams (2011) in New Zealand finds that there are positive possibilities from STEM integration, including:

— Energizing the learning environment with real-world relevance,
— Igniting learners' desire to explore and investigate,
— Seeing learners develop confidence and self-direction,
— Building a pathway to technological literacy,
— Encouraging students to think with flexibility and confidence, and
— Reducing the dropout rate (p. 31).

Steiner and Posch (2006) argue that approaches such as transdisciplinary case studies in sustainable development require teachers to abandon their roles as the information providers and students to abandon their roles as consumers of information. What emerges instead is a new learning paradigm focused on "ecological, economic and social development" (p. 878) where each of these three concepts have equal importance. This transdisciplinary learning paradigm is so complex that it cannot be approached by traditional class instruction where knowledge is segmented by discipline. Instead, because of the challenges of the topic and the significance of the conclusions, there is a mutual search for sustainable solutions to the world's problems. The learning is not focused on gaining factual knowledge but on building capacity to solve complex, authentic problems through planning, decision-making, and project management skills. A key sustainable development skill is self-regulated learning: students are more active than their instructors in seeking information and applying critical thinking in what Steiner and Posch (2006) describe as "mutual self-responsible learning" (p. 881). Unlike PBL where the students work to solve problems, in sustainable development, all of the participants (teacher/researchers, students, and practitioners) seek to build their capacity to solve complex and ill-defined problems.

Boy (2013) reminds us that we are only beginning to understand how the shift from manufacturing to information technologies is changing how we work, learn, and live. He argues eloquently that education systems need to be investigated and updated. The Internet now allows knowledge beyond memory as we can access information literally at the touch of a button (or a voice command). He argues for *understanding* over knowing because the age of the Internet has introduced more complex systems, requiring students to think more critically about the available information. Students, now more than ever, need to be concerned with who is sending the information and if it is supported by respected institutions. Students also need to understand core concepts of their disciplines and consider how to apply them in real life.

Boy also posits that students need opportunities to embrace and work in the complexity which is the reality of today's existence. Today's issues for scientists, such as sustainable energy, are complex and will require global responses. Students need to know how to be social and how to communicate and they must work creatively and collaboratively to share knowledge in ways that target information differently to different audiences. He finds also that the Internet has had a democratizing effect on education, allowing knowledge to be more accessible to increasing populations (Boy, 2013, p. 7).

To assist in demonstrating how these multiple, different imperatives and suggestions have emerged for improving learning in STEM subjects through active learning approaches, a framework of sample studies and recommendations was created. While this synthesis cannot claim to be definitive, it does provide indications of some of the trends present in STEM higher education today (Table 2).

Reaching Reasoned Conclusions about Active Learning

There has been a steady march over the past several decades toward the democratization of education. Whether or not higher education classes are conducted online, partially online, or in physically co-located settings, instructors must still come to terms with the reality that students have unlimited access to multiple, sometimes competing, sources of information on the Internet. This, alone, does not render the lecture-mode as such obsolete, but it should encourage instructors to question whether or not their role is to select the most important information from a chapter or readings, and talk about it at sufficient length that students will study the topic further.

Access to information does not necessarily equate with the ability to organize and critically analyze information sources so that the knowledge can be applied in other contexts or communicated creatively by students using digital tools. Students are shifting from their role as consumers of information to becoming collaborative learners and the producers of new media. In order for this to happen, students need to construct their own understandings of knowledge so that they become, in essence, knowledge workers. If we want students to be constructors of knowledge and creative communicators, then education has to change to model these approaches through active learning, self-regulation, and

Table 2. Active Learning Framework: Key Elements of a STEM Active
Learning Epistemology.

Active Learning Elements	Key Instructional Imperatives
Student-centered focus	Students as active learners (Freire, 1970; Wieman, 2007)
	Personalized education (Freire, 1970; Hornsby & Osman, 2014; Pellegrino, 2006; Summerlee, 2013)
	Student voice (Freire, 1970)
	Students are producers of their education (Jourdan et al., 2004)
	Build new learning on the prior learning of the individual (Chickering & Kuh, 2005; Wieman, 2007)
	Student ownership of the learning (Bransford et al., 2002; Chickering & Kuh, 2005; Koohang et al., 2016; Steiner & Posch, 2006)
	Safety in learning (Biggs, 1999; G. Catalano & K. Catalano, 1999)
	Construction of meaning through active engagement (Wieman, 2007)
	People learn by creating their own understanding (Wieman, 2007)
Authentic (messy, complex) tasks	Higher-order thinking skills (Bloom, 1956; G. Catalano & K. Catalano, 1999)
	Meaningful, relevant learning (Prince, 2004)
	Authentic tasks (Koohang et al., 2016; Wieman, 2007)
	Build relevance, authenticity, and complexity into work in classrooms (situated cognition) (e.g., Bednar et al., 1992; Koohang et al., 2016; Lave & Wenger, 1998; Lombardi, 2007)
	Problems should have real-world relevance and require sustained investigation (Lombardi, 2007)

Table 2. (*Continued*)

Active Learning Elements	Key Instructional Imperatives
Innovation skills/Career focus	Ability to learn on the job (Cukier, 2016)
	Adaptive expertise (Pellegrino, 2006)
	Flexibility, adaptability, initiative, self-direction (Trilling & Fadel, 2009)
	Work skills, e.g., productivity (Trilling & Fadel, 2009)
More diverse instructional approaches	Employ more diverse instructional approaches, larger repertoire (Chickering & Kuh, 2005; Pellegrino, 2006)
	Uncover students' misconceptions in order to build on them (Pellegrino, 2006; Wieman, 2007)
	Increase retention by moving from the lecture to more engaged types of learning (Wieman, 2007)
	Case studies (Gottschlich, 2000; Zuelke & Willerman, 1995)
	Culturally responsive teaching (Haak et al., 2011)
	Clickers or personal-response systems and consensus groups to discuss the responses (Smith et al., 2009, 2011; Wieman, 2007)
	Discussion case studies (Gill, 2011)
	Model how to organize learning (G. Catalano & K. Catalano, 1999; Pellegrino, 2006)
	Model the use of technology applications that students employ in their out-of-school online learning (Jacobsen & Lock, 2004; Voogt, Erstad, Dede, & Mishra, 2013)
	Organize the lecture around 7–10 key concepts (Wieman, 2007)
	Problem-based learning (Barrows & Tamblyn, 1980; Pellegrino, 2006; Prince, 2004; Savin-Baden, 2007)

Table 2. (*Continued*)

Active Learning Elements	Key Instructional Imperatives
	Problem and project-based learning activities (Haak et al., 2011; Lombardi, 2007; Pellegrino, 2006; Prince, 2004)
	Transdisciplinary case studies (sustainable development) (Lozano et al., 2013; Steiner & Posch, 2006; Williams, 2011)
	Uncoverage: some content covered out of class (Walker et al., 2008)
Communication skills/ ICT skills	Communication skills (Prince, 2004)
	Digital literacy skills (Pellegrino, 2006; Trilling & Fadel, 2009)
	Social and cross-cultural skills (Trilling & Fadel, 2009)
	Situated learning; communities of practice (Lave & Wenger, 1998)
	Collaboration with peers (Biggs, 1999)
	Teamwork and knowledge work for the global digital era (Olson, 2015)
Concept mapping, models	Students need assistance and models to organize learning: find patterns, build models of learning and conceptual frameworks to help them with knowledge retrieval (G. Catalano & K. Catalano, 1999; Pellegrino, 2006; Wieman, 2007)
Digital literacy skills: information literacy, media literacy, ITC literacy	Students need to learn how to approach cognitive dissonance (Pellegrino, 2006)
	Instructors should scaffold the task (Koohang et al., 2016)
	Students should encounter multiple perspectives and a variety of resources in order to discern the relevant information (Bednar et al., 1992; Lombardi, 2007)
	Learn how to determine an expert view (Dede, 2008)

Table 2. (*Continued*)

Active Learning Elements	Key Instructional Imperatives
	Conscious awareness of the sources of messages, their quality, and consequences of attending to them (Flavell, 1979)
	Use technology to support communication and learning (Dede, 2008; Garrison et al., 2001; Jacobsen & Lock, 2004; Lombardi, 2007; Pellegrino, 2006)
	ITC literacy (Cukier, 2016; Trilling & Fadel, 2009)
Complexity	Conscious awareness of sources of information and consequences of attending to each (Flavell, 1979)
	Ethical complexity (Fuchs, 2011)
	Help students gain the skills of inquiry learning (Lombardi, 2007; Pellegrino, 2006)
	Encourage higher-order thinking (Bloom, 1956; G. Catalano & K. Catalano, 1999; Koohang et al., 2016).
	Problems should be complex, require sustained investigation and collaboration (Lombardi, 2007)
Collaborative learning, co-operative learning, positive interdependence	Encourage collaborative and co-operative learning – opportunities for productive group work (Bednar et al., 1992; Biggs, 1999; G. Catalano & K. Catalano, 1999)
	Positive interdependence (D. Johnson & R. Johnson, 2009; Johnson et al., 1984).
	Mutual, self-responsible learning (Steiner & Posch, 2006)
Metacognition/ Monitoring own learning	Metacognition includes knowledge of one's capacity and how one (self) learns, reflections on past learning, conscious awareness of understanding or lack of, setting learning goals (Flavell, 1979)

Table 2. (*Continued*)

Active Learning Elements	Key Instructional Imperatives
	Clarity around learning objectives (Biggs, 1999; Bransford et al., 2002)
	Build skills of metacognition (Bednar et al., 1992; Bransford et al., 2002; Lombardi, 2007; Pellegrino, 2006; Prince, 2004)
	Make thinking visible (Pellegrino, 2006)
	Develop metacognitive skills through peer collaboration (Wieman, 2007)
	Students need to know how learning happens, including their own learning (Trilling & Fadel, 2009)
	Realistic self-assessment (Cukier, 2016)
	Self-regulated learning, mutual self-responsible learning (Steiner & Posch, 2006)
Alignment between learning and assessment	Ensure transparency and alignment among the learning objectives, learning plan, and assessments (Biggs, 1999)
	Critical forms of assessment including peer assessment and self-assessment (Wiggins & McTighe, 2005)
Continuous, personalized feedback, assessment to inform instruction	Assessment should be continuous through carefully designed homework, grading policies, and feedback (Lombardi, 2007; Wieman, 2007)
	Assessment should inform the teachers about student learning so that they can give better feedback to teachers (Pellegrino, 2006)
	Monitor student attainment of key concepts (Wieman, 2007)
	Provide prompt, detailed, and personalized feedback (Chickering & Kuh, 2005)

metacognition. Both instructors and students need to embrace these new realities. As more students enroll in higher education, instructors will become more responsive to increasing student diversity. Students will also need to be more responsive to diverse perspectives and acknowledge that there may be more than one right answer.

In reviewing the present trend toward what she terms as "consumerism" in higher education, Regan (2012) wrestles with the functional and moral roles of instructors and students. She concludes that the *role of the instructors is to use their abilities to facilitate optimal learning*. In turn, the role of the students should be to *do their best to learn* (Regan, 2012). To this I would add that, in order to preserve what is best in humanity and meet the needs of future generations, today's students need to embrace the complex nature of problem-solving and decision-making and view higher education as an opportunity *to learn how to learn*. Active learning engages them in this process.

References

Barrows, H. S., & Tamblyn, R. M. (1980). *Problem-based learning: An approach to medical education*. New York, NY: Springer Publishing Company.

Bednar, A. K., Cunningham, D., Duffy, T. M., & Perry, J. D. (1992). Theory into practice: How do we link. *Constructivism and the technology of instruction: A conversation*, 17–34.

Biggs, J. (1999). What the student does: Teaching for enhanced learning. *Higher Education Research & Development, 18*(1), 57–75.

Bloom, B. S. (1956). *Taxonomy of educational objectives. Vol. 1: Cognitive domain* (pp. 20–24). New York, NY: McKay.

Boy, G. A. (2013). From STEM to STEAM: Toward a human-centred education, creativity & learning thinking. *Proceedings of the 31st European Conference on Cognitive Ergonomics* (p. 3). ACM.

Bransford, J., Vye, N., & Bateman, H. (2002). Creating high-quality learning environments: Guidelines from research on how people learn. In *The Knowledge Economy and Postsecondary Education: Report of a Workshop* (pp. 159–198). Washington, D.C.: National Academy Press.

Catalano, G. D., & Catalano, K. (1999). Transformation: From teacher-centered to student-centered engineering education. *Journal of Engineering Education, 88*(1), 59–64.

Chickering, A. W., & Kuh, G. D. (2005). *Promoting student success: Creating conditions so every student can learn* (Occasional Paper No. 3). Bloomington, IN: Indiana University Center for Postsecondary Research.

Cukier, W. (2016). Bridging the skills gap. Retrieved from http://www.hrpatoday.ca/article/bridging-the-skills-gap.html

Dede, C. (2008). A seismic shift in epistemology. *EDUCAUSE review, 43*(3), 80.

Dewey, J. (1910). Science as subject-matter and as method. *Science, 31*(787), 121−127. Retrieved from http://www.jstor.org/stable/1634781

Flavell, J. H. (1979). Metacognition and cognitive monitoring: A new area of cognitive-developmental inquiry. *American psychologist, 34*(10), 906.

Freire, P. (1970). *Pedagogy of the oppressed.* New York, NY: Herder & Herder.

Fuchs, C. (2011). WikiLeaks: Power 2.0? Surveillance 2.0? Criticism 2.0? Alternative media 2.0? A political-economic analysis. *Global Media Journal: Australian Edition, 5*(1), 1−17.

Garrison, D. R., Anderson, T., & Archer, W. (2001). Critical thinking, cognitive presence, and computer conferencing in distance education. *American Journal of distance education, 15*(1), 7−23.

Gill, T. G. (2011). What is a discussion case? Retrieved from http://mumacasereview.org/what-is-a-discussion-case

Gottschlich, M. (2000). Writing basics: Elements of the case study. *Journal of the American Dietetic Association, 100*(11), 1293−1295.

Haak, D. C., HilleRisLambers, J., Pitre, E., & Freeman, S. (2011). Increased structure and active learning reduce the achievement gap in introductory biology. *Science, 332*(6034), 1213−1216.

Hornsby, D. J., & Osman, R. (2014). Massification in higher education: Large classes and student learning. *Higher Education, 67*(6), 711−719.

Jacobsen, D. M., & Lock, J. V. (2004). Technology and teacher education for a knowledge era: Mentoring for student futures, not our past. *Journal of Technology and Teacher Education, 12*(1), 75.

Johnson, D. W., Johnson, R., Holubec, E., & Roy, P. (1984). *Circles of learning. Cooperation in the classroom.* Alexandria, VA: Association for Supervision and Curriculum Development.

Johnson, D. W., & Johnson, R. T. (2009). An educational psychology success story: Social interdependence theory and cooperative learning. *Educational Researcher, 38*(5), 365−379.

Jourdan Jr, L. F., Haberland, C., & Deis, M. H. (2004). Quality in higher education: The student's role. *Academy of Educational Leadership Journal, 8*(2), 17.

Koohang, A., Paliszkiewicz, J., Goluchowski, J., & Nord, J. H. (2016). Active learning for knowledge construction in e-learning: A replication study. *The Journal of Computer Information Systems, 56*(3), 238−243.

Lave, J., & Wenger, E. (1998, 2008). Communities of practice. Retrieved from http://www.valenciacollege.edu/communities

Lombardi, M. M. (2007). Authentic learning for the 21st century: An overview. *Educause Learning Initiative, 1*(2007), 1−12.

Lozano, R., Lukman, R., Lozano, F. J., Huisingh, D., & Lambrechts, W. (2013). Declarations for sustainability in higher education: Becoming better leaders, through addressing the university system. *Journal of Cleaner Production, 48*, 10−19.

Olson, M. P. (2015). A multilateral approach to bridging the global skills gap. Retrieved from http://www.cornellhrreview.org/a-multilateral-approach-to-bridging-the-global-skills-gap/

Pellegrino, J. W. (2006). *Rethinking and redesigning curriculum, instruction and assessment: What contemporary research and theory suggests.* National Center of Education and the Economy for the new commission on the skills of the American workforce. NCEE. Retrieved from http://www.skillscommission.org/

Prince, M. (2004). Does active learning work? A review of the research. *Journal of engineering education, 93*(3), 223–231.

Regan, J.-A. (2012). The role obligations of students and lecturers in higher education. *Journal of Philosophy Education, 46*, 14–24. doi:10.1111/j.1467-9752.2011.00834.x

Savin-Baden, M. (2007). *A practical guide to problem-based learning online.* New York, NY: Routledge.

Smith, M. K., Wood, W. B., Adams, W. K., Wieman, C., Knight, J. K., Guild, N., ... Su, T. T. (2009). Why peer discussion improves student performance on in-class concept questions. *Science, 323*(5910), 122–124.

Smith, M. K., Wood, W. B., Krauter, K., & Knight, J. K. (2011). Combining peer discussion with instructor explanation increases student learning from in-class concept questions. *CBE-Life Sciences Education, 10*(1), 55–63.

Steiner, G., & Posch, A. (2006). Higher education for sustainability by means of transdisciplinary case studies: An innovative approach for solving complex, real-world problems. *Journal of Cleaner Production, 14*(9), 877–890.

Summerlee, A. (2013). Lectures: Do we need them at all? In D. J. Hornsby, R. Osman, & J. De Matos-Ala, *Large-class pedagogy: Interdisciplinary perspectives for quality higher education* (pp. 21–31). Stellenbosch, South Africa: African Sun Media.

Trilling, B., & Fadel, C. (2009). *21st century skills: Learning for life in our times.* San Francisco, CA: John Wiley & Sons.

Voogt, J., Erstad, O., Dede, C., & Mishra, P. (2013). Challenges to learning and schooling in the digital networked world of the 21st century. *Journal of Computer Assisted Learning, 29*(5), 403–413. Retrieved from http://ai2-s2-pdfs.s3.amazonaws.com/5113/5f0cd1fad2cfe00b26c531ccfd8bbc4a1280.pdf

Vygotsky, L. (1978). Interaction between learning and development. *Mind and society* (pp. 79–91). Cambridge, MA: Harvard University Press.

Walker, J. D., Cotner, S. H., Baepler, P. M., & Decker, M. D. (2008). A delicate balance: Integrating active learning into a large lecture course. *CBE-Life Sciences Education, 7*(4), 361–367.

Wieman, C. (2007). Why not try a scientific approach to science education? *Change: The Magazine of Higher Learning, 39*(5), 9–15.

Wiggins, G. P., & McTighe, J. (2005). *Understanding by design.* Alexandria, VA: Association for Supervision and Curriculum Development.

Williams, J. (2011). STEM education: Proceed with caution. *Design and Technology Education: An International Journal, 16*(1).

Zuelke, D. C., & Willerman, M. (1995). The case study approach to teaching in education administration and supervision preparation programs. *Education, 115*(4), 604–612.

Chapter 2

Designing for Active Learning: A Problem-Centered Approach

Susan Stetson-Tiligadas

Abstract

This chapter outlines potential steps to take in designing active learning experiences based on several theories underlying the learning process. The chapter examines theories of learning and instruction including information processing, schema acquisition, and cognitive load theory. Next follows an explanation of how these theories support problem-centered learning as well as a rationale for the need to help learners develop domain-general, flexible problem-solving skills that will transfer to future needs and contexts. The second half of the chapter focuses on designing active learning experiences based on the selection of real-world problems as the foundation for learning, activating prior knowledge, demonstration of the process or concept, multiple opportunities for practice with relevant scaffolding, and the chance to integrate that knowledge into the learners' own context based on M. D. Merrill's (2002) First Principles of Instruction. Examples of assessments, strategies, and activities to foster active, problem-centered learning drawn from the literature are also provided.

Keywords: Active learning design; problem-centered learning; flexible problem solving; cognitive load; instructional theory; first principles of instruction

Active Learning Strategies in Higher Education: Teaching for Leadership, Innovation, and Creativity, 45–71
Copyright © 2018 by Emerald Publishing Limited
All rights of reproduction in any form reserved
ISBN: 978-1-78714-488-0

Part One: Theories and Approaches

The theories underlying learning and instruction are continually evolving and developing. Just as basic quantitative research witnessed the arrival of a subjective turn supporting increased emphasis on qualitative methods, so has education experienced a subjective turn from the dominance of behaviorist instructivist theories to greater emphasis on cognitive constructivist approaches. Significantly, the emergence of the constructivist paradigm has shifted educational methods from an emphasis on the delivery of instruction aimed at bringing about an observable change in behavior signifying learning to the design of learning activities based on cognitive processes (Boghossian, 2006; Bruning, 1983), where "relevant, meaningful knowledge is created by the individual" (Sims, 2009, p. 386). Constructivist approaches, which steadily gained acceptance over the second half of the 20th century, lead to a more holistic, interdependent, and active learning process which more closely mirrors real-world learning and interaction. An example of this is when someone declares that better learning often results from performing on the job rather than from being lectured to in a classroom. On the job, learners are actively engaged in completing processes and solving problems which require a hands-on approach, either mentally or physically. Conversely, in a classroom lecture someone else, a content area expert, is relating the product of their own experience so that those in attendance can gain an understanding of the concept or process. Indeed learning can and does happen this way, but this more passive form of learning prevents the learners from gaining that active hands-on experience of interpreting and making meaning for themselves that can result in longer lasting learning and transfer to learners' actual contexts.

Moving the learner to the center of the meaning-making process has direct implications for the cognitive processes used in learning and, by extension, for the way the learning is structured. In other words, "knowledge relative to human learning helps shaping instructional methods that mesh with human beings' learning capacities and limits" (Pasquinelli, 2011, p. 190). To better understand learning through constructivist approaches, it can be useful to examine the cognitive architecture of the mind from an information processing theory perspective and to examine the affordances and limitations of this architecture on learning. Approaching learning through the lens of information processing theory with its focus first on the learner and subsequently on the instruction can contribute to more active and effective learning environments (Bruning, 1983). The information processing model in combination with cognitive load theory and schema theory affect how learning environments and activities should be structured based on how information is encoded and stored in memory. The first part of this chapter will endeavor to explain the information processing model, cognitive load theory and schema theory and will describe the use of problem solving as an instructional framework to promote active learning. The second half of the chapter will highlight evidence-based approaches to designing instruction for active learning.

Information Processing, Schema Acquisition, and Cognitive Load Theory

The information processing model derives from several parallels drawn between humans and computers. Martinez (2010) presents three common areas between humans and computers: both have different types of memory, both transform information into new information, and both are open systems that receive information as input and can produce some form of output to interact with the outside world. In educational terms, learners take in information, store it to a greater or lesser extent, oftentimes transform it into something new through analysis and synthesis, and may share the analysis, synthesis, or simple reproduction with peers or the instructor. Limitations connected to the first two types of memory, short-term memory and working memory, impact how successful encoding information into long-term memory will be (Demetriou, Spanoudis, & Mouyi, 2011). The transfer and encoding of information into the vast stores of long-term memory is arguably the purpose of all education; that is when learning has occurred. It is, therefore, important to recognize constraints on information processing and retention and to work within the boundaries of those constraints to design instruction aimed at long-term retention.

To arrive at learning transfer into long-term memory the other two types of memory first play their role. To begin with, short-term memory, sometimes called the sensory register (Demetriou et al., 2011), has an extremely limited duration. An example could be taken from online shopping when a six-digit one-time code is sent to a mobile phone for a user to complete a purchase. The code arrives and is entered into the appropriate field. If the buyer were asked even half a minute later to repeat the one-time code, chances are the individual would not be able to remember it accurately because it had been held temporarily in short-term memory. Thus, short-term memory is a rather efficient way of dealing with temporarily needed or inconsequential information to save cognitive processing power. Information regarded as more important moves in working memory, but working memory is also quite limited. One of the most frequently cited pieces of research in Psychology is from a 1956 book entitled *The Magical Number Seven, Plus or Minus Two: Some Limits on Our Capacity for Processing Information*. In the book, G. A. Miller reported on the number of items that can be processed in working memory at one time: seven items, perhaps five, perhaps nine. More current research puts the number of items working memory can process even lower (Cowan, 2015; Demetriou et al., 2014).

In many college classrooms, in one brief instructional period, students receive a deluge of concepts, facts, and figures, far more than the five or seven items that can be effectively processed. Adding new information before previous information has been effectively processed and encoded may effectively displace the previous information to make room for the new. For instance, when students leave a classroom, they may have firm grasp on the ideas discussed, but unless the information was properly encoded, new information in the form of conversations with friends or concepts from the next course may soon occupy the space in working memory, effectively pushing out the previous information. Fortunately, through the processes of rehearsal and repetition, single pieces of information presented together begin to form chunks. Understanding chunks impacts how load is placed on working memory, known as cognitive load, which is explained further down. The size of chunks is important because:

> An element or a chunk of information for particular learners and specific tasks is determined by the organized knowledge structures (schemas) the learners hold in their long-term memory base. With the development of expertise, the size of a person's chunks increases: many interacting elements for a novice become encapsulated into a single element for an expert. (Kalyuga, 2011, p. 2)

In a car driving example, a new driver's working memory is busy processing multiple separate chunks of information to start driving, such as attach seat belt, make sure the car is in neutral, put the key in the ignition, depress the clutch (while turning the key), check the rearview mirrors, select a gear, let up on the clutch, and engage the accelerator. Each individual piece places a heavy load on working memory, which Demetriou et al. (2011) described as a "holding system for pointers to schemas in long-term memory" (p. 612). Consequently, as the new driver gains more practice with this initial process, the individual pieces begin to form larger chunks. So instead of more than seven separate items to deal with, the working memory recognizes the pre-driving process as one chunk of information. New individual smaller chunks of information can then be processed together with larger chunks, facilitating schema acquisition, leading, in this example, to a complete "car-driving" schema. Building schemata, or mental models, is beneficial because they "tend to be more stable and resist forgetting" (Merrill & Gilbert, 2008, p. 201).

Schema Theory and Cognitive Load Theory

Additionally, van Merriënboer and Ayres (2005) noted that learners cannot manipulate new information effectively until that information has been encoded in schemata of long-term memory, and schema theory posits that knowledge is stored in long-term memory in the form of various groupings of related concepts, processes, items, or characteristics (Demetriou et al., 2011; Martinez, 2010; Paas & Sweller, 2012). Demetriou et al. (2011) described working memory as a "holding system for pointers to schemas in long-term memory" (p. 612). Therefore, to accommodate new knowledge, skills, or attitudes, learners should be encouraged to incorporate new concepts or features into existing schemata. Schema theory is in turn related to cognitive load theory, which posits that any form of new knowledge increases the cognitive load of the learner (Kalyuga, 2011; Paas, 1992; Paas & Sweller, 2012; Sweller, 1994). Cognitive load is considered "the major factor in determining the success of instructional intervention in attaining transfer of knowledge and skills" (Paas, Tuovinen, van Merriënboer, & Darabi, 2005, p. 26). Cognitive load theory points to two types of load on working memory: intrinsic load and extraneous load, and as Sweller (1994) noted, any information that leads to high cognitive load, no matter which type, constitutes a significant challenge to effective learning. It should be noted that some literature refers to a third type, called germane load in the literature (Morrison & Anglin, 2005), although its inclusion as a separate type of load is a matter of discussion (de Jong, 2010; Kalyuga, 2011). Nonetheless, the differences between intrinsic load and extraneous load have important implications for designing active and lasting learning.

Managing the two types of cognitive load can facilitate schema acquisition leading to learning. Of the two types of cognitive load, extraneous load is within instructors' control to decrease, while intrinsic load originating from the learning content itself is more difficult to attenuate. Intrinsic load is produced by what is to be learned, and the intrinsic load placed on working memory processing varies according to the prior knowledge and experience of the learner and to the nature of the content (van Merriënboer & Ayres, 2005). Intrinsic load processing could be perceived as positive load, in that working memory is being used to activate existing schemata and acquire new schemata. In contrast, "engaging in complex activities [...] that impose a heavy cognitive load and are irrelevant to schema acquisition will interfere with learning" (Sweller, 1994, p. 301). Extraneous load falls into this latter category. Extraneous cognitive load is the load placed on working memory, not by the learning content itself, but by instructional methods, activities, and presentation (Kalyuga, 2011). Sweller (1994) further remarked that "extraneous cognitive load, by definition, is entirely under instructional control" (p. 303) and that instructional methods "not directed at schema acquisition and automation, frequently assume a processing capacity greater than our limits and so are likely to be defective" (p. 299).

In sum, understanding the role of these cognitive theories in the learning process helps instructors improve the structure and types of learning activities provided to students. As Sweller (1994) argued, the processes of automation and schema acquisition are the primary foundation on which learning is built. Schemata, which may contain enormous amounts of information as illustrated in the car driving example, can be processed as whole chunks as opposed to isolated pieces of information, thereby improving the processing required to facilitate learning by reducing the cognitive load (Paas & Sweller, 2012; van Merriënboer & Ayres, 2005). Furthermore, schema theory and cognitive load theory can be related to flexible expertise used in problem solving (Kalyuga, Renkl, & Paas, 2010). Incorporating instructional elements aimed at building problem-solving skills into instruction can facilitate long-term learning and transfer and is the focus of the next section.

Problem-Based and Problem-Centered Learning

The quest to help learners acquire knowledge and skills has generated wide interest in the topic of problem solving. Problem solving, whether approached from a behavioral/instructivist or cognitive/constructivist perspective, is well supported in the research literature as an effective instructional strategy to promote learning and transfer (Demetriou et al., 2011; Kalyuga et al., 2010; Kuruganti, Needham, & Zundel, 2012). There is some confusion, however, regarding the terms used to discuss problem solving, with problem-based learning and problem-centered learning frequently being conflated and used interchangeably. Therefore, the first part of this section is an attempt to make the differentiation between the two types clearer. This clarification will be followed by a focus on the role of problem-centered learning and the construction of domain-general knowledge in problem solving. This section will conclude with a rationale for helping learners develop cognitive flexibility and enhance their flexible problem-solving skills.

At the outset of discussing the use of problems in learning, it is important to make a distinction between problem-based learning and problem-centered learning. As an approach adhering to the constructivist belief, the problem-based approach to instruction is inherently one which focuses on the learner and the active role the learner plays in building knowledge (Savery, 2009). Moreover, Kalyuga et al. (2010) estimated that the metacognitive processes essential to acquiring problem-solving expertise could be adequately fulfilled in mainly learner-controlled environments. True problem-based learning, however, presupposes highly trained tutors and a significant investment into facilities and support materials so that a small group of learners, no more than seven have access to resources as and when they deem appropriate in the course of solving the central problem (McCaughan, 2013). Howard Barrows (2002), the individual who is arguably founder of problem-based learning, briefly summarized problem-based learning as the use of ill-structured problems presented as they would appear in actuality, learners' almost complete responsibility for the learning process including negotiating the course of action and resources needed to reach a solution, a tutor trained in problem-based learning to facilitate the learners and prompt reflection, and the selection of authentic real-world problems (p. 119). However, research has shown that allowing learners complete control in directing their own learning processes with minimal guidance can be problematic and ineffective (Kirschner, Sweller, & Clark, 2006; Merrill, 2007; Merrill & Gilbert, 2008) since learners may expend their efforts and attention in unproductive directions. On the contrary, problem-centered learning does not require a rigid process and can be used to describe learning environments where knowledge and skills are acquired through solving authentic problems with appropriate support and scaffolding used when necessary. Information in the remainder of this chapter uses the perspective of problem-centered rather than that of problem-based learning.

Using problems as a basis for learning appears to be one of the more broadly applicable strategies to promote active learning. Problems constitute an effective starting point for learning because daily life is filled with a variety of problems which learners must face. Moreover, the array of authentic problems to choose from provides opportunities to build both content-specific and general problem solving skills. Jonassen (1997) noted that problems have a domain, a type, a process, and a solution, which together constitute the problem space (p. 66). Jonassen (2011) further described a continuum of problems from well-structured to ill-structured, shown in Figure 1. Well-structured problems generally have a specific correct solution and a clearly defined process to arrive at that solution (Jonassen, 2011). Ill-structured problems, on the other hand, have neither a clearly defined solution, nor a clear way to arrive there. Choosing problems appropriate to the content and to the learners' level is a key point in promoting active learning to help build problem-solving skills.

Building Flexible Problem-Solving Skills

Helping learners develop robust problem-solving skills in one particular domain, while beneficial, can be limiting. Domain-specific problem-solving helps build knowledge and skills in a specific area, but the skills may not transfer effectively to other problem domains. In other words, concepts gained in one situation may not apply at all or in the same way as in a previous situation. Kalyuga et al. (2010) claimed that the skills needed in the modern era in a world where technological change is a constant will lead learners to "dynamically adjust cognitive activities based on flexible knowledge, [and] nonroutinely approach new tasks and ideas" (p. 175). The authors therefore advocated for the acquisition of flexible problem-solving skills to give active learners some degree of

Figure 1.   A Continuum of Well-Structured to Ill-Structured Problems.
Source: Adapted from Jonassen (2002, 2011).

control over the direction of their learning and help them become more capable of transferring those skills and strategies to new problem-solving situations. Likewise, Demetriou et al. (2011) pointed out that it is important for educators to highlight the metacognitive aspects of learning and build reflective capacities so that learners can "swing between the domain-specific and the domain-general operation as efficiently and profitably as possible" (p. 643). Thus, helping learners develop cognitive flexibility and flexible problem-solving skills is a worthy goal in learning.

Cognitive Flexibility Theory

Cognitive flexibility theory (Spiro, Coulson, Feltovich, & Anderson, 1988) was originally founded on seven overarching principles: simple, regular problems should be avoided; problems should be approached from a variety of perspectives and levels; the application of concepts is highly dependent on the problem context; learners need to actively construct solutions; concepts should be examined in the context of the current problem − not prior ones; emphasis on highly focused schemata should be avoided as focused schemata are not applicable across a broad range of domains; and flexible thinking should be encouraged. If the problems seem simple on a surface level, an effort should be made to expose and probe their complexity. It is in searching for the complexity of a problem and deconstructing it that learners will be more effective at assembling a solution to the problem. Representing the problem from a variety of angles and perspectives will allow the learners to build a more comprehensive knowledge base to construct solutions to the problem. Examples or precedents, rather than the elaboration of theory and principles, are necessary to solve novel problems because the unpredictability of the concepts that will be pertinent to solving a novel problem precludes the anterior presentation of fixed materials (i.e., theories or principles). Learners need to assemble their solutions from the bottom up (Spiro et al., 1988, pp. 6−9).

Domain-General Skills

Furthermore, in describing cognitive flexibility theory, Spiro et al. (1988) advocated that "knowledge that will have to be used in many ways has to be learned, represented, and tried out (in application) in many ways" (p. 5). Providing multiple opportunities for learners to practice the developing skills will enhance schema formation while at the same time allowing for a variety of surface features to improve learner's flexible cognitive skills so that the learning will be applicable in a variety of as-yet undetermined situations (Clark & Mayer, 2008). Consequently, the use of well-established schemata should be de-emphasized due to the high probability of their not being applicable across various domains. Instead, the use of flexible, smaller knowledge structures which can be combined in myriad ways should be emphasized. Kalyuga et al. (2010) acknowledged that flexible problem-solving skills place a heavy cognitive load on working memory. Searching for a potential solution when the solution is ill-defined significantly increases the cognitive processing or thinking demands placed on the learner. Kirschner et al. (2006) claimed that "while working memory is being used to search for problem solutions, it is not available and *cannot be used to learn*" (p. 77, emphasis added). It could be argued, however, that while memory is being used to search for problem solutions, it is actively matching what it knows in the form of established schemata against potential "fits" and the cognitive load is an intrinsic rather than extraneous one. Through the application of flexible problem-solving skills, learners are extrapolating the relevant points or processes from one schema and trying to apply them to a novel situation (Kalyuga et al., 2010). In other words, working memory is busy evaluating and manipulating schemata to overlay onto the current problem, building sought-after cognitive flexibility. In other words, the search *is* learning because as learners are looking for a solution or set of principles to apply to a given problem, they are reinforcing existing knowledge while at the same time creating new connections across and among different concepts.

In conclusion, an understanding of learning theories and how they are interwoven with instructional theories can increase the likelihood of designing learning environments that lead to effective and long-lasting learning. Problem-centered learning has been described above as an effective approach to fostering active learning and enhancing both learners' knowledge and their metacognitive skills. More specifically, the act of problem-solving helps to develop higher-order cognitive skills, meta-representation, and personal and interpersonal skills (Demetriou et al., 2011; Kalyuga et al., 2010; Kuruganti et al., 2012). The limitations of working memory and cognitive load also play a significant part in the problem-solving process since higher-order thinking skills are made possible when working memory and long-term memory combine. Cognitive load theory posits that working memory can be easily overloaded by new information which decreases efficiency and hinders learning. The purposive use of instructional design strategies can help attenuate cognitive load and improve learner outcomes when learners are faced with novel problems and situations. The following section is intended to highlight particular guidelines and strategies as well as potential activities to incorporate when designing instruction for active learning.

Part Two: Design Guidelines for Active Learning

Introduction – Instructional Design

From the theories described in the first part of the chapter, the question turns to how those theories are applied in practice within that theoretical framework. In other words, it is important to consider which factors and approaches can effectively promote active learning. Common points can be derived from different types of effective instruction across different content areas and domains. M. D. Merrill (2002) in an article aptly entitled *First Principles of Instruction* presented a set of design-oriented principles to follow to create effective learning experiences. The *First Principles* framework will form the basis for an active learning design process described in this section, which among other points will analyze the types of problems to choose, how to sequence the problems, how and what kinds of scaffolding to use – and when to reduce scaffolding, and transfer of learning with the integration of the content or skill into the learner's own context. Lastly, a variety of different research-based learning activities, strategies, and assessment strategies for problem-centered learning will be described to provide instructors with a range of methods and approaches to choose from depending on the needs of the learners and aims of the course.

First Principles of Learning and Instruction

The five principles included in the First Principles of Instruction originated from a synthesis of other instructional design theories. As design-oriented strategies, the first principles can be applied to creating learning experiences across multiple domains and contexts (Merrill, 2002). The five principles can be briefly summarized as follows. Learning is promoted when: (1) learners work with authentic problems, (2) new knowledge is introduced after prior knowledge has been activated, (3) new knowledge is demonstrated to the learner (rather than simply being told to the learner), (4) the learner can practice applying the new knowledge, and (5) there is integration of the new knowledge into the learner's context (Merrill, 2002, pp. 44–45). Each of the principles and how they relate to designing active problem-centered learning will be described below.

Choose an Authentic Problem

The four principles of activation, demonstration, application, and integration proceed from an initial premise that effective learning can be fostered when the learning experiences are based on an authentic problem that learners are likely to encounter in the course of professional practice in the content area or in their own context. This point jibes well with the problem-centered approach explained previously. Merrill (2002) defines the term *problem* as one that includes:

> a wide range of activities with the most critical characteristics being that the activity is some whole task rather than only components of a task and that the task is representative of those the learner will encounter in the world following instruction. (p. 45)

In addition to the selection of a problem with real-world application, including the whole problem or task in the learning process rather than disjointed pieces of different problems or tasks can help with learning, developing flexible skills, and transfer (Kalyuga et al., 2010). Overall, using an authentic problem as a basis to design an active learning experience can help increase both motivation and transfer.

Transfer, the ability to take skills and concepts learned in one context and apply them in a new context, is arguably "the ultimate goal of education" (Martinez, 2010, p. 111). Near transfer and far transfer are both worthy goals of learning. Near transfer allows learners to apply principles from one concept, problem, or skill and apply them to a similar one, while far transfer is the ability to apply those same principles in a different way to a concept, problem, or skill which is quite different from the original (Smith & Ragan, 2005). Explicit reference to and discussion about the transfer of learning can greatly improve opportunities for transfer. Wiggins and McTighe (2011) pointed out that explicit and regular reference is important because most students do not realize that [transfer] is the goal of learning. They are quite convinced — from prior experience and, especially, typical tests — that the aim is to recall and plug in what was previously taught. [Instructors should] make clear that the "transfer" game is very different from the "recall and plug in" game. (p. 114)

A point of congruence between a principles-based approach and constructivist models is the need for the learning task to be based on learning experiences to which the learner can directly relate. Similar to Merrill (2002), Silber (2010) advocated that the instruction provide learners with a "realistic problem/case situation" (p. 38). Likewise, van Merriënboer et al.'s (2002) model emphasized that learning tasks represent "whole tasks that experts encounter in the real world" (p. 44). In other words, the problem must represent one which they would likely encounter during the actual course of events if they were already proficient in the knowledge or skills being learned. It would be ineffective to base instruction off an artificial problem which, while encouraging the learners to employ all the relevant skills, would be one they would not likely encounter in an actual situation. Therefore, the problem choice on which the learning will be based needs to be reflective of how that learning will be performed in the future if there is to be an expectation of transfer (Merrill, 2002, 2007).

An explicit explanation of the problem choice to the learners can help increase learners' active participation in the whole process. As experts in the field, instructors are deeply familiar with the problems, skills, and processes used during professional practice and may take for granted the fact that learners will appreciate or understand the importance of the chosen task, skill, or process. For novice learners, such as those at the general education level, it is likely that the relevance between the chosen problem (or theory) and practice is not apparent. When the instructor is transparent about the practical applications — even in situations where the broader scope may be beyond the learners' current abilities — learners can make a connection to the "bigger picture," potentially increasing engagement and enhancing far transfer. General education courses, as a foundation and introduction to a discipline, frequently focus on helping learners acquire the basic terminology for the processes and concepts at the expense of relaying why or how those concepts may relate to learners or to the broader professional field. Bannier (2010) concluded, in studying general chemistry courses, that as a consequence of waiting until higher-level courses to discuss the questions of why and how, "learners often feel disenfranchised, as if the course had no relevance to them whatsoever" (p. 227). Consequently, active learning will be improved if the problem choice is based on an authentic situation and if its practical applications are explained to learners. Active learning can also be promoted if the learners are asked to generate and predict practical potential applications of the problem, which are then confirmed or refined by the instructor.

Activate Prior Knowledge

Before introducing a new concept, process, or skill, it is useful to help learners recall, discuss, or explain what they already know about the topic that may be similar to the new content. The activation of prior knowledge provides an opportunity both for learners to recall past information and experience and to retrieve the associated memory structure or schema to use as a foundation for new knowledge (Merrill, 2002). Beginning the learning process in a way that allows learners to explicitly retrieve and activate existing schemata facilitates cognitive processing by reducing cognitive load (de Jong, 2010; Morrison & Anglin, 2005) and can foster higher learner performance. Hatsidimitris and Kalyuga (2013) noted that the depth or breadth of a learner's prior knowledge will determine "whether complex information is processed as many interacting low-level elements of information or as a single complex schema incorporating many interacting lower-level elements that have effectively been chunked into a single unit" (p. 93). Thus, activating prior knowledge helps reduce cognitive load and facilitates schema acquisition. From a different perspective, reflecting on prior knowledge can help establish a forthcoming cognitive dissonance (Glisczinski, 2011) where the learners perceive a potential disconnect between the known – or assumed – information and the introduction of new knowledge. As Glisczinski (2011) pointed out, such a situation can open the door for "scholarly teachers [to] model and then facilitate critical reflection" (p. 9) throughout the learning process to incorporate new knowledge into existing schemata. Smith and Ragan (2005) advocated using advance organizers, metaphors, and general review strategies to activate prior knowledge. An advance organizer can simultaneously prompt what learners already know on a topic and provide a preview of the whole task or lesson to facilitate schema acquisition. A metaphor or an analogy can be used to relate an abstract or complex concept or process to a more familiar cognate with similar features or processes. Merrill (2002) emphasized that, depending on the complexity and familiarity of the content, the use of pretests to activate prior knowledge can be frustrating and counterproductive. In sum, it is important to consider effective ways for learners to recall and activate their prior knowledge to establish active learning experiences.

Demonstrate the Problem

Demonstrating the problem for the learners is essential to allow learners to see a whole task, to gain an expert view of and approach to the problem, and to enhance cognitive flexibility by providing purposeful sequencing and multiple representations of the problem. Merrill (2002) pointed out that much more effective than mere information transmission through lecturing is actually demonstrating what is to be learned. Merrill (2002) further emphasized the need for consistency between the content being demonstrated and the goal of the learning, such as "(a) example and non-examples for concepts, (b) demonstrations for procedures, (c) visualizations for processes, and (d) modeling for behavior" (p. 47). Demonstrating new learning content can also foster learning through cognitive apprenticeship, in which learners gain from hearing the instructor as expert think aloud and apply expert steps and strategies (Martinez, 2010; Smith & Ragan, 2005), for example while demonstrating a process, procedure, perspective, or argument. Merrill (2002) concluded that demonstration strategies using specific portrayals of the information resulted in more effective learning than simply presenting "information followed by a few remember-what-you-were-told questions" (p. 48). Gaining an expert view of how to approach or solve a problem can strengthen learners' higher-order thinking skills because through cognitive apprenticeship, learners gain an expert view of the whole task rather than being left "struggl[ing] to discern and reconstruct the teacher's oftentimes invisible mental actions in their own mind" (Immordino-Yang, 2011, p. 101).

Sequencing

The issue of how to effectively divide and sequence the learning content also arises when focusing on the demonstration principle. In problem-centered learning, the sequencing of problems may significantly impact the acquisition and further development of higher-order thinking skills (Kalyuga et al., 2010), and there are a number of sequencing strategies an instructor might follow. Van Merriënboer and Ayres (2005) observed that presenting all of the relevant information at once can place a heavy burden on learners' cognitive load and that presenting information in stages with increasing levels of detail can help manage the cognitive load to make learning more effective (p. 9). Similarly, Kuruganti et al. (2012) supported that problem-centered learning is sequential according to skill and remarked that the sequencing of problems can have a serious impact on student success; if the problems increase in difficulty too rapidly, student output will decrease. The sequencing of the problems should therefore be simple-to-complex (Kuruganti et al., 2012). Kalyuga et al. (2010) provide evidence for two contrasting sequences, stating that a general-to-specific approach may be useful for novice learners as it does not require a high cognitive load up front. In contrast, Kalyuga et al. (2010) suggested that following a specific-to-general approach can build skills through practice and free up working memory resources which can engender the further development of higher-order skills (p. 181).

Demetriou et al. (2011) approached the sequencing issue from a different angle, focusing not on the way that the problems themselves are laid out, but on a student's developmental age as a measure of how learners advance their problems-solving skills. The authors explained that the acquisition of problem-solving skills progresses continually through an age-related developmental phase until it reaches the threshold of the next phase where the process recommences, building in scope and complexity until the cycle repeats itself (Demetriou et al., 2011, p. 618). Overall, there is not one best problem-solving sequence; there are sequences which work better in some situations than in others depending on the content and on the learner level. Consequently, it is incumbent upon the instructor as designer to have a solid basis for choosing a given sequence.

In addition to sequencing considerations, instructors should aim to incorporate multiple problem representations into the demonstration process to help learners develop and strengthen cognitive flexibility and flexible problem-solving skills. By providing multiple representations of problems, instructors introduce elements enhancing both near and far transfer. For example, by varying the surface features of problems at the outset, the instructor helps with the near transfer of skills to the next phase of learning, the application phase. On the contrary, a progression of problem types with more fundamental differences can encourage far transfer as learners are required to consider approaches and outcomes rather than simply applying the same process to a similar problem. However, it is important to note that an explicit explanation of the common features among various problem types is necessary to help learners build their flexible problem-solving skills by recognizing the domain-general features common to each problem. As experts in the field, instructors may take for granted or deem obvious common points that novice learners may overlook. In contrast, explicitly drawing learners' attention to common, domain-general features can help prevent misunderstanding or misinterpretation while improving the cognitive flexibility and flexible problem-solving skills that will lead to better transfer of learning to contexts beyond the classroom.

Support (Timely) Application

Merrill's (2002) fourth principle of instruction relates to the application of knowledge. Practice consistency in the application phase is equally important as described in the previous demonstration phase. Practice consistency might also be referred to as alignment among the learning goals, the practice activities, and the assessment strategies. It is logical that learners should practice applying new concepts, skills, or knowledge in a manner consistent with the way that the learning will be assessed, and by extension, in a way consistent with how the learning will be applied beyond the classroom environment. Merrill (2002) provided examples of specific strategies related to practice consistency, including:

> (a) information-about practice — recall or recognize information, (b) parts-of practice — locate, and name or describe each part, (c) kinds-of practice — identify new examples of each kind, (d) how-to practice — do the procedure [or process] and (e) what-happens practice — predict a consequence of a process given conditions, or find faulted conditions given an unexpected consequence. (p. 49)

Independent of the type of practice chosen, it is also important that the practice be timely. Half a semester of lecture classes during which students remain silent and take notes followed by an expectation of relevant or meaningful application on a midterm or final exam without previous opportunities to actively apply the knowledge is inconsistent with a desire for long-lasting learning. Timely, regular practice in applying the skills with the ability to receive feedback and guidance from the instructor is an important precondition to foster long-term learning. Appropriate scaffolding strategies described below can also facilitate the application of new learning.

The Use of Scaffolding

According to Demetriou et al. (2011), "when processing efficiency and working memory are weak, guidance is necessary to compensate for the students' weakness to construct the necessary relations themselves" (p. 638), an idea also supported previously by Paas (1992). This guidance is also known as scaffolding. In the application phase, learners can benefit from various types of scaffolding, for example from the use of templates or worked examples. First, the use of templates can free up more cognitive resources by allowing learners to focus on the learning content (intrinsic load) rather than directing cognitive processing power to non-content-related issues such as format, or interpreting complex directions, which are both areas that produce extraneous cognitive load. As Sweller (1994) observed, "extraneous cognitive load, by definition, is entirely under instructional control" (p. 303). For example, supplying an essay outline template (or lab report template, etc.) allows learners to focus their cognitive resources on the learning task rather than on extraneous-load factors such as proper use of Roman numerals, lettering, and indenting. Templates can lighten the cognitive load imposed by the instruction, in this example by the format, and help ensure that learner attention and focus are not diverted and expended in an unproductive direction.

The use of worked examples can also be a useful scaffolding technique. Kirschner et al. (2006) noted that worked examples "reduce working memory load [i.e. cognitive load]" (p. 80). Clark and Mayer (2008) advocate striking a balance between instructivist and constructivist strategies, stating that more directed strategies, such as worked examples, can facilitate learners at the beginning better than immediate application can. Accordingly, worked examples can be a particularly useful scaffolding technique for novice learners (Kirschner et al., 2006; Sweller, 2010). Nonetheless, although Merrill (2002) referred to the need to provide both scaffolding and coaching through feedback during the application phase, he also advocated the gradual removal of both to allow the learner space to become more independent in the learning process. Another reason to decrease scaffolding relates to the diminishing returns for learning as the learners become more competent in the content area. In other words, more expert learners may be hindered by including too much scaffolding of any type. This is known as the expertise reversal effect, which stipulates that the increased guidance and scaffolding that are helpful to the novice learner increase the expert learner's extraneous cognitive load by redirecting processing power to redundant, previously known information (Hatsidimitris & Kalyuga, 2013; Kirschner et al., 2006; Sweller, 2010). Jonassen (2010), Clark and Mayer (2008), and Van Merriënboer and Ayres (2005) each pointed to the expertise reversal effect as an issue to be aware of when designing learning experiences. Like Merrill, Jonassen (2010) and Hmelo-Silver, Duncan, and Chinn (2007) also supported the use and corresponding gradual removal of scaffolding in constructivist and problem-based learning environments. In sum, supporting learners through scaffolding and gradually reducing the scaffolding and coaching support can help learners build skills and gain confidence in applying their new knowledge.

Reflection

Designing opportunities for reflection should be an integral part of any learning experience. Merrill (2002, 2009) noted that reflection has a particular place in the integration phase of learning, while other research points to the importance of integrating reflective points throughout the learning process (Askell-Williams, Lawson, & Skrzypiec, 2012). As a metacognitive strategy, reflection deepens understanding and knowledge construction and helps with self-regulated learning and evaluation processes (Magno, 2010). Demetriou et al. (2011) supported reflection as playing an important role in developing learning to learn skills and critical thinking and noted that reflection is "the mental tool for the activation, refreshing, comparison, variation, and mapping representations onto each other in order to deal with novelty" (p. 624). In problem-centered learning, ongoing reflection is indeed useful for looking back over the process so far to evaluate and consolidate decisions made, avenues not followed, and the ongoing results. Reflecting forward is also a useful tool to design into the learning process. By reflecting forward, learners can predict other uses of the current process or skill and, more importantly, envision how that particular learning will be relevant to their lives in the future. This may be especially useful for learners completing the general education requirements of their studies. Learners in general education courses may experience low motivation to achieve the course outcomes because they perceive the course content to be entirely irrelevant to them and unrelated to their academic goals (Hawthorne, Kelsch, & Steen, 2010; Jessup-Anger, 2011; Warner & Koeppel, 2009).

The instructor can easily provide a number of ways the concepts or skills will be useful in the future, but to do so preempts the constructive, personalized aspect of the learning process. Using forward reflection, the instructor is leaving a space for the learners to fill in a projected need or relevance relating to their own context. In general, building in pauses to reflect − both forwards and backwards − on learning can keep learners active in the process and make learning more effective and relevant.

Design for Integration Based on Learner Context

Merrill's final principle of instruction relates to the integration of the instruction into the learner's individual context. This final phase of instruction has important implications for learner motivation and for long-term learning and transfer. As Merrill (2002) highlighted, "learning is the most motivating of all activities when the learner can observe his or her own progress" (p. 50). Motivation can be further enhanced when learners have the opportunity to personalize that learning to their own context. Sims (2014) in his support of the learning design process as a combination of science and art that could be termed *design alchemy* pointed to increased motivation that accompanies learning experiences when learners have the opportunity to personalize and contextualize their learning. Likewise, Kalyuga et al. (2010) emphasized that flexibility and the resulting transfer are also enhanced when the learners have some amount of control in determining some steps or choosing some personalized features in the learning process. Active learning is not likely to be promoted when learners show their knowledge in a multiple-choice assessment. A short-answer assessment as evidence of learning integration can be enhanced by allowing learners to explain the relevant concepts as they can be applied within the learner's own context. Assessments that better mirror practical application (e.g., portfolios, projects) may be more difficult to evaluate yet may provide learners with more effective means to integrate their learning in a meaningful way (Berg, 2006; Lombardi, 2008; Mislevy, 2007). As a result, learners will be more likely to take an active role in the learning process when they see the practical implications of the learning not only for completion of a particular course, but for their lives beyond the classroom.

In conclusion, Merrill's (2002) First Principles are domain-general concepts for designing active learning. They are broadly applicable across a wide range of learning domains and content areas. Using a First Principles of Instruction framework, instructors have a basic map to follow when designing learning experiences for students. By carefully selecting problem types, sequencing and learning strategies with an eye to transfer and cognitive load, instructors can create effective learning experiences that promote active learning. Furthermore, Sims' (2014) Design Alchemy pedagogy is also an effective framework to foster active learning through approaches such as problem-solving. Sims (2014) summarizes the learner-centered Design Alchemy pedagogy as:

> Focus[ing] on the learner in such a way that the activities the learner engages in, and the people and resources they interact with, result in the creation of assessment artefacts that demonstrate the achievement of learning outcomes and the ability to apply the knowledge in a context relevant to the individual learner. (p. 125)

This approach allows for the personalization and contextualization that are fundamental to designing experiences which keep learners actively engaged and which lay the foundation for long-lasting transfer of learning to life beyond the course or program.

What about Technology?

Readers may be wondering why technology has not yet been mentioned in the chapter. Indeed, technology is such a focus of instruction and can be a point of frustration and apprehension among instructors that it oftentimes seems to occupy a central role in learning today. However, it is worth remembering that technology should be used in service to learning rather than as a driver of learning. Sims (2014) warned of the ineffective learning that may result from designs based on technology rather than pedagogy and Merrill (2002) reported that incorporating flashy high-tech multimedia tools as a way to improve learner motivation would have a very limited effect, if any, on learner motivation. Furthermore, the potential technology needs and tools available vary widely from discipline to discipline preventing recommendations for a particular technology strategy or tool to include in learning. Sims (2014) supported that "a strong pedagogy can embrace any technological innovation" (p. 19) and further advocated following "a design practice that is pedagogically driven and technology enabled" (p. 98). Certainly technology is important to education today, but the design of effective active learning should begin with the learner and with pedagogical considerations foremost and technology considerations as an ancillary issue rather than a primary one.

Conclusion

Understanding the learning process has been greatly facilitated by research into cognitive processes and the acceptance of a constructivist learning paradigm. An awareness of the way in which information is processed, the limitations of processing power, and the cognitive load imposed on learners by instruction can inform and positively influence the way that instructors design learning for their students. Problem-centered strategies can be useful in designing active learning experiences because problems are almost universally applicable across disciplines as well as are imminently applicable to professional and personal contexts. Therefore, careful consideration of what types of problems to choose and how to help learners develop and strengthen domain-general as well as domain-specific problem-solving skills should be a focal point of an instructor's design process. Furthermore, incorporating strategies such as scaffolding and reflection can support learners in the acquisition and consolidation of new knowledge and skills. Lastly, using theory as a springboard for analyzing learning along with a framework such as Merrill's First Principles can constitute a useful guide to help instructors in designing active, meaningful, and long-lasting learning experiences for their students.

References

Askell-Williams, H., Lawson, M. J., & Skrzypiec, G. (2012). Scaffolding cognitive and metacognitive strategy instruction in regular class lessons. *Instructional Science, 40*(2), 413−443. doi:10.1007/s11251-011-9182-5

Bannier, B. (2010). Motivating and assisting adult, online chemistry students: A review of the literature. *Journal of Science Education & Technology, 19*(3), 215−236. doi:10.1007/s10956-009-9195-x

Barrows, H. (2002). Is it truly possible to have such a thing as dPBL? *Distance Education, 23*(1), 119−122. doi:10.1080/01587910220124026

Berg, S. (2006). Two sides of the same coin: Authentic assessment. *The Community College Enterprise, 12*(2), 7−21.

Boghossian, P. (2006). Behaviorism, constructivism, and Socratic pedagogy. *Educational Philosophy and Theory, 38*(6), 713−722.

Bruning, I. L. (1983). An information processing approach to a theory of instruction. *Educational Technology Research & Development, 31*(2), 91−101.

Clark, R. C., & Mayer, R. E. (2008). *E-learning and the science of instruction: Proven guidelines for consumers and designers of multimedia learning.* Hoboken, NJ: John Wiley & Sons.

Cowan, N. (2015). George Miller's magical number of immediate memory in retrospect: Observations on the faltering progression of science. *The Psychological Review, 122*(3), 536−541. doi:10.1037/a0039035

de Jong, T. (2010). Cognitive load theory, educational research, and instructional design: Some food for thought. *Instructional Science, 38*(2), 105−134. doi:10.1007/s11251-009-9110-0

Demetriou, A., Spanoudis, G., & Mouyi, A. (2011). Educating the developing mind: Towards an overarching paradigm. *Educational Psychology Review, 23*(4), 601−663. doi:10.1007/s10648-011-9178-3

Demetriou, A., Spanoudis, G., Shayer, M., van der Ven, S., Brydges, C. R., Kroesbergen, E., Podjarny, G., & Swanson, H. L. (2014). Relations between speed, working memory, and intelligence from preschool to adulthood: Structural equation modeling of 14 studies. *Intelligence, 46*(1), 107−121. doi:10.1016/j.intell.2014.05.013

Glisczinski, D. J. (2011). Lighting up the mind: Transforming learning through the applied scholarship of cognitive neuroscience. *International Journal for the Scholarship of Teaching and Learning, 5*(1), 1−13. Retrieved from doi:10.20429/ijsotl.2011.050124

Hatsidimitris, G., & Kalyuga, S. (2013). Guided self-management of transient information in animations through pacing and sequencing strategies. *Educational Technology Research & Development, 61*(1), 91−105. doi:10.1007/s11423-012-9276-z

Hawthorne, J., Kelsch, A., & Steen, T. (2010). Making general education matter: Structures and strategies. *New Directions for Teaching & Learning, 121,* 23−33. doi:10.1002/tl.385

Hmelo-Silver, C. E., Duncan, R., & Chinn, C. A. (2007). Scaffolding and achievement in problem-based and inquiry learning: A response to Kirschner, Sweller, and Clark (2006). *Educational Psychologist, 42*(2), 99−107. doi:10.1080/00461520701263368

Immordino-Yang, M. H. (2011). Implications of affective and social neuroscience for educational theory. *Educational Philosophy and Theory, 43*(1), 98−103. doi:10.1111/j.1469-5812.2010.00713.x

Jessup-Anger, J. E. (2011). What's the point? An exploration of students' motivation to learn in a first-year seminar. *The Journal of General Education, 60*(2), 101−116. doi:10.1353/jge.2011.0011

Jonassen, D. (2003). Using cognitive tools to represent problems. *Journal of Research on Technology in Education, 35*(3), 362−381.

Jonassen, D. (2011). Supporting problem solving in PBL. *Interdisciplinary Journal of Problem-based Learning, 5*(2). doi:10.7771/1541−5015.1256

Jonassen, D. H. (1997). Instructional design models for well-structured and ill-structured problem-solving learning outcomes. *Educational Technology Research & Development, 45*(1), 65–94.

Jonassen, D. H. (2002). Engaging and supporting problem solving in online learning. *Quarterly Review of Distance Education, 3*(1), 1–13.

Jonassen, D. H. (2010). Assembling and analyzing the building blocks of problem-based learning environments. In K. Silber & W. Foshay (Eds.), *Handbook of improving performance in the workplace* (Vol. 1, pp. 361–394). San Francisco, CA: Pfeiffer.

Kalyuga, S. (2011). Cognitive load theory: How many types of load does it really need? *Educational Psychology Review, 23*(1), 1–19. doi:10.1007/s10648-010-9150-7

Kalyuga, S., Renkl, A., & Paas, F. (2010). Facilitating flexible problem solving: A cognitive load perspective. *Educational Psychology Review, 22*(2), 175–186. doi:10.1007/s10648-010-9132-9

Kirschner, P. A., Sweller, J., & Clark, R. E. (2006). Why minimal guidance during instruction does not work: An analysis of the failure of constructivist, discovery, problem-based, experiential, and inquiry-based teaching. *Educational Psychologist, 41*(2), 75–86. doi:10.1207/s15326985ep4102_1

Kuruganti, U., Needham, T., & Zundel, P. (2012). Patterns and rates of learning in two problem-based learning courses using outcome based assessment and elaboration theory. *Canadian Journal for the Scholarship of Teaching and Learning, 3*(1), 4. doi:10.5206/cjsotl-rcacea.2012.1.4

Lombardi, M. M. (2008). Making the grade: The role of assessment in authentic learning. *EDUCAUSE Learning Initiative.* Retrieved from http://net.educause.edu/ir/library/pdf/ELI3019.pdf

Magno, C. (2010). The role of metacognitive skills in developing critical thinking. *Metacognition and Learning, 5*(2), 137–156. doi:10.1007/s11409-010-9054-4

Martinez, M. E. (2010). *Learning and cognition: The design of the mind.* Upper Saddle River, NJ: Pearson.

McCaughan, K. Dr. (2013). Barrows' integration of cognitive and clinical psychology in PBL Tutor guidelines. *Interdisciplinary Journal of Problem-based Learning, 7*(1). doi:10.7771/1541–5015.1318

Merrill, M. D. (2002). First principles of instruction. *Educational Technology, Research and Development, 50*(3), 43–43. doi:10.1007/BF02505024

Merrill, M. D. (2007). A task-centered instructional strategy. *Journal of Research on Technology in Education, 40*(1), 5–22.

Merrill, M. D. (2009). Finding e3 (effective, efficient and engaging) instruction. *Educational Technology, 49*(3), 15–26. Retrieved from http://mdavidmerrill.com/Papers/Finding_e3_instruction_EdTech%5BFinal%5D.pdf

Merrill, M. D., & Gilbert, C. G. (2008). Effective peer interaction in a problem-centered instructional strategy. *Distance Education, 29*(2), 199–207. doi:10.1080/01587910802154996

Miller, G. (1956). The magical number seven, plus or minus two: Some limits on our capacity for processing information. *The Psychological Review, 63,* 81–97.

Mislevy, R. J. (2007). Validity by design. *Educational Researcher, 36*(8), 463–469.

Morrison, G. R., & Anglin, G. J. (2005). Research on cognitive load theory: Application to E-learning. *Educational Technology, Research and Development,* 53(3), 94–104.

Paas, F. (1992). Training strategies for attaining transfer of problem-solving skill in statistics: A cognitive load perspective. *Journal of Educational Psychology,* 84(4), 429–434.

Paas, F., & Sweller, J. (2012). An evolutionary upgrade of cognitive load theory: Using the human motor system and collaboration to support the learning of complex cognitive tasks. *Educational Psychology Review,* 24(1), 27–45. doi:10.1007/s10648-011-9179-2

Paas, F., Tuovinen, J. E., van Merriënboer, J. J. G., & Darabi, A. A. (2005). A motivational perspective on the relation between mental effort and performance: Optimizing learner involvement in instruction. *Educational Technology, Research and Development,* 53(3), 25–34.

Pasquinelli, E. (2011). Knowledge- and evidence-based education: Reasons, trends, and contents. *Mind, Brain & Education,* 5(4), 186–195. doi:10.1111/j.1751-228X.2011.01128.x

Romoszowski, A. (2009). Fostering skill development outcomes. In C. Reigeluth & C. Carr-Chellman (Eds.), *Instructional-design theories and models: Building a common knowledge base* (Vol. 3, pp. 199–224). New York, NY: Routledge.

Savery, J. R. (2009). Problem-based approach to instruction. In C. Reigeluth & C. Carr-Chellman (Eds.), *Instructional design theories and models* (pp. 143–165). New York, NY: Routledge.

Silber, K. H. (2010). A principle-based model of instructional design. In K. Silber & W. Foshay (Eds.), *Handbook of improving performance in the workplace* (Vol. 1, pp. 53–92). San Francisco, CA: Pfeiffer.

Sims, R. (2009). From three-phase to proactive learning design: Creating effective online teaching and learning environments. In J. Willis (Ed.), *Constructivist instructional design (C-ID): Foundations, models, and examples* (pp. 379–391). Charlotte, NC: Information Age Publishing.

Sims, R. (2014). *Design alchemy: Transforming the way we think about learning and teaching.* Switzerland: Springer.

Smith, P. L., & Ragan, T. J. (2005). *Instructional design* (3rd ed.). Hoboken, NJ: Wiley.

Spiro, R. J., Coulson, R. L., Feltovich, P. J., & Anderson, D. K. (1988). Cognitive flexibility theory: Advanced knowledge acquisition in ill-structured domains. *Report from the Center for the Study of Reading.* Technical Report 441, ERIC Report ED 302 821.

Sweller, J. (1994). Cognitive load theory, learning difficulty, and instructional design. *Learning and Instruction,* 4(4), 295–312.

Sweller, J. (2010). Element interactivity and intrinsic, extraneous, and germane cognitive load. *Educational Psychology Review,* 22(2), 123–138. doi:10.1007/s10648-010-9128-5

van Merriënboer, J. G., & Ayres, P. (2005). Research on cognitive load theory and its design implications for E-learning. *Educational Technology, Research and Development,* 53(3), 5–13.

van Merriënboer, J. G., Clark, R. E., & de Croock, M. B. (2002). Blueprints for complex learning: The 4C/ID-model. *Educational Technology, Research and Development, 50*(2), 39.

Warner, D. B., & Koeppel, K. (2009). General education requirements: A comparative analysis. *The Journal of General Education, 58*(4), 241–258.

Wiggins, G. P., & McTighe, J. (2011). *The understanding by design guide to creating high-quality units.* Alexandria, VA: ASCD.

Wiske, M. S., & Beatty, B. J. (2009). Fostering understanding outcomes. In C. Reigeluth & C. Carr-Chellman (Eds.), *Instructional-design theories and models: Building a common knowledge base* (Vol. 3, pp. 225–247). New York, NY: Routledge.

Appendix: Activities to Promote Active Learning Using Problem Solving

Activities to promote active learning using problem solving

	Skills Learning	Learning for Understanding	Emotion/ Affective Learning	Integrated Learning
Learning Domains & Outcomes	Reproductive skills (algorithmic based, automatic skills) or productive skills (heuristic based, creative skills)	Knowledge (Theories & Concepts) Methods Purposes	Forms of expression	Combinations of learning domains listed to the left
Assessments	Report Multi-media project Use of questions to assess individual's understanding of group work Creation of a product Elaboration of concepts leading to product Comparison to expert solution of problem-type Performance Argumentation			
Strategies	Carefully select, organize, and represent the problem Promote causal reasoning Incorporate questions throughout Build in continuous monitoring (instructor) & reflection (learner) of the learning process			
Activities	Building real-world representations of model problems (quantitative & qualitative) Analogy to prior experience Worked examples Structural analogues Case studies Presentation of alternative perspectives Argumentation Simulations			
Source :	Savery (2009), Jonassen (2003), Jonassen (2011), Romiszowski (2009), **and Wiske and Beatty (2009)**			

Figure A1. A Matrix of Learning Domains and Approaches to Promote Learning through Problem Solving.

This matrix represents a list of specific strategies derived from the literature to facilitate the assessments, guiding strategies, and types of activities which can further learning in problem-centered environments and which are applicable to a variety of different learning domains.

SECTION II
ACTIVE LEARNING STRATEGIES
IN HIGHER EDUCATION:
"STORIES" AND LESSONS LEARNT

Chapter 3

Active Learning Stories in Higher Education: Lessons Learned and Good Practices in STEM Education

Anastasia Misseyanni, Paraskevi Papadopoulou,
*Christina Marouli and Miltiadis D. Lytras**

Abstract

Active learning is not a simple practice. It is a new paradigm for
the provision of high-quality, collaborative, engaging, and motivating education. Active learning has the capacity to respond to most
of the challenges that institutions of higher education are facing in
our time. In this chapter, we present active learning strategies used
in STEM disciplines and we analyze the potential of active learning
to redefine the value proposition in academic institutions. After
providing the theoretical underpinnings of active learning as an
evolving practice, an attempt is made to connect it with different
learning theories and present an integrative model in which institutional strategies, learning strategy and information, and communication technologies work synergistically toward the development of
knowledge and skills. We then present the results of a survey examining "stories" of active learning from the STEM disciplines, identifying good teaching practices, and discussing challenges and lessons
learned. The key idea is that active engagement and participation
of students is based on faculty commitments and inspiration and

---

*The three co-authors after the first one have contributed equally to the chapter.

Active Learning Strategies in Higher Education: Teaching for Leadership,
Innovation, and Creativity, 75–105

mentoring by faculty. We finally present a stage model for the implementation of active learning practices in higher education. Emphasis is put on a new vision for higher education, based on systematic planning, implementation, and evaluation of active learning methods, collaboration, engagement with society and industry, innovation, and sustainability, for a better world for all.

Keywords: Active learning; learning stories; STEM disciplines; mentoring; information and communication technologies; higher education; management of education; future of education

Introduction

Today, there is a global debate around the directions that higher education should take. The previous decade was characterized by a content-centric philosophy to justify the value of higher education. A lot of research was conducted globally for programs and curriculum design, for new studies in emerging fields but with a continuous monolithic emphasis on knowledge transfer and preparation of content for narrow learning objectives. In our view, elements such as creativity, collaborative work, intrinsic motivation to study, cultivation of research culture, and embodiment of social values in programs should be emphasized more. This content-driven paradigm of higher education has a number of limitations. In fact, it becomes obsolete day-by-day due to the fast evolution of content management technologies and with the great evolution of the internet and the social networks. Knowledge today is everywhere. Students become familiar with the existence of Knowledge Archives, huge open educational resources and teaching materials as well as thousands of massive open online courses. It seems that the traditional classroom model of instructor-led instruction becomes less and less motivating for students. The Generation XYZ consists of young people who are fanatical about using technology, used to fast transition of information in the internet highways, and maybe less familiar with collaboration and joint work. At the same time, instructors feel the static, slow-moving, and reluctant-to-change administration in higher education institutions as a key obstacle in the adoption of new teaching scenarios. In parallel, their academic load in teaching, scholarship, and service in their institutions increases anxiety, decreases self-esteem, and creates a context of tension and uncertainty. Within this complicated context, we support that active learning is a sound proposition.

Active Learning as an Evolving Practice: Theoretical Underpinnings and Propositions

The literature on active learning is spread across several disciplines. Several learning theories contribute to the main propositions of active learning. What is evident in the literature is an ongoing exploratory discovery of significant interventions among the teachers, learners, context, and content. While for many years the focus of studies was on deterministic approaches where the outcome of learning should be attached to specific learning tasks, nowadays we realize a shift in engaging scenarios where nothing is considered as predefined or in the context of cause and effect relationships.

At the same time, in the scientific domain of Educational Data Mining, the emergence of Learning Analytics sets new interesting challenges. The discovery of personal characteristics of learners and the understanding of hidden behavioral patterns as recorded in unexplored data sets of the educational practice provide a new wide area for the provision of active learning based on scientific findings in critical problematic areas of Higher Education, e.g., retention rates in programs, personal development plans, and the enhancement of policy making based on educational data. In the next section we elaborate on basic aspects of active learning based on different literature sources and different perceptions. The main purpose is to provide a common ground of agreement about the basic characteristics of active learning. This will be used for the development of an abstract model for active learning.

Active Learning Underpinnings

Many people consider active learning to be a recent and innovative approach to teaching, while thinking of lecturing as the traditional and oldest teaching method, dating back to the European Middle Ages. However, active learning as a phenomenon in which learners do things and reflect on what they are doing seems to have emerged before lecturing (Corrigan, 2013). As a philosophy and movement, active learning dates back to the last two centuries and decades, respectively

(Page, 1990). But as a practice and phenomenon, it is probably as old as learning itself. It is an innate process through which humans come to know things by doing and through experience. In the past few decades, it has received increasing attention in higher education as an approach that offers new insights into teaching practices; in reality, this trend toward active learning just renews our attention to some of the oldest methods of deep learning.

Research shows that the "traditional" lecture approach which is convenient for delivering large volumes of information cultivates passive learning, with students acting as mere "receptacles of knowledge" (Ryan & Martens, 1989). Such teaching may fail to develop skills that are essential for professional success such as the ability for collaborative work, critical and creative thinking, as well as problem solving. Furthermore, as learners have varying learning styles (Belenky, Clinchy, Goldberger, & Tarule, 1997), the traditional lecture approach may be appropriate only for a small number of learners. A variety of teaching methods is advisable to stimulate knowledge creation and retention. Studies show that lectures are the least efficient method of knowledge retention, when compared to reading, use of audiovisual material, demonstration, discussion, practice by doing, and teaching others (Sousa, 2001). A summary of the different types of evidence offered to support this assertion is provided by Bligh (2000). The superficial learning cultivated in lectures may also fail to stimulate student motivation and enthusiasm (Weimer, 2002). Over the years, the importance of employing active learning instructional strategies to maximize student learning in the college or university classroom has been emphasized (Chickering & Ehrmann, 1996; Chickering & Gamson, 1987; Cross, 1987).

Active learning describes a more learner-centered approach to teaching, an approach that fosters student engagement in their learning. Active learning is a key principle of "pedagogies of engagement," a term introduced by Edgerton (2001) to emphasize the need for a mode of learning that will allow students to acquire the abilities and skills they will need in the 21st century. It "involves students in doing things and thinking about the things they are doing" (Bonwell & Eison, 1991). Active learning strategies may include in- and out-of-class activities, and cooperative and collaborative learning, and may involve the use of technology tools. Instructors who employ active learning strategies spend less time lecturing and transmitting information and more time helping students develop their understanding and other skills which promote deeper learning. They thus resume the role of a facilitator in the learning process.

Extensive literature exists on different instructional strategies focusing on active learning (Bonwell & Eison, 1991; Doyle, 2008; Faust & Paulson, 1998). Some examples of such methods include:

- *Interactive lectures:* Interactive lectures may include a variety of active learning methods such as question-and-answer sessions (Socratic method), providing wait time for students to respond (pause procedure), student summary of another student's answer, brainstorming on a topic, interactive discussion, creating quiz questions. Icebreaker activities, in-class contests, and guest speakers can also be used to increase student motivation in a lecture.
- *Visual-based active learning:* Films and in-class demonstrations followed by class discussion or assignments in which students reflect on the audiovisual material are examples of visual-based active learning that can prove to be both effective and enjoyable.
- *Classroom assessment techniques (CATs):* The "minute" paper in which students are asked to summarize class content and the "muddiest point" activity in which students identify the most difficult point are good classroom assessment techniques that help develop active listeners and writers. Additionally, flash cards, clicker questions, and other personal response systems may provide immediate feedback to students on what they have learned.
- *Experiential learning:* Lab experiments, simulations, field work, and field trips are good examples of experiential learning in which students learn by doing, understand the practical applications of theoretical concepts, and become capable of connecting course material to real-life situations.
- *Problem-based learning:* A form of enquiry-based learning that reverses the traditional teaching approach, as students are given a problem and are asked to develop a procedure to solve it. It can be an individual or a group activity.
- *Flipped classroom activities*: In a flipped classroom, the typical lecture and homework elements of a course are reversed. Students view short video lectures and do assignments at home before the class session. In-class time is used for exercises, projects, or discussions.
- *Case study analyses:* The discussion of specific real-life cases allows students to apply the knowledge they have learned to a real-world situation and understand actions and consequences.
- *Creative activities:* Students may undertake creative projects (e.g., creative writing, production of artwork, audiovisual material, creation of games, web sites, presentations, performances, etc.) and integrate them with course material.

- *Game-based learning and gamification:* Using games to enhance the learning experience is an old practice that may increase excitement in the classroom. Classroom versions of TV game shows, electronic or board games, as well as role playing can be used for this purpose. Students can also be asked to develop their own games for the course. Alternatively, gamification is the idea of adding game elements to a non-game situation; it also seems to increase student engagement.

- *Cooperative and collaborative learning*: Collaborative learning involves joint intellectual efforts by students, or students and teachers together, toward a common goal. Cooperative learning is more structured: each student is assessed individually and is held responsible for contributing to the success of the group. There are many activities that can involve collaborative learning: brainstorming in groups, active review sessions, concept mapping (students create a concept map by connecting terms and indicating relationships between them), problem solving, visual lists (e.g., with the pros and cons of a topic), jigsaw projects (each student is asked to complete a discrete part of a group assignment), in-class role playing, panel discussion, debates, games, etc. In think-pair-share exercises, students work in pairs to discuss topics, compare/share notes, or evaluate another student's work. Assessed group projects are another example of collaborative learning.

- *Community-based learning:* This method involves teaching and learning methods that connect course material with the surrounding community (including history, cultural heritage, and natural environment). It is based on the belief that the learning experience of students can be enhanced by using intrinsic educational assets and resources that communities offer.

- *Service learning:* A teaching and learning strategy that includes community service as one of its essential elements. Students may engage in projects that have both learning and community-based goals. Through such projects, they may gain a broader appreciation of the discipline, and an enhanced sense of civic responsibility. Service learning enriches the learning experience for students, and strengthens communities.

- *Research-based learning:* Students are actively involved in research projects, often in collaboration with faculty; in this way, they get exposed to the most recent findings on a topic. Such projects help them develop their ability for critical analysis and synthesis as well as important transferable skills.

Some of the above activities can be incorporated into the formative or summative assessments of a course. Different active learning approaches have been used by the authors of this chapter in several studies, aiming at enhancing the learning experience of students: examples include experiential learning (Misseyanni & Gastardo, 2017; Misseyanni, Marouli, Papadopoulou, Lytras, & Gastardo, 2016), visual-based learning (Lytras & Papadopoulou, 2017; Lytras et al., 2017; Misseyanni & Gastardo, 2017), collaborative learning (Marouli & Misseyanni, 2017; Misseyanni, Marouli, Papadopoulou, & Lytras, 2017b), use of ICTs tools to promote and enhance learning (Marouli, Lytras, & Papadopoulou, 2016; Marouli, Misseyanni, Papadopoulou, & Lytras, 2016a), game-based learning (Marouli, Misseyanni, Papadopoulou, & Lytras, 2016b), research-based learning (Lytras, Misseyanni, Marouli, & Papadopoulou, 2016), and a combination of other methods (Lytras, Papadopoulou, Marouli, & Misseyanni, 2018; Misseyanni, Daniela, Lytras, Papadopoulou, & Marouli, 2017a; Misseyanni et al., 2016; Papadopoulou, Lytras, & Marouli, 2016).

Prince (2004) has summarized important benefits of active learning based on research findings. Active learning significantly improves not only the recall of short-term and long-term information, it also improves understanding of concepts and student academic performance, increases attention, promotes student engagement, develops enhanced critical thinking skills, improves students' self-esteem, and improves interpersonal relationships as well as teamwork skills. Retention in academic programs is also better when active learning strategies are employed. According to Schreiner (2010), "students who are thriving academically are psychologically engaged in learning and take charge of their own learning process." Several studies show that active learning in STEM disciplines increases student performance and improves student attitudes (Armbruster, Patel, Johnson, & Weiss, 2009; Cudney & Ezzell, 2017; Freeman et al., 2014; Preszler, Dawe, Shuster, & Shuster, 2007; Prince, 2004).

When it comes to selecting and implementing an active learning method, the risk that the activity may fail to achieve its purpose has to be taken into consideration. Simple activities such as pause procedure and class discussion are short and low risk, while longer-lasting activities such as experiential, cooperative, or problem-based learning entail higher risk for instructors (Bonwell & Sutherland, 1996). Other factors that increase the probability for successful outcomes (in terms of both student engagement and achievement of learning outcomes) when implementing active learning strategies are the degree of planning and preparation from the instructor, the degree of structure of the activity, the concrete nature of the subject matter, the student's prior knowledge of the subject matter and of the teaching technique used, the instructor's prior experience with the particular technique, as well as the encouragement of interaction among instructor and students (Bonwell & Eison, 1991; Svinicki & McKeachie, 2012).

A number of obstacles to active learning have been reported by instructors, including not being able to cover sufficient content in class within the time available, demanding pre-class preparation, the difficulty of implementing active learning strategies in large classes, instructors' pre-conceptions (some consider themselves good lecturers), lack of resources (equipment, technology), student resistance to non-lecture approaches (Bonwell & Eison, 1991; Svinicki & McKeachie, 2012). Another element that inhibits effective teaching, as reported by instructors is the "performativity" culture, where the pressures of performance and competition, with focus on high achievements in research, come in conflict with teachers' preferred ways of operating (Carnell, 2007).

The previous discussion of perceptions about active learning leads the discussion to the connection of active learning with some of the dominant learning theories. In the next section we elaborate further on this requirement with a focused strategy.

Connection of Active Learning to Basic Learning Theories – Grounding the Proposition of Active Learning Stories

There are so many learning theories that it is difficult to select one of them as the most influential, with greater impact on learning outcomes. The world of today requires a different perspective. The complexity and multiple dimensions of contemporary issues in higher education pose a challenge of looking for synergies and integration among the learning theories. This new approach fits with the main scope of active learning. The enhancement of interaction of learners in collaborative learning, the provision of cognitive exploration, the linkage between learners as social peers in social phenomena, and the great evolution of media and emerging communication and collaboration technologies link most of the major learning theories to active learning.

In this section, we provide our critical overview on the major categories of learning theories that provide useful insights for the planning, design, and implementation of any active learning strategy in higher education. Additionally, such a discussion automatically leads to a critical inquiry related to which is a flow, non-sequential model that guides active learning in real higher education environments.

In our perception, active learning is linked to most of the major learning theories and their consideration should inform our teaching strategy. Several categories of learning theories provide a context for critical discussion about the purpose of learning, with the most important examples being constructivism, behaviorist theories, cognitivist theories, motivation and humanistic theories, design theories, media and collaboration theories, and theories of identity (Table 1).

The interpretation of the basic value propositions of these theories in the context of active learning implies that an integration of learners' identity with behavioral, cognitive, and social elements requires a sophisticated design of contexts, media, and collaboration models. Finally, within this integrative view to active learning it is critical to envision a shift from content-intensive strategies to interaction-intensive strategies. Our exploration of the connection of learning theories with active learning goes beyond a discussion of how learning theories serve as reference theories. Thus, in Table 1, we outline the implications of major categories of learning theories for active learning. We also present active learning methods that, in our view, are associated with these theories. Our purpose is to use elements of this discussion as a guide that will inform several key requirements for the development and implementation of an active learning strategy. In the next step, we proceed a step further, by proposing an integrative model for the planning, design, and implementation of active learning in Higher Education.

Active Learning Integrative Model

Through the analysis of "stories" of active learning, we attempt to develop an integrated model for the adoption of active learning in STEM education, discuss scenarios for good practices, and provide guidelines for STEM courses. In our model, shown in Figure 1, learning strategy, technology enablers, and institutional strategies are the key parameters leading to student development and acquisition of knowledge, cognitive, practical, and transferable skills.

Institutional Strategic Fit is an important element of our model. Active learning can be seen as a well-justified institutional act in higher education. In most cases though, it is supported by enthusiastic and passionate individuals who feel the pressure of a static, slow-moving,

Table 1. Connection between Learning Theories and Active Learning.

Learning Theory	Description of the Theory	Implications for Active Learning	Active Learning Methods Associated
Constructivism	The learner is an information constructor. People actively construct or create their own subjective representations of objective reality (Piaget, 2013; Vygotsky, 1980). Examples of constructivist theories are discovery-based learning and problem-based learning.	The learner participates in the construction of knowledge. This implicates active engagement and participation which leads to more ownership of knowledge from the part of the learner.	Research-based learning; project-based learning; problem-based learning.
Behaviorist Theories	Learning is defined as a change in the behavior of the learner. Response to environmental stimuli produces learning. Positive reinforcement or negative reinforcement shape behavior (Watson, 2013).	Student—student and student—instructor interaction shape the behavior of the student. Positive reinforcement increases student engagement and improves attitude toward learning while negative reinforcement usually has the opposite effect.	Interactive class sessions in which students receive feedback from instructor and peers; collaborative learning; peer teaching; constructive instructor feedback on student work (positive reinforcement is particularly important).
Cognitivist Theories	Exploring mental processes such as thinking, memory,	Students receive information from different sources and are	Mind maps; concept maps; critical essays; project work;

	knowing, and problem solving is important for understanding how people learn. Knowledge is defined as a change in a learner's schemata or symbolic mental constructions (Cooper, 1993; Ertmer & Newby, 1993). The learner is viewed as an information processor.	asked to process this information, critically evaluate it, and use it to synthesize their own work.	literature reviews; case study analysis; and decision making.
Motivation and Humanistic Theories	In humanism, people act with intentionality and values (Huitt, 2001) and one should study the person as a whole (self, motivation, goals) to better understand how learning takes place. The purpose is the development of self-actualized, autonomous people (Rogers & Freiberg, 1994) in a cooperative, supportive environment (DeCarvalho, 1991). Learning is student-centered and personalized, and the educator's role is that of a facilitator.	Humanism theories are in perfect accordance with what is considered active learning in education. Students are engaged in the learning process and develop autonomy as learners. Support from and cooperation with instructors and peers seem to be important in this self-actualization process. More specifically in experiential learning, observation and experimentation are key steps of the scientific method; active	Collaborative learning; project-based learning; research-based learning; experiential learning (lab and field activities; visual-based learning).

Table 1. (*Continued*)

Learning Theory	Description of the Theory	Implications for Active Learning	Active Learning Methods Associated
	As an example of a humanistic theory, experiential learning theory postulates that "learning is the process whereby knowledge is created through the transformation of experience" (Kolb, 1984, p. 38).	learning includes any activity in which students have the chance to learn through "experience."	
Design Theories	Design-based Research (DVBR) is an important methodology for understanding how, when, and why educational innovations work in practice and aims at finding relationships between educational theory and practice (Brown, 1992; Collins, 1992).	Designing active learning environments based on educational theories, implementing them and evaluating the outcomes, is an important process that leads to a connection between theory and practice.	All active learning methods can be tested through design-based research.
Media and Technology Theories	Examples include theories on e-learning, game-reward and gamification, online collaborative learning.	ICTs have a great potential in promoting active learning; this potential needs to be explored. Additionally, game-reward systems or gamification could	Use of ICTs tools such as online interactive tools and collaborative platforms (online discussion boards, blogs, etc.) through course management

E.g. E-learning theory describes how electronic educational technology can be used and designed to promote effective learning (Mayer & Moreno, 2003).

Game-reward theory is based on the idea that game elements such as rewards and incentives increase intrinsic motivation in players while also offering extrinsic rewards (Wang & Sun, 2011). Gamification refers to the process of applying games or game-based elements in non-game contexts such as education (Leaning, 2015).

Online collaborative learning is based on instructor-led group learning online (Harasim, 2012).

be used as a means to increase motivation and engagement. Online collaborative platforms can also facilitate student–student and student–instructor interaction. These methods/tools will enhance creativity and innovation in the classroom.

systems or social media; use of videos, animations, computer models, and any technology that will enhance learning; game-based learning.

Theories of Identity	Such theories examine the relationship between mind and body.	Through active learning methods, learners are engaged in the learning process: they do things and reflect on what they do; thus, they understand	Reflective essays; projects in which some form of self-evaluation takes place; collaborative learning (any form of group work).

Table 1. (*Continued*)

Learning Theory	Description of the Theory	Implications for Active Learning	Active Learning Methods Associated
	E.g. Self-perception theory describes the process in which people observe their own behavior and come to conclusions as to what attitudes must have driven that behavior (Bem, 1972). Social identity theory, on the other side, proposes that a person's sense of who they are depends on the groups to which they belong (Turner & Tajfel, 1986).	better how they learn, and this shapes their character and identity. Also, the interaction with other students and the instructor through collaborative learning helps students develop a social identity.	

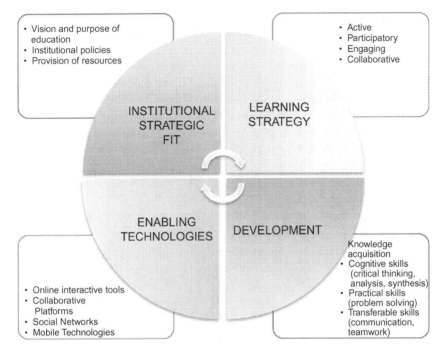

Figure 1.   Active Learning Integrative Model.

non-evolving learning context in higher education. In our perception, higher education administrators will sooner or later face the challenge of setting active learning the top priority for attracting talented students.

Learning Strategy is our means to achieve student learning and development. The learning strategy that we envision focuses on active learning, with interactive lectures, class discussion, problem-based learning, and collaborative learning. It is a strategy that promotes student engagement and participation in the learning process. Examples of active learning methods have been described in the previous section.

Technology Enablers are an essential tool toward the development of 21st century digital learners. Online interactive tools delivered through course management systems, collaborative platforms, social networks, and mobile technologies should be integrated into the teaching process to enhance collaboration and promote student engagement.

Development of Skills and Competencies is the aim of our integrative model. Our goal is not only the acquisition of knowledge but also the development of cognitive, practical, and transferable skills and competencies such as the ability for problem solving and decision making, teamwork skills, communication skills; all are essential for professional development and future careers.

Institutional strategic fit, learning strategy, and technology enablers act in a concerted manner to promote learner development; the evaluation of the outcome of this development becomes the driving force that can lead to further enhancement of the first three elements, leading to a reconception of institutional policies, learning strategies, and development of further technology tools.

Active Learning Stories: A Qualitative Analysis of Lessons Learned and Experiences Gained

The Methodology

A main purpose of the chapter is to discuss and compare active learning strategies in STEM disciplines. An extensive literature review was conducted to identify active learning methods used by instructors. In parallel, two open-ended questionnaires with similar questions on active learning were distributed to STEM faculty from different universities and colleges in two different periods, the results of which are presented in the section that follows in the form of stories. Each active learning story refers to a specific course and the teaching and learning strategy followed in this course; instructors were asked to discuss their overall teaching goals, the specific teaching goals for the course, the active learning methods they used, how these methods were evaluated, and what were the lessons learned. Each active learning story, thus, provides unique insights into teaching and learning in STEM education. Our sample is not a representative sample; it is a snowball sample. However, given that our purpose was to explore instructors' understanding and opinions relating to different aspects of active learning and the possible obstacles they face, this is considered adequately enlightening. We received a total of 23 responses (10 more analytical responses from the first survey and 13 from the second survey) from instructors in the STEM disciplines (environmental science, biology, chemistry, information systems, information technology, mathematics, and engineering) from different countries. Our aim is not to generalize but to contribute to a nuanced understanding of active learning, its richness, and the conditions that make it possible.

The Main Findings

1. *Goals in Teaching*
The answers of instructors concerning their teaching goals showed similarities and differences. Transmission of knowledge, but also development of other skills such as critical evaluation, analysis, application to everyday life, as well as practical and transferable skills were major goals of environmental science and biology instructors. Connection with real life and society and use of modern pedagogical approaches were also considered important by science instructors. Helping students develop ownership of basic knowledge in a field as well as develop critical thinking and the ability to challenge taken-for-granted ways of being in society was the focus of another science instructor. Understanding of quantitative information, application in real-life situations, and provision of opportunities for authentic learning using active learning methods were the goals of a math instructor. Knowledge, ability to communicate, development of critical thinking and research skills, empowering students, and enabling them to seek knowledge on their own were the focus of information systems instructors. Less content-focused and more skills-oriented teaching was mentioned as a goal for higher level courses. Setting challenges for students and making the subject appealing were additional goals of instructors. Development of skills and knowledge, and ability to apply them in real-life situations, awareness raising, and ability for problem solving and for working with scientific literature were the goals of other instructors in the STEM disciplines.

As a conclusion, it was obvious that all instructors who participated in the survey have teaching goals that aim not only to transmit knowledge, but also to cultivate cognitive skills (e.g., ability for critical thinking and evaluation), practical skills (application to real-life situations), and transferable skills (e.g., ability for communication and teamwork).

2. *Definition of Active Learning*
It is interesting to compare the definitions of active learning by the 10 instructors who participated in the first survey. Three instructors define it as learner-centered, in which students learn by experience and by "doing" things, while the instructor acts as a facilitator in the learning process (action-based and experiential learning). In an active learning classroom, students are actively engaged in various in-class activities − a form of learning that develops students' understanding and skills other than knowledge; problem-based,

cooperative, and collaborative learning were definitions given by two other instructors. Students being involved in the teaching process, being prepared enough for class, learning that promotes a proactive and participatory approach, learning in which students engage in reading, writing, discussion, problem solving, and case studies are some other key points in the different definitions of active learning. Similar answers were given by the 13 participants of the second survey. The greater level of student engagement, "more space and time for students to express their opinions and teach other students," students being active participants instead of recipients of knowledge, and student investment and involvement were some of the elements that, according to the participants of the survey, distinguish active learning from traditional learning practices.

Common elements in the answers of all instructors is the student-centered approach to teaching and learning, the engagement of students with a variety of activities other than listening to a lecture, and the development of skills other than knowledge such as critical thinking, analysis, synthesis, and evaluation of course-related material.

3. *Specific Goals for the Course*

The different nature of the courses examined (science, information systems, engineering, math) accounts for the variations in the specific goals for each course. Scientific literacy, resolving misconceptions about scientific issues, understanding of the human impact on the environment and of the impact of scientific developments on society, experiential learning, action research, application of course content to real-life situations, critical thinking ability, development of research skills, teamwork skills, knowledge transfer and knowledge discovery by students, awareness of the importance of social issues, increasing success rate in exams were some of the course-specific goals listed by instructors. Preparation for careers was mentioned as a goal in higher level courses.

As a general conclusion, the teaching goals for each course are related to the overall teaching goals and philosophy of each instructor and also depend on the nature and level of the course.

4. *Active Learning Methods Used*

A wide spectrum of active learning methods was used by the instructors who participated in the survey. Question and answer, brainstorming and class discussion, in-class debate, lab and field activities with teamwork, lab reports, group discussion based on video screenings, pause and in-class summaries, problem solving as well as use of online technologies (Blackboard, discussion boards, online quiz-zes, etc.) were some of the methods used in introductory science clas-ses. Collaborative work and action research through group projects involving field work, creative projects, and interviews, individual port-folios with journal entries and essays, as well as game-based learning were additional elements of a Greening the Campus course, with emphasis on experiential learning. Flipped lessons, problem solving with think-pair-share, collaborative learning, instructor feedback, and online technologies were used in introductory math classes. Flipped lessons and peer teaching were used by a variety of other instructors as well (biology, environmental science, and information systems). Case study analysis, class discussion, and collaborative development of students' research models were additional elements of more advanced information systems classes. Other courses examined used reading, writing, discussion, self-evaluation and collaborative work, role play and reflective assessment, tutorials, feedback sessions, multi-media content, brainstorming, as well as technologies and learning analytic tools to address students' questions and to solve problems.

Most instructors used ICT tools to enhance learning. Course man-agement systems such as Blackboard or Moodle and online interac-tive tools (discussion boards, blogs, and wikis) were extensively used by the participants of the survey. Use of social media (Facebook pages) was also mentioned by one instructor.

A conclusion that can be drawn is that the selection of the active learning method depends on the instructor's teaching goals as well as the specific goals of the course. Instructors' preferences and skills also affect the learning approach they will follow. Similarities and differences in the methods used and in the way they were implemen-ted were observed among instructors.

5. *Assessment of Active Learning*

The effectiveness of the active learning methods used was assessed by examining student performance in formative and summative assess-ments. ABET (Accreditation Board for Engineering and Technology, Inc.) key indicators were used in an Algorithm Design class. Student feedback obtained through official or informal course evaluation sur-veys, senior exit surveys, or informal discussions with the instructor provided a measure of student satisfaction with the methods used. Free journal entries and student self-reports used in some courses allowed students to reflect on the course and express themselves on their experiences and the active learning methods used.

6. *Evaluation of Methods Used*

When instructors were asked to evaluate the methods used, the following interesting conclusions could be drawn:

- Some activities such as group projects and flipped lessons promoted a higher level of student engagement and cultivated more student autonomy, as assessed by instructors and students (Misseyanni et al., 2016, 2017a, 2017b; Misseyanni & Gastardo, 2017). Lab and field activities and reports also involved significant engagement and also helped students develop practical and transferable skills such as the ability for teamwork and for scientific writing. They were characterized as very effective by instructors of science courses and by students of environmental science classes.

- For many instructors, it is difficult to decide which method produced more learning, so it can be concluded that a combination of different active learning methods can prove effective. For example, flipped lessons with follow-up in-class activities positively affected both students' perception of the course and student learning, as assessed by a survey (Misseyanni et al., 2016). Both visual methods (followed by class discussion) and experiential learning methods (through lab and field work) were rated as effective and enjoyable by students of an environmental science class (Misseyanni & Gastardo, 2017). Problem solving seems to be a successful learning method in math classes. Also, a combination of class discussion, case study analysis, and student project presentations proved effective in an information systems class.

- Using online technologies, mobile technologies, and multimedia content; exchanging opinions; solving students' real-world questions; and employing a toolbox acquired during the lectures.

Toward an Integrated Model for the Adoption of Active Learning in STEM Education

Lessons for STEM Disciplines

Taking into consideration the results of the survey, some general conclusions can be drawn (Misseyanni et al., 2016, 2017a, 2017b; Misseyanni & Gastardo, 2017):

- The subject of the course plays a role in the selection of the appropriate active learning method. Experiential learning through lab and field work as well as visual methods (videos, animations) are widely used in science courses, while problem solving and peer teaching is widely used in math courses.

- The level of the course is also important. It is easier to implement active learning practices in higher level courses, in which more autonomy and a higher level of maturity is expected from students; such courses also prepare students for their professional careers. Project-based learning (individual or group projects), role playing, and case study analysis are methods used in higher level courses, as these methods cultivate higher order learning skills. A challenge associated with introductory science classes is that of having to deliver large volumes of information while also trying to achieve depth, stimulate student interest, and combat students' pre-conceptions about science. However, students' previous experience with active learning methods greatly facilitates such endeavors at any educational level (see the Finnish educational system).
- Collaborative learning is widely used by instructors in the STEM disciplines and is characterized as an effective method of student learning. Instructors should be ready to address issues of group dynamics that may lead to conflict, disagreement, and feelings of resentment (Misseyanni et al., 2017b).
- The potential of ICTs to enhance active learning is huge and seems not to be fully explored by instructors who mention using ICTs mostly in the form of course management systems, to upload information and resources, and less to promote interaction and collaboration. Development of suitable computer applications would save time for instructors in the preparation and delivery of their courses.
- The composition of the student population (age, educational and cultural background, major) and group dynamics are important. Challenges include meeting the needs of all students in heterogeneous groups, such as the ones in introductory science classes, as well as adjusting to the different types of learners.
- Time management and use of more time-efficient active learning methods are important as time is limited and material of the syllabus needs to be covered.
- Active learning implies more democratic class settings – living with uncertainty. However, classroom management while implementing the active learning method is essential so that students feel it is not just a "fun" activity, unrelated to learning.
- Maintaining student motivation and engagement with the active learning method throughout the course is necessary. If students don't

engage sufficiently with the learning method, no active learning can be achieved.

- Mentoring and guidance are needed; students feel more secure when expressing their ideas in a group; group work should be enhanced for this purpose. A balance between guidance and freedom to think, learn, and connect ideas should be established.

General Lessons Learned

In order to effectively move toward a more engaging and socially useful education that can foster more collaborative and integrated societies, we need to consider how active learning can become the major paradigm in education − including higher education − and what elements should be present or emphasized. Our model presented in Figure 1 stresses the interplay of institutional strategic fit, learning strategy, and technology enablers in the development of skills and competencies.

Active learning is both a pedagogic paradigm/theory and a teaching and learning process. Active learning as a process is guided by a theory of learning that places students and everyday experience at the center of the learning process. It is also assessed as an outcome, as it is translated into specific skills and knowledge.

In our view and based on the results of our research, active learning as a process implies a combination of the following parameters:

- *Institutional aspects*: Given that active learning accepts unpredictability in the class, the educational institution in which the course takes place should support flexible learning processes in terms of both curriculum design and institutional support.
- *People involved*: Instructors and students with prior exposure to student-centered and experiential learning methods are more open to active learning. Instructors with prior skills in different alternative pedagogies are often more willing and capable of introducing active learning techniques in their courses. Students with prior exposure to active learning methods can more quickly appreciate these methods and can effectively participate more readily. Individual predispositions of instructors and students are also a significant parameter that colors their reaction to such teaching/learning approaches.
- *Resources*: As highlighted from the responses of the instructors in our research, incorporating active learning in the learning process implies

increased lesson preparation as well as use of information and communication technologies. Thus, certain resources are required or at least advisable for the promotion of active learning pedagogies in an educational institution.

- *Design of active learning strategy*: Active learning activities should be well integrated in the course's learning plan. Thus, any activity should be preceded with needed preparatory activities and follow-up activities that facilitate reflection and connections with other course materials. Ideally, active learning activities are also well integrated with social—environmental concerns of the local community, leading to actual problem solving.
- *Stages*: Given that active learning is a process, the stages of planning, doing, checking, and revising are important and should be consciously incorporated in curriculum development.
- *Flexibility*: Active learning is characterized by flexibility as it is based on integration of unforeseen events in the learning process, rather than control of the process to avoid unpredictability. Flexibility also implies the ability to use a variety of teaching/learning approaches.
- *Education in society*: Active learning comes as a requirement in our time, given the new role that education has in society: problem solving of significant social and environmental problems; more integral connection between education and society; connection of different aspects of society and economy; innovative approaches to contemporary concerns.

A Stage Model for the Adoption of Active Learning in STEM Disciplines

We propose a stage model for the adoption of active learning in STEM disciplines that comprises the following steps (Figure 2):

1. *Goal/vision clarification*
   Setting goals and clarifying the vision in teaching and learning is an important first step at the level of the course, the program, and the institution. At the level of the course, the instructor should have a clear vision and teaching pedagogy that will guide him/her in the selection of the appropriate teaching and learning strategy. At the program level, teaching methods should satisfy the learning outcomes and help students develop important transferable skills. Institutions, on the other side, should aim at cultivating a culture of engagement that leads to the creation of informed global citizens.

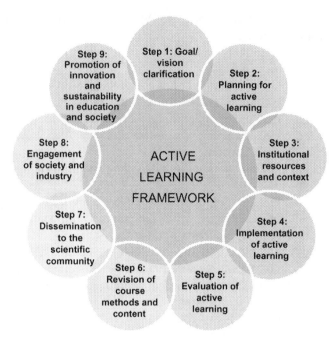

Figure 2.   A Stage Model for the Adoption of Active Learning.

2. *Planning for active learning*

Planning is an important step in the adoption of an active learning approach. The appropriate selection of teaching methods is an essential step in the planning process; these should reflect the teaching goals and help achieve the learning outcomes of the course. The assessment strategy of the course should also support the active learning approach. Our study shows that the nature of the course (discipline, level) plays an important role in the selection of the appropriate teaching strategy. Suitable teaching materials also need to be selected and developed, as needed. Resources needed also have to be identified.

3. *Institutional resources and context*

The institution should be ready to provide the appropriate resources for the implementation of the active learning approach: technology, physical resources (facilities, space), instructor training, and library resources. Course release time for instructors designing active learning strategies and engaging in the scholarship of teaching and support to faculty for attending related conferences and adopting active learning practices at the institutional level are some of the institutional aspects that should be considered.

4. *Implementation of active learning*

The active learning component and strategy must be integrated into the teaching of the specific course; they must become part of the learning process. Some challenges instructors have to face are maximizing student engagement, providing the appropriate guidance and support throughout the activity, time management, addressing issues of conflict, and maintaining overall control of the classroom.

5. *Evaluation of active learning*

Active learning methods should be evaluated in terms of their effectiveness in achieving learning outcomes, the impact of the method on student attitudes, and the suitability of resources used (technology, physical resources). Student performance in assessments, official course evaluation surveys, as well as senior exit surveys provide a measure of student learning and satisfaction with the teaching methods used. Surveys in which students are asked to evaluate specific active learning methods in terms of how effective and how enjoyable they were provide additional information about specific methods used in a particular course and may allow instructors to connect particular methods with the achievement of specific learning outcomes of the course. Surveys in which instructors are asked to evaluate the methods used provide additional insights into how particular methods affect student learning.

6. *Revision of course methods and content*

The results from the evaluation of the active learning approach should be used to revise course methods and content. This may lead to a redesign of the course syllabus to incorporate active learning methods into the teaching and learning strategy of the course. Introduction of more projects, problem-based learning, collaborative learning, role playing, as well as use of ICTs in the learning process would promote more active student engagement and autonomy. Assessment methods may also need to be reconsidered, as our study indicates that some assessment methods such as exams based on memorization do not seem to support an active learning approach (Papadopoulou, Lytras, Misseyanni, & Marouli, 2017).

Course content may also need to be revised; our experience shows that heavy course content is a barrier to active learning. An issues approach, with case studies and problem solving, would be more suitable for higher level courses and would certainly promote critical thinking and increase student engagement if connected with the appropriate teaching and assessment methods. More difficult appear to be the cases of large classes in introductory survey courses that cover a big breadth of topics. Achieving student engagement in such cases may be a really challenging task.

When courses are an integral part of academic programs, revisions to the whole program may be considered necessary, in order to incorporate a philosophy of active learning and an overall pedagogy of engagement into the program. Such revisions should be discussed at program level and institutional level and should be communicated to the academic community through program committees and curriculum committees.

7. *Dissemination to the scientific community*
Disseminating the results of the active learning approach to the scientific community would be an important stage. This could happen through participating in workshops and conferences, writing academic papers, and engaging in the scholarship of teaching. Exchange of information and ideas among academics and development of collaborations at international level would help develop and improve teaching competence. Institutional support in the form of training workshops, establishment of teaching and learning centers, course release time for faculty, and funding for participation in international conferences would be essential for developing a culture that fosters pedagogies of engagement across the institution and helping in the dissemination of research findings to the scientific community.

8. *Engagement of society and industry*
The next important stage would be to try to integrate the learning process with society and industry. Higher education today is asked to provide more than knowledge transfer; it should aim to strengthen its connection with the world of work and address societal needs (UNESCO, 1998). Active learning leads to the creation of more civically engaged and creative individuals. It provides skills that are important for students' professional development. The connection with industry and society should be taken into consideration in the design of active learning strategies. Projects conducted in collaboration with the industry and the world of work, or within the framework of work–study programs and apprenticeships, will bring students in confrontation with real-life problem solving and will

enhance their employability skills. Creative projects in which students develop entrepreneurial skills will also help students not only seek better jobs but also become job creators.

Connections and synergies should be developed between higher education institutions and the world of work at the level of the course, the program, and the institution. Additionally, social responsibility should be cultivated throughout the curriculum. Active learning strategies based on collaborative learning, service learning, or community-based learning would strengthen this sense of social responsibility and promote the desirable connection of higher education with society.

9. *Promotion of innovation and sustainability in education and society*
   In the 21st century knowledge society, higher education is called to play an enhanced role, promoting innovation and interdisciplinary/transdisciplinary work (UNESCO, 1998). Furthermore, in contemporary society which faces urgent environmental problems and increasing social inequalities, sustainability has become an important social goal, with higher education institutions aiming to "green" their campuses and curricula. Sustainability requires integrated approaches, involving knowledge and innovation, new practices and emotional involvement. Action research, a form of active learning that involves learning via committed action and research, is tightly connected with such efforts. Learning for sustainability involves emotions, aside of the mind, and looks for innovation in thinking, formulating, and solving problems and in choosing technologies (Marouli et al., 2016a). Innovation in teaching and learning brings innovation in the curriculum and in the vision and mission of higher education institutions.

Conclusion – Future Research Directions

With this chapter, we introduced the main dimensions of active learning and we set the ground for scientific discussion for the past, present, and future of it. Supported by a large number of learning theories, active learning can be seen not just as a simple practice, but as a new paradigm for the provision of high-quality, collaborative, engaging, and motivating education. From our discussion, based on "stories" of active learning in STEM disciplines, we learned lessons on effective teaching strategies and discussed challenges that instructors face and implications for higher education institutions.

From our lessons learned, it seems that instructors should carefully select the active learning methods to use, depending on teaching goals and course learning outcomes. Ways to maximize student engagement with the active learning method and thus maximize its success and effectiveness should be explored. The potential of ICTs to enhance active learning and foster more student-centered and collaborative approaches is huge and presents an area for further research. A redesign of the course syllabus might be necessary, to include active learning elements in the teaching strategy and the assessment of the course. Support from the administration would be a key factor for the successful implementation and further enhancement of active learning approaches at institutional level.

Future studies should focus on further exploring effective active learning strategies using large samples of students and classes and comparing classes with and without active learning; measuring student performance in courses where specific active learning methods are implemented; evaluating student satisfaction on the active learning approach used; and exploring instructors' perception on innovative teaching and learning strategies.

We conclude that active learning has the potential to redefine the value proposition in academic institutions by bringing together students, instructors, higher education administration, society, and industry toward a new, integrative model of teaching and learning. And this model sets the grounds for the new era that we envision in higher education; an era with emphasis on collaboration, cultural integration, and human development, toward a better world for all.

References

Armbruster, P., Patel, M., Johnson, E., & Weiss, M. (2009). Active learning and student-centered pedagogy improve student attitudes and performance in introductory biology. *Cell Biology Education, 8*(3), 203–213.

Belenky, M. F., Clinchy, B. M., Goldberger, N. R., & Tarule, J. M. (1997). *Women's ways of knowing: The development of self, voice, and mind* (10th Anniversary Edition). New York, NY: Basic Books/Harper Collins.

Bem, D. J. (1972). Self-perception theory. *Advances in Experimental Social Psychology, 6*, 1–62.

Bligh, D. A. (2000). *What's the use of lectures?* San Francisco, CA: Jossey-Bass Publishers.

Bonwell, C., & Eison, J. (1991). *Active learning: Creating excitement in the classroom (ASHE-ERIC Higher Education Report No. 1)*. Washington, DC: George

Washington University. Retrieved from http://www.ed.gov/databases/ERIC_ Digests/ed340272.html

Bonwell, C. C., & Sutherland, T. E. (1996). The active learning continuum: Choosing activities to engage in the classroom. In T. E. Sutherland & C. C. Bonwell (Eds.), *Using active learning in college classes: A range of options for faculty — New Directions for Teaching and Learning* (Number 67, Fall, pp. 3−16). San Francisco, CA: Jossey-Bass Publishers.

Brown, A. L. (1992). Design experiments: Theoretical and methodological challenges in creating complex interventions in classroom settings. *The Journal of the Learning Sciences, 2*(2), 141−178.

Carnell, E. (2007). Conceptions of effective teaching in higher education: Extending the boundaries. *Teaching in Higher Education, 12*(1), 25−40.

Chickering, A. W., & Ehrmann, S. C. (1996). Implementing the seven principles: Technology as a lever. *AAHE Bulletin, 49*(2), 3−6.

Chickering, A. W., & Gamson, Z. F. (1987). Seven Principles for Good Practice in Higher Education. *American Association for Higher Education, 39*, 3−7.

Collins, A. (1992). Towards a design science of education. In E. Scanlon & T. O'Shea (Eds.), *New directions in educational technology* (pp. 15−22). Berlin: Springer.

Cooper, P. A. (1993). Paradigm shifts in designed instruction: From behaviorism to cognitivism to constructivism. *Educational Technology, 33*(5), 12−19.

Corrigan, P. T. (2013). Active learning has an ancient history. *Teaching and Learning in Higher Education.* Retrieved from https://teachingandlearninginhighered.org/2013/11/30/active-learning-has-an-ancient-history/

Cross, P. (1987). Teaching for learning. *AAHE Bulletin, 39*(8), 3−7.

Cudney, E. A., & Ezzell, J. M. (2017). Evaluating the impact of teaching methods on student motivation. *Journal of STEM Education, 18*(1), 32−49.

DeCarvalho, R. (1991). The humanistic paradigm in education. *The Humanistic Psychologist, 19*(1), 88−104.

Doyle, T. (2008). *Helping students learn in a learner centered environment: A guide to teaching in higher education.* Sterling, VA: Stylus.

Edgerton, R. (2001). *Education White Paper.* Retrieved from http://www.pewundergradforum.org/wp1.html

Ertmer, P. A., & Newby, T. J. (1993). Behaviorism, cognitivism, constructivism: Comparing critical features from an instructional design perspective. *Performance Improvement Quarterly, 6*(4), 50−72.

Faust, J. L., & Paulson, D. R. (1998). Active learning in the college classroom. *Journal on Excellence in College Teaching, 9*(2), 3−24.

Freeman, S., Eddy, S., McDonough, M., Smith, M., Okoroafor, N., Jordt, H., & Wenderoth, M. (2014). Active learning increases student performance in science, engineering, and mathematics. *Proceedings of the National Academy of Sciences, 111*(23), 8410−8415.

Harasim, L. (2012). *Learning theory and online technologies.* New York, NY: Routledge.

Huitt, W. (2001). *Humanism and open education — Educational psychology interactive.* Valdosta, GA: Valdosta State University.

Kolb, D. A. (1984). *Experiential learning: Experience as the source of learning and development*. Englewood Cliffs, NJ: Prentice-Hall, Inc.

Leaning, M. (2015). A study of the use of games and gamification to enhance student engagement, experience and achievement on a theory-based course of an undergraduate media degree. *Journal of Media Practice, 16*(2), 155–170.

Lytras, M., Misseyanni, A., Marouli, C., & Papadopoulou, P. (2016). Integrating research to teaching in Higher Education: A value chain model for academic excellence and student development. *ICERI2016 Proceedings*, 5332–5342. doi:10.21125/iceri.2016.2296

Lytras, M., & Papadopoulou, P. (2017). Virtual reality systems for introductory biology labs: An integrated survey of industry solutions. In J. Beseda, L. Rohlikova, & J. Bat'ko (Eds.), *Disco 2017: Open education as a way to a knowledge society, 12th conference reader* (pp. 421–435). Prague, Czech Republic: Center for Higher Education Studies.

Lytras, M. D., Papadopoulou, P., Marouli, C., & Misseyanni, A. (2018). Higher education out-of-the-box: Technology-driven learning innovation in higher education. In S. Burton (Ed.), *Engaged scholarship and civic responsibility in higher education* (pp. 67–100). Hershey, PA: IGI Global. doi:10.4018/978-1-5225-3649-9.ch004

Marouli, C., Lytras, M., & Papadopoulou, P. (2016). Design guidelines for massive open online courses (MOOCS) in STEM: Methodological considerations towards active participatory teaching and learning. *EDULEARN16 Proceedings*, 5686–5693. doi:10.21125/edulearn.2016.2359

Marouli, C., & Misseyanni, A. (2017). Sharing knowledge in higher education: Collaborative teaching, collaborative learning and ICTs. In J. Beseda, L. Rohlikova, & J. Bat'ko (Eds.), *Disco 2017: Open education as a way to a knowledge society, 12th conference reader* (pp. 313–322). Prague, Czech Republic: Center for Higher Education Studies.

Marouli, C., Misseyanni, A., Papadopoulou, P., & Lytras, M. (2016a). ICT in education for sustainability: Contributions and challenges. In *Proceedings of the International Conference on the Future of Education*, 6th edition (pp. 189–193).

Marouli, C. Misseyanni, A., Papadopoulou, P., & Lytras, M. (2016b). Game-based learning and gamification: Towards the development of a how-to guide in STEM education. *ICERI2016 Proceedings*, 5343–5352. doi:10.21125/iceri.2016.2299

Mayer, R. E., & Moreno, R. (2003). Nine ways to reduce cognitive load in multimedia learning. *Educational Psychologist, 38*(1), 43–52.

Misseyanni, A., Daniela, L., Lytras, M., Papadopoulou, P., & Marouli, C. (2017a). Analyzing active learning strategies in Greece and Latvia: Lessons learned and the way ahead. *INTED2017 Proceedings*, 10117–10124. doi:10.21125/inted.2017.0940

Misseyanni, A., & Gastardo, M. T. (2017). Active learning in the sciences: The case of an undergraduate environmental science class. *Academic Journal of Science, 07*(02), 207–216.

Misseyanni, A., Marouli, C., Papadopoulou, P., & Lytras, M. (2017b). Exploring collaborative learning as an active learning approach in higher education. *EDULEARN17 Proceedings*, 8041–8050. doi:10.21125/edulearn.2017.0479

Misseyanni, A., Marouli, C., Papadopoulou, P., Lytras, M., & Gastardo, M. T. (2016). Stories of active learning in STEM: Lessons for STEM education. In *Proceedings of the International Conference on the Future of Education*, 6th edition (pp. 232–236).
Page, M. (1990). Active learning: Historical and contemporary perspectives. Dissertation, University of Massachusetts. Retrieved from http://files.eric.ed.gov/fulltext/ED338389.pdf
Papadopoulou, P., Lytras, M., & Marouli, C. (2016). Capstone projects in STEM education: Novel teaching approaches, mentoring and knowledge management for empowering students. *EDULEARN16 Proceedings*, 5675–5685. doi:10.21125/edulearn.2016.2358
Papadopoulou, P., Lytras, M., Misseyanni, A., & Marouli, C. (2017). Revisiting evaluation and assessment in STEM education: A multidimensional model of student active engagement. *EDULEARN17 Proceedings*, 8025–8033. doi:10.21125/edulearn.2017.0477
Piaget, J. (2013). *The construction of reality in the child* (Vol. 82). Milton Park, Abingdon, Oxon: Routledge.
Preszler, R. W., Dawe, A., Shuster, C. B., & Shuster, M. (2007). Assessment of the effects of student response systems on student learning and attitudes over a broad range of biology courses. *CBE Life Sciences Education*, 6 (1), 29–41.
Prince, M. (2004). Does active learning work? A review of the research. *Journal of Engineering Education*, *93*(3), 223–231.
Rogers, C., & Freiberg, H. J. (1994). *Freedom to learn* (3rd ed.). New York, NY: Macmillan.
Ryan, M. P., & Martens, G. G. (1989). *Planning a college course: A guidebook for the graduate teaching assistant*. Ann Arbor, MI: National Center for Research to Improve Postsecondary Teaching and Learning.
Schreiner, L. (2010). Thriving in the classroom. *About Campus*, *15*(3), 2–10.
Sousa, D. A. (2001). *How the brain learns* (2nd ed.). Thousand Oaks, CA: Corwin Press.
Svinicki, M., & McKeachie, W. (2012). *McKeachie's teaching tips: Strategies, research and theories for college and university teachers*. Belmont, CA: Wadsworth Cengage Learning.
Turner, J. C., & Tajfel, H. (1986). The social identity theory of intergroup behavior. *Psychology of Intergroup Relations*, 7–24.
UNESCO (1998). *World declaration on higher education for the twenty-first century: Vision and action*. Retrieved from http://www.unesco.org/education/educprog/wche/declaration_eng.htm
Vygotsky, L. S. (1980). *Mind in society: The development of higher psychological processes*. Cambridge, MA: Harvard University Press.
Wang, H., & Sun, C. T. (2011, September). Game reward systems: Gaming experiences and social meanings. In *Proceedings of DiGRA 2011 Conference: Think design play* (pp. 1–12).
Watson, J. B. (2013). *Behaviorism*. Redditch, Worcestershire: Read Books Ltd.
Weimer, M. (2002). *Learner-centered teaching: Five key changes to practice*. San Francisco, CA: Jossey-Bass.

Chapter 4

Concepts and Communication in the Early Stages of an Environmental Science Degree: A Case Study of Formative Activities and Tasks

Peter J. Shaw

Abstract

To meet the needs of the professional environment sector, environmental science graduates need to be suitably equipped in terms of their knowledge, understanding, and skills. At the University of Southampton, the first-year module *Environmental Science: Concepts and Communication* aids students in their journey into Environmental Science by preparing them to face the challenges of university study and beyond. This module thus engages students in independent learning and provides them with opportunities to develop and enhance the skills necessary to do so. Formative and student-led activities and tasks are considered important tools to achieve this aim. This review provides an overview of selected formative and student-led activities with focus on methods and approaches, values and benefits, and the practicalities of delivery. Three assessments are reviewed: a practice essay, a communication exercise, and a practice presentation. The intended benefits and value of these assessments are (1) engagement with environmental issues and topics and (2) development and enhancement of study skills. The value of such work is only realized, however, with student engagement. Delivering this module has demonstrated that

Active Learning Strategies in Higher Education: Teaching for Leadership,
Innovation, and Creativity, 107–131
ISBN: 978-1-78714-488-0

formative elements are most effective when orientated to tutor group activities. Motivation for engagement appears most effective when the visibility – or absence – of students' work is brought to the foreground through working in small groups. There is added value in that the collation and sharing of feedback within a small group permits students to learn not only from their own work but also from their peers.

Keywords: Active learning; environmental science; formative assessment

Introduction

As highlighted in other chapters of this book, there is an established need for active learning elements and approaches in higher education (Bonwell & Eison, 1991). Environmental science and related degrees are no exception in this regard; the demands of multi- and interdisciplinary study are many and various (Hansman, 2009). The environmental employment sector commonly seeks committed, flexible, and adaptable graduates with the "can-do" attitude to take on roles and responsibilities in a vibrant, dynamic, and challenging sector. The breadth of environmental and related degree specifications is also a key asset from employers' perspectives (Brown & Clarke, 1997), whilst "soft skills" can be seen as lacking amongst environmental science graduates (Donnan & Carthy, 2011).

Within higher education itself, there are other factors that influence the landscape of curriculum design and delivery. The arrangements for funding undergraduate study in the United Kingdom (i.e. increased marketization of higher education) are driving a progressive shift toward "student consumers" (Tomlinson, 2017). The costs of delivery are also a consideration to higher education institutions – means of reducing "seat time" without impacting on students' learning experience and their achievement of learning outcomes (Baepler, Walker, & Driessen, 2014) have obvious appeal in that reduced staff–student contact time has financial benefits. Shifts toward "nontraditional" arrangements for teaching do, however, need to be carefully planned if they are to support effective learning (Moffett, 2015).

If graduates with environmental degrees are to meet the needs of the professional environment sector (Hansman, 2009; Thomas, 2003), their experience in higher education should equip them with the necessary knowledge, understanding, and skills (Green, Hammer, & Star, 2009). To achieve this, environmental science degrees must – unquestionably – provide students with the "must-have" attributes (e.g. practical skills: Jones, 2000). In terms of how students acquire core knowledge and understanding, there is a necessity for some learning to be undertaken on a prescriptive basis. The aims, principles, and practices of Environmental Impact Assessment, for example, need to be taught and learned such that students are conversant with industry practice and regulatory processes (Morris & Therivel, 2001). At the same time, an environmental science degree that relied exclusively upon learning and teaching orientated around prescriptive approaches may fail to capitalize on the opportunities for and benefits of student-centered learning (Lord, 1999).

Clearly, there are opportunities and needs for learning activities within environmental degrees that actively engage students in learning and, simultaneously, lead to more and better outcomes from the activities and tasks undertaken (Lord, 1999). The development of critical thinking skills in the early stages of environment-related degrees, for example, may be fostered by collaborative learning activities which lead onto and underpin subsequent study (Whiley, Witt, Colvin, Sapiains Arrue, & Kotir, 2017). Critical skills development may be positively influenced by activities undertaken within group-based activities (Kim, Sharma, Land, & Furlong, 2013). Students also need to acquire and develop competencies to navigate interdisciplinary problems – such as those encountered in environmental science – in order to realize the potential of interdisciplinary learning (Stentoft, 2017). More generally, evidence has shown that students studying STEM (Science, Technology, Engineering, and Mathematics) subjects benefit from active learning practice in terms of their performance (Freeman et al., 2014). Students' responsibility and accountability for their work may be enhanced through exposure to nontraditional teaching methods (Breunig, 2017). Progression through stages of undergraduate study may also be positively influenced by collaborative learning (Loes, An, Saichaie, & Pascarella, 2017).

The Environmental Science degrees at the University of Southampton are orientated around a model that delivers core knowledge, understanding, and skills alongside specialization. This approach can be viewed as comprising complementary components that permit students to explore and develop a thematic area as a means to develop specialization, whilst acquiring "must-have" attributes (Figure 1). The curriculum in the early stages of the degree comprises mainly core modules, with the intention

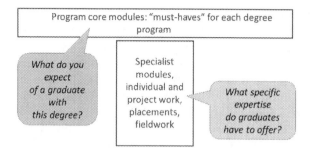

Figure 1. The Overarching Structure of University of Southampton Environmental Science Degrees. *Note*: The curriculum is designed such that major learning components are aligned with graduate attributes.

that students are prepared for subsequent study in terms of skills, knowledge, and understanding. In the first year of study, the core curriculum includes four such modules with specific focus on Environmental Science *per se*:

— Quantitative Methods
— Environmental Science: Research and Applications
— Environmental Field Techniques and Applications
— Environmental Science: Concepts and Communications

The role and purpose of each of these modules is discrete, and there are complementarities between them. In the context of Environmental Science degree courses at the University of Southampton, the *Environmental Science: Concepts and Communication* module serves two key purposes:

— To encourage students to think, read about, and discuss current environmental issues on an inter- and multidisciplinary basis.
— To provide, in early stages of study, a framework for enhancement and development of students' generic study and subject-specific skills that will support students' learning in subsequent stages of study.

As with many environmental science degree courses, early stages of study comprise mainly prescribed modules; optional modules and associated specialization (Figure 1) increase progressively through higher levels of study. The intention is therefore that engagement with environmental issues during early stages of study exposes students to their range and nature such that they are well positioned to take responsibility for subsequent self-selected thematic work and self-directed study. Hence, decisions regarding future focus (Figure 1) are underpinned by an informed view and awareness of the "realm" of environmental science.

The intention of this specific module to enhance and develop skills is, likewise, intended to underpin future study. Learning activities and tasks are intended to acclimatize students to the nature and demands of work in a university, including expectations, standards, and necessary skills. Moreover, activities undertaken within this module are orientated in part to the longer term "journey" to possible professional roles in the environmental sector after graduation. In this regard, a key intention is to draw students' attention to the skills agenda, including their awareness of the skills needs in the short-term (during undergraduate study) and longer term (with career focus and workplace orientation). At early stages of undergraduate study, the view is taken that engagement with the skills agenda has a critical function in fostering effective approaches to study and developing a portfolio of career- and employability-focused skills and attributes. Students' development of their employability is partially underpinned by activities in the first year of study. A range of subsequent activities and efforts − formal and informal − builds upon, extends, and expands the skills acquired through the module considered in this study.

The structure and composition of the module (Figure 2) provide for the delivery of its overarching purposes. This current approach reflects some 20 years of progressive enhancement, driven and informed by student feedback and periodic review, and changes in the external environment (e.g. in preuniversity education and employers' needs and expectations). Moreover, the module has multiple learning outcomes (Table A1) which reflect its multiple roles within the degree. Likewise, there are multiple activities, tasks, and assessments associated with the module (Figure 2).

Overview of the Module: Aims, Structure, and Roles of Learning Activities

Delivery of the module commences with an overview lecture in which the aims, purposes, content, and assessments are set out to the class. This overview outlines:

− How the module focuses on environmental issues across a range of themes.

— How society has accrued knowledge and understanding of the environment, and how information about the environment is obtained and used.
— How information can be combined and analyzed to enable prediction of environmental change and responses to interventions.
— How information can be drawn together to understand environmental processes and to inform decisions about how we deal with and interact with the environment.

In this first session of the lecture series, the role and purpose of formative and summative assessment are also set out, and the timing and nature of feedback are described and explained. The intention is that students are fully aware of not only *what* they will be required to do but also *why* they are required to do so. Students are also guided regarding the content, role, and purpose of individual, tutorial, and classroom-based activities (Figure 2) and the links and complementarity between them. It is stressed that formative work and activities do not contribute

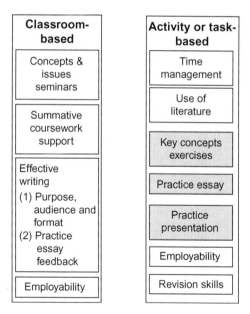

Figure 2. Schematic Representation of the *Environmental Science: Concepts and Communication Module* at University of Southampton, Divided into Classroom-Based and Activity or Task-Based Work. *Note*: Links and interactions between elements are described in the text. This case study review focuses on the three tasks/activities highlighted.

directly to the summative mark for the module. It is explained that (1) the formative work is intended to give feedback to help students become more efficient and able in their studies and (2) the role of formative activities and tasks is to aid development of skills and efficiency. The benefits of formative work are explained in terms of how students are helped to meet academic and (ultimately) professional standards and achieve higher levels of performance in their studies. Module learning outcomes are mapped in relation to module assessments and activities (Table A1).

The present review of this module focuses in detail on a sample of formative exercises and activities. To set these activities in context, it is instructive to provide a brief commentary on other module elements to hand (Figure 2).

With regard to classroom-based sessions, the majority comprise seminars presented by Environmental Science and associated staff; the themes are not prescribed but selected and devised by the staff themselves. These seminars act as exemplars of contemporary environmental problems and emphasize the process of acquiring, analyzing, and interpreting information as a means to effect problem solving. The staff-led seminars are augmented by a series of student-led seminars in the following semester.

The topics for student-led sessions are devised by each of the tutor groups and delivered to the rest of the class by every tutor group in the year class; these presentations largely adopt the emphasis of staff-led seminars in terms of information, analysis, interpretation, and evaluation. Tutor groups comprise usually 4–6 students who have interests in the same area, as evident by their chosen area for specialization within the degree. The tutor provides academic and pastoral support for tutees; academic support in the first year of study is largely orientated to group tutorials of 45 minutes duration that take place at around weekly intervals for the first semester. Tutorials take place in small groups and emphasize interactive discussion, the intention being to provide an opportunity for learning that contrasts and complements whole-class activities.

This module is perhaps unusual with regard to summative assessment; the main summative assignment does not relate directly to any of the formal teaching sessions. This work focuses on the UK National Park closest to Southampton (the New Forest) and requires students to work toward making a prediction of a specific facet of the future for this National Park, 50 years hence. Facets of the New Forest addressed typically include, for example: floods and flooding; broad-leaved woodland, tourism, waste management, transport, birds, and coastal ecosystems. These areas are intended to provide the students with work that is sufficiently narrow in scope to permit detailed scrutiny of specific factors, attributes, and interactions, whilst incurring a need to identify and select those themes or aspects that merit (or do not merit) inclusion in the work. There are no formal content-based classroom sessions on the topic of this work; this approach is adopted specifically as a means to foster and enhance the students' independent learning skills. The students' work is, however, supported by training and guidance in (1) academic writing skills and (2) using scenarios to build and deploy frameworks for making predictions.

In terms of academic writing skills, there are synergies between tutorial activities and class-based sessions. In particular, two of the tutorial activities (the practice essay and key concepts exercises; see below) are connected with classroom-based workshops that focus on written communication skills. Notably, a workshop considering purpose, audience, and format offers insight and ideas that support the key concepts exercises, whilst a workshop on effective writing reflects on class-scale feedback on the practice essays produced (see below). In addition, there are skills-focused sessions in the tutorial sessions that underpin the summative coursework assignment and, in due course, other written assignments. A time management exercise in a tutorial session provides an overview of methods and approaches to effective time management, with specific focus on researching and preparing academic work within a specified timeframe. The illustrative example of a GANTT chart that students are required to create provides, in principle, a template for completion of their summative assignment for this specific module. Likewise, students are guided in good practice for learning from literature via the "reading for your degree" exercises through which strategic approaches to the use of literature are explored and developed.

Given the importance of careers to prospective environmental science professionals, sessions on employability are provided across class-based and tutorial sessions. Links between class-based and tutorial activities are explicit. Classroom sessions on the *Curriculum Vitae* and shortlisting protocols, for example, are reinforced by follow-up activities in tutor groups that explore individuals' profiles and self-presentation of skills and competencies.

To ensure that the content and coverage of tutorial sessions is uniform and consistent (i.e. independent of the individual tutor), a week-by-week schedule is prescribed and detailed in the module guide. The series of tutorials is set out on a thematic basis, with guide notes on students' tasks (before, after, and during tutorials) and associated time-lines. Accompanying notes include details of all tasks and activities, background reading, and supporting reference materials. Use is also made of electronic repositories (i.e. a Virtual Learning Environment: *Blackboard Learn* in this instance) as a means to make available supporting materials and information.

The Practice Essay

The first formative exercise that students are required to complete is a practice essay. Within the structure of the module and its overall purposes, the practice essay provides a vehicle for students to acclimatize to university work in two regards.

First, each student is tasked, individually, to consider environmental issues or themes that are of interest to them. At a subsequent tutor group meeting, members of the group discuss the topical environmental issues or themes that they have identified, aiming to select a subject that is of mutual interest. With guidance from the tutor, a title for the practice essay is composed. Experience has shown that the tutor's role is often to adjust the proposed title such that the scope of the title is suitable for the length of the essay (the main body of which should be 1,500 to 2,000 words). The tutor may also need to intervene if the group needs to be reminded of team skills and roles, notably regarding inclusion and participation. This process presents an early opportunity for students to select their own focal point for their work and acts as a precursor to self-selection of work at higher levels of study such as final year individual research projects.

Secondly, the practice essay offers a vehicle for skills development and formative feedback at an early and critical stage of undergraduate study. To this end, students are required to submit work in two phases. Initially, they are asked to prepare an outline plan for the work, which provides tutors with an opportunity to give feedback on the proposed plan in terms of structure, content, and supporting information. For this purpose, students are provided with a *pro forma* to use as a guide for the outline plan. The *pro forma* requires students to identify the specific purpose of each section of their planned essay and to align key reference materials with each section. Having received feedback on their outline plan, students then compose the full essay and are able to respond to and incorporate the comments and suggestions they have received.

The requirements for this work are aligned with expectations and conventions in university standard work, i.e. the aim is to produce work of an appropriate academic standard. Students are instructed that their essays should be fully and properly referenced and word-processed. Other conventions and expectations are also highlighted, including, for example, presentation, labeling, and referencing for tables, figures, and other illustrative materials, plus use of language and accuracy in writing. The timing of this task is important: by phasing this work early after commencement of undergraduate study, this work is completed and associated feedback provided before summative assessments for this and other modules have to be submitted. The practice essay therefore serves as an early opportunity for mistakes to be made; means to rectify such errors can thus be identified before subsequent summative work is submitted in this module or others.

> *The practice essay was useful, in particular the essay*
> *plan we completed before we attempted the essay.*
> Undergraduate Environmental Science student,
> March 2017.

The practice essay also enables delivery of feedback via different means and on different attributes of students' work. As noted, feedback is provided on both the outline plan and the completed essay, which may, for example, highlight aspects of essay structure, technical skills, content, referencing, use of supporting evidence, and writing style. The two-stage submission of an outline plan and a complete essay also permits provision of (1) individual feedback (outline plan and essay), (2) tutor group feedback (via tutorial-based comparison and discussion of essays), and (3) class feedback.

Whilst feedback on individual work is specific to the specific work at hand, group feedback extends the range and nature of comments and suggestions that can be made. Within tutor groups, discussion of individuals' work provides tutees with insight to what others have done (or not done) when working to the same title. Differences in content and structure, for example, are invariably revealed and ideas shared. Feedback is provided to the whole class in generic form after tutors have contributed notes to the module coordinator. This approach permits students to learn from each other by highlighting common attributes of essays in terms of both strengths and weaknesses. The lecture via which class feedback on practice essays is covered forms part of a series of sessions focusing on written communications skills (Figure 2) which, cumulatively, underpin writing skills and approaches for other work, in other, contemporaneous modules and in subsequent study.

Communication Exercises: Key Concepts in Environmental Science

Having completed their practice essays and received feedback in different forms, students focus their attention on more specific facets of written communication skills. The intention of "key concepts" exercises within the module (Figure 2) is to enable students to develop and refine their written communication skills through a task orientated around notable concepts in environmental science. The motivation for this exercise is two-fold and borne of long-term experience in undergraduate teaching: (1) encouragement to engage fully and deeply in literature is often needed and has clearly identifiable benefits and (2) the default for undergraduates' academic work is often an essay style that is not necessarily fit-for-purpose other than for essay writing. To an extent, this situation is rooted in preuniversity education in which assessments are guided – justifiably and correctly – with the purpose to hand and often require an essay format to be used. As noted, the Environmental Science courses at Southampton adopt the principle that variety in assessment methods and styles has merit in terms of the ensuing academic challenge and preparation for the workplace. The purposes and contexts of undergraduate assignments thus vary considerably, and students' skills in adapting to requirements are paramount.

Prior to individuals undertaking these exercises within tutor groups, a classroom-based workshop introduces and explores how purpose, audience, and format shape and form communication. In particular, this workshop session focuses on short-form communication, this often being an area of which early-stage undergraduate students have relatively little experience. The workshop thus considers how purpose, audience, and format influence approaches that may be adopted and how work produced might be best fitted to the situation in terms of the key message, language, and terminology. An important facet of short-form communication is that students are challenged to decide not only what information and ideas to include but also which to omit.

The first two key concepts exercises comprise prescribed topics, work on which is carried out in tutor groups. This is a formative role-playing exercise involving preparation of work by individuals with subsequent group discussion. In tutor group meetings, students consider the concepts to hand and related literature, in combination with discussion of the challenges, considerations, and approaches to communicating environmental science concepts with respect to purpose, format, constraints, and audience. Feedback is given on individual work and to the tutor group during tutorial sessions and includes both peer and tutor input.

The role-playing aspect of this exercise offers opportunities to compare and contrast how audience, purpose, and format guide and influence communication of an environmental concept. The roles given to each student (Table 1) provide a structure in which purposes and audiences contrast; the formats also contrast (i.e. written and verbal) but are all in short, concise form. The constraints — in time or words — emphasize the specific challenge(s) of achieving conciseness and also reduce the time necessary to produce and present the work. As is perhaps more generally observed, there is commonly reluctance on the part of the student to complete formative work, so participation may perhaps be encouraged by adopting a less onerous requirement. Each member of the group is allocated one of the roles and associated tasks by the tutor; tutees take on a contrasting role for the different exercises.

The choice of topics for the key concepts exercises (Table 2) is specifically made to enable comparisons and contrasts. The first session focuses on a notable peer-reviewed academic research paper (Table 2) that — arguably — is a benchmark in environmental science literature that led to extensive research and impact within its field. On the other hand, the second session focuses on a book (Table 2) in which the complex notion of limits to growth is set out in a format, form, and structure orientated to an audience of young children. Both sessions thus have common challenges, in that the key messages must be understood and the statements must meet the specified requirements (Table 1).

With respect to the adjustment of terminology and language, the two topics present contrasting challenges. To illustrate, communication of the *Tragedy of the Commons* to an audience of children requires the key message to be distilled from the research paper and termed in words and phrases that align suitably with a specific age group. At the same time, a briefing note on the *Tragedy of the Commons* for a member of parliament should aim to distill key message(s) of relevance to government and policy, whilst recognizing and adapting to the knowledge of a politician can be assumed to possess.

Table 1. Illustrative Roles and Tasks for *Key Concepts in Environmental Science* Exercises.

Role	Task	Audience	Constraint
Children's TV Presenter	Write a script for a short piece on this book for a children's TV program on current affairs.	4−6 or 11−16 year olds	60 seconds
Parliamentary Researcher	Write a briefing note on the book, article or topic to outline its contemporary political context.	Member of Parliament	300 words
Television News Editor	Write a script for a piece for a topical TV news program; introduce the subject at hand prior to a longer discussion and debate involving interviews	Adults	90 seconds
Newspaper Editor	Write an editorial outlining the contemporary significance and value of this book, article, or topic.	Newspaper readers (Tabloids, quality left-wing or quality, right-wing)	100 words
Seminar Publicist	Write a short piece to publicize a forthcoming environmental science seminar and persuade people to come and listen it.	Undergraduate students	150 words
College Tutor	Write a summary for colleagues teaching Environmental Sciences that outlines	University tutors leading tutorials with 16−18 year old students	500 words

Table 1. (*Continued*)

Role	Task	Audience	Constraint
	the key themes of the book, article, or topic so they are adequately informed to lead small group tutorials on the subject to hand.		

The roles and tasks present contrasts in terms of the challenges, considerations, and approaches to communicating environmental science concepts with due respect to format, constraints, and audience. The role, task, audience, and constraint can be readily adjusted or augmented to alter the specific nature and demands of the task.

Table 2. Examples of Key Environmental Concepts that Serve as Foci for Exercises in Communication.

Environmental Concept	Key Literature (Indicative)	Notes and Comments
The *Tragedy of the Commons*	Hardin (1968) Pearce (2012)	This is arguably a relatively simple concept that was initially delivered in a formal, peer-reviewed paper and has since been interpreted and reinterpreted by other authors.
Limits to growth	Dr Suess (1971). Godfray et al. (2010). Turner (2014)	This can be viewed as a complex concept that was delivered (by Dr Suess) in a children's book and has a body of academic work in the same realm.

For each concept, roles of tutees (Table 1) are allocated by the tutor. Key challenges are (1) to identify the key message(s) of the concept, (2) deliver this message in a concise form that complies with the stated constraints (Table 1), and (3) to adjust the terminology and language such that they are appropriate to the context and the audience.

> *Some tutor activities e.g. tragedy of the commons didn't do that much to improve knowledge/skills base but took a lot of time.*
>
> Undergraduate Environmental Science student,
> March 2017.

There is a further, third, exercise that adopts the structure (Table 1) of the key concepts exercises. For the theme selected by the tutor group for their practice presentation (see below), the group are tasked with preparing statements on a role-by-role basis (Table 1). This exercise has two important functions: (1) members of the tutor group are required to research and locate key literature for their chosen topic and (2) selection of relevant key messages or themes assists the group in identifying and developing key areas for the content of their presentation. Furthermore, this exercise brings to the fore how tutor groups need to recognize and adapt to the time constraint to hand, the audience, and their likely knowledge and understanding of the subject.

The Practice Presentation

After completion of formative and summative work in the first semester, Environmental Science students' efforts are devoted to practice presentation in the period between the start of Semester 2 and the Easter vacation. As with the practice essay, the practice presentation provides a vehicle for students to acclimatize to university work in two regards. Each student is first tasked to consider again which environmental issues are of particular interest to them and that they would find valuable as a topic for a presentation. The group members discuss individual suggestions and ideas at a tutor group meeting and select a subject of mutual interest. The tutor's role is to guide discussions and advise on a suitable working title that is appropriate to the time available (up 20 minutes + time for questions). This process also presents a second opportunity for student-led selection of thematic independent work and acts as an opportunity to develop further skills and approaches to self-selection of work that will be encountered in greater measure at higher levels of study.

Research for and preparation of this presentation also incorporates and relies upon other tasks and activities within the module (Figure 2). Application of techniques and methods of time management, for example, assists in planning work toward the presentations, whilst many aspects of good practice in academic writing (e.g. technical skills, data handing and presentation) are relevant to both paper-based work and oral presentations. Likewise, the focus on message and content within formative work (notably the practice essay and key concepts exercises) underpins research for and preparation of the presentation. As noted earlier, the final exercise in the series key concepts exercises focuses upon the topic of the presentation and directly informs the presentation in terms of content and message, in relation to the context and audience.

Presentation skills specifically are first introduced and considered in a workshop session during the first semester. The first stage of the workshop comprises a "how not to give a lecture" demonstration in which an academic deliberately makes mistakes that can and do commonly occur when making presentations. The class is not forewarned that this will occur but are expecting one of a series of topical seminars presented by a member of staff. The deliberate mistakes are used as cues for class discussion of presentations skills, building guidelines for good practice that are generated and agreed by the class. The guidelines are written up by the staff member and made available to the group for reference and reflection.

The tutor group presentations are made to the rest of the class early in Semester 2, after completion of the Semester 1 examinations. At this stage, students have completed all the summative assessments for the module; all subsequent activities and tasks are formative. To ensure breadth in students' learning, they are required to ensure that their practice presentation is not closely related to their practice essay. The topic as selected thus extends the knowledge and understanding gained through preparation of prior student-led formative assessments and tasks. Tutor group meetings are held in the second semester on an as-needed basis. Timings and tasks are arranged and coordinated by tutor groups, with input and attendance of the group's tutor at the behest of the group. Tutor groups are encouraged to discuss what needs to be done, by when and by whom, and to decide on the form and function of their tutor's contributions. It is obligatory for tutor groups to take part in this exercise and for all tutor group members to participate at all stages, including delivery of the presentation to class peers.

The preparation of the practice presentation offers a further vehicle for formative feedback at an early stage of undergraduate study, leading to skills development. Given the nature of tutor group work in preparing their presentation and the as-needed input of tutors, the feedback is tailored to the students' needs. Typically, tutors will provide feedback in the intended message, structure, content, visual materials, and delivery of presentations during the preparatory phase. Tutor groups are also encouraged to arrange a rehearsal of the full presentation, with optional attendance of the group's tutor. With or without the tutor in attendance, a rehearsal is considered to give ample opportunity for reflection on and analysis of the presentation and its delivery. To augment and refresh students' presentation skills and awareness of good practice, a surgery session takes place during the period that the presentations are being prepared. This session is student-led, themes and focus being formed around suggestions elicited from the class and building upon the outcomes and messages of the earlier, Semester 1 workshop on presentation skills.

> *Tutor group presentations were interesting and built a lot of confidence.*
> > Undergraduate Environmental Science student,
> > March 2017.

Student feedback on the practice presentation is largely positive; there is a clear view that completion of this task has merit and value as a means of enhancing presentation and related skills through practice, leading to higher levels of confidence. There are also positive informal comments on the subject matter of the tutor group presentations: student-led selection of topics takes a substantial element of the module content away from the control of the academic lead and orientates content to the cumulative interests of the tutor groups.

Observations, Outcomes, and Lessons Learned: The Enabler's View

The value and effectiveness of a module must, of course, be considered in relation to its aims. As noted, this module has specific roles in the first-year curriculum of Environmental Science degrees at the University of Southampton, vis-à-vis:

– To encourage students to think, read about, and discuss current environmental issues on an inter- and multidisciplinary basis.
– To provide, in early stages of study, a framework for enhancement and development of students' generic study and subject-specific skills that will support students' learning in subsequent stages of study.

For the purposes of the present review, the focus is upon selected formative exercises and tasks, which do not, in isolation, reflect the full range of module elements and activities that contribute to the students' learning. With regard to engagement with current environmental issues, the early stages of these Environmental Science courses focus mainly on "must-haves" (Figure 1). There is consequently an important role for student-selected work in these early stages of study. The tasks as set preview possible areas of specialization in subsequent study, whilst self-determination and self-direction in study builds skills and confidence for independent and/or individual work later in study.

In this regard, the selection of topics or themes for the practice presentation and practice essay offer students a chance to take ownership of their work in a manner that is not necessarily fostered by prescriptive, tutor-led activities and tasks. Strong self-motivation for study often follows: it is no surprise that those students who have selected topics that they are interested in are enthused by the topic and keen to find out more. Similarly, by attending the practice presentation series, students are exposed to topics and themes in areas that are not necessarily covered in other modules. The students' perspectives on these topics and themes are also unconstrained, in that they do not follow – nor need to follow – prescriptive syllabi as long as there is a substantive connection with environmental science in its broadest meaning.

Likewise, the group approach to work on student-selected topics leads to inter- and multidisciplinary perspectives. By virtue of 4–6 different individual perspectives, tutor groups will naturally refer to and incorporate multiple facets when discussing environmental issues. It is notable in this respect that the preuniversity qualifications of environmental science students are often highly varied. The past experience and knowledge to hand in a tutor group consequently tend to be multidisciplinary by default.

For the practice essays, the exposure to current environmental issues is group-specific; the content of these essays is not explicitly discussed at a broader level when cumulative feedback is given to the whole class. In contrast, the practice presentations engage students' inter- and multidisciplinary perspectives at two scales. First, preparation of the presentation draws on the tutor group's experiences of often differing subject study prior to undergraduate study. The subsequent presentation to the class opens the subject for discussion through the question and answer session. At this point, contributions of the rest of the class invariably develop and extend the theme(s) of the presentation on an inter- and multidisciplinary basis. For the tutors in attendance, to witness the question and answer sessions is a highlight of the module, in that evidence of critical thought and insight is often evident in the questions asked and the answers given.

In terms of the module's intentions regarding generic study and subject-specific skills, the formative activities and tasks outlined in this case study are critical (Table A1). The foregoing commentary on and

Table 3. Examples of Informal Comments on the Case Study Module Made by First-Year Environmental Science Students at the University of Southampton, March 2017.

Comments	
Negative	"...didn't help much — content was not in exams."
	"Too much formative."
	"...took up lots of time, not that relevant."
	"A lot of formative activities that sometimes seemed irrelevant."
Positive	"...helped improve communication and confidence."
	"...enjoyable and informing."

appraisal of three exemplar formative activities provides an outlook on their role and purpose with regard to development and enhancement of skills, but those working in the higher education sector will be familiar with the notion that formative exercises and assessments are by no means guaranteed to engage students. There is a clear risk, therefore, that reliance on formative activities and tasks for skills development and enhancement may be doomed to failure unless students are suitably engaged. Indeed, as indicated by informal feedback (Table 3), there is a considerable range of perceptions in this regard.

Given that there can be considerable educational merit and value in work orientated to study skills, what are the options to encourage or assure student engagement? The problem can, arguably, be expressed as:

1. Summative assessment of skills encourages students to engage.
2. Formative skills assessment risks low student engagement.

Summative assessment at the cost of formative is perhaps attractive, in that there is explicit motivation for students to complete and submit the work. Moreover, such summative assessments can be set to test explicitly students' achievements with respect to learning outcomes. These are obvious merits, but summative assessment denies students the opportunity to learn through making mistakes without impacting their performance — and denies tutors opportunity to provide formative, constructive feedback at an early stage of students' university experiences.

Obviously, formative skills-orientated assessments need to be completed by students if their value is to be realized. In offering opportunities for mistakes to be made without adversely impacting on marks awarded, there are clear benefits to students, but the connections and interactions between formative and summative assessments are not always apparent to students (Table 3). Although the students are informed of the formative work at the beginning of the module, there has not been an evaluation of whether providing the overview has effects – positive or otherwise – on student participation in formative work. In principle, knowledge of the intended benefits of engagement in this formative work should promote and encourage participation, but 100% engagement of all students in all tasks and activities does not occur.

It should also be noted that there is neither direct penalty nor direct consequence for failure to complete formative work described and evaluated in this paper. The module can be successfully passed without completion of the formative work; completion of formative work is not a formal criterion for demonstration that learning outcomes have been achieved. The module grade awarded to students relies exclusively on the summative assessments; these are criterion-referenced and do not directly take into account completion of formative work or the quality of formative work when completed. There has, as yet, been no formal attempt to assess quantitatively whether and how engagement in formative assessments leads to higher performance in summative work. Anecdotally, the small number of students whose attendance at tutorial sessions is infrequent tend to perform less well; a causal link has not been established in this respect.

With regard to students' acquisition of employability skills, it cannot be stated unequivocally that the formative tasks and exercises presented in this study lead directly to enhancement. Whilst there is some confidence that these tasks incur a need to apply skills that are valued in the professional workplace, the specific tasks form part of a longer and diverse set of formal and informal opportunities to enhance employability. The key role in this regard is that study and employability skills are set in place as part of the agenda for undergraduate learning and should, in principle, lead to engagement in employability-related activities at subsequent stages of study.

There are valuable lessons to be learned from the module to hand. First, it is not always necessary to allocate a summative mark as a means to engage students in assessments. By orientating formative activities and tasks around tutorial groups, those who do not engage are highly visible to their tutor and peers; there is consequently motivation to engage. For tutor group work, this visibility has variable effects, depending much on individuals and their response(s) to peer and other pressures. If − or when − students do not see the value of formative exercises (e.g. Table 3), there may be less incentive to complete them. In overseeing the practice presentations, it has become highly apparent that peer pressure at class scale is a powerful incentive for engagement.

As noted, it is obligatory for students to participate in the preparation and delivery of the practice presentation, which is made to the whole year class. This arrangement means that the quality of the presentation is highly visible to the year group. The level of effort in preparing these presentations is invariably high, as is their standard. There is a strong element of competition amongst tutor groups, none of whom appear to be prepared to look weak before their peers.

In conclusion, this case study provides insight to exemplar methods for engaging early-stage undergraduate students in formative assessments, the benefits and value of which are outlined. The critical matter is whether students actively do, in reality, engage with such activities. In this regard, it is recommended that activities and tasks are orientated around tutor groups. The visibility − or absence − of students' work is thereby brought to the foreground, and there is a consequent motive for engagement with the work at hand. Moreover, the sharing and collation of feedback offers added value to individuals. Learning from mistakes is a default for formative activities; learning from the mistakes that others make is an added benefit of group-based activities and review.

Acknowledgments

The author would like to acknowledge and thank many and various colleagues who have contributed to the progressive development and enhancement of *Environmental Science: Concepts and Communication* over many years. Without their valuable and creative contributions, this module would have been very different.

References

Baepler, P., Walker, J. D., & Driessen, M. (2014). It's not about seat time: Blending, flipping, and efficiency in active learning classrooms. *Computers and Education, 78,* 227−236.

Bonwell, C. C., & Eison, J. A. (1991). *Active learning: Creating excitement in the classroom*. Washington, DC: George Washington University.

Breunig, M. (2017). Experientially learning and teaching in a student-directed classroom. *Journal of Experiential Education, 2017*, 1–18.

Brown, A. L., & Clarke, S. (1997). Employability of environmental science graduates in Australia. *Enviornmentalist, 17*, 45–55.

Donnan, A., & Carthy, R. (2011). *Graduate employment and internships : Issues form the environmental science and sustainability sectors*. London: Institution of Environmental Sciences. Retrieved from https://www.the-ies.org/sites/default/files/reports/Graduate%20Employment%20%26%20Internships.pdf

Freeman, S., Eddy, S. L., McDonough, M., Smith, M. K., Okoroafor, N., Jordt, H., & Wenderoth, M. P. (2014). Active learning increases student performance in science, engineering, and mathematics. *PNAS, 111*, 8410–8415.

Godfray, H. C. J., Beddington, J. R., Crute, I. R., Haddad, L., Lawrence, D., Muir, J. F. ... Toulmin, C. (2010). Food security: The challenge of feeding 9 billion people. *Science, 327*, 812–818.

Green, W., Hammer, S., & Star, C. (2009). Facing up to the challenge: Why is it so hard to develop graduate attributes? *Higher Education Research and Development, 28*, 17–29.

Hansman, R. (2009). Linking the components of a university program to the qualification profile of graduates: The case of a sustainability-orientated environmental science curriculum. *Journal of Research in Science Teaching, 46*, 537–569.

Hardin, G. (1968). The tragedy of the commons. *Science, 162*, 1243–1248.

Jones, A. (2000). *Practical skills in environmental science*. Harlow: Pearson Education.

Kim, K., Sharma, P., Land, S. M., & Furlong, K. P. (2013). Effects of active learning on enhancing student critical thinking in an undergraduate general science course. *Innovative Higher Education, 38*, 223–235.

Loes, C. N., An, B. P., Saichaie, K., & Pascarella, E. T. (2017). Does collaborative learning influence persistence to the second year of college? *The Journal of Higher Education, 88*, 62–84.

Lord, T. R. (1999). A comparison between traditional and constructivist teaching in environmental science. *The Journal of Environmental Education, 30*, 22–27.

Moffett, J. (2015). Twelve tips for "flipping" the classroom. *Medical Teacher, 37*, 331–336.

Morris, P., & Therivel, R. (Eds.). (2001). *Methods of environmental impact assessment* (2nd ed.). London: Spon Press.

Pearce, F. (2012). What tragedy? Whose commons? Conservation. Retrieved from http://www.conservationmagazine.org/2012/09/what-tragedy-whose-commons/. Accessed on September 7, 2012.

Stentoft, D. (2017). From saying to doing interdisciplinary learning: Is problem-based learning the answer? *Active Learning in Higher Education, 18*, 51–61.

Suess, Dr. (1971). *The Lorax*. New York, NY: Random House.

Thomas, I. (2003). Employers' expectations of graduates of environmental programs: An Australian experience. *Applied Environmental Education & Communication, 2*, 49–59.

Tomlinson, M. (2017). Student perceptions of themselves as 'consumers' of higher education. *British Journal of Sociology of Education, 38*, 450–467.

Turner, G. (2014). *Is global collapse imminent?* MSSI Research Paper No. 4, Melbourne Sustainable Society Institute, University of Melbourne. Retrieved from http://sustainable.unimelb.edu.au/sites/default/files/docs/MSSI-Research Paper-4_Turner_2014.pdf

Whiley, D., Witt, B., Colvin, R. M., Sapiains Arrue, R., & Kotir, J. (2017). Enhancing critical thinking skill sin first year environmental management students: A tale of curriculum design, applications and reflection. *Journal of Geography in Higher Education, 41*, 166–181.

Appendix A

Table A1. Mapping of Learning Outcomes to Learning Activities for the Module Environmental Science: Concepts and Communication (summative individual work: I_s; formative individual work: I_f; formative group work: G_f).

Learning Outcome	Assessment	Classroom Sessions	Tutorial Tasks & Activities
To know and understand:			
The importance of environmental concepts, terms, principles and methods, and the need for multi- and interdisciplinary approaches.	I_s, I_f, G_f	✓	✓
The value of an holistic approach to environmental science by using techniques and ideas in different subject disciplines.	I_s, I_f, G_f	✓	✓
The contribution of the sciences to the identification, understanding and, where appropriate, resolution of environmental issues and concerns.	I_s, I_f, G_f	✓	✓
Human causes and consequences of environmental impacts.	I_s, I_f, G_f	✓	✓

Table A1. (*Continued*)

Learning Outcome	Assessment	Classroom Sessions	Tutorial Tasks & Activities
General environmental concerns, which may include: biodiversity; environmental limits to economic or population growth; demand for, and consequences of, water, resource utilization; energy and material production and use, including alternatives; air, land, and water pollution; climate change; environmental change.	I_s, I_f, G_f	✓	✓
To be able to:			
Use facts and data properly to support arguments and assemble and critically evaluate relevant information from several sources and develop a personal point of view.	I_s, I_f		✓
Analyze, synthesize, and summarize information critically, including prior research.	I_s, I_f, G_f		✓
Collect and integrate several lines of evidence to formulate and test hypotheses.	I_s		✓
Produce reasoned arguments, justifying conclusions and recommendations by reference to appropriate analytical frameworks and supporting evidence.	I_s, I_f, G_f		✓
Communicate ideas and arguments effectively in a variety of written formats, orally, and in the context of formal presentations.	I_s, I_f, G_f	✓	✓

Table A1. (*Continued*)

Learning Outcome	Assessment	Classroom Sessions	Tutorial Tasks & Activities
Select, gather, evaluate, and synthesize information from a range of sources (printed, electronic, and other material) and make evidence-based assessment and judgments.	I_s, I_f, G_f		✓
Use information and communication technology to acquire, collate, process, and analyze data and information and to make the results available to others in written and/or electronic form.	I_s, I_f		✓
Prepare, process, interpret, and present data, using appropriate qualitative and quantitative techniques and ICT packages.	I_s, I_f, G_f		✓
Use the Internet critically as a source of information.	I_s, I_f, G_f		✓
Work effectively as a member of a team by identifying individual and collective goals and responsibilities and recognizing and respecting the views and opinions of other team members.	G_f		✓
Evaluate your approach to your work in terms of key skills, identify the skills necessary for self-management, and work toward targets for personal, academic, and career development.			✓

Chapter 5

Active Learning Strategies: Stories and Lessons Learnt – Studying Environment in the Field

Daniel Moscovici and Emma Witt

Abstract

Field-based education for environmental studies has been a foundational principle for the Environmental Studies program at Stockton University, which began in 1971. Located within the 445,000 hectare Pinelands National Reserve, on an 800-hectare campus near Atlantic City, New Jersey, USA, two professors in the program discuss our rationale and experiences teaching students about the environment within the environment. Expounding on the interdisciplinary literature of field-based learning, we present four unique case studies including local and regional experiences, as well as student learning abroad. The first case proposes that learning outdoors might be beneficial for students with learning disabilities. This is exemplified during a one-week field study to the 2.4 million hectare Adirondack Park & Preserve. The second instance reveals the benefits of working with local towns and environs acting as consultants in a multidisciplinary capstone experience. Next, we show how on-campus data collection and hypothesis formulation help students to learn about environmental design and statistical analysis. Finally, an international trip to the Caribbean opens the minds of students through a service learning project. While on campus, in

Active Learning Strategies in Higher Education: Teaching for Leadership,
Innovation, and Creativity, 133–150
ISBN: 978-1-78714-488-0

town, across the United States or at an international destination, learning in the field gives students the opportunity to expand their knowledge through field-based active learning strategies.

Keywords: Environmental studies; field work; active learning; sustainable education; experiential capstones; international study; service learning; engagement; hands-on learning; edu-venture

Introduction

The limits of traditional lecture approaches for information delivery in environmental science, as well as many other STEM (Science, Technology, Engineering, and Math) disciplines, are quickly reached. Courses that primarily emphasize one-way information exchange (professor tells student) are less effective at achieving student learning goals than those that incorporate active learning strategies (Freeman et al., 2014). Incorporating field components in environmental science courses is an essential tool that naturally forces active learning. It is here where students are compelled to apply knowledge obtained from "traditional" approaches (lecture/textbook) to analyzing and understanding a variety of concepts while physically in the environment. In addition to the educational benefits to students, field exercises are generally an enjoyable experience for students (Boyle et al., 2007). A number of approaches will be discussed in the chapter. They are related to the strategies identified in the literature as being effective in environmental education (i.e. Sauve, 2005; Thomas & Munge, 2015). Our case will be focused on our work at Stockton University, in and near Atlantic City, New Jersey, USA.

The Pinelands National Reserve of New Jersey is unique in a number of respects. The region is a designated and protected rural area of greater than 445,000 hectares (ha), occupying more than 20% of the land area of the most urbanized state in the country. The Pinelands is not a national park or national forest, rather a federal, state, county, and local partnership – unlike anything in the country and maybe in the world. The Pinelands were designated a Biosphere Reserve by UNESCO in 1988, and the area includes 850 plant species, two wild and scenic rivers, and extensive groundwater resources (Mason, 2004). In total, the unique landscape that is the Pinelands serves as an excellent outdoor classroom.

In the heart of the region, not far from the Atlantic coast is Stockton University. The university has roots in general education, an interdisciplinary focus, and one of the oldest environmental studies programs nationwide. The 800 ha campus is largely forested and includes two lakes, Atlantic white cedar swamps, a variety of wildlife habitats, and a diversity of soil types. In addition to this exceptional outdoor classroom in the heart of the Pinelands preservation area, students have opportunities working with local businesses, partnering with towns and communities, as well as studying in other states and internationally. Using this combination of resources, the faculty and students engage practically through hands-on education. By studying the environment in the field, students and faculty can connect ideas and reality through a multidisciplinary, multidimensional pedagogical experience.

Using a variety of case studies in this chapter, we demonstrate that learning in the field provides opportunities unavailable to those working solely in classrooms. We note a number of impacts of field-based learning on students. First, students come alive in the field. Students that do not adapt well to classroom settings, either due to documented learning disabilities or general apathy may be far more engaged in field settings. Second, being in the field increases their environmental awareness, particularly of the sustainable fragility of ecosystems as well as allowing for hands-on evaluation of environmental properties and processes. Third, the needed balances between the environment, businesses, and people around them are highlighted, promoting the formation of connections to issues separate from the primary subject of the course. In addition to the impacts mentioned above, learning in the field promotes both deep learning and active learning. Out of the classroom the who, what, where, why, and how are exposed. One goal of environmental education at Stockton is ensuring that students become professionals committed to the local environment and people, wherever they end up. This type of purposeful pedagogical experience successfully develops the environmental stewards needed for the environmental tasks ahead.

Beyond the impact of field-based learning on the development of educated, engaged environmental stewards, field activities can reinforce or more strongly demonstrate concepts first introduced in the classroom or via independent assigned readings. Observing environmental phenomena in the field physically translates words from a page or a lecture to measurable, tangible outcomes. The increased depth of learning using field-based techniques helps students to grasp frequently complex concepts.

Case studies presented in this chapter will cover a range of issues, techniques, and outcomes of field experiences used in teaching environmental science. Topics include: impact of field experiences on students with learning disabilities, international field experiences, teaching environmental science to interdisciplinary students, field projects in capstone courses that integrate a range of environmental disciplines, and using field work to introduce and improve understanding of statistics and scientific concepts.

This chapter identifies strategies for teaching environmental science in the field. Powerful experiences for the students and professors have happened on campus, in nearby communities, in the Adirondacks Park and Preserve, and the Commonwealth of Dominica. However, it is not only travel and sun that opens student minds. A day full of grit, odor, cold, and hunger may be just as powerful, or more so.

Literature Review

Field work is an essential part of environmental science curricula. The design of field activities varies with the specific subject matter, course goals, and the professor. However, learning in the field usually incorporates one or more of the following educational strategies: problem-based learning, active learning, experiential learning, and constructivist learning. The objective of this chapter is to describe the benefits of field-based learning for environmental science undergraduates at a regional, public university in New Jersey, USA.

Field-based learning promotes student education in a number of ways. Due to the nature of field experiences, a deep approach, rather than a surface approach is favored. As described by Entwistle (1987) and Stokes and Boyle (2009), characteristics of deep-learning approaches include a high level of student interaction with content, integrating previous and new knowledge and using new concepts to draw conclusions and apply to real-life situations. Deep learning promotes student learning through self-motivation and an objective to understand material, while surface learning relies on external motivation (general completion of a task to avoid failure) and memorization of material (Entwistle & Ramsden, 1983; Entwistle & Smith, 2002; Stokes & Boyle, 2009). Essentially, the deep approach to learning integrates learning at both the cognitive and affective levels, in which examinations of cognitive learning focus on how students learn and examination of affective learning focus on why students learn (McConnell & van Der Hoeven Kraft,

2011). Strategies to promote affective learning include: ensuring students can relate the material to situations beyond the classroom, are interested in the material or have freedom to choose topics they are interested in, and that they understand the expectations of the overall project (McConnell & van Der Hoeven Kraft, 2011).

Increasing cognitive and affective learning is a benefit of experiential, active, and constructive learning approaches, all of which are useful in field-learning situations. In all of these methods, emphasis is placed on connecting students to material and requiring reflection to draw conclusions and make connections based on their engagement. Millenbah and Millspaugh (2003) present an experiential learning process adapted from Kolb (1984) consisting of four steps: experience, reflection, generalization, and experimentation. Steps one and two provide students with an experience and opportunity to reflect, followed by the opportunity in steps three and four to understand the underlying principle of the activity and predict the outcome of similar activities (Millenbah & Millspaugh, 2003). Based on the definition of active learning, provided by Faust and Paulsen (1998), which places all activities other than listening to a lecture in the category of active learning, experiential and constructive learning approaches certainly integrate active learning fully into the curriculum. Constructive learning is related to experiential learning and focuses on students discovering concepts and instructors facilitating their discovery (Cooperstein & Kocevar-Weidinger, 2004). Constructive learning techniques are highly student centered and have minimal reliance on lecture as an information delivery technique (Lord, 1999; McLaughlin & Johnson, 2006). Each of these approaches have applicability to field learning, provided the activity is appropriately designed and implemented.

Strategies for promoting deeper learning through field experiences are highly varied based on the specific field being taught, but a number of traits are common to successful activities. First, development of field activities require planning and direction on specific outcomes. This can ease apprehension and self-doubt which may hamper learning (McConnell & van Der Hoeven Kraft, 2011; Stokes & Boyle, 2009). Second, journaling or recording experiences in a field notebook helps reinforce what students learn through reflection (Carlson, 1999; McLaughlin & Johnson, 2006; Millenbah & Millspaugh, 2003). Third, it is important to structure activities that engage students. These are most effective when they perceive the problems to be applicable beyond the classroom. This increases learning and self-efficacy (Dunlap, 2005; Manner, 1995; Stokes & Boyle, 2009). Effective field activities that incorporate the preceding three components have a range of benefits to students beyond improved cognition.

Improved student learning is one benefit of field-based learning, but there are a number of other skills students can gain from the experience. Learning to work as effective team members is a common outcome of field-based learning (Carlson, 1999; Stokes & Boyle, 2009). Learning to work well with others is a skill that is necessary postgraduation. An improved understanding of the complexities of and the value of the environment is another learning outcome of field-based research (Manner, 1995; McLaughlin & Johnson, 2006). Finally, an increased understanding of the scientific method and how to develop appropriate research design are important outcomes (Carlson, 1999; Millenbah & Millspaugh, 2003).

Among the high-impact educational practices identified by Kuh (1998), this paper discusses four of them. These include: collaborative assignments and projects, global learning through study abroad programs, community-based learning, and capstone projects. The following examples of field-based learning include the observed benefits to students.

Case Studies

Learning Disabilities No More?

Adirondack Mike (a pseudonym created for student anonymity and protection) was only known as Mike during the regular semester. He was an outsider and a bit of a troublemaker; frequently late or absent for class with disruptive excuses. He had difficulty partnering with other students during group work sessions. In addition, he often arrived without his homework and was behind on the readings; it seemed certain that this student would not be eligible for the 7-day field study within the largest park in the lower 48 contiguous United States — The Adirondack Park and Preserve. Here students would have hands-on experiences, full days in the field, to see, experience, learn, and understand land and resource planning in a protected forested area spanning almost 2.4 million ha.

Mike had a learning disability, recognized by the State through our Learning Access Program (LAP). The LAP seeks to comply with the standards of the American with Disabilities Act and Section 504 of the Rehabilitation Act. In short, LAP gives students with all disabilities, including learning disabilities, support services for equal access to education. Our Environmental Studies department always happily receive students from LAP, and they can have many options for classroom accommodation. Some students have notetakers, while others get special testing times and locations. It is understood that at a public institution of higher learning, it is everyone's job to help educate all of our children. Unfortunately, even with accommodation from LAP, Mike was not likely to pass the course.

As the final paper and presentations before the trip loomed, Mike knew he was in danger of failing the course and missing the experience. In fear of not graduating in time, and with some extra academic work and a stern warning, Mike was allowed to travel with the group to the Adirondacks. He was forced to sign an extra letter knowing his parents might pick him up mid-trip. It was important for the professor to keep a close eye on Mike during our trip north. We were invited guests at our site visits including the Olympic Centers, The Uihlein Sugar Maple Research facility, Paul Smith's College, the wood biomass facility, through the wild mountains and rivers and other locations. Not to mention students could run wild in the hamlet of Lake Placid if they decided to ignore all warnings, deadlines, and social norms and just party all night. I was worried that Mike would be their leader, and our reputation for the future would be ruined.

When we arrived to our destination, I realized I was both right and wrong. Mike did become the leader, but not with any of the negativity anticipated. He became the top student, with the greatest enthusiasm and motivation. It was not just to boost his grade; it was genuine – as if he just came alive. He even began doing research on the region with the many field guides I bring along to teach the other students. We were having class outside for 12 hours per day climbing peaks over 1,300 meters. Students were chasing professors and professionals through the forests, in rivers, and across rugged landscapes. Now nicknamed Adirondack Mike, by the group, this student made sure everyone was on time every day for our departure, that students did not stay out too late. He even became our official map reader – helping me navigate the drive. In addition, he took lead on our wilderness hikes and canoe trip, while I stayed with students struggling at the rear. It was as if he was the teaching assistant for the course, having taken it multiple years – in fact, he was a completely different person. This transformation is an example of the deep learning and affective learning that arises from self-motivated students. Adirondack Mike clearly benefitted from the constructive and experiential learning approach favored by this field experience. He excelled in environmental education, ready to become a professional. Upon our return from our edu-venture, I wrote a strong recommendation for Adirondack Mike to work with the US Fish & Wildlife Service in Alaska – the job required long days outside, map work, surveying of wild areas. I knew that he would again come alive in the work.

Is Adirondack Mike an anomaly or does studying in the field aid some with learning disabilities when studying the environment? I have observed other instances over the years where students identified through LAP thrive on these field study courses. However, in other instances, they struggle with the social manifestations that come while students study and travel together away. None have been as successful as Adirondack Mike, but certainly more research is needed into this correlation. Given the confidentiality surrounding learning disabilities and medical records, great care and attention will be needed to evaluate this important topic further. However, in the meantime, the authors recommend that faculty take chances on students who might not traditionally learn well in the classroom. Take them outside to learn locally, with an active, constructive, deep learning approach. Then, if the opportunity arises out of city, state, or country, watch them come alive and thrive.

Field-Based Capstone Course

Many environmental and natural resource curricula incorporate a senior capstone class or project. These initiatives compel students to integrate their experiences and knowledge in a transition from education to employment. Developing semester-long projects where students have a "client" and work flow that mimics what they may see after graduation is one strategy for ensuring they remain engaged and are prepared for their careers. This approach incorporates problem-based and experiential learning.

Bridgeton, NJ is the poorest city in the poorest county in New Jersey (U.S. Census Bureau, 2013) and has struggled since manufacturing left the area in the 1980s. While the city has struggled economically and is experiencing a shift in demographics, it has a number of features on which to build. These include a 450 ha park and New Jersey's first zoo. In addition, the Cohansey River runs through the park, and Sunset Lake is one of its centerpieces. Unfortunately, recreational opportunities in the lake are limited due to bacterial contaminants. The

Bridgeton City Park served as the setting for a semester-long project undertaken by the Stockton University environmental science/studies capstone students.

I assigned students teams based on courses they had completed and their stated area of interest related to environmental science. Additional grouping considerations incorporated overall GPA and my knowledge of student personalities. The subfocus of the individual teams included: hydrology and water quality of Sunset Lake and the Cohansey River; aquatic, avian, and terrestrial wildlife; forest resources; and GIS, trails, and recreation. I tasked each group with developing a written proposal for their semester-long activities and presenting their plans to the class. After feedback from their classmates and me, the student proposals were implemented at the park. At the end of the semester, the students presented their findings to the mayor, other Bridgeton city officials, interested community leaders, and Stockton community members.

Over the course of the semester, three student engagement and active learning themes emerged. First, connection is important. Connecting student work to the community and the entire project motivates the students. This connection relates to two crucial facets of the process described by Kolb (1984) and Millenbah and Millspaugh (2003): experience and reflection. Second, group success was often determined by the presence of strong leadership within the group. Meanwhile, individual success was more prevalent in groups lacking such a leader. Finally, undertaking these types of semester-long projects requires a rethinking of the traditional classroom model.

Prior to the first field visit to Bridgeton City Park, during the phase of proposal development, I asked students to consider the topic of environmental injustice, specifically the value of parks to urban and economically disadvantaged communities. In general, the classroom-based discussions on environmental injustice resulted in a palpable sense of anger among the students. The faculty worked to ensure students understand that having a functioning park in Bridgeton is more than just evaluating an ecosystem, it includes the rights of those community members to open space and environmental health. Upon our first visit to the park, many of the students were dismayed by the condition of some facilities and reacted negatively to the litter. Negative aesthetics in parks impact all park users, not just the students conducting research (McCormack, Rock, Toohey, & Hignell, 2010).

It was difficult to have students connect the dilapidated park conditions and the financial realities of the city. However, one group, the GIS, trails, and recreation group, was able to recognize these issues in their proposal and presentation. They also made concrete suggestions for facility upgrades, proposed diversification of recreational opportunities, and addressed issues of litter management. These students were better able to articulate the connection between the status of the community (i.e. economic status, substance abuse issues, unemployment) and the importance of the park as a community asset. Another group, the forestry group, was very successful at translating their knowledge from forestry-based classes to develop a forest management plan for the city park. Of all the groups, these two groups was most successful at drawing generalizations from their observations and recommending concrete actions for park improvement.

Following our first field visit, the mood of the class seemed to shift from being optimistic to being overwhelmed. The students learned the park presented a complex problem, and simple solutions would not come easily. Furthermore, all of the problems would not be solved in the space of a semester. Groups that were most successful at overcoming their initial shock had a strong group selected leader and cohesion among members. Several commonalities were observed between the two groups with strong leadership. First, neither had a single dominant personality in the group, but both had unofficial leaders. These leaders were academically high-achieving students, conveyed confidence, and their fellow group members trusted their instincts. Second, neither of the groups were overwhelmed by the task assigned and were able to formulate a plan that focused on one or two important issues to the park. Third, these groups agreed early on to what they felt was an equitable division of labor. The overall group satisfaction was communicated effectively in the biweekly group assessment each student was required to complete.

In addition to these groups, several individual students were able to form personal connections with their work in the park and successfully apply knowledge learned in other classes as well as expand on their existing knowledge. Interestingly, three of these students were slightly older than most of their classmates, and two of the three were veterans (our university is a strong supporter of veteran education). A combination of their maturity and experiences prepared them for independent learning, project definition, and goal setting. Other common themes of personal connection from this experience emerged. There was a willingness to explore new areas of interest, communicate with me as well as with the client, and achieve a successful outcome. Nevertheless, there were some problems with the course design.

Using client-based, real world, field work scenarios do not always lend themselves to the traditional classroom meetings with laboratory exercises. A more contemporary approach that would have fewer meetings, but for longer time periods, would be more successful. Instructors have used a variety of approaches to ensure adequate time to complete field work, including Saturday classes, full days of class during the week, scheduling multiweek trips outside of the regular semester, or dedicating an entire semester to the capstone experience. Students, on the other hand, must confront that only so much could be accomplished in a 15-week semester and that they will not solve all of the problems in this period of time.

In summary, creating career-based learning, as part of a capstone course, provides multiple benefits to students. First, they are required to develop teamwork skills. Sometimes they learned to work together, other times they acquire insight into what went wrong. Second, students were forced to make proposals and then scale them appropriately to the stakeholder needs. This included developing appropriate field techniques, collecting data, or designing projects that could continue for future students or citizens. Finally, giving students a real client to work with gives them more than just a grade. They are accountable to a third-party and a great responsibility comes with this.

Using Field Data to Introduce Statistics

In STEM fields, it is vital that students have a basic understanding of statistics and experimental design. These skills allow them to think critically and evaluate scientific data. However, given that even basic statistics can be difficult to learn, it is less realistic that students will understand the well-designed, executed, and statistically sound methods of published researchers without first-hand experience. Our effective approach requires them to design, implement, analyze, and write about field studies carried out over the course of multiple lab sessions.

Physical Geography is a required course for environmental science/studies majors at Stockton University, taken in either the freshman or sophomore year. Learning objectives for the lab component of the course include: developing familiarity with field techniques used by environmental science professionals, acquiring data management skills including using spreadsheets for organizing, analyzing, and displaying data, as well as introducing spatial analysis using geographic information systems (GIS) software. These skills are required for success in junior and senior level courses as well as upon graduation. Students in the course typically spend the first two to three weeks of the course learning aspects of both spreadsheet and GIS software. The majority of students in Physical Geography have, at most, a basic understanding of spreadsheet software and generally have no prior experience with GIS software. After some familiarity, a field scenario is a next logical step.

Students have transitioned their computer skills into the field on a variety of assignments. These include: measuring the influence of forest management (clear-cut, thinning, and no cutting) on temperature, and evaluating the impact of forest management and prescribed fire on soil moisture. These activities promote student learning in field techniques, statistical analysis, and scientific writing.

First, due to limits on time and resources, students are required to work in groups to accomplish their objective. They are forced to develop effective teamwork habits not only with their members but with all groups in the class – ensuring consistency and accuracy. By collaborating across groups they can ensure, for example, that soil samples were taken at similar depths or soil temperatures were measured at a consistent depth. This part of the experimental design eliminates errors and extraneous variables. This activity provides techniques for randomization and emphasizes how important it is to avoid sampling bias. They can begin to experiment with scientifically sound design.

Through this project, students are also required to learn hypothesis formulation and testing. Many students are equipped in articulating basic hypotheses. For example, they might say "I expect soil moisture to be greatest in clear-cut, burned areas" at the beginning of the semester. Less common, however, is an understanding of null and alternate hypotheses as they apply to statistical tests. A null hypothesis could include: "there is no difference in soil moisture in clear-cut, thinned, and unharvested areas." An alternate hypothesis may be: "there is a difference in soil moisture in clear-cut, thinned, and unharvested areas." Going in the field and seeing the differences in harvesting techniques, for example, allows students to move the hypotheses from abstract to tangible. Simply seeing the landscape and taking the samples can transition the basic hypotheses to statistical-testing-based hypotheses. This is an example of constructive learning working to move from abstract statistical concepts to applied research and deeper learning.

Once the hypotheses have been formed, students must consider the statistics. They learn basic statistical techniques to analyze their data, including t-tests, ANOVA, and regression analysis. The first step in this process includes developing data analysis skills. Our experience has been that students are most challenged when dealing with large datasets. However, they become familiar with organizing these data to determine summary variables including treatment means, standard deviations, and making histograms for normality testing. The second step is performing the statistical tests and interpreting the results. This requires developing an understanding of alpha levels (or p-values). Again we have noticed difficulty understanding the variance between measured differences in the variable of interest and the statistically significant difference between treatments. Having the students involved in the design, and particularly the in-field collection of the data, is helpful in overcoming these barriers. Finally, students completing this exercise develop skills in scientific writing. Their time in the field is essential to writing. They are required to accurately describe the field and statistical methods used to evaluate their hypotheses, as well as provide appropriate context (i.e. descriptions of the field sites and treatments). This step has been identified as being important, relying on student-centered observation to interpretation in constructive learning.

Overall, learning about experimental design by implementing field experiments provides students a number of benefits. First, they have ownership over the experimental design with peer collaboration, as has been identified as a crucial step in many active learning techniques. Second, they gain experience with field sampling techniques and the level of detail required to avoid bias and error. Third, their collected environmental data helps them understand variability and the complexities in evaluating these datasets. Overall, the field exercises, statistical analyses, and writing allows them to critically evaluate all scientific experiments and deepens their understanding of environmental science.

International Environmental Service Learning

We finally met as a group of 10 students and one faculty, in Newark International Airport, New Jersey. Past the train stop, ticketing, and TSA (Transportation Security Administration) security, the students were surprisingly quiet and very nervous. Of the enrollees, only two had previously left the country and some had never left the state (or not that they could remember). New Jersey is a region of convenience. Given the proximity to New York City and Philadelphia across the Hudson and Delaware Rivers, respectively, almost every city or town has the amenities of the suburbs or big city close by — but without the buildings, crowds, and traffic. New Jersey has some of the most impressive interstate highways in the world, public transportation that is good by American standards, and interestingly New Jersey is one of only two states where it is illegal to pump your own gas. All of these students had cars, but none had ever pumped their own gas!

The juxtaposition of visiting and studying on an island where there was not even a stoplight would open their minds to possibilities and global struggles. To arrive in the Commonwealth of Dominica, we would fly to Puerto Rico, then on a small plane to Anguilla, only then to board another small plane to Dominica. This last flight would only continue if conditions were just right. Douglas–Charles Airport did not have night landings, and the strip was just below a very steep mountain where wind was severe. Dominica is only 751 square kilometers, with a population of 70,000 people, known as the "Nature Island of the Caribbean" (Moscovici, 2017).

Our class in Dominica was focused on the environmental impacts from different types of tourism development including UNESCO world heritage sites, ecotourism, historical tourism, resort tourism, and particularly cruise ships. This required immersion in the local environment of the island to understand those impacts. Our activities included hikes through cloud forests and to other protected sites, meetings with ministers of the government and associations, and a walk onto a cruise ship for a tour while passengers disembarked. But, the impact was greatest during our day of service. During the rest of the field portion of this course, students sometimes acted like tourists, but I wanted them to begin the journey of becoming citizens of the world. Following the professor or guide and asking some questions was not enough. It was easy to be disconnected, to return to a comfortable hotel room with cable and wi-fi, to see or hear from home.

It is important to emphasize that prior to the field study portion of the course, students had read many articles and books, participated in multiple lectures, worked on a research project and presentation, and had successfully passed an exam on the material. The course was rigorous both mentally and physically. Stateside, so much was demanded of them with respect to research and preparation. While abroad, our days were very long, outdoors, often requiring strenuous physical activity. While students grumbled about the intense workload and itinerary (as students will often do), it wasn't until our last day on the island that students became both mentally and physically exhausted. This would be a day of service at Scotts Head, the southern tip of the island near Soufriere Bay. In conjunction with the Dominica Water Sports Association, the Discover Dominica Authority (the national tourism board) and the Ministry of Tourism, our students would lead a beach clean-up. We were provided the gloves, bags, lunch, and the government would remove all of our trash for free. The media was there too — international kids cleaning beaches was certainly newsworthy. The students were excited at the idea.

Scotts Head is an incredible place. A promontory connected by a narrow strip of land leads to a small hike with amazing views. Standing here you see the rough Atlantic Ocean on one side and the calm Caribbean Sea on the other with views of the mountains and island for miles. This peninsula also locks in Soufriere Bay which is home to the Soufriere-Scotts Head Marine Reserve (SSMR), a tentative-listed United Nations Educational, Scientific, and Cultural (UNESCO) site. SSMR is most unique as the bay is an extinct volcano crater with walls dropping to unmeasurable depths within a lava chute (UN, 2017). However, when storms and tides are strong — the peninsula becomes a catchall for waste of the Caribbean Sea. The moment we arrived, the students were overwhelmed.

They had studied about waste and recycling and even the problems with illegal dumping, but could not believe what they saw. This was one of the most famous views on the island, adjacent to a UNESCO candidate site, yet all they could see was an overwhelming quantity and quality of trash. The sheer abundance was staggering. Weary and tired by the end of the day, we had filled all of the bags that were provided to us and heaped them into a giant pile that the waste company would later haul away. However, it was what we picked up that led to the greatest discussion — one that seemed to change the discourse of the entire class. Of course, we had the usual trash including: food waste, paper products, bones of animals, plastics of all kind, wood, metals, styrofoam, plastic bags, debris, etc. However, we also had many products which the students could not move safely: car engines/parts, construction equipment, mattresses, appliances, and so many tires, etc. These we would not expect to see in the sea. The thoughts of hikes in the wilderness, tropical fish, the indigenous Carib, and the historical sites were replaced by piles of waste. Furthermore, they learned that after the next big storm, the headland would be filled with trash and debris all over again. We did not solve the problem, only cosmetically improved it for a short time.

The sense of hopelessness and reality affected the students personally through first-hand experience working in the field. As they got their hands dirty (with protective gloves of course), they imagined the stories behind these pieces of trash and thought about how, until this point, the group were merely passengers on an international field study paradise course. Now, they were awakened to an issue that they also have to face at home. However, it was the international experience that allowed the students to make that connection directly and to care.

The short-term study abroad achieved all of the goals of academic scholarship: discovery, integration, application, and teaching (Boyer, 1990). By transcending the discipline and the classroom setting, it allows the students to gain a deeper understanding of the material. Furthermore, by working in the natural environment on real problems through a service capacity sparks new interests and develops continuity. This continuum could be achieved by students participating on the eduventure, year after year, adding to past research (Moscovici, 2013). Or, it could be that the students awaken a passion that they can repatriate in their communities, or beyond, as they become professionals. By learning in the field, in an international setting, students are able to connect the material to their lives, to their communities, to their professional careers, and with the people they will meet.

Conclusion

Whether collecting data for statistical analysis on campus, acting as consultants for a local city, exploring the wild of one of the biggest parks in the country, or traveling to an international destination, in the field students are able to engage with environmental science/studies and achieve learning objectives that a normal classroom setting cannot provide. The deep, hands-on learning is not a replacement for traditional classrooms, but in combination with the multiple in and out of the classroom, students can better learn holistically and prepare for careers in the environment.

Through our experiences, we have seen students come alive in the field, especially those that struggle with normal classroom settings. We have increased environmental awareness of our local surroundings and the environmental issues the world faces collectively. We have seen students engage with local communities and clients. By working in the field, getting dirty, cold or hot, and covered in bugs, we firmly believe students can connect the material to fully understand the who, what, where, why, and how of the environmental issues we are teaching. We need fully trained environment stewards to fight the complex transdisciplinary problems of the future. This active learning strategy, learning in the field, will educate, engage, and reinforce the curriculum needed within the STEM fields.

References

Boyer, E. L. (1990). *Scholarship reconsidered: Priorities of the professoriate*. San Francisco, CA: Jossey-Bass, 147 pp.

Boyle, A., Maguire, S., Martin, A., Milsom, C., Nash, R., Rawlinson, S. ... Conchie, S. (2007). Fieldwork is good: The student perception and the affective domain. *Journal of Geography in Higher Education, 31*, 299−317.

Carlson, C. A. (1999). Field research as a tool for learning hydrogeochemistry and scientific-writing skills. *Journal of Geoscience Education, 47*, 150−157.

Cooperstein, S. E., & Kocevar-Weidinger, E. (2004). Beyond active learning: a constructivist approach to learning. *Reference Services Review, 32*, 141−148.

Dunlap, J. C. (2005). Problem-based learning and self-efficacy: How a capstone course prepares students for a profession. *Educational Technology Research and Development, 53*, 65−85.

Entwistle, N. (1987). A model of the teaching-learning process. In J. T. E. Richardson, M. W. Eysenck, & W. Piper (Eds.), *Student learning. Research in education and cognitive psychology* (pp. 13−28). Milton Keynes: Open University Press and SHRE.

Entwistle, N., & Ramsden, P. (1983). *Understanding student learning*. London: Croom Helm, 248 p.

Entwistle, N., and Smith, E. (2002). Personal understanding and target understanding: Mapping influences on the outcomes of learning. *British Journal of Educational Psychology, 72*, 321−342.

Faust, J. L. and Paulsen, D. R. (1998). Active learning in the college classroom. *Journal on Excellence in College Teaching, 9*, 3−24.

Freeman, S., Eddy, S. L., McDonough, M., Smith, M. K., Okoroafor, N., Jordt, H., & Wenderoth, M. P. (2014). Active learning increases student performance in science, engineering, and mathematics. *Proceedings of the National Academy of Sciences, 111*, 8410−8415.

Kolb, D. A. (1984). *Experiential learning: Experience as a source of learning and development*. Edgewood Cliffs, NJ: Prentice Hall.

Kuh, G. D. (1998). *High-impact educational practices: What they are, who has access to them, and why they matter*. Washington, DC: AAC&U, 34 pp.

Lord, T. R. (1999). A comparison between traditional and constructivist teaching in environmental science. *Journal of Environmental Education, 30*, 22−28.

Manner, B. M. (1995). Field studies benefit students and teachers. *Journal of Geological Education, 43*, 128−131.

Mason, R. J. (2004). The Pinelands. In *Big places, big plans*. Burlington, VT: Ashgate Publishing.

McConnell, D. A., & van Der Hoeven Kraft, K. J. (2011). Affective domain and student learning in the geosciences. *Journal of Geoscience Education, 59*, 106−110.

McCormack, G. R., Rock, M., Toohey, A. M., & Hignell, D. (2010). Characteristics of urban park use and physical activity: A review of qualitative research. *Health and Place, 16*, 712−726.

McLaughlin, J. S., & Johnson, D. K. (2006). Assessing the field course experiential learning model: Transforming collegiate short-term study abroad experiences into rich learning environments. *Frontiers: The Interdisciplinary Journal of Study Abroad, 13*, 65—85.

Millenbah, K. F., & Millspaugh, J. J. (2003). Using experiential learning in wildlife courses to improve retention, problem solving and decision-making. *Wildlife Society Bulletin, 31*, 127—137.

Moscovici, D. (2013). Boyer Plus: Field study courses for sustainable education. *Journal of Sustainability Education, 5*, 7pp.

Moscovici, D. (2017). Environmental impact of cruise ships on island nations. *Peace Studies Review, 29*(3), 366—373.

Sauve, L. (2005). Currents in environmental education: Mapping a complex and evolving pedagogical field. *Canadian Journal of Environmental Education, 10*, 11—37.

Stokes, A., & Boyle, A. P. (2009). The undergraduate geoscience fieldwork experience: Influencing factors and implications for learning. In S. J. Whitmeyer, D. W. Mogk, & E. J. Pyle (Eds.), *Field geology education: Historical perspectives and modern approaches* (pp. 291—311). Geological Society of America Special Paper 461. doi:10.113012009.2461(23).

Thomas, G., & Munge, B. (2015). Best practices in outdoor environmental education: Pedagogies for improving student learning. In M. Robertson, R. Lawrence, & G. Heath (Eds.), *Experiencing the outdoors*. doi 10.1007/978-94-6209-944-9_14.

United Nations. (2017). Description: Soufriere-Scott's head marine reserve. *United Nations Educational, Scientific and Cultural Organization World Heritage Convention*. Retrieved from http://whc.unesco.org/en/tentativelists/6022/. Accessed on March 3, 2017.

U.S. Census Bureau. (2013). Median household income-American Community Survey. Social Explorer. Retrieved from https://www.census.gov/censusexplorer/censusexplorer.html. Accessed on March 17, 2017.

Chapter 6

Online Learning as the Catalyst for More Deliberate Pedagogies: A Canadian University Experience

Lorayne Robertson, Wendy Barber and William Muirhead

Abstract

This chapter explores issues of quality teaching, learning, and assessment in higher education courses from the perspective of teaching fully online (polysynchronous) courses in undergraduate and graduate programs in education at a technology university in Ontario, Canada. Online courses offer unique opportunities to capitalize on students' and professors' digital capabilities gained in out-of-school learning and apply them to an *in-school*, technology-enabled learning environment. The critical and reflective arguments in this paper are informed by theories of online learning and research on active learning pedagogies.

Digital technologies have opened new spaces for higher education which should be dedicated to creating high-quality learning environments and high-quality assessment. Moving a course online does not guarantee that students will be able to meet the course outcomes more readily, however, or that they will necessarily understand key concepts more easily than previously in the physically copresent course environments. All students in higher education need opportunities to seek, critique, and construct knowledge together and then transfer newly-acquired skills from their coursework to the worlds of work, service, and life. The emergence of new online learning spaces helps us to reexamine present higher education

Active Learning Strategies in Higher Education: Teaching for Leadership,
Innovation, and Creativity, 151–168
ISBN: 978-1-78714-488-0

pedagogies in very deliberate ways to continue to maintain or to improve the quality of student learning in higher education.

In this chapter, *active learning in fully online learning spaces* is the broad theme through which teaching, learning, and assessment strategies are reconsidered. The key elements of our theoretical framework for active learning include (1) deliberate pedagogies to establish the online classroom environment; (2) student ownership of learning activities; and (3) high-quality assessment strategies.

Keywords: Online learning; polysynchronous learning; higher education pedagogies; deliberate pedagogies; quality in online learning

Introduction

This chapter explores issues of quality teaching, learning, and assessment in higher education courses using a comparative perspective and reflecting on the transition of moving from the face-to-face graduate seminar classes to teaching synchronous online courses. Our faculty of education in Canada offers one fully online graduate and one fully online undergraduate program as well as one blended program. The university is technology-focused and had, as its founding feature, an emphasis on the development of technology-rich learning environments – known as the TELE program (Muirhead & Robertson, 2017). One of the founding principles of the TELE program is to fully integrate technology into program and curriculum design. As such, our courses are, of necessity, focused in education but they are also deliberately techno-centric in their program delivery, curriculum, and assessment.

The university initially had a STEM-focused emphasis but recently there has been an impetus to move from STEM to STEAM, with considerations that Science, Technology, Engineering, and Mathematics courses can become broader spaces for student inquiry, problem-based learning, critical thinking, and creativity where the social implications of innovations can be studied. The shift toward thinking about design and automation as, first and foremost, an enterprise that impacts people has been termed *human-centered design* (Boy, 2013). The creation of integrated spaces for problem solving and critical thinking is important because it signifies a trend toward more holistic approaches to learning and problem solving. An integrated learning environment which includes a range of backgrounds and subject specialties can be a more creative and fruitful learning environment. Boy (2013) reminds us that the age of the Internet has introduced active learning or *learning by doing* as well as learning to understand more complex systems. Students need to think critically based on the wealth of information available on the Internet, and they can be supported in this by other learners. They also need to learn to work collaboratively and creatively to share knowledge in ways that are compatible with the audiences who are receiving the information. According to Boy (2013), integrated approaches to learning, active learning, understanding complex systems, exploring possible futures and creativity are newer elements of human-centered design that can apply to education.

Earlier research on educators' responses to moving into fully online teaching reveals that it offers both opportunities and challenges for instructors. It offers the opportunity to pause and reflect more deeply on pedagogy, choices, and resources around curricula. The switch to a new modality of teaching and learning also has challenges because change is disruptive and leads to its own learning and implementation curves (Robertson & Hardman, 2012). In the process of adapting to new methods of delivery, some educators take the opportunity to reconsider key aspects of the instructional design: the environment, the learning activities, and the assessment activities. This chapter elaborates on each of these three key areas.

Deliberate Pedagogy: The Structure of the Online Environment

The first disruptive aspect of our course design and its resultant opportunities came in the form of a new teaching, learning, and assessment environment. In the baccalaureate and graduate programs, the classes are held in a synchronous online environment. Students meet with the instructors in real time using the affordances of software provided by the university (Adobe Connect). There are multiple functions with this software, and many have implications for learning and teaching. For example, this particular software includes back channels. Students are able to chat with each other using a (nonverbal) visible chat function in the online classroom, and they can also hold private instant message conversations during class. Students can post written questions, information, and web links to the class or the instructor without interrupting the conversations happening in the synchronous classroom. Kellogg et al. (2006) have investigated the complexity of the backchannel as a communication space, finding that the backchannels can serve many purposes: steering the group back on track with the process; providing content; and helping users to participate, for example. Backchannels can also be employed for tangential, unrelated types of conversations as well as untimely interruptions (Kellogg et al., 2006).

The backchannel can also serve important social functions. Erickson and Kellogg (2000) find that the visible backchannel can provide clues to highlight awareness of the student, thus increasing accountability. They describe this as *social translucence*. Kellogg et al. (2006) find that the backchannel can raise a student's visibility and copresence, enabling students to build common ground. They find that these features enhance the user experience and the effectiveness of the online interaction (Kellogg et al., 2006). The digital backchannel in our courses is a multidirectional space where students can make comments, share resources, hold discussions, and ask questions, as well as raise their visibility in the online classroom.

The synchronous elements of our classes are not confined to the whole class space, however, as the software affords opportunities for the students to meet and video chat in small groups in real time through a breakout room feature. We find that breakout rooms mimic the practices of the smaller, graduate seminars of yesteryear. The breakout room feature immediately became popular with the students for two reasons. Firstly, there were more opportunities for students to speak with each other in smaller groups, and secondly, for students who were reluctant to try out ideas in the context of the full class (for example, students who were not working in their first language or students who are generally quiet), the breakout rooms provided them with opportunities to propose ideas with less perceived risk.

There are also a-synchronous communications happening before and after course times. A program decision was made to offer the students and professors an Adobe Connect meeting room which is open 24/7 for collaboration and discussion, as it allows the students the opportunity to rehearse if they are planning to lead a presentation or discussion in class. It is essentially a synchronous practice room that they can use a-synchronously to prepare for the scheduled class time. We have found that students find ways to combine technologies to enhance their learning and productivity for learning, and then they share these digital tools with other students through the online meeting room or in the synchronous classroom. The digital room is also used for the thesis presentations and defenses.

Other a-synchronous features include a class-only email in the learning management system (LMS) and communication is encouraged through questions or topics assigned in the Discussion Board in the LMS (Blackboard). In the a-synchronous discussion board, students may choose their groups and decide to interact with large groups or smaller groups. We encourage students to choose a group of peers with similar interests for interaction on the discussion board, but we leave the full discussion board visible for students who want to see all of the communications of the other groups and their posted assignments.

Our impression is that most of the students easily adapt to the multiple modes of digital communication, and some students will initiate additional communication venues such as sharing documents in the cloud, trying new applications, or using other means of online communication such as WhatsApp or Google hangouts from the Google apps for education. Occasionally, students will offer views about the level of technology – sometimes asking us to "keep it simple" so we have learned that the amount of new technology needs to be monitored through student feedback.

Dalgarno (2014) defines learning environments such as the one we employ for our courses as *polysynchronous*. These are environments which blend together the multiple channels of communication experienced in face-to-face (f2f), asynchronous, and synchronous teaching in order to provide more opportunities. Essentially, Dalgarno argues that these newer types of student interaction patterns allow students more options to communicate and collaborate with each other and thus encourage deeper levels of engagement. We concur that the opportunities of the f2f synchronous, online environment do allow our students to problem-solve and discuss in real time with their peers, but we ponder whether or not these elements, of themselves, create more or deeper engagement.

We have discovered, however, that the synchronous online environment can become more of a site for student-to-student discussion if we provide some *deliberate elements* in the course design to establish this environment. First, we give students access to all of the production controls in our online classrooms so that they are able to discuss, produce, and interrogate peers using the identical affordances to those used by the course instructors. Using a function of the software, we "promote" students so that they can present their learning, organize their peers into work groups, speak when their turn is recognized, and even set up the design of the classroom environment in advance of the class. The students may "own" the online room in which they will present and discuss. In doing so, we model that we are a community of learners, and our collective enterprise is to support and construct learning together.

The concept of an invisible type of pedagogy, which is the deliberate setup of the classroom environment was earlier theorized by Bernstein (1975) in the context of K-12 education. According to Bernstein, who studied the pedagogy underlying the setup of the learning environment for young children, the teacher uses a deliberate and almost invisible pedagogy when structuring the learning environment by offering a range of activities within the learner's expected capacity. The learner exercises choice within the learning environment and is self-regulating. The instructor not only establishes the learning environment and the learning activities, but also does not take center stage. The instructor observes the learner who is interacting with the environment in order to determine the learner's understanding of concepts and readiness for new concepts. The image below (Figure 1) displays many aspects of this deliberate type of pedagogy taking place in one of our online classes.

Barber and vanOostveen (2016) describe a related type of invisible pedagogy in online problem-based learning courses. They define invisible pedagogy as one which requires the online instructor to support the learning from the background, not the foreground. It requires the online instructor to be fully present in multiple ways such as social, emotional, pedagogical, and technical. In their view, the instructor is invisible only with respect to leading but is fully a participant as a cocreator of learning in a community of inquiry (Barber & vanOostveen, 2016).

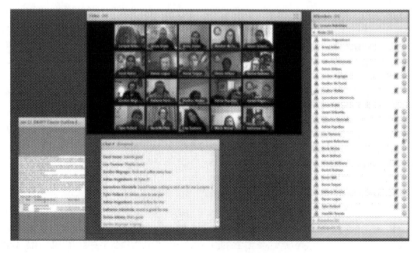

Figure 1.   An Online Class (Deliberately Blurred to Protect Identity).

Figure 1 is a screen shot of a moment in an online graduate class. The images have been *deliberately blurred* to protect the students' personally identifiable information.

There is a list of attendees in the class which helps to build social presence and is therefore significant. Often, a list of names is not provided in classes where students are expected to work together and share knowledge. The attendee list shows that many of the students have their microphones muted at the point that the screen shot was captured, but their rights to speak in class are clearly in evidence. Secondly, there are green checkmarks beside students' names indicating that they have responded to a quick online poll asking if they have understood a question or have voted on a decision about what is to happen next in class. Most of the students (20 out of 24) have their video cameras on, and they are broadcasting live. Several students at this point in time have chosen to pause their cameras (which students are encouraged to do for short time periods so that they do not disrupt the class with, for example, the sudden appearance of one of the student's children saying good night). Live chat is in evidence in the chat box which appears below the pictures of the students. A shared content note pod is also open, and it is showing content, likely in order to respond to a student question. The students have unrestricted rights to share resources and comments in class.

In an analysis of four case studies which outline online classroom scenarios encountered in polysynchronous learning environments, Dalgarno (2014) finds that real-time interaction activities such as responding to multiple choice questions through status visibility features (like the green check marks beside the students' names in Figure 1) can change the student learning experience in significant ways. Students are constructing meaning and making their learning and thinking visible, rather than waiting until they are called upon individually to respond to a question. Multiple forms of interaction allow for a more active learning experience, because students take what was previously a private activity (viewing content or listening to content) and then, in the online setting, they transform it into a social activity where learning, understanding, and experiences are shared (Barber & vanOostveen, 2016; Dalgarno, 2014).

Student Ownership of the Learning Activities

Not all instructors who switch to online classrooms embrace the use of the affordances of the new technologies, however. In a review of research on e-learning in higher education, Flavin (2012) finds that instructors who employ digital technologies have tended to *duplicate rather than transform existing pedagogies* for adult learners. In Flavin's research, higher education instructors who switched to online courses relied on one or two tried-and-true technologies rather than attempting new technological innovations as they emerged. Flavin describes the technology as *disruptive* to the instructor because the students are more familiar with the affordances of the technologies than the instructor and this causes the instructor to "relinquish some authority" (2012, p. 104). Barber and vanOostveen (2016) address this issue directly, arguing that an invisible pedagogy which puts the instructor into the supporting role also puts the power into the hands of the learner – power to brainstorm solutions, make choices, and take direction in problem solving.

In our courses, we generally let the students create and demonstrate what they know about different online applications and how these can be productively employed for learning and communication in the online classroom. This alternate approach allows students to use their technology knowledge and builds their ownership and expression of voice within digital spaces. In order for this to happen, as higher education instructors, we need to carefully establish the environment that allows the students to show what they know and encourage students to "own" the online classroom for purposes of constructing effective colearning experiences for their peers. In other words, we rely on our students to raise the level of the quality of the learning in the class whenever it can benefit others in the class.

In the past, the academy focused on and recognized individual student achievement over collective learning, but in the real world, many problems require collective insights and strong communication skills in order to challenge and test theories or to verify direction and seek alternatives. Our perception is that students have developed many technology-intensive skills in their out-of-school lives, and we believe that academic courses should offer students opportunities to showcase and apply their digital communication skills to bring out-of-school learning closer to in-school learning.

We acknowledge that, although digital technologies open new spaces for learning, teaching and assessment in higher education, we need to carefully monitor whether or not these spaces translate into more enabling, higher quality student learning environments. Employing an online space and using the tools of online learning do not necessarily predict that students will more easily meet course outcomes, achieve stronger understandings of key concepts, or transfer their learning to new areas. The presence of e-learning alone does not predict that students will learn more deeply or more critically. Although the learning environment is significant, and it can be deliberately constructed to encourage student ownership of learning, the student learning activities and the assessment of student learning are critical elements also. In the next section, accordingly, we outline some of the deliberate elements of online course design and assessment.

Online Course Design

Less dependence on lecture: We purposefully structure our courses so that they are *not lecture-dependent.* We concur with Garrison and Anderson's (2003) contention that, although the technology may be novel, if the teaching remains mostly transmission-based, then there exists the possibility that the student learning may be focused on more traditional knowledge transfer, acquisition, and recall. To make the claim that our classes are not lecture-intensive is not to say that there is less content or less learning in our courses, but we structure our classes in different ways so that the focus of the in-class time is on discussion and engagement with the content at the higher levels of Bloom's (1956) taxonomy. Rather than asking students about knowledge recall, for example, we expect students to prepare for class with readings and assignments, and we deliberately use the time in class for students *to apply their new knowledge* in assignments that require application, critical analysis, and problem solving, using a range of discussion, problem-based learning, project-based learning, and case studies.

Flipped classroom: When active learning was integrated into large lecture courses in introductory biology, Walker, Cotner, Baepler, and Decker (2008) found that the Biology students in the active learning classes performed as well if not better than the control groups of students in the more traditional, lecture-intensive classes. They found that less content was covered in the active learning classes, meaning that some of the content had to be covered through readings and assignments (Walker et al., 2008). In our programs, students know that they need to come to class prepared for discussion and active learning. To a significant degree, we employ Mazur's (2009) *flipped classroom* model, encouraging students to prepare by working and/or collaborating outside of class (and prior to class) to understand the assigned chapters or readings. This approach encourages students to take more ownership of their learning and it also encourages them to acquire and organize the new information at their own pace and in their own way outside of class, so that they can use class time for application and consolidation.

Anytime minilectures: There is some disagreement about the role of the higher education instructor. For example, Barber and vanOostveen (2016) see the instructor role as that of a colearner. In our experience, there is an assessment aspect to the instructor role also, which requires the higher education instructor to monitor and assess understandings during class time and attempt to encourage more clarity or clear up any misconceptions if they exist. Occasionally, instructors identify common themes or misconceptions emerging from student contributions that require a brief explanation or exploration outside of class. When this occurs from time-to-time, a minilecture or a brief video will be added to help students understand a concept with which they have been wrestling or explain an assignment. The flexibility of the LMS in the online environment makes the use of new video-based technologies such as Kaltura to record just-in-time online minilectures both feasible and desirable. Another key feature available with online video-based classes and minilectures is that students can access the recordings of the classes anywhere and anytime and view them again to increase their comprehension. This is helpful for students such as those who are new to the language of presentation or students who benefit from review and clarification of the course material.

In-school learning resembling out-of-school learning: We want our students to feel that we are preparing them for the world in which they will work and learn rather than looking through the rear view mirror and focusing on how learning has traditionally happened in the academy in the past. In order to do this, we work toward the model that *in-school learning* needs to more closely resemble *out-of-school learning*. As such, we expect the students to employ many of the technologies they use outside of class in order to seek, verify, and share information in their fully online worlds. In addition, if we want to prepare students for the world of work, then we need to keep the focus on *applying* theories and concepts, and giving students opportunities to transfer their learning as they wrestle with real-world problems.

Smith, Douglas, and Cox (2009), concerned with improving STEM education specifically, and higher education in general, wrestle with the issue of students dropping out of STEM programs and apply the How People Learn (HPL) framework (Bransford, Vye, & Bateman, 2002) to improve teaching and learning in STEM and address the needs of individual learners. The HPL framework was developed by Bransford and colleagues in a landmark review of the research on learning and

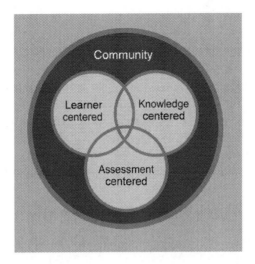

Figure 2. The Four Lenses of the How People Learn Framework (Bransford et al., 2002).

development and it can be applied to guide learning design. It can also be applied to analyze the quality of the learning experience. The framework has four lenses, indicating that high-quality classrooms should be learner-centered, knowledge-centered, and assessment centered, and take place within a community of learners (See Figure 2).

Within the HPL framework, a *knowledge-centered* environment is transparent about what students should know and be able to do, and identifies the foundational and enduring knowledge, skills, and values. These are what Wiggins and McTighe (2005) would characterize as the *enduring outcomes* of the course. According to Bransford and colleagues, if a course is *learner-centered*, the plan of the learning should focus on meeting the learners at their individual levels of understanding and capitalize on the individual learner's strengths, interests, previous assumptions, and preconceptions. This necessitates the provision of learning activities which help the students understand their level of cognition as they approach the learning. When learning is *community-centered*, the learning community is supportive and students feel safe to ask questions; learn to work collaboratively; use the technology; and build their learning skills. Finally, a learning environment should be *assessment-centered* – providing students with many opportunities to *make their thinking visible* so that they can receive feedback (Bransford et al., 2002).

Garrison and Anderson (2003) build on the theory of the HPL framework and apply it to online learning. They argue that the semantic web allows higher education instructors to tailor the content more closely to support the learning needs of individual students and the students as a learning community. Students create, personalize, annotate, and reuse content, working within a community of learners, thus improving the depth of understanding for what students learn. The affordances of Web 2.0 allow real-time access to subject experts and allow students to time shift and listen (or listen again) to key presentations when they are most open to learning and able to learn. Garrison and Anderson also theorize that online learning allows both time and place shifting opportunities to provide "just-in-time" feedback in an assessment-centered learning environment.

We find in our online courses that when students are encouraged to work together in small groups to solve problems, they become more comfortable voicing their opinions and asking questions. Students have both a *social presence* online and a *cognitive presence* (Garrison, Anderson, & Archer, 2001). The provision of small groups and a problem-solving orientation may also support the building of community. Barber (2017) also reports that when the online environment becomes more of a familiar space to them, students use the online affordances and work together to build community.

In summary then, the move to online teaching has encouraged us as higher education instructors to reconsider present research on how people learn, and in particular how the benefits of *active learning in online courses* emerge in courses characterized by student engagement, participation, and democratic norms. In our classes, we engage students in setting personal learning goals, encourage them to participate in knowledge construction and dissemination, and prompt them to assess and reflect on their learning. Moving to online learning helps us to see that students can become more empowered and enabled to consider the quality of their own learning and contributions and the contributions of their peers in higher education. In the next section of the chapter, we review the third aspect of teaching online, exploring assessment-centered learning in higher education.

Quality Assessment Practices

If we are making a commitment to provide learning environments that build collaboration and critical reflection skills in order to meet 21st century learning outcomes, then the assessments of the learning outcomes need to align with how students learn in digital spaces (Barber, 2017; Voogt, Erstad, Dede & Mishra, 2013). This change includes a reexamination of who has the power in the community of learners. In a more democratic digitally-driven pedagogy, students should build skills of self-assessment and reflection of their own and their peers' learning on authentic tasks (Barber, 2017).

As we deliberated on the assessment practices for our online courses, we considered whether or not the assessment in the online space should align with traditional assessment practices or whether the assessment practices should change. As instructors, we knew that higher order thinking skills needed to factor heavily in the assessment design. We wanted to build student engagement and interaction into our assessments. In addition, we wanted to help students build their skills of self-assessment and self-awareness. We also wanted to try some of the newer technological affordances to build an assessment repertoire and dialogue with our students.

One of the deliberate pedagogical elements of our online courses became adherence to quality assessment practices. As a theoretical framework, we decided to utilize the *backward design model* developed by Wiggins and McTighe (2005) which encourages the course instructor to begin with the end of the course (the course outcomes or the program outcomes) in mind. In our discussions, we find that this model aligns with the HPL framework (Bransford et al., 2002) as well as Garrison and Anderson's (2003) theories of online learning and assessment. In this model, the higher education instructor and the student identify the significant understandings that a learner would want to have upon completion of the course. These enduring outcomes have also been identified as the concepts that are at the *heart of a discipline* or concepts that require the support of the higher education instructor to be learned because of their complexity (Smith et al. 2009). According to Pellegrino (2006), higher education instructors can help students organize their learning by helping them to identify these key concepts and connect their learning using theoretical frameworks.

When we first meet with the students, we provide the graduate outcomes for the program and align these with the course learning outcomes. We do this so that students can see clearly how the learning in the course aligns with the learning in the program. We also match each assignment in the course to the learning outcomes for the course and the graduate outcomes. This provides our students with clear *alignment* and *clarity* surrounding the purposes for the learning and the purposes for assessment.

There should also be alignment between the way students are assessed and how the course is structured for their learning. In other words, if the course is 100% discussion, and the students are assessed only on their written work, there is a disconnect. Also, students arrive into a course with different prior experiences and knowledge, and the role of the higher education instructor is to help students understand what they need to do in order to develop skills and competence, even if the students are setting personal goals. One of the key elements of our course design is to offer the students choice in the pathways that they take toward mastery of the learning outcomes. Assignments are individual, paired, or group assignments. Students can also choose their group work partners for multiple class assignments or elect to work alone for most of them. As instructors, we connect elements of choice to empowerment and deeper engagement with student learning.

Helping students develop skills of metacognition (helping students understand their own thinking and learning development) is a higher order skill that can be developed through self and peer assessment, as well as deliberate efforts to help students understand the assessment in a course. This focus on metacognition also empowers higher education students to monitor their own progress in the course and understand how they learn. In order for students to acquire metacognitive understanding, higher education instructors need to give detailed and targeted feedback.

Wiggins and McTighe (2005) identify this type of assessment-focused learning as "uncoverage" (p. 21). The role of the teacher is to *uncover* students' thinking by asking questions, encouraging them to try out new ideas, and rethinking when concepts are not connected and meaningful to them. Regular, ongoing assessment also performs the role of uncovering student misconceptions. While it is a learner-focused activity, it is a deliberate pedagogy for the teacher who already understands the key concepts and understandings of the course or program. Smith et al. (2009) advocate for more of an emphasis on formative or ongoing assessment than summative assessment, because formative assessments encourage instructors to identify potential challenges with student understanding and revise the learning activities accordingly, thus supporting a student-centered approach to learning as well as an assessment-centered approach (and reflecting the HPL framework).

In our reflective practice, we have come across other descriptions of the concept of *uncoverage*. Tomlinson (2001), while concurring that there is a need for knowledge or standards, encourages instructors to also think about the skills that can be modeled and assessed in instruction such has how to observe, question, plan, and analyze. She argues that every discipline has its own set of skills which are used by practitioners as the "intellectual building blocks" of a profession (p. 40). The role of the instructor is not to cover the content but *to uncover* the meanings within the discipline (Tomlinson, 2001; Wiggins & McTighe, 2005).

Pellegrino (2006) theorizes that technology-supported learning environments have enhanced our capacity as instructors to help students deeply understand concepts (comprehensiveness), align their learning with the purpose of the course and the learning outcomes (coherence) and view their progress through continuous assessment over the duration of the course (continuity).

Assessment should not only be beneficial to students in their learning but it should be a transparent process that students understand well. In Canada, an advisory committee developed principles for fair student assessment which provide guidance for educators from all levels of education (Rogers, 1993). More importantly, however, these principles provide students with more safety in their learning because they are based in fairness. One of the principles of fair assessment is alignment or the notion that the learning methods and assessment methods should match. Another *fair assessment principle* recommends that student performance should be judged on multiple work efforts, rather than large, single assessments in order to build more quality, validity, and confidence into the assessments. In addition, students should be given the option to demonstrate their understandings in multiple creative ways. Students can exercise choice in how they demonstrate their learning and choice in the group makeup.

Students who participate in a transparent assessment environment assume most of the responsibility for their individual and collective progress. Skills of metacognition that assist with student-centered learning include the ability for students to set learning goals and monitor their progress. Instructors may need to support students in the development of metacognition skills where students monitor their own learning and understand more deeply how they learn as individuals. Metacognition and self-regulation skills can be taught, but monitoring achievement is a key responsibility of the student (Flavell, 1979; Pellegrino, 2009). Steiner and Posch (2006) describe this type of *mutual learning* as "self-regulated and self-responsible learning" (p. 877).

We have carefully considered how technology can enable assessment to happen in more transparent and innovative ways to help students construct their own understanding. At the present time, we are working to develop more *assessment dialogues* with students rather than using the traditional transmission method from instructor to student as a means of communicating an assessment result. Here, again, we are exploring with the use of Kaltura to use video to support our assessment comments and encouraging students to respond. This type of dialogic assessment model that has been used in the Oxford tutor–student system has been found to have its advantages. Beck, for example, finds that assessment dialogue has been seen to support a closer monitoring of student progress. It also has advantages for the student, such as encouraging students to think for themselves. The one-to-one contact also lowers the emotional barriers and encourages students to find their voices (Beck, 2007). We would not have considered this new approach to an assessment dialogue without the efficiencies of the new technologies to allow us to have "conversations" with students without the barriers of geography and time.

Conclusion

In summary, we concur with Jacobsen and Lock (2004) that instructors need to consider how students are prepared to work in the knowledge era where the communications are interactive and just-in-time. Our students not only need to know how to locate information but they need to know how to publish and exchange information. To quote Jacobsen et al., "An important job for all educators is to enable learners to author using the media of their time" (2004, para. 2). Students need to be taught in new ways and not necessarily the ways that we were taught. Our students will not only locate global information but they will also become global authors and publishers and they need to learn how to exchange and construct deeper understandings across the globe.

Our deliberations on our pedagogy suggest that it would be prudent to maintain an open, investigative stance toward the potential of e-learning environments as spaces for more deliberate, active learning pedagogies such as problem-based learning, project-based learning, case study discussions, and multiple other activities which encourage the learners to take responsibility both for their own learning and also for monitoring what gets accomplished in the learning community of their peers.

References

Barber, W. (2017). Critical play in fully online learning communities. In R. V. Nata (Ed.), *Progress in education* (Vol. 43). ISBN: 978-1-53610-561-2. Retrieved from https://www.novapublishers.com/catalog/product_info.php?products_id=60364

Barber, W., & vanOostveen, R. (2016). Invisible pedagogy: Developing problem-based learning in digital contexts. In R. Henderson (Ed.), *Problem-based learning: Perspectives, methods and challenges* (pp. 18–31). New York, NY: Nova Publishers.

Beck, R. (2007, March). The pedagogy of the Oxford tutorial. In *Tutorial education: History, pedagogy, and evolution conference*. Appleton, WI: Lawrence University.

Bernstein, B. (1975). Class and pedagogies: Visible and invisible. *Educational studies, 1*(1), 23–41.

Bloom, B. S. (1956). *Taxonomy of educational objectives. Vol. 1: Cognitive domain* (pp. 20–24). New York, NY: McKay.

Boy, G. A. (2013). From STEM to STEAM: Toward a human-centred education, creativity & learning thinking. In *Proceedings of the 31st European Conference on Cognitive Ergonomics* (p. 3). ACM.

Bransford, J., Vye, N., & Bateman, H. (2002, May). Creating high-quality learning environments: Guidelines from research on how people learn. In *The Knowledge Economy and Postsecondary Education: Report of Workshop* (pp. 159–198).

Dalgarno, B. (2014). Polysynchronous learning: A model for student interaction and engagement. *Rhetoric and reality: Critical perspectives on educational technology. Proceedings Ascilite Dunedin 2014*, 673–677. Retrieved from http://ascilite.org/conferences/dunedin2014/files/concisepapers/255-Dalgarno.pdf

Erickson, T., & Kellogg, W. A. (2000). Social translucence: An approach to designing systems that support social processes. *ACM transactions on computer-human interaction (TOCHI), 7*(1), 59–83.

Flavell, J. H. (1979). Metacognition and cognitive monitoring: A new area of cognitive-developmental inquiry. *American psychologist, 34*(10), 906.

Flavin, M. (2012). Disruptive technologies in higher education. *Research in Learning Technology, 20*. Retrieved from http://www.tandfonline.com/doi/full/10.3402/rlt.v20i0.19184

Garrison, D., & Anderson, T. (2003). Introduction. In D. R. Garrison & T. Anderson (Eds.), *E-learning in the 21st century: A framework for research and practice*. New York, NY: Routledge.

Garrison, D. R., Anderson, T., & Archer, W. (2001). Critical thinking, cognitive presence, and computer conferencing in distance education. *American Journal of distance education, 15*(1), 7–23.

Jacobsen, D. M., & Lock, J. V. (2004). Technology and teacher education for a knowledge era: Mentoring for student futures, not our past. *Journal of Technology and Teacher Education, 12*(1), 75.

Kellogg, W. A., Erickson, T., Wolf, T. V., Levy, S., Christensen, J., Sussman, J., & Bennett, W. E. (2006, November). Leveraging digital backchannels to enhance user experience in electronically mediated communication. In *Proceedings of the 2006 20th anniversary conference on computer supported cooperative work* (pp. 451–454). ACM.

Mazur, E. (2009). Farewell, lecture. *Science, 323*(5910), 50–51.

Muirhead, W., & Robertson, L. (2017). Invisible pedagogies in online learning. Presented to INTED, Valencia, Spain, March 2017. Retrieved from https://library.iated.org/view/MUIRHEAD2017SIL

Pellegrino, J. W. (2006). *Rethinking and redesigning curriculum, instruction and assessment: What contemporary research and theory suggests. A paper commissioned by the National Center of Education and the Economy for the new commission on the skills of the American workforce.* NCEE. Retrieved from http://www.skillscommission.org/

Rogers, T. (1993). *Principles for fair student assessment practices for education in Canada.* Edmonton: Joint Advisory Committee. Retrieved from http://www.bced.gov.bc.ca/classroom_assessment/fairstudent.pdf

Smith, K. A., Douglas, T. C., & Cox, M. F. (2009). Supportive teaching and learning strategies in STEM education. *New Directions for Teaching and Learning, 2009*(117), 19–32.

Steiner, G., & Posch, A. (2006). Higher education for sustainability by means of transdisciplinary case studies: An innovative approach for solving complex, real-world problems. *Journal of Cleaner Production, 14*(9), 877–890.

Tomlinson, C. A. (2001). Standards and the art of teaching: Crafting high-quality classrooms. *NASSP Bulletin, 85*(622), 38–47.

Voogt, J., Erstad, O., Dede, C., & Mishra, P. (2013). Challenges to learning and schooling in the digital networked world of the 21st century. *Journal of Computer Assisted Learning, 29*(5), 403–413.

Walker, J. D., Cotner, S. H., Baepler, P. M., & Decker, M. D. (2008). A delicate balance: Integrating active learning into a large lecture course. *CBE-Life Sciences Education, 7*(4), 361–367.

Wiggins, G. P., & McTighe, J. (2005). *Understanding by design.* Virginia: ASCD.

Chapter 7

Active, Cooperative Learning in Online Higher Education. The Learning Design for "Change Management" at the Universitat Oberta de Catalunya

Eva Rimbau-Gilabert

Abstract

This chapter describes and analyzes the result of an active, cooperative learning design adopted in "Change Management," an elective
course at the Universitat Oberta de Catalunya (UOC), which is a
fully online university. The paper describes the context and foundations that support the learning design, outlines the learning activities and their evolution, and presents the results of a student survey
to assess the design's effectiveness in reaching its main goals. The
results of the survey suggest that students perceived this design
as enhancing their teamwork abilities, while being interesting and
motivating, as well as useful in learning the course's content.
Therefore, the desired goals were attained and the design was kept,
with minor changes, in subsequent editions of the course. In addition, students without prior teamwork experience valued the collaborative activities more than students who had previously worked in
teams in other subjects of their degrees. In contrast, no differences
were found for individual learning activities. This suggests that the
design can be useful in introductory courses where students are
asked to learn in virtual teams for the first time.

Keywords: Case-based learning; collaborative learning; e-learning;
virtual teams; teamwork; change management

Active Learning Strategies in Higher Education: Teaching for Leadership,
Innovation, and Creativity, 169–185
Copyright © 2018 by Emerald Publishing Limited
All rights of reproduction in any form reserved
ISBN: 978-1-78714-488-0

Introduction

Active learning in the virtual environment is no different from active learning in face-to-face classrooms. The definition of active learning as "anything that involves students in doing things and thinking about the things they are doing" (Bonwell & Eison, 1991, p. 2) can be applied no matter what the student's learning environment. Its defining feature is adopting instructional practices that engage students in the learning process, so that they develop a deep understanding of the important ideas to be learned (Prince, 2004) through their engagement in higher order thinking, such as analysis, synthesis, and evaluation (Koohang, Paliszkiewicz, Gołuchowski, & Nord, 2016, p. 17). Such practices and activities can be performed in all kinds of contexts (face-to-face or online) and concerning any content (natural or social science, humanities, etc.). There is now abundant literature describing how active learning can be developed online (e.g. Bolliger & Armier, 2013; Koohang, 2012; Koohang & Paliszkiewicz, 2013; Salmon, 2013; Trentin, 2010), but, as of yet, detailed case studies of active learning in online higher education are uncommon. Thus, this chapter describes what is considered to be a good practice in this context.

The chapter outlines and analyzes the result of an active learning design adopted in "Change Management," an elective course within the bachelor's degrees in Business Administration and Management and Labor Relations and Employment of the Universitat Oberta de Catalunya (Open University of Catalonia, UOC), which is a fully online university. We thus examine the learning that took place in a web-based environment with no face-to-face meetings between students or between instructors and students. The learning design included the analysis of real case studies, with a strong constructivist approach in three of the learning activities.

The description adopts the levels suggested by Zabalza (2012) to describe good teaching practices in higher education: context, foundation, learning activities (called "evolution" in Zabalza's model), assessment ("impact and results" in Zabalza's model), current situation, and transferability.

Context: The University and the Course

An educational initiative can only be considered "good" if it fits the needs and constraints imposed by its context. Therefore, here

I introduce the main traits of the university and the course where the active learning experience took place.

The Universitat Oberta de Catalunya

The Universitat Oberta de Catalunya (UOC) (http://www.uoc.edu/portal/en/index.html) is a fully online university with headquarters in Barcelona, Spain. It was founded in 1995 by the regional government of Catalonia with the mission of "providing people with lifelong learning and education through the intensive use of information and communication technologies." The UOC was the first fully online university designed from scratch. Since its beginnings, in the academic year 1995/1996, the UOC has grown consistently, from just 200 students to a University community of over 200,000 people, 54,022 of which are students and 3,692 teaching staff. The courses offered are official and endorsed by the Catalan University Quality Assurance Agency (AQU Catalunya) and the Spanish Quality Assessment and Accreditation Agency (ANECA), which ensure academic rigor and compliance with the standards required by the European university system.

At the UOC, the student learns actively, mentored at all times by the teaching staff and in cooperation with his or her fellow students, supported by tools and resources and competency-based assessment. UOC students have a particular profile, since they usually are not full-time students but have other professional or personal commitments to attend to. They chose the UOC to update their skills and competence because it allows them to overcome time and space constraints (Mor, Guerrero-Roldán, Hettiarachchi, & Huertas, 2014).

The UOC has a student-centered educational model based on activities. The whole learning process takes place through its virtual learning environment, comprising a learning management system, learning materials, a digital syllabus, and assessment tools. The assessment is continuous and formative and has an impact on the continuous improvement of students' learning. The assessment activities help ensure that learning objectives are achieved and skills developed.

The model is oriented toward collective participation and knowledge building and embraces the students' learning, social and working experiences. It is committed to a learning process that balances the personal engagement of the student with collaboration, enriching the student's learning process with the knowledge, opinions, and experiences of their fellow students and developing their teamwork skills in preparation for the professional world.

In summary, the learning model of the UOC demands an active learning approach from its teaching staff and fosters the use of collaboration as a learning context. These traits were adopted in the design of the Change Management course, as explained below.

The Change Management Course

"Change Management" is an elective course that is part of the bachelor's degrees in Business Administration and Management and in Labor Relations and Employment. The chapter's author was the course's coordinating professor. I developed the course's learning goals, content and learning activities. Following the idea of constructive alignment (Biggs, 1999), I had to design learning activities and assessment tasks that facilitated the learning outcomes I wanted the students to attain. This section presents the learning outcomes for the course on Change Management at the UOC and explains the rationale that led to choosing an active learning design, based on teamwork and case studies.

In the cognitive domain, the learning goals were the following:

- Explain the different forms of change, the forces that drive organizational change and its main elements.
- Explain what novelty is, how it is generated, and how it spreads.
- Distinguish the various roles that people involved in change can have.
- Explain the role of people's human needs, personality, and emotions when faced with changes in their organization.
- Identify which model of organizational change is the most adequate for different types of problems and expose in detail the main models of planned change.
- Identify and analyze behaviors that are considered as being resistant to change and propose ways to prevent them from appearing.
- Explain what characteristics should be present in someone who is responsible for organizational change and what measures they should take.
- Analyze the political interests surrounding a process of change and identify some ways in which to fulfill these interests.

- Discuss the relationship between culture and change in organizations.
- Explain how learning can be both an enabler and an obstacle for organizational change.
- Analyze organizational changes to detect their strengths and weaknesses and make proposals for improvement.
- Design plans to carry out organizational changes of different levels of complexity.

In the interpersonal domain, students were expected to develop their ability to work in virtual teams, thus being able to cooperate with other students to reach a shared goal.

The first difficulty in achieving the stated knowledge goals was the markedly theoretical approach of the course's content. It included topics such as Change and Novelty, Models for Change Management, Individual Aspects of Change, Resistance to Change, Leadership and Politics, and Learning and Organizational Culture. The learning materials as they were did not include enough examples to allow students to connect the concepts with the reality of organizational change. Such an abstract approach harbored a considerable risk of hindering students' meaningful learning and their attainment of the learning goals mentioned above. To offset this difficulty, I decided that knowledge construction by students would revolve around "credible" applications of the theory to real or realistic situations. The broad definition of active learning encompasses very diverse activities, among which case-based learning offers learners an opportunity to work on authentic and complex problems, and aims to support the application and transfer of knowledge to real professional situations (Kopp, Hasenbein, & Mandl, 2014, p. 352). Thus, the course adopted an active learning approach whereby all learning activities would include the analysis of real cases of organizational change.

A second route to improving students' engagement with the content was based on their characteristics. As the UOC is a fully online university, its students tend to be people with personal and/or professional responsibilities, who cannot or do not want to attend face-to-face courses at a brick-and-mortar university. Therefore, it was safe to assume that the course's students probably had experienced organizational changes in their own professional life. Taking advantage of this experience, the students provided examples of organizational changes that they or a person close to them had undergone recently.

Finally, since the course learning goals included the ability to work in virtual teams, a collaborative element was included in the design. According to Magzan, Aleksić-Maslać, and Jurić (2010):

> ... the inclusion of teamwork as a learning strategy in business education has multiple benefits. Involving students in collaborative projects helps them to recognize, value and capitalize on the strengths of other people in interactive business situations. Also, it helps their understanding and experience of cooperative group processes by thus providing them with essential team skills suitable for different types of employment. As crucial stakeholders in higher education, prospective employers continue to demand graduates who are experienced in team work.

However, in the current globalized work context, many teams are composed of members that work in separate locations and have to collaborate via communication technologies. Thus, not only teamwork but virtual teamwork skills are needed from college graduates to succeed in their future jobs.

As a result of combining real cases with teamwork, the course activities asked students to share their change cases with their teammates, choose two of the cases, analyze them and compare them using the course's concepts so that they could provide suggestions for improvement that could have been useful in the real cases. This collaborative construction of new knowledge by learners is the key feature of constructivist learning and was used in three of the five learning activities proposed during the semester.

In summary, this course was designed by adopting an active approach that used real and personal case studies and a combination of individual and collaborative work as a means of reaching its goals, namely: enhancing comprehension of the content, motivating and engaging students in their learning process, and improving the students' competence in virtual teamwork.

Foundation: Active, Collaborative Learning in Online Education

This section describes how the two main traits of the adopted design — active learning and collaboration — can be implemented in an online environment and provides some particulars about the design used in

Change Management, although the full details of the course's activities are given in the subsequent section.

Active e-Learning

Koohang (2012) proposed a systemic model for active learning in e-learning, comprised of three stages that are internal to learning (underpinning, ownership, and engaging) and a group of prerequisite elements that are external to learning (class size, active and responsive support services, standard course policies, and e-learning courseware usability). According to Koohang (2012, p. 70), "the three stages and the prerequisite elements must, in their entirety, be present in an e-learning environment for successful learning to occur."

- The underpinning stage creates the basis and the groundwork for learning. The elements of this stage are real world and relevant examples, exploration, higher order thinking skills (analysis, evaluation, and synthesis), and scaffolding that can be used to make learners think above and beyond what they normally know. These elements create the environment in which learners can become active learners and have to be built into course activities by the instructor.
- The ownership stage promotes learners' self-confidence and empowerment so they begin and take control of their learning. The instructor has to design activities that allow for self-reflection and self-awareness, let learners include their own experiences in solving case-based activities and guide the learner to actively participate and present their ideas.
- The engaging stage actively builds a community of learners that collaboratively and actively engage in the construction of new knowledge. It includes: (1) learners' active engagement in analysis, evaluation, and synthesis of multiple perspectives and (2) learners' collaborative assessment. The instructor's responsibility is not merely facilitating the learning process; he or she actively coaches, guides, mentors, tutors, assesses, and provides feedback to learners.

In Change Management, students had to use their experience or explore others' experience to provide real-world examples. As will be explained in the next section, they were provided step-by-step instructions so that they progressed from the mere description of a change case, through the analysis and comparison of cases, to the elaboration of suggestions to improve such cases. Students proposed and agreed upon rules to regulate the functioning of their teams, which proved to be useful when any team member didn't perform as needed. The class instructors guided all this activity; they also provided feedback on the quality of team processes and assessed the teams' final reports.

Regarding the prerequisite elements, Koohang (2012) asserts that "large class sizes do not allow for the construction of meaningful knowledge. For learning to occur successfully in e-learning, an online class should be 15 to 20 students for undergraduate courses and 10 to 15 students for graduate courses." Class sizes for the UOC's Change Management course were around 60 students. Therefore, classes were divided into work groups of 4−5 people so that teamwork could advance smoothly. A second key element for Koohang is standard course policies, ones that help keep the learner on-task and contribute to the success of learning. The syllabus and other documents provided in Change Management included the purpose and structure of the course, a clear explanation of how the course would be given, due dates for completing all activities, guidelines for online team collaboration, and the main traits of assessments. Through their advisor, students could get information on the courseware platform, the expectations for UOC students, and the methods of regular communication between students and instructors and among students.

The other two prerequisite elements proposed by Koohang (2012) − namely active and responsive support services and e-learning courseware usability − were also present as default features of the UOC's offer for all its students.

Collaborative e-Learning

One particular approach to active learning involves collaboration, which Palloff and Pratt (2005, p. 4) define as "an educational approach to teaching and learning that involves groups of learners working together to solve a problem, complete a task, or create a product." As is the case with face-to-face teams, virtual teams utilized in online distance education programs consist of a group of people interacting to accomplish goals that require a high degree of interdependence (Williams, Duray, & Reddy, 2006, p. 593). Team members have a shared responsibility in performing the tasks required to attain team goals.

Collaborative learning provides ample benefits for the student. Brookfield (1995), for example, contends that collaborative processes promote initiative, creativity, critical thinking skills, and dialogue on the part of the learners. When developed online, collaboration enhances learning outcomes and reduces the potential for learner isolation that can occur in the online environment. By learning together in a learning community, students have the opportunity to extend and deepen their learning experience, test out new ideas by sharing them with a supportive group, and receive critical and constructive feedback (Palloff & Pratt, 2005, p. 8).

The use of teamwork in an online class can, in addition to assisting with knowledge generation, prepare today's learners for today's work world, since virtual teams are ubiquitous nowadays. A 2016 survey (RW3, 2016), which had 1,372 respondents from 80 countries, indicated that corporate teams were by that time almost entirely virtual, with 41% never meeting in person. What was significant is that virtual teams were found to be even more global, with members located in more countries than in prior editions. In the 2016 survey, 48% of respondents revealed that more than half of their teams included members from other nations. In 2014, that figure had been only 41%, and in 2012, only 33%. Therefore, future graduates should develop the skill of working effectively in online teams. A fully online educational setting is particularly well-suited for training in such a skill, since neither students nor instructors ever meet face-to-face.

In online collaborative activities, the instructor is responsible for creating the context through which collaboration can happen efficiently. Consequently, the instructor needs to set the stage for teamwork by focusing on the development of a learning community and creating the adequate environment by encouraging collaborative activity from the first day of the course and explaining and modeling its importance (Palloff & Pratt, 2005, p. 10). In Change Management, this was accomplished via the various communication spaces available in the virtual classroom. Students were encouraged to introduce themselves and explain their interests regarding the course in the class forum. Instructors explained in their virtual boards the relevance of teamwork for learning and employability. Also, the students got a document that guided them in the process of carrying out virtual teamwork, including the attitudes that enhance virtual teamwork, creating and reaching initial agreements in a new team, and how to communicate while the team was working. Team activity took place in closed forums, one per team. They could also use other communication media (such as chat apps and tools for collaborative documents), but they had to provide a record of what had been discussed outside of the spaces provided by the UOC's Virtual Campus.

Learning Activities

Students' knowledge construction was developed through five learning activities, four of which were based on case studies. To reach the general goal of offering "credible" applications so that students saw the presented concepts as useful in understanding the reality of change management, three of the cases were real cases of organizational change supplied by students, because they personally or some close acquaintance had experienced them. Since the UOC's students usually have some professional experience, they were able to provide an interesting and diverse set of examples of real organizational changes. To offer the students adequate exposure to real cases of organizational change, students worked in teams to apply the subject's concepts to their cases, to exchange information about each other's cases, and to analyze the cases together. Therefore, the adopted approach combined case analysis with collaborative learning. The necessary teamwork took place through technology-mediated communication in the UOC's Virtual Campus.

Table 1 describes the five learning activities of the course and their assessment structure. Activities 1, 3, and 4 were based on the collaborative approach just described.

- Activity 1 asked students to reach a consensus on operational agreements that would guide their ensuing collaborative work. They were asked to choose a coordinator and establish team rules about the values espoused by the team, the expected dedication from team members, and what would the team do in case any member breached its agreements. Then, students shared their change example with their teammates and asked any questions they might need to perfectly understand each other's cases. After that, every student separately analyzed the similarities and differences between the cases and proposed some general, theoretical principles that they thought emerged from that evidence.
- In activities 3 and 4, each team had to choose two of its change cases, compare them along the dimensions indicated by the instructor, and suggest ideas that would have improved the changes' results. In activity 3, the comparison was centered on individual issues such as

Table 1. Learning Activities in "Change Management."

Learning Activity	Description	Assessment
1[a]	Explain your change situation to the team and analyze one of your teammates. Draw up a theory from everyone's examples. (Attention to team creation and reaching of operational agreements.)	Individual (60%) Group (40%)
2	Conceptual map connecting several theoretical chapters and readings.	Individual
3[a]	Compare the managerial aspects in the change situations provided by two teammates, offering suggestions to the organization.	Individual (25%) Group (75%)
4[a]	Compare the individual aspects in the change situations provided by two teammates, offering suggestions to the organization.	Individual (25%) Group (75%)
5	Teacher-provided case study. Global view of the subject.	Individual

[a]Activities based on cases provided by students and with collaborative work.

resistance to change and the role of human needs, personality, and emotions. In activity 4, the comparison focused on the actions that managers took to implement the changes.

The degree of team interdependence increased progressively from the first to the following activities, in a strongly structured fashion. In the first activity, only exchange of information was needed, and each student drew up their own analysis. In contrast, in the other two collaborative activities, the main goal was to develop a shared analysis of two cases selected by the team in question from the cases submitted by its members.

Collaborative activities were assessed along two dimensions: the output delivered by the team and the teamwork process. Outputs took the form of submitted documents which analyzed a number of issues (posed by the teacher) as they applied to the students' cases, and their content was assessed in a traditional fashion. The teamwork process was assessed by observing each student's participation and performance in the group.

This design presents the main implications of constructivism for instructional design, as described by Jonassen (1994, cited in Koohang et al., 2016, p. 39):

- Provide multiple representations of reality: all team members shared their change experiences with their teammates, so there was a diverse representation of how change unfolds in real organizations and how real people react to such changes.
- Represent the natural complexity of the real world: the descriptions did not perfectly fit the course's conceptual classifications, so the students had to negotiate uncertainties to make sense of the information provided by their peers.
- Focus on knowledge construction, not reproduction: there was no interest in knowledge reproduction; the tasks were focused only on analysis, comparison, and producing suggestions.
- Present authentic tasks (contextualizing rather than abstracting instruction): this was the underlying goal of the design – bridging abstract concepts to real-life situations.
- Provide real-world, case-based learning environments, rather than predetermined instructional sequences. Real-world case studies were the basis for four out of five learning activities. However, the learning sequence was significantly preestablished by the instructor as a means of providing structure for the students' work, as a scaffolding to make learners think above and beyond what they normally know.
- Foster reflective practice: students were first asked to reflect on their own experience with organizational change and, later, with virtual teamwork in the course.
- Enable context- and content-dependent knowledge construction: each group constructed their reflections differently, as a result of the different cases they were analyzing.
- Support collaborative construction of knowledge through social negotiation: each team had to establish a set of "team agreements" that would regulate their interactions and potential conflicts. Also, for each team assignment, each group submitted only one joint report that they elaborated through negotiation and consensus.

Assessment

An online survey was sent to the students at the end of the semester to assess the effectiveness of this design. It asked the students about their experience with virtual teamwork in the university and required their assessment of each learning activity regarding its interest and motivational potential, its usefulness in learning the course's content, and its value in enhancing the students' teamwork skills.

All 124 students received the survey, for which 65 valid responses (52.4% response rate) were received. Respondents and nonrespondents did not differ in terms of their gender or the number of semesters they had studied at the UOC. The results of the survey suggested that students perceived this design as enhancing their teamwork skills (3.90 on a 5-point scale), while being interesting and motivating (3.79) and useful in learning the course's content (3.85). Therefore, the desired goals were attained and the design was kept, with minor changes, in subsequent editions of the course.

Such assessments were often higher for students without prior experience in collaborative learning, compared to those students that had already taken courses which involved teamwork (see Tables 2 and 3). According to Table 2, students without prior teamwork experience might value more the contribution of collaborative activities to their teamwork skills. Table 3 shows that students without prior teamwork experience valued the collaborative activities' degree of interest and contribution to learning more than students who had previously worked in teams for other subjects of their degrees. In contrast, there was no difference for individual learning activities. These results suggest that those

Table 2. Students' Evaluation of Collaborative Activities as Useful in Improving their Teamwork Skills (Average, 5-Point Scale).

	Students with Prior Teamwork Experience $N = 53$	Students without Prior Teamwork Experience $N = 12$	Sign.
Learning activity 1	3.79	4.17	
Learning activity 3	3.83	4.25	
Learning activity 4	3.79	4.23	.087

Table 3. Students' Evaluation of Learning Activities as Interesting and Motivating, and Useful in Learning the Content (Average, 5-Point Scale).

	Students with Prior Teamwork Experience $N = 53$	Students without Prior Teamwork Experience $N = 12$	Sign.
Learning activity 1 (teamwork)	3.74	4.13	.065
Learning activity 2	3.47	3.45	
Learning activity 3 (teamwork)	3.74	4.24	.022
Learning activity 4 (teamwork)	3.73	4.08	.095
Learning activity 5	4.14	4.44	

who most benefitted from this design were students without prior virtual teamwork experience.

The low significance of the differences between the two groups of students may be due to the small sample size and, in particular, of the small subsample of students without prior teamwork experience. This notwithstanding, the assessment for learning activity 3 is highly significant and suggests that it very much made a difference for students without prior teamwork experience.

It must be noted, too, that an activity being individual or team-based had no impact on students' assessment of its degree of interest or learning and motivating potential. Activity 2 consisted in the elaboration of a conceptual map and obtained the lowest evaluation, while activity 5 was a case study and obtained the highest praise from students. Team activities received assessments in between the two.

Current Situation

The basic design of the course activities was kept for subsequent editions. However, the first activity was not developed in teams, but individually, and it was in the second, third, and fourth activities that teamwork was used. This change was deemed necessary as a result of two factors. First, the official number of course students is unstable during the first two weeks of the semester, thus making the creation of teams difficult. Second, students need some time to get to know each other and establish trust. In the new design, this is accomplished through natural interactions that take place during the first learning activity. As a consequence, students are more confident that teamwork will progress smoothly when the second learning activity begins.

Transferability

The learning design adopted in the Change Management course is transferable to other courses where competence in virtual teamwork is to be developed. Any course with content that has a clear correspondence with real-world situations may adopt the proposed structure of presenting and comparing cases suggested by the students. In particular, it seems useful when students do not have prior experience with online collaborative learning.

Expensive or hard-to-find technology is not necessary for the design to be successful. Virtual forums are enough to get the tasks done and are available in any learning management system, many of which can be used for free. Students can also use other free systems to communicate and cooperatively elaborate documents, such as text apps (WhatsApp, Telegram) and collaborative documents (like Google Docs, Microsoft Word Online, or Etherpad). Therefore, the design is transferable to any context in which instructors and students have a reliable Internet connection.

Conclusions

This paper contributes to two streams in educational research: the study of active learning as a means of interpersonal skill development in online contexts (in this case, teamwork skills) and the study of adequate methodologies for specific subjects (in this case, Change Management).

First, while the literature on interpersonal skills such as teamwork is quite abundant, more examples of good practices for online settings are needed. This paper contributes to this stream with an active learning design that can be applied in a variety of online courses to improve teamwork competence. In particular, since students without prior teamwork experience rated collaborative activities higher than students who had some prior experience with online collaborative learning, this approach can be useful in courses that introduce teamwork for the first time as part of a degree program.

Second, Change Management as a discipline is quite recent in university degrees, and its adequate pedagogical approach is far from established. However, such courses often include case studies to enhance understanding of otherwise abstract concepts such as "resistance to change" or "emergent change." This paper contributes to the limited literature on how to teach Change Management, with a description and assessment of an innovative learning design that combines case studies with virtual teamwork, which students have valued as being motivating and improving comprehension of theory. More generally, this learning design may be useful in courses that need to convey an applied flavor to their otherwise too theoretical content.

References

Biggs, J. (1999). *Teaching for quality learning at university*. Buckingham: The Society for Research into Higher Education and Open University Press.

Bolliger, D. U., & Armier Jr, D. D. (2013). Active learning in the online environment: The integration of student-generated audio files. *Active Learning in Higher Education, 14*(3), 201–211.

Bonwell, C. C., & Eison, J. A. (1991). *Active learning: Creating excitement in the classroom.* 1991 ASHE-ERIC Higher Education Reports. ERIC Clearinghouse on Higher Education, The George Washington University, Washington, DC.

Brookfield, S. D. (1995). *Becoming a critically reflective teacher*. San Francisco, CA: Jossey-Bass.

Koohang, A. (2012). Active learning in e-learning: Advancing a systemic moddel. *Issues in Information Systems, 13*(1), 68–76.

Koohang, A., & Paliszkiewicz, J. (2013). Knowledge construction in e-learning: An empirical validation of an active learning model. *Journal of Computer Information Systems, 53*(3), 109–114.

Koohang, A., Paliszkiewicz, J., Gołuchowski, J., & Nord, J. H. (2016). Active learning for knowledge construction in E-learning: A replication study. *Journal of Computer Information Systems, 56*(3), 238–243.

Kopp, B., Hasenbein, M., & Mandl, H. (2014). Case-based learning in virtual groups – Collaborative problem solving activities and learning outcomes in a virtual professional training course. *Interactive Learning Environments, 22*(3), 351–372. doi:10.1080/10494820.2012.680964

Magzan, M., Aleksić-Maslać, K., & Jurić, V. (2010). Teamwork in relation to quality of e-learning: Business education context. In *Advances in Business – Related Scientific Research Conference 2010* (ABSRC2010). Olbia, Sardinia, Italy.

Mor, E., Guerrero-Roldán, A. E., Hettiarachchi, E., & Huertas, M. A. (2014). Designing learning tools: The case of a competence assessment tool. In

P. Zaphiris & A. Ioannou (Eds.), *Learning and Collaboration Technologies: Designing and Developing Novel Learning Experiences: First International Conference, LCT 2014, Held as Part of HCI International 2014,* Heraklion, Crete, Greece, June 22–27, 2014, *Proceedings* (Vol. 8523), Part I. Zürich: Springer.

Palloff, R. M., & Pratt, K. (2005). *Collaborating online: Learning together in community* (Vol. 32). San Francisco: John Wiley & Sons.

Prince, M. (2004). Does active learning work? A review of the research. *Journal of Engineering Education, 93*(3), 223–231.

RW3 Culture Wizard. (2016). Trends in global virtual teams. Retrieved from http://cdn.culturewizard.com/PDF/Trends_in_VT_Report_4-17-2016.pdf. Accessed on May 10, 2017.

Salmon, G. (2013). *E-tivities: The key to active online learning.* New York: Routledge.

Trentin, G. (2010). *Networked collaborative learning: Social interaction and active learning.* Oxford: Elsevier.

Williams, E. A., Duray, R., & Reddy, V. (2006). Teamwork orientation, group cohesiveness, and student learning: A study of the use of teams in online distance education. *Journal of Management Education, 30*(4), 592–616.

Zabalza Beraza, M. A. (2012). El estudio de las "buenas prácticas" docentes en la enseñanza universitaria. *REDU. Revista de Docencia Universitaria, 10*(1), 17–42.

Chapter 8

Engaging the Nonart History Student: A Tale of Five Football Players (and Others) in Roman Art

Gretchen Kreahling McKay

Abstract

How was I going to engage the students in my ancient Roman Art and Architecture course, especially the five football players who had signed up in the fall of 2015? In this chapter, I will discuss the commitment I made to the students and myself to ensure that each class period was one in which an active learning technique was used, often paired with some lecture, and sometimes not, to engage students and help them learn about Roman Art and Architecture. I will discuss what assignments I chose based on research and my own observation, as well as the results of a focus group held with the football players a year later about what they remembered. Football players tend to be kinetic learners and thus were chosen as the follow-up to see how the active learning techniques in this class met objectives. Specifically, this chapter will discuss the inclusion of a Reacting to the Past role-playing game, a research project on "Daily Life in Ancient Rome," and presentations on different methodologies of interpreting an image from a Pompeiian tavern.

Keywords: Active learning; reacting to the past; kinetic learners; instructor immediacy

Active Learning Strategies in Higher Education: Teaching for Leadership,
Innovation, and Creativity, 187–209
ISBN: 978-1-78714-488-0

In the fall of 2015, I attempted to insert an active learning technique into every class session of the semester for my class on ancient Roman Art and Architecture. I made this decision for active learning inclusion after learning that I had five members of the NCAA Division Three football team in my class. I needed to find a way to keep them, and all the other students, engaged in the class. I kept in touch with these five players in the semesters after the class ended and asked them to participate in a focus group a year later, which they did. The results of that focus group and the outcomes from that class are explored in this chapter, which will also note some of the active learning techniques I used that other faculty might consider implementing.

In the fall of 2015, I walked into the first day of my scheduled class on Roman Art and Architecture. When I arrived at the classroom a few minutes early, which I always do, I noticed that there were some very large male students sitting in the back of the room. Based on their physique, I thought they were likely athletes, and perhaps football players, but I did not ask them right away about what sport they played. A week or so into the semester, I was invited by our president to be his guest at our first home football game of the season. Before that game, I did talk to those five students and found out that they were, indeed, all on the football team. When I arrived at the game at the presidential suite, I bought a program right away to identify the players that I had in the Roman Art class. It turns out that all five players were starters on the team, which meant they got a lot of playing time, three of them as key leaders of the offense and two on defense. I learned their numbers and watched them on the field that day. I witnessed from them a high level of commitment and leadership. The defensive leader who plays linebacker led the team in a goal-line stand on a crucial fourth-down and was so emotional about it, I saw him rip off his helmet and proceed to rejoice and hug his fellow teammates.

Witnessing that instance of engagement and leadership, and watching the other players' devotion and tenacity, I decided to take what was for me a dramatic step in my teaching. While I had been experimenting with active learning methods for some time, I had not attempted to teach that way in every class period for the entire duration of the semester. I began incorporating active learning in my classes in 2007 when I first used Reacting to the Past, an immersive role-playing pedagogy, which will be discussed in more detail later in this chapter. In addition to teaching with Reacting, I had also changed some of my lecture-based art history class periods to involve students more actively in learning the material. But I hadn't changed every class for an entire semester.

But that Saturday on the football field, after watching my five Roman art student athletes, I made a vow: I would find a way to incorporate at least one active learning technique into every class period of the Roman Art and Architecture course for the entirety of the semester. While a lecture would sometimes be necessary to introduce a concept or idea, there would always be at least one activity that would actively involve students in their learning.

Part of my reasoning was that I knew those five football players loved their sport. It was quite evident by the way I saw them act on the field on game day and how they talked about practice as I interacted with them before and after class as the weeks went on. I also knew that they were taking my class as a liberal arts general education requirement. Like most liberal arts colleges, our specific general education plan has a lot of flexibility within the different requirements, and students can choose from a myriad of courses to fulfill them. There is no doubt: these students were taking my Roman Art and Architecture class to fulfill one of those requirements. There were many courses offered that semester that fulfilled "International Western Perspectives," and "Social, Cultural, and Historical Understanding." And yet, they chose my Roman art class. I doubted — and still doubt — that they will ever love Roman art as much as they do the sport of football. But I knew there was a reason that they took the class; some amount of interest or curiosity in the subject matter led them to me. It was my supposition that day on the football field that *the way* I taught the class could perhaps sustain or continue their level of initial interest, and perhaps even increase it. It seemed to work.

The class went well, which was confirmed by positive course evaluations, but also by a sense of energy and enthusiasm, and a lack of absences that I encountered during that semester. After the class concluded in the fall of 2015, two of the players went on to take other classes with me, and through social media and being at a small campus, I followed up with all of them. They remembered a lot about the class, which led me to propose a talk for the College Art Association's annual meeting (2017), which is one of the major conference gatherings for art historians. I proposed a pedagogy talk on the Roman art class with the same title as my chapter here. It was accepted and I gave that talk in February of 2017.

To find evidence for my talk and to back my suppositions of the learning that went on in that class, I asked a colleague of mine to convene and lead a focus group with the five football players to ask them questions and to assess if the active learning techniques that I employed had a bearing on their learning. Four of the five football players attended the focus group that was convened in late October of 2016, which was one year after the class on Roman art had met. I have given these four players the pseudonyms of Ed, Brian, Fred, and Tom for this chapter. While admittedly this is a small pool, these findings suggest that active learning helps certain kinds of students and offers up some conclusions that would benefit from follow-up studies.

I am using the findings from the focus group to develop the following headings for this chapter, which will examine what active learning techniques were employed and the type of reaction that resulted as recorded by these football players in the focus group. We will start with some basic descriptions of the type of learners these students turned out to be. Then, the chapter will examine the following topics that the focus group identified: (1) enthusiasm of the instructor, (2) goal-setting for various in-class assignments, (3) creating arguments, (4) museum visit and knowledge acquisition, (5) lessons for other instructors.

Basic Characteristics of Kinetic Learners

From the focus group, these students were expressing the characteristics of kinetic or kinesthetic learners, who tend to require movement, change, and action to facilitate their understanding of the material. They like competition. Setting up debates or games in class can ignite their enthusiasm for learning the material. As Tranquillo (2008) has explored, kinetic learners typically need to move around. I found that during the times when I added an active learning component to the class, the more these students could pay attention. Mobley and Fisher (2014) found similar results with kinesthetic activities in various levels of their political science courses. In the focus group for my course, the students specifically noted that they loved the Reacting to the Past game we played. Reacting to the Past is an immersive role-playing game pedagogy that requires students to take on a character, read primary texts from the period, and debate through speeches.

Reacting to the Past as a pedagogy began around 2000 in the classroom of Mark Carnes, Professor of History at Barnard College. In his book, *Minds on Fire*, Carnes (2014) describes his earliest attempts at creating a Reacting game, particularly during the play of a game set in Ming China (Gardner & Carnes, 2014). Rather than a typical discussion seminar, Carnes made each student a character from the period and assigned them reading from the *Analects*. The students one day took it so seriously that when the class ended, they all stayed. They were still debating. Reacting to the Past has over a dozen games published and many more in the path of development.

It was perhaps not surprising that my students, who play on the football team and are motivated by team work and competition, rated Reacting so highly. Reacting to the Past games require working in teams and are competitive by their nature. These games also require critical thinking, and McBride and Reed (1998) have indicated that athletes struggle with this important skill. Perhaps more classes that include Reacting games could ignite more critical thinking among student athletes in collegiate classrooms. More research is needed to delve into the motivating factors of Reacting to the Past games with football players specifically and student athletes more broadly. Reacting to the Past and football players will be a focus of my future research; as of now, unfortunately, not much research has been conducted on Reacting and athletes.

In my Roman Art class, I used the *Beware the Ides of March* game, a game still in development and authored by Carl Anderson (University of Michigan) and Keith Dix, with substantial editing by Naomi Norman (both from the University of Georgia). The *Ides of March* game opens after the death of Julius Caesar. The Senate, packed with Caesar's supporters as well as those who wish to save the Republic, must decide what to do with Caesar's dead and bloody body.

I chose the Rome game for inclusion in my class for several reasons. In the discipline of art history, context is paramount. Thus, my first reason for choosing a game for this course is to help students understand the context for the art and architecture that we study. For instance, to call a meeting of the Senate in the game, the students must also research a space for the Senate to meet, which helps them to understand which buildings were available in 44 BCE. They also learn by experience that Rome was a culture predicated on oral speeches, that power was not centered with one person until this period, and that the situation with Caesar was one that threatened the power of the Senate in Rome.

In the focus group, the students noted that they loved that they were on a team, or "faction" in Reacting parlance. Most Reacting games have two or more "factions" or characters that feel similarly about enough topics that they form a group of the like-minded. In the Rome Game, there are essentially two factions, one of which included followers of Caesar and the other group loyal to the Republic. In the latter faction, many fear Caesar has permanently threatened the Senate and its role in the Republic by his play for unlimited power. In the focus group, Brian noted that he didn't want to "let his faction down." To not let the faction down, Tom explains, they "*had* to do extra research." When class time came around, they felt that they *had* to be prepared and have their speeches ready. They did not want to let down others who were relying on them. They also wanted to win, which once again connects back to the competition and team work that inspires them to want to learn. In my experience with Reacting, many students, not just athletes, thrive on the competition that a game setting provides in the classroom. It makes sense that for student athletes this would have a positive effect, though future research could further illuminate this area. The remainder of the chapter will investigate the four broad themes that the focus group brought to light, beginning with instructor enthusiasm, which plays an important role in student learning.

Enthusiasm of the Instructor

The issue of "instructor enthusiasm" has always been an area with which I personally struggle. The question on course evaluations, which asks if the instructor demonstrated enthusiasm for the material and/or class, has, frankly, always bothered me; I have long wondered what *my* enthusiasm has to do with student learning. However, quotations from the focus group included statements such as, "McKay was 100% the reason it was successful" (Ed.) and, "She was always so enthusiastic and wanted you to participate, too." (Brian.) Another said, "She was very genuine" (Fred.) in both my interest in the material and what they correctly perceived was my desire for their learning. Apparently, they could pick up on the fact that I really wanted them to learn about Roman art and to appreciate it. They noted that I "knew that people would overlook elements" (Tom.) when doing the visual analysis of a work of art in class through discussion, but that my constant support and enthusiasm for the material and them as learners − helped students to participate more in the class. As Zhang (2014) points out, "when students perceive their teachers as enthusiastic and energetic, they are more likely to be intrinsically motivated to learn, and engage behaviorally, cognitively, and emotionally." Similarly, Umbach and Wawrzynski (2005) emphasized in their work that there is measurable higher student learning when faculty members are "highly involved" in teaching.

Although unbeknownst to me on a conscious level, through the focus group, I learned that I had built an environment for, and with, these students where they felt it was okay to be wrong. They commented that in other lecture-dominated classes, the only time they can see if they are wrong is on a high-stakes test, which is normally a memorization exam. In my class, we were always presenting, discussing, and building interpretations from visual analysis. Sometimes I had to push to get them to look more closely and think more deeply, which they soon learned meant that they hadn't *quite* gotten the point, which in turn led them to "want to be the one to get it right." (Tom.) To be the one to "get it" was, in a way, tapping into that competition factor that comes from their love of games and sports. But, I made the class a place where they could express enthusiasm and curiosity for the content, which was encouraged, embraced, and modeled by me.

For students to take ownership of the class and make educated guesses to meanings of the works of art, it was important to encourage and support them. As noted above, in their vocabulary, this was a class where "it was ok to be wrong." (Ed.) I worked to structure the class and develop activities that would help them understand the content, which often challenged them to think, often deeper than usual, and certainly more deeply than if I had been lecturing content to them. In turn, they gradually assumed responsibility for their role in the class. They liked the competition and the challenge and did not want to let their faction-mates down. They also began to like to see if they could be the one to "get the answer." (Tom.) Although these students learned that there is always more than one answer when interpreting works of art, they soon learned that there are some interpretations that make more sense, and when we were building to one, and I encouraged more or deeper thinking on a topic, they wanted to be the "one to get it."

Fred noted that it was a class that you did not want to miss because you wanted to see what we would do and what I had planned. This suggests that a certain enthusiasm was building through the semester, which from this comment seemed to be infectious, drawing these students into a class for which they had some initial interest and curiosity. Their initial curiosity, it would seem, held or maybe even grew over the semester through their participation in the activities I planned for each class, as well as by their witnessing my joy at their discoveries and understanding.

I want to return to the specific issue of instructor enthusiasm. The findings from the focus group blur a bit between my personally expressed *enthusiasm* (for them and the material) and the *active learning elements I chose* to incorporate into the course as the instructor. I am not sure whether it was solely my enthusiasm *as the instructor* that facilitated the learning or rather it was *what I did* in each class and that involved them. I say this because one of the other comments from the focus group was this: "Other teachers could do it, too." (Tom.) And I do not think they meant, "be more enthusiastic."

Instead, I think they were indicating a belief that other teachers could demonstrate more clearly and transparently an obvious and genuine interest in students' learning. I would contend that one way to reveal a genuine interest in student learning would be for faculty to incorporate more active learning techniques into their classes. Thus, if faculty were to "do it, too" – "it" being the choice to include active learning techniques – that decision would likely be viewed by students as indicative of the instructor's desire to really want students to learn. My choice of including active learning pedagogies into every class seemed to them to be an expression of my genuine interest in student learning and their retention of the material. According to these students, if they sense this choice on the part of the professor, the dynamic then shifts. They, in turn, "Do not want to let the professor [who is utilizing the active learning technique] down." (Brian.) This is again the "team" mentality; if students feel like the professor wants them to learn, by displaying a genuine desire for their learning, being enthusiastic, and taking a chance with active learning, that faculty member is viewed by these students as one of their "team." Subsequently, they will not want to let that instructor down.

There are many ways that faculty can show interest in students. Hawk and Lyons (2008) offer a table listing course attributes that indicate faculty interest, as well as other characteristics of "pedagogical caring." Something as simple as asking students about their lives outside of the classroom can express a faculty's attentiveness to student learning. Following up on something a student says in class, or asking about their extracurricular activities, can sometimes help kindle a further engagement in a student who suspects the faculty member cares about their learning.

Goal-Setting for Various In-Class Assignments

One of the ways in which a faculty member can begin to insert more active learning pedagogies into a class is by setting learning goals not only for the course but also for each session of the class. Goals for the course are nearly universally expected on syllabi, which are discussed the first day and often forgotten by students. But if each class is conceived as having a specific learning goal, rather than the topic to "cover" for the day, class planning can shift substantially. Johnson, Johnson, and Smith (2013) talk about cooperative learning and tying activities to larger course goals. This is also discussed by Mobley and Fisher (2014), mentioned above, who talk about the importance of connecting individual class goals and projects back to the overall learning objectives of the course.

For my class, when I teach about the Emperor Augustus, I want to tie his sculptural and architectural project meanings back to one of my main course themes, which is how Roman rulers used art and architecture for propagandistic purposes. Augustus was careful about what he built and what subjects decorated his monuments. When it came to his own commissioned portraits, he similarly controlled his visage. Augustus produced a carefully programmed portrait program that continued to show a youthful, vigorous emperor, from the beginning of his reign in 27 BCE to his death in 14 CE. I could certainly lecture my students and tell them about the propaganda that is embedded into Augustus' artistic and architectural programs, but I have found that they learn it better when they research it themselves. Thus, I have developed an active learning class structure that has them engage deeply with one monument of importance during Augustus' reign.

The class begins with a discussion of the shift in portraiture from the realism of the Republican period to the youthful vigor displayed in different images of Augustus. First, in groups that I presort, they analyze a text from Suetonius that describes how Augustus looked. They then compare that text to examples of his portraits, which display an idealistic youth compared to Suetonius' description. Comparing and discussing Suetonius while visually examining the sculptures helps them to begin to understand the issues of propaganda and how art can influence viewers' perceptions of reality. According to Suetonius, near the end of his life, the Emperor Augustus was suffering from skin diseases and was infirmed. Yet, Augustus' portraits never relay this fact to the Roman public.

After this part of the class finishes, each group is assigned an Augustan monument from the following: Augustus' *Forum*, *House*, and his *Mausoleum*, or the *Ara Pacis*. I provide images for their monument that they download from our course management site. Students researched the monument during class and then presented "their" monument during the next class meeting. They were also required to produce a bibliography in proper citation that was to be turned in when they presented. Their presentation needed to identify the message(s) of propaganda that were emphasized on or in their monument.

When the presentations were held, I made it clear that everyone was to take notes, looking specifically for similar themes or meanings amongst Augustan buildings. This was necessary, since after the presentations, I led the class in a discussion to determine which of the monuments was most successful at portraying Augustus' propagandistic messages and why. This led to a discussion of which monument had "the best" or most successful propagandistic message, with students not always voting for their "own" monument. Unwittingly, the presentations about propaganda had turned into a contest or debate. Probably not coincidentally, this was after the Reacting to the Past game chronologically in the scope of the class.

During the focus group, one of the first topics that came up was how much they remembered about propaganda. The focus group leader followed those comments about what they recalled and it was eventually revealed that they learned the most from *doing*. "If I can apply the information and do something with it, I remember it better." (Fred.) From the comments these students were making during the focus group, it was clear that they remembered the complexities, but also the success, of Augustus' propaganda messages in the monuments. A couple of students echoed this comment, saying that they felt that through these types of assignments they were "living through it," (Tom.) and "a lived experience makes it stick." (Brian.)

This also led to a student lament. Why, they wondered, when classes are around 20–25 students, was active learning not more often experienced? Why was my class such an anomaly? Since the classes are small, which was one the reasons they chose their college, they wondered why more classes were not more "hands-on," (Tom.) giving students a chance to "live the experience," (Brian) rather than just have the information imparted to them through a lecture by the professor. Brian also indicated that a class in his major, sports training, would have been more successful for him if he had been put in situations where he had to use knowledge of the physiology of the body to solve problems with clients. He noted specifically that he would have liked to have learned a lot more in that class and if the course had been more than lectures, he believes he would have retained more information. The focus group students noted that leaving everything just to the memory, without a chance to apply the information, limited their chances to learn the material more deeply. This led to some comments about internships, which all admitted were important. But they reiterated several times that they felt that more faculty could come up with ways to structure the class to have students engage more deeply with the material, rather than just experiencing it passively in a lecture format.

Another goal I set for this class is for the students to understand what it was like to live in the busy city of Rome, but to understand also that one's lived experience would have varied widely depending on one's social status. I refer to this as my "Daily Life in Ancient Rome" assignment and it has two parts. The first part is a written research assignment that they do individually (see Appendix A). Students are asked to research what it would be like on a typical day in Rome in 120 CE. What would you see? Where would you go? What would you do?

I chose that date as it is near the apex of Rome's expansion and wealth, and it is also when the assignment fits best into the class chronologically. There is another element to the assignment, however, which makes it more akin to the role-playing games: students are also randomly assigned a social status from among the patrician, plebeian, freedman, soldier, and slave societal classes. Students must research Roman rituals, the built environment, as well as the dangers and entertainments that were present in ancient Rome. But not all spaces were open to all Romans. The randomly assigned social status determined how much the students can report in his or her paper that was seen or experienced and what was off limits because of societal constructs.

After this assignment is turned in, I grade it and give feedback on it to each student. Then the assignment goes into a Part II (Appendix B). For this part of the assignment, they must get with other students and give a public presentation about their experiences in Rome. I give them some time in class to figure out how they might work together, what scenario might bring them together, but they still need time outside of class to prepare the assignment. On one of the last days of the semester, the groups present. Since I tell them they are not allowed to have a PowerPoint presentation and lecture to us, most of the students gravitate toward a kind of "skit" that they write and perform. Some of the skits in the past included students who were randomly assigned the role of slave and researched and wrote about their lives as gladiators who fought in the arena. In another skit, the patricians teamed up as a married couple and worked with two other students who were slaves in the household and acted out a family drama.

For this part of the assignment, I am less concerned about historical details, though I do tell them that they should try to make it as true to the time as possible. Since it is one of the culminating days of the class, and there is usually by now a camaraderie built up among the students, it becomes a way for them to "wrap up" their learning in a collective and collaborative way. Some take videos on their phones of the skits as they are performed. The students in the focus group remembered this and noted that it was one of the elements of the class that they remembered most fondly. Since there is a traditional research component that must be created prior to the skit, I feel comfortable with them sometimes leading into erroneous statements or actions. I always make sure there is a day remaining after the skits so that I can talk to them about any truly egregious ahistorical action that they might have expressed. Except for minor infractions, I have not had to intervene or explain much. My view is that this assignment provides another way for them to apply the research that they do individually to a team-based activity, and a way for them to "live the experience," so that they remember it, which in the case of the focus group, they did.

Faculty interested in integrating active learning into their classes might reflect on one topic of the course and work backwards from the goals for that subject. What do you want students to learn about the topic for that day? Once you reach the goal, you can then work backwards to design a debate, role-play, or other type of scenario to help get to the students to that answer without simply telling them. While this does take a bit more time during the class, the students retain the information more deeply, as was evidenced in the focus group a year later and the amount of information that was shared with the convener about propaganda.

Creating Arguments

Another topic that came up in the focus group that seemed to help students retain information and "change things up" (Tom.) to keep their attention, focused on in-class exercises that required them to think critically about an image or problem and find an interpretation or a solution. My Roman Art course that fulfills the requirement for "Social, Cultural, Historical Understanding" requires students to learn about different disciplinary methods or "how we know what we know." I will talk about two distinct ways I provided for this aspect of the requirement in the ancient Roman Art course. First, students lead the class in the creation of a possible hypothesis of the meaning of a work or art (as opposed to a presentation after formal research) after having time in pairs to analyze the work visually. Second, students come to understand that there are different interpretive methods in art history through an analysis of one image from three disciplinary perspectives.

The first of these types of critical argument exercises, coming up with a possible hypothesis for a meaning of a work of art and discussing that with the class, is carried out chronologically in the class immediately after the presentations of the Augustan monuments. After discussing Augustus' imperial works of art, explaining classical elements and allusions, the class immediately following emphasizes abstract funerary art of the lower classes in Rome. Students are assigned a work of art to interpret by using only the visual analysis skills we have been developing all semester. Assigned an image from a PowerPoint, students examine the images carefully in class, usually in pairs or groups, depending on the size of the class, and begin to develop a working hypothesis of possible meaning from those observations. They can use books and/or Google search to help them find out basic elements of the image, but there really isn't time for them to "find the answer" on the web. But because most of my choices are rather obscure, and information on the web limited, this requires them to spend significant time analyzing the image on their own using their visual analysis and discussing what they see with each other.

After they spend some time examining the image and coming up with a working hypothesis, they lead the class in a discussion of that work to try to help the class as a whole to see that potential meaning. I start this class off by leading the class and modeling for them what I want them to do by discussing with them a work of plebeian funerary art that shows one of the officials of the Circus Maximus standing next to a statue of his deceased wife, while chariots are shown during a race in the arena.

It was about this assignment that Ed in the focus group commented, "She makes it OK to be wrong." During the focus group, the convener of the group asked what one of the students meant by that, and the student went on to describe how he and his partner (both in the focus group) were assigned a small plaque that was carved in Ostia, the port city of Rome, which depicted a man selling poultry. When they first looked at the image, they had no idea what to do with it. I think Tom even called it "ugly." Because of the lack of perspective and other more typical Western, Renaissance-like renditions of space, they were at a loss as to how to even begin to read the image, let alone come up with a full meaning of the work. However, the goal for that day was twofold: to get them to look and to begin to understand abstract spaces and to begin to see the difference between presenting information, and leading a discussion of it.

While the two football players that led the class discussion on this poultry seller sign from Ostia did not get the image "right," they remembered it a year later. When pressed in the focus group, they admitted that they learned more because while they initially read the image "wrong," the other students' suggestions made when they led the discussion in class helped them see more. Because those ideas were not coming from me, the "authority", but rather, their classmates, they felt freer and more "in charge" of this image. They learned, remembering it a year later. The active learning activity of developing a hypothesis for meaning and then asking the class to engage with the same work of art helped these students learn about several abstract images.

The Ostian Poultry Seller is not the most important in the library of Roman images that professors tend to teach. But I was amazed at the details that they remembered in the focus group about the image a year later: the poultry man, the baskets, and the counter. They also informed the focus group facilitator that as I sorted them into pairs to begin the activity, I quipped, "And it's OK if you get it wrong" or something to that effect. It sounded to me as if I made it as a secondhand and off-the-cuff remark, which admittedly does sound like something I might utter while sorting everyone into the activity for the day. While I do not *specifically* remember saying that, to the football players who were assigned the poultry seller plaque from Ostia, this statement alleviated pressure and helped create an atmosphere where being wrong was not a penalty, but rather a catalyst for learning. In fact, when Tom was assigned the poultry seller image, he said that he muttered to his partner, Ed, "thank goodness [we can be wrong], because there's no way we're getting this one right."

In the focus group, the recall of this image and the class assignment around it made them contemplate more deeply about learning from mistakes. They commented that in lecture-dominated classes the only time they can see if they are wrong is on a high-stakes test, and that by then, "it's too late." (Brian.) Most of the time, they admitted, if they didn't learn something correctly for the test, they had to move on to new information and were not able to go back to try to learn from that mistake. Interestingly, they also said that they learned from my class that there is "more to everything." (Fred.) One of the students, assigned the Ostian poultry seller image, said he thought at first that it was "just an ugly sculpture," (Tom.) but through this exercise, he learned that there is a story behind it, "a reason for all of it." He continued, "You start to realize there is more to it and understand the meaning behind it." (Tom.) They were emphatic that it was the *getting up* and having to discuss with classmates that made them remember this, as well as being free to be wrong.

As for my own reflection on that day's class, I noted that some of the students were not able to shift out of presentation mode. They simply presented what they came up with as a possible interpretation. I did not chastise them for this, nor did I take off points for their participation that day. But I did make a mental note for the next time I do this, to talk a bit ahead of time about the differences in skills of presenting and leading others in a discussion. I always have this discussion on the differences *after* the exercise; but this experience makes me think doing so on both ends of the assignment might be worthwhile. Perhaps even adding a reflection piece to this assignment asking students to comment specifically on presenting versus leading discussion could be helpful in the future.

While the exercise of looking at abstract funerary art emphasizes the first step of the discipline of art history, which is always visual analysis, other activities are incorporated into the class to have students engage in another course goal: understanding different disciplinary methods. To help them see that art can be interpreted in different ways, I assign in class an article by John R. Clarke about a painting from the exterior wall of a Pompeiian tavern that depicts a donkey penetrating a lion anally. Once again, a student in the focus group brought up this assignment spontaneously; there were no leading questions about what they thought about it specifically. The article is entitled "The Philological, the Folkloric and the Site-Specific: Three Models for Decoding Classical Visual Representation" (in *Role Models in the Roman World: Identity and Assimilation*, eds. S. Bell and I.L. Hansen, 2008). In it, Clarke presents three different interpretive methods to "decode" the meaning of a Pompeiian tavern painting. This painting was taken from Pompeii and is now in the Naples Archaeological Pornography museum. The shock value of this painting is one reason I chose it, but there is another more salient reason; it is one of the few published works by a scholar in the field that interprets one painting, as the title alludes, from three different methodological perspectives that is also accessible to undergraduate nonmajors. I put a lot of information about the context of the Pompeii tavern on our online class site, which they access during the class activity, such as an interactive map that shows the location of the tavern on the block in Pompeii, as well as the paintings (surviving only in sketches) that were also on either side of it the exterior walls of the tavern.

In class, the students are divided into groups. Each group takes one of the three interpretive models. I give them Xeroxed pages from Clarke's work only on their assigned interpretive method, which is about three to four pages to read and work through as a group. They are then asked to figure out how their interpretive disciplinary model interprets the painting and then present their method to the class. When presenting their disciplinary method to the class, they must also identify the strengths and drawbacks of their assigned interpretive method. Asking them to grapple with the concepts in class creates a more communal experience rather than working alone. Having the class engage in the interpretation of an unusual image helps to actively engage them in the creation of meaning and helps them understand the discipline of which they are a taking part during the course.

While the focus group participants did not remember the names of the different interpretive models, they did recall that there were different methods. They also connected that exercise in the class later in the semester when they were suggesting meanings for the poultry seller plaque, the Augustan monument they were assigned, and other works of art. These in-class exercises and assignments, taken together, helped these students understand that there is no "right" answer to interpreting works of art. However, they understood that you must be able to defend your argument and interpretation with evidence. They began to see the building of argument and support with evidence as the key to the discipline of art history. This discussion of scholarship within the confines of the classroom allows faculty to be on hand and answer questions as students attempt to analyze, synthesize, and evaluate, all of which are elements that active learning helps to increase in students as Bonwell and Eison (1991) explain.

I believe that group reading and comparison activities help students learn the important skills of synthesis, analysis, and evaluation. These are higher level skills than memorizing and understanding, and thus the presence of the instructor in the classroom while students wrestle with these issues can be helpful. Finding ways to stage in-depth analysis in the class where you can guide students is a way to make active pedagogy work for higher order learning. While I am not advocating for no individualized work, or that understanding and learning facts are not also important, having students work in groups to form judgments and analysis can often be helpful, especially with the faculty member on hand for questions.

Museum Visit and Knowledge Acquisition

Because of our geographical proximity to Baltimore and Washington, D.C., our department makes a commitment to be sure that each class has at least one field trip per semester to area museums. For the Roman class, the Walters Art Museum in Baltimore is a perfect location. At the Walters, students experience a small but fantastic collection of art spanning from the Republic to the end of the Empire. The main purpose of the trip to the Walters Art Museum was not meant to be an assessment opportunity, but the focus group comments helped me use it as such. During the focus group, Brian noted, "I can remember tons of stuff from that class. I feel like I was a part of it [the class], and when I then saw the sculptures [at the museum], it related back to the game...I just *knew* the sculptures." I am still not precisely sure how the game specifically related to this students' recall of the sculptures in the museum, but he noted that he had to find "different works in the museum." The museum assignment itself required them to find three works in the museum and compare them to images we had seen in class.

The members of the focus group commented that seeing these works in person made the museum experience more vivid, but they also think it was because of the way that they had interacted with the material before they got there, that made the museum experience more memorable. For instance, when they saw the portrait of Augustus displayed at the Walters, they recognized him in part not because I had showed that specific image in class to prepare them for the trip, but because they had spent time thinking of the propagandistic messages encoded in similar Augustan portraiture through the in-class activity I described above. When they saw the bust of one of the Flavian emperors (identity is not clear), they had a similar reaction. Since a previous in-class exercise had them grouped as "advisors" to the emperor Vespasian, they had already spent time thinking about the characteristics that would be the "right" portraiture for him, a new emperor in a new dynasty. The Flavians, the first dynasty after the Julio-Claudians, have a chance to change the message. The students recognized how portraiture – and propaganda messages – had shifted under the new Flavian regime, and they saw immediately how this was manifested in the Flavian portrait at the Walters.

Another focus group topic of discussion that indicated to me the learning transpired over the course of the semester was a student's mention of Trajan's "Pole." [sic]. Of course, the student meant Trajan's *Column*, but the fact that this work of art came up in a completely organic way happily surprised me. That is because when this class — on Trajan and his Column — came in November, I felt like I could not come up with anything interactive for them to do. It was late in the semester and I was tired. I nearly gave up and resorted back to passive lecturing. I didn't, though, and I describe the class activity below. But for me, this part of the focus group was particularly ironic and gratifying.

For the class on Trajan's Column, students were paired up and had to examine different scenes from the sculptural relief on the column. They were told to identify the emperor in their assigned scenes and try to figure out what was happening around him. Then, after the students all presented "their" scenes to the entire class, we discussed commonalities and themes began to emerge. They immediately began to see Trajan's Column as another form of propaganda, with the emperor manipulating the meaning of the work. At this point in the focus group, they continued to discuss more about propaganda, noting that these scenes on the column, and in other imperial monuments, were not true and not meant to be accurate. They were visual manipulations meant to sway the people of Rome and others to see a certain meaning or meanings. This even led to a short discussion in the focus group of the current crop of candidates for the presidential election in the United States (the focus group was convened in October of 2016), and how their images and messages were being manipulated by and for the media today.

The students mentioned Trajan's Column when the conversation steered to discuss the experience of shy students, and if they are left behind in class like this, which could favor the more verbal students in the class. Most agreed that nearly any student could learn from this method, and they collectively mentioned again the importance of a supportive environment. Brian said, "She set the tone," indicating that a friendly atmosphere and communal approach can help students come out of their shells. All of them agreed that for shy students, this class would give them more confidence. This was said in part to explain the supportive environment I worked to create, but it was also clear from what they were saying that while I "set the tone," peers teach peers through the group work. They all indicated that working in groups in class, when no grade was specifically attached, helped them get to know each other and to become more comfortable with each other.

Incorporating activities where there is a focused question can keep learners more engaged in the learning process if the instructor makes sure to create a goal that can be managed in the class period. As the example with Trajan's Column indicates, having time alone to ponder and analyze, and then share, and then discuss with the whole class, changes the dynamic of the class significantly in terms of structure, and allows for shifts in focus that can facilitate learning.

Lessons for Other Instructors on Active Learning

The students at different points in the focus group lamented the fact that there were not more classes such as mine that made use of active learning. One went so far as to wonder why that is, being that most of their classes are relatively small. But they also realized that they were part of something that could educate more faculty members. They know from our personal discussions outside of class that I want to help other faculty find ways to make their classrooms more active. They uttered hope that the paper I gave at the conference in February 2017 and any subsequent work I do, such as the opportunity to contribute to this volume, would help other faculty learn how to change their classes to actively engage students more substantially.

Our students are savvy. They noted with dismay that faculty are not expected when they are in graduate school to "learn how to teach." They understand that graduate students are in school to master content, but all of them wondered why some expectations about learning how to teach students was not also fundamental to their training. A few of them are elementary and secondary education minors, and they note the rigors that those students go through to learn how to teach. They wonder why it is so much less for college faculty. They hoped that other faculty might reflect more on the ways that college students learn. Since my five football players now know I presented a short paper on this topic and am contributing to this volume, their hope is that their experiences with me might change some faculty attitudes about how they approach their individual classrooms.

Other publications on the scholarship of teaching and learning that offer examples of active learning include Bain's seminal work (2004) on *What The Best College Teachers Do*, as well as a Bowen's *Teaching Naked* (2012). Bowen's latest in that series, coauthored with Watson, *Teaching Naked Techniques* (2017), includes practical tips for faculty on how they might implement active learning into their classrooms.

As this chapter has attempted to show, in my class on Roman Art and Architecture, I attempted to "change things up" with active learning techniques that I swapped out from day to day. While there was no set rule about how I would do that, on days when a Reacting game was not used, the class generally went like this:

- Lecture from me on the material, setting the context.
- Break up into groups or pairs to work on a problem.
- Come back and present or discuss as a larger group.
- Evaluate as a class.
- Revisit idea from group work.
- Sometimes write a reflection at the end of the class.

While I did not always follow this exact formula, and nearly resorted back to lecturing when I was tired and out of gas when Trajan's Column was due to be covered that fall of 2015, I found a way to keep them engaged. This engagement was confirmed a year later through the focus group. It is hoped that the ideas shared here might lead others to consider active learning in their classrooms as well, to engage students more deeply and meaningfully in their studies.

Acknowledgments

I would like to thank the five football players that took my Roman Art course in the fall of 2015. You know who you are! I would also like to thank my colleagues in the social sciences for helping this art historian with research in this discipline. Specifically, I would like to thank Dr. Robert Trader, Dr. Lauren Dundes, and Dr. Sara Raley, all of whom are wonderful and generous colleagues.

References

Bain, K. (2004). *What the best college teachers do*. Cambridge, MA: Harvard University Press.
Bonwell, C. C., & Eison, J. A. (1991). *"Active Learning. Creating Excitement in the Classroom." ASHE- ERIC Higher Education Reports*. Washington, DC: George Washington University.
Bowen, J. A. (2012). *Teaching naked. How moving technology out of your classroom will improve student learning*. San Francisco, CA: Jossey-Bass.
Bowen, J. A., & Watson, C. E. (2017). *Teaching naked techniques*. San Francisco, CA: Jossey-Bass.
Carnes, M. C. (2014). *Minds on fire: How role-immersion games transform college*. Cambridge, MA: Harvard University Press.

Clarke, J. R. (2008). The philological, the folkloric and the site-specific: Three models for decoding classical visual representation. In S. Bell & I. L. Hansen (Eds.), *Role models in the Roman world: Identity and assimilation* (pp. 301–316). Ann Arbor, MI: University of Michigan Press.

Gardner, D. K., & Carnes, M. C. (2014). *Confucianism and the succession crisis of the Wanli Emperor, 1587.* New York, NY: W.W. Norton.

Hawk, T. F., & P. R. Lyons (2008). Please don't give up on me: When faculty fail to care. *Journal of Management Education, 32*(3), 316–338.

Johnson, D. W., Johnson, R. T., & Smith, K. A. (2013). Cooperative learning: Improving university instruction by basing practice on validated theory. *Journal on Excellence in University Teaching, 25*(4), 1–26.

McBride, R. E., & Reed, J. U. D. Y. (1998). Thinking and college athletes: Are they predisposed to critical thinking? *College Student Journal, 32,* 443–450.

Mobley, K., & Fisher, S. (2014). Ditching the desks: Kinesthetic learning in college classrooms. *The Social Studies, 105,* 301–309.

Tranquillo, J. (2008, June), Kinesthetic learning in the classroom. Paper presented at 2008 Annual Conference & Exposition, Pittsburgh, Pennsylvania. 2017. Retrieved from https://peer.asee.org/3389. Accessed on June 6.

Umbach, P. D., & Wawrzynski, M. R. (2005). Faculty do matter: The role of college faculty in student learning and engagement. *Research in Higher Education, 46*(2), 153–184.

Zhang, Q. (2014). Assessing the effects of instructor enthusiasm on classroom engagement, learning goal orientation, and academic self-efficacy. *Communication Teacher, 28*(1), 44–56.

Appendix A: Daily Life in Ancient Rome Writing Assignment

You live in Rome and it is the year 120 CE. You are to write a three (3) page paper that describes a day in the life of the city from your social perspective. This "perspective" will be your social class, which you will choose randomly from a hat I will pass around. You will be one from one of these social classes:

- Patrician man
- Patrician woman
- Plebeian (you may choose your gender)
- Freedman (male)
- Soldier (male)
- Slave (you may choose your gender)

Once you have chosen your identity, you will need to do some research to become familiar with what you would experience in a typical day:

- Where do you go?
- What do you do?
- How do you spend your time?
- Where do you spend most of your time?
- How much of the city do you ever get to see?
- What, specifically, do you see?

Your paper should consider Roman rituals, the built environment, as well as the dangers and entertainments that were present in Rome at this time. Your social standing as a Roman will determine how much you can see and how much is off limits to you.

Goals/Learning Objectives of the Assignment

Students will:

- Demonstrate understanding of living in the ancient city of Rome;
- Conduct research of primary and secondary sources;
- Create a bibliography of sources; and
- Use footnotes in an appropriate manner.

Appendix B: Daily Life in Ancient Rome

Part II: Presentation

Using your individual writing assignment as a guide, you will work with the other of your social standing to create a presentation about what life is like in Rome for those like you.

You will be presenting/performing these presentation on Wednesday, December 2.

Please think beyond PowerPoint presentation: we already know the facts from class. What I will be grading you on is:

- Engagement in the period by demonstrating research that was gathered.
- How your social class influenced how you interacted with the built environment in Rome every day.
- Creativity in presenting the material.

Different groups can work together if it is likely that there was some crossover in their daily activities.

You will have the remaining class period today (11/23) to begin to work on these presentations that will be given on the last day of class (December 2).

Grade: 10% of your overall grade for this presentation.

Chapter 9

Preservice Teachers and Active Learning in Technology-Enhanced Learning: The Case of the University of West Bohemia in the Czech Republic

Zbyněk Filipi and Lucie Rohlíková

Abstract

This chapter presents innovative approaches to active learning that were introduced into the teaching of preservice teachers at the Faculty of Education of University of West Bohemia, Pilsen, in the Czech Republic. Over the last three years, the Technology-Enhanced Learning course has seen substantial innovations in both the content and use of teaching strategies designed to prepare the students for their professional lives. The whole update of the course was implemented using the results of action research — all individual changes were rigorously tracked and analyzed. The state of the art in the active learning domain in education of preservice teachers is presented in this chapter.

There is a description of the procedure to update the course, based on the reflections of teachers and feedback from students, gathered during action research. Detailed evaluations of particular methods of active learning that have been proven in teaching are provided.

Besides practical activities with tablets and smartphones, during which students familiarize themselves with various types of applications and reflect on their use in teaching, the course was extended

Active Learning Strategies in Higher Education: Teaching for Leadership,
Innovation, and Creativity, 211–245
Copyright © 2018 by Emerald Publishing Limited
All rights of reproduction in any form reserved
ISBN: 978-1-78714-488-0

by the use of practical aids for the efficient inclusion of mobile technologies for teaching – the Czech version of Allan Carrington's Padagogy Wheel. This aid is derived from the revised Bloom's taxonomy and SAMR model and helps the systematic reflection of preservice teachers when preparing for technology-enhanced teaching.

A significant part of the teaching consists of cooperative projects between preservice teachers and pupils of elementary schools – for example, the preservice teachers help elementary school pupils discover possibilities of virtual reality during Google Cardboard activities, or preservice teachers in teams with elementary school pupils create digital stories together on the topic of Internet safety.

The innovative approach to active teaching in the Technology-Enhanced Learning course is apparent even during the exam. In the course of the exam, students process, present, and defend a lesson plan for the implementation of an activity using digital technologies.

Throughout the learning, as well as at the end, preservice teachers are encouraged to reflect on the teaching in the Technology-Enhanced Learning subject.

Keywords: Active learning; higher education; technology-enhanced learning; preservice teachers

Introduction

Active learning engages students in the learning process, requires students to do meaningful learning activities, and think about what they are doing (Bonwell & Eison, 1991). A whole host of prior studies have confirmed that active learning is the most effective learning approach in order to promote students' learning (e.g., Crouch & Mazur, 2001; Deslauriers, Schelew & Wieman, 2011; Haak, Hillerislambers, Pitre, & Freeman, 2011; Hake, 1998; Hsieh, 2013; Naiz, Aguilera, Maza, & Liendo, 2002; Nehm & Reilly, 2007). The basic findings on active learning were summarized by Michael (2006) and Prince (2004) in their work.

The theory of active learning derives from two basic assumptions. First, that learning is by nature an active endeavor, and second, that different people learn in different ways (Meyers & Jones, 1993). Active-learning techniques move students from passive learning to active learning (Meyers, 1986), produce higher achievement, more positive relationships among students, and healthier psychological adjustment (Johnson, Johnson, & Smith, 1998), and are based on learner-centered as opposed to content-centered instruction (Halonen, Brown-Anderson, & McKeachie, 2002). Students are engaged in more activities than just listening. They are involved in dialogue, debate, writing, and problem solving, as well as higher order thinking (Bonwell & Eison, 1991). Bean (2011) describes many active-learning exercises as strategies that make students more powerful thinkers and better arguers. He recommends the use of case studies, role-playing, work in small groups, and creative activities, which stretch the thinking skills that can be applied to given situations. Yoshida (2016) found that students who learned actively in a small group significantly increased their understanding and skills in curriculum management week by week.

Active learning has been studied extensively across multiple disciplines, and a vast amount of research has identified a variety of approaches to enhance teaching and learning in the classroom. The most common active-learning techniques are cooperative learning, collaborative learning, problem-based solving, discovery/inquiry-based learning, challenge-based learning, and concept mapping (Hsieh, 2013). In each discipline, the use of these techniques is different and reflects a specific field. Many studies point to the fact that active learning influences not only remembering the study materials but also primarily the relationship among the students and between the students and the teacher (Braxton, Milem, & Sullivan, 2000; Prince, 2004).

The strength of the active-learning classroom is that it facilitates personal involvement with the materials, thereby provoking students into relevant discussion and evaluation (Browne & Freeman, 2000) and maximizes the impact of the learning upon the learners themselves (Meyers, 1986). Retention levels are enhanced when active learning methods are used (Halonen et al., 2002; Silberman, 1996).

These are all important reasons why active learning became the basis for changing the subject of Technology-Enhanced Learning taught at the Faculty of Education at the University of West Bohemia in Pilsen in the Czech Republic.

The aim of this chapter is to present in detail active-learning techniques that have been, over the last two years (academic year 2015–2016 and 2017), integrated into the courses to enhance students' motivation, teamwork, and for gaining practical skills. The experience gained during our research can be an inspiration for all those involved in the preparation of future teachers for the field of ICT in education.

In the next part of the chapter, a literature review focuses on active learning in preservice teacher–technology integration. After that, the methodology of action research is introduced at the Faculty of Education at the University of West Bohemia in Pilsen in the Czech Republic, with a detailed description of the curriculum and the active-learning techniques used in preservice teacher education.

Active Learning in Preservice Teachers–Technology Integration

The Technology-Enhanced Learning subject is designed for preservice teachers, the target group, for which it is possible to choose the appropriate active-learning techniques, relies on a wide range of specifically targeted previous research. The aim of this subchapter is a literature review specifically focused on active learning in preservice teacher–technology integration.

Many authors state that preservice teachers' preparation in the integration of technology could be aligned closely with pedagogical issues and curriculum integration (Agyei & Voogt, 2011; Ottenbreit-Leftwich, Glazewski, Newby, & Ertmer, 2010; Sang, Valcke, van Braak, & Tondeur, 2010). A crucial factor influencing new teachers' adoption of technology is the quantity and quality of preservice technology experiences included in their teacher education programs (Agyei & Voogt, 2011; Drent & Meelissen, 2008). Many programs have attempted to develop preservice teachers' technology skills through an introductory educational technology course (Polly, Mims, Shepherd, & Inan, 2010) and have tried to select and implement the most effective strategies on how to prepare preservice teachers to integrate technology into their future lessons (Goktas, Yıldırım, & Yıldırım, 2008). By taking an educational technology course, preservice teachers are expected to transfer knowledge and skills to their future classrooms (Brush et al., 2003).

If we focus on learning strategies in educational technology courses, we often meet with active-learning techniques. Admiraal et al. (2017) present two main enablers of student teachers' learning to teach with technology, which refers to: (1) teaching practice to enact what was learned in teacher education, as well as to receive feedback from students on this enactment and (2) modeling of teacher educators and teachers in school. Tearle and Golder (2008) stressed that "watching" technology being used could not substitute for actual "doing." Preservice teacher educational technology programs must therefore be highly practically aimed and provide a wide range of approaches throughout their curriculum (based on Ottenbreit-Leftwich et al., 2010; Polly et al., 2010): information delivery of technology–integration content (e.g. lectures, podcasts), hands-on technology skill-building activities (e.g., workshops), practice with technology integration in the field (e.g. field experiences), and technology-integration reflections (e.g. electronic portfolios). Lavonen, Lattu, Juuti, and Meisalo (2006) suggested a mixture of short lectures or demonstrations, along with practical work. So and Kim (2009) integrate problem-based learning with the aim of better preparing future teachers to have pedagogically sound technology integration or technological pedagogical content knowledge. Albion and Gibson (2000) combine interactive multimedia packages based on problem-based principles to help preservice teachers integrate technology into their teaching and learning sessions, and to develop their knowledge in technology, self-organization, and classroom management. The study by Sahin (2003), who explored the preservice teachers' perceptions of the instructional development course, reports that among others, there are two inspirational comments by students concerning active learning:

- *I used my skills. I used a computer, video, etc. I enjoyed being active. We have to be active as the teachers of future.*
- *I made my own materials. I was an active learner. After I made my materials, I presented them to my friends as an example elementary course. I learned about the preparation of different materials with different technologies. Also, I observed my friends and evaluated their materials with my class and my lecturer.*

One of the challenges identified for a teacher education program is the difficulty of engaging preservice teachers and teacher educators in conversations about their attitudes regarding the role technology should play in teaching and learning (Goktas, Yildirim, & Yildirim, 2009). Discussion groups, observation, and writing seem to help preservice teachers reflect on the role of technology in education (O'Reilly, 2003; Tearle & Golder, 2008). According to Angeli and Valanides (2009), collaboration with peers appeared to provide a time effective, high-challenge, low-threat learning environment for preservice teachers, contrary to many technology learning experiences that can induce anxiety and failure avoidance. Brush et al. (2003) recommend providing the necessary scaffolds, such as additional support during the planning and preparation stages. Recent studies emphasized technology training in authentic teaching situations and have revealed that the best practices provided to preservice teachers with regard to technology training include authentic experiences in real K-12 classrooms (Goktas et al., 2008; Ottenbreit-Leftwich et al., 2010).

Tondeur et al. (2011) points out that active-learning techniques in preservice teachers' education lead to a move from traditional assessment to continuous feedback, from tests without the relationship with what is needed in order to make progress in using technology in the classroom to formative assessment (Barton & Haydn, 2006). The Lavonen et al. (2006) study showed that evaluation data should be continually collected by discussions, questionnaires, interviews, and observations in order to follow how staff members have adopted technology, how they use technology, and how their ICT competence has developed, as well as what kind of problems and visions they have had with technology use. Sahin (2003) implemented assessments based on the process (the efforts of the students, active participation and material development processes, cooperation, etc.), and preservice teachers were evaluated by their peers and their instructors.

The abovementioned studies were a form of inspiration and support for changes to the Technology-Enhanced Learning subject, which we describe in the following sections of the chapter.

Adopting New Strategies

The Technology-Enhanced Learning subject has been included in the Master's program at the Faculty of Education University of West Bohemia in Pilsen for preservice teachers who are preparing to teach computer science at elementary and high schools. Computer science teachers often act as ICT coordinators in these schools and are expected to encourage other teachers to use digital technology in other subjects (languages, science, and others). In our subject, we have focused primarily on the fact that after starting work, its graduates could explain to their colleagues (future teachers) how to properly incorporate digital technology into the classroom. At the same time, however, we assume that they themselves will be able to enjoy the introduced teaching strategies in teaching computer science.

Technology-Enhanced Learning has been taught as a subject since 2008, organized in two semesters of the first year – in winter, traditionally a lecture (2 hours) and a seminar (1 hour), and in summer, a 3-hour seminar. In the winter semester, teaching was concluded by a credit test form, realized through LMS Moodle and an oral examination, in the spring semester, by a test in the form of a presentation of credit tasks. Note: At universities in the Czech Republic, at the end of the semester, an exam is taken (which is a more demanding option) or a credit on the basis of fulfilling a predefined credit task (seminar paper, assignment, test) is carried out.

Lessons were in the form of lectures, usually implemented with the support of a PowerPoint presentation and practically-oriented seminars. Students worked with the teacher on seminars on various time-consuming tasks in the field of technology-enhanced learning.

Among shorter tasks was, for example, acquaintance with Crowder's branched program (Crowder, 1959), which served as a still good usable product from the beginning of the use of digital technologies in education. Students also tried creating different types of test questions in LMS Moodle and through a digital literacy test. They included discussion of the theoretical basis for the use of digital technologies in the classroom. Among the more time-consuming tasks were creating concept maps, Webquest, and a tutorial program.

Creating concept maps was included in teaching to support one of the six principles of teaching and learning by J. D. Novak, namely that "teachers should organise the conceptual knowledge they want to teach" (Novak, 2010). The function of concept maps was described in the lecture, and additional resources were made available to students. Students created concept maps with the specified course of study outside of computer science. They had to justify the choice of topic selection, from which content subsequently resulted. The reasons for selecting the software chosen for creating the concept maps were also evaluated. The resulting product was handed in with accompanying documentation which suggested the methodology of work with the conceptual maps created in the lesson.

Webquest is one of the first attempts to use the Internet in education, and was known as early as the mid-90s of the 20th century, and is still very inspiring today. Research has shown that Webquest can positively influence factors that often precede or promote learning, such as increased motivation and the integration of technology into teaching and learning (Abbit & Ophus, 2008). Technology-Enhanced Learning students should first familiarize themselves with the structure of WebQuest and the taxonomy of tasks that it can perform (Dodge, 2002). Instead of lectures led by teachers, they themselves in groups subsequently conducted an evaluation of one given and one selected

Webquest in the roles of didactic, innovator, and technologist, and coordinator. Presenting their assessment was accompanied by discussions during the seminar. Armed with this practical experience, they could proceed to the subsequent task. In it, they first justified the selection of a crosscutting theme (e.g. environmental education, media education, and more), which was considered appropriate for WebQuest. They created it in WebQuest in a classical structure (motivation description, task, process, information sources, evaluation, conclusion, guidance), including their own websites. The teacher assessment was conducted in the same manner that they tried themselves at the beginning, in order to become familiar with the inquiry-based learning activity.

The most challenging task in the Technology-Enhanced Learning subject was to create a training program for second-degree-course students – Physics, Mathematics, Biology, etc. (NB. In the Czech Republic, preservice teachers always study two fields that will later be taught at schools). First, the students set goals that they want to use the tutorial to fulfill. In the first document, they were asked to describe the theme and what age pupils the teaching program is intended for. In the second document, they describe in detail the content of the teaching program at the level of educational scenarios (a sequence of interpretive materials with activation elements, including diagnostics, etc.). In the third document, students justify the choice of hardware and software for creating the teaching program. In accordance with all three documents, they subsequently come to their own creation of the teaching program. When submitting each individual part, the students receive feedback from the teacher, to which he responds with appropriate modifications. The students then rate each other's resulting teaching programs. When preparing the final classification, the teacher considers the student peer assessments.

Fulfilment of practical time-demanding tasks was difficult for the students for various reasons. Students fulfilled them away from full-time teaching, at home, which led to frequent underestimation of the time required to develop quality tasks. The number of time-demanding tasks was also too large to provide good feedback for the gradual creation of tasks and justifying each step. Primarily, the creation of the teaching program will then be shown in the case of student teachers in a certain contradiction with the levels of previously developed skills in their future professions as applicable competencies.

Basic Changes to the Subject and Methodology

Since 2008, evaluation has been carried out by students regarding teaching methods, and the students' results in exams were monitored. The feedback from students clearly shows the need to further enhance students' motivation for the active use of technology in teaching, to develop students' practical skills in this area, and to set educational activities in a real context. If the students do not have the opportunity to verify the impact of activities prepared in school practice, everything depends on the evaluation of the teacher in the class, and the students' motivation to actively carry out the tasks is much lower.

The Technology-Enhanced Learning subject must be continuously modified and improved on content and methodology, so that it affects the rapid development of technology-enhanced learning, while retaining a certain timelessness. In 2015, we therefore asked for accreditation of the subject in a modified form and we proceeded to make a number of changes, not only in the content of the subject but especially in teaching methods and evaluation. For new methods of active learning, we also continuously closely monitor the impact of implemented changes.

Since 2016—2017, the two subjects merged into one, in the range of a 2-hour lecture and a 3-hour seminar. Merging subjects and their time allotment concentrated into one semester now allows more intensive work and the realization of the projects and activities. Changes made in time allocations, organization, content, and method of evaluation of the course are shown in Table 1.

As described in the table, new course contents been modified and accredited, including changing the method of evaluating students. Topics related to e-learning and open and online education is a newly independent E-learning subject in education. The main topics of the course are complemented by conceptual maps, microworlds, simulation, multiuser virtual environments, and digital storytelling.

Two teachers began teaching the subject, one of whom is focused more on the theoretical basis of the subject (primarily leading lectures) and one more on active learning methods and links with practice (leading seminars). Merging the time allotment for two semesters enabled significantly changing the methods by which students become acquainted with the subject. Teaching in the Technology-Enhanced Learning subject is implemented in small groups of up to 15 students, so that there is enough space for an individual approach to teaching teamwork in small groups, discussing, and challenging hands-on

Table 1. The Basic Characteristics of Technology-Enhanced Learning.

	to 2015–2016	since 2016–2017
Time allocation	2-hour lecture + 1-hour seminar in the winter semester 3-hour seminar in the summer semester	2-hour lecture + 3-hour seminar in the winter semester
Teaching organization	1st year Master's studies (winter and summer semester)	1st year Master's study (only winter semester)
Number of teachers	1	2
Course content (Didactic principles of teaching selected thematic units)	Historical development of the use of computer systems in education and current trends. Internet and didactic aspects of its use in teaching. Projects teaching with Internet support.	Historical development of the use of computer systems in accordance with various theories of learning and their reflection in the present. Internet and didactic aspects of the use of its components and associated activities in the classroom. Projects teaching with Internet support.

Diverse computer-aided teaching individual educational areas and crosscutting themes.	Diverse computer-aided teaching individual educational areas and crosscutting themes.
Didactic analysis of multimedia tutorials.	Didactic analysis of multimedia tutorials.
Computer literacy.	Digital literacy.
Open technologies in education.	
The possibilities of e-learning in education.	**Conceptual maps.**
	Microworlds, simulation, and multiuser virtual environments.
	Digital storytelling.

activities that require a teacher with individual students, or less available material equipment (technology), which students must take turns with.

A very important factor leading to the improvement of education is continuous cooperation of teachers, in terms of which the pros and cons of innovative methods used were closely continually debated. The process of improvement of the course has not been completed, the first experience with adapting the subject in 2015–2016 led to adjustments to the implementation of the subject in 2016–2017, and further changes for the year 2017–2018 are currently being discussed and prepared.

The main objective of the changes in the content and methods of teaching of Technology-Enhanced Learning is to significantly enhance the practical focus of the course and introduce students to relevant pedagogical communities of teachers, thereby giving them a basis for lifelong learning in information and communication technologies in education.

Within the framework of the course are the following active learning techniques:

- cooperative learning – students work together toward a common goal and being evaluated individually (Dougherty et al., 1995),
- collaborative learning – students work together toward a common goal (Lumpe & Staver, 1995),
- discovery/inquiry-based learning – students are exposed to situations, questions, or tasks that allow the discovery of intended concepts (Wilke & Straits, 2001),
- problem-based learning – problems are introduced at the beginning of the instruction, and motivated students' learning followed (Dochy, Sergers, Van den Bossche, & Gijbels, 2003), and
- challenge-based learning – students are presented with a scenario in which they work toward a solution with others (Roselli & Brophy, 2006).

Changes implemented in the academic year 2015–2016 and 2016–2017 and their impact are closely monitored and evaluated. We also continuously asked the students for feedback.

Action research included evaluation of students' results, evaluation of the students' progressive and final questionnaires, and continuous evaluation carried out by way of discussions with both teachers of the subject.

If we look at students' test results over the last few years (see Figure 1), it is evident that after the change of the method, there was perhaps a definitive reverse in the trend of deteriorating academic performance. Due to the changing requirements for credits and exam, this is rather tentative as an indicator. Despite this, the improvements can be seen in two directions. Despite maintaining sufficient demands, there are decreases in those who in a given year never succeed in the subject. For example, in 2013, the successful pass rate for the subject was less than 40%, in 2016 it was as much as 80% of the students. At the same time, there are increases in the representation of the proportion of students who manage to achieve excellent results. Excellent results were achieved before 2015 by less than 10% of students, but in 2015 and 2016 approximately 40% of students achieved excellent results.

One very important fact is that this subject is now completed by students who are motivated and equipped with practical experience and competence. This derives not only from their interest in other activities

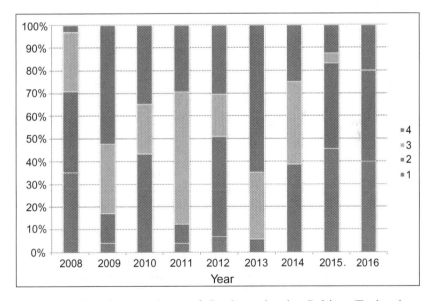

Figure 1. The Success Rate of Students in the Subject Technology-Enhanced Learning. *Notes*: Figure 1 shows a comparison of students' success in the years 2008—2014 (before adjusting the subject) and between 2015 and 2016 (after adjusting the subject). Evaluation scale applicable to universities in the Czech Republic 1 — excellent, 2 — praise-worthy, 3 — good, 4 — fail.

in the field of digital technologies in education but also from the feedback provided by the teacher in the evaluation of teaching quality (see Table 2).

The practical focus of the course was positively evaluated by most students, stating that this concept of teaching is unusual for them, and that they do not encounter it in other subjects.

Table 2. Examples of Final Evaluation Comments by Students.

Feedback #1	*For me, I took more away from the subject than from any other subjects. I am taking practical experience with technology to my work experience (Google Cardboard, tablets), but also with planning various activities.*
Feedback #2	*I certainly acquired the knowledge, skills, and ideas that I can use as a teacher, if I actually go this way.*
Feedback #3	*Thank you for my new knowledge. I could always look forward to lessons with you. It was interesting, useful, and fun ... :)*
Feedback #4	*Working with a tablet, work with many devices, experience with children during the project, a lot of new knowledge about applications, knowledge for the creation of a methodological sheet, and its application in practice.*
Feedback #5	*I am very glad that I was able to complete the subject under your leadership, all the hours and materials produced in the lessons have some sense, and are not just put away in a drawer like in other subjects. I very much also appreciate the efforts to learn something practical, as well as the final exams, where one is not as stressed as in other tests.*
Feedback #6	*I am taking away experience with technologies and applications that I would probably not have gained by myself. In addition, I learned how it could be meaningfully used in the classroom.*

Note: Free expression of students in a questionnaire after completing the course.

Active Learning Strategies Implemented in the Technology-Enhanced
Learning Subject

The following subchapters present in detail the activities that were
newly incorporated or adapted within the scope of the subject, and in
which we feel active learning brings the most significant added value,
and this being:

- practical activities using technologies (on and off campus),
- reflections based on the Padagogy Wheel,
- school projects,
- formative assessment, and
- reflection and evaluation of teaching quality.

Description of activities and explanation of the reasons for their
inclusion in teaching in the text is supplemented by relevant feedback
from students that we have gained through students filling out questionnaires at the end of the course or at the conclusion of each activity.

Practical Activities Using Technologies (On and Off Campus)
Good activities develop deep understanding of the important ideas to
be learned. To do this, the activities must be designed around important
learning outcomes and promote thoughtful engagement on the part of
the student (Wiggins & McTighe, 1998). It is not enough to merely
introduce the activity into the classroom, but it needs to be promoted
by student engagement and encouraging the students to think about
what they are learning (Prince, 2004).

Within the scope of Technology-Enhanced Learning, students
have the opportunity to work with different types of technologies
and reflect their potential application in teaching different subjects.
Teaching involves mainly work with Internet applications, with tablets,
and mobile phones, with interactive whiteboards, as well as Google
Cardboard.

Students are encouraged to invent their own activities to be implemented in the teaching process, along with methodology sheets for the
implementation of these activities. During the course, they are also
made familiar with technologies that are not commercially available,
but the main part of suggestions for teaching is focused on technologies
and activities which are widely available. The emphasis is on Internet
applications and activities that can be implemented on multiple platforms (i.e. we are looking for activities such as touch tablets and

phones, in order to be implemented on devices running iOS, Android, and Windows).

An example might be the preparation of articles on the Web site *Have fun with science*, aimed at popularizing science, where students are authors of elementary and high school tips for interesting activities in the use of technology. The attractiveness of prepared articles is intended to be discussed directly with the target group, and according to the feedback received, the materials can be fine-tuned. Another example is a project during which students created and deployed in a university building educational posters with QR codes and then observe and reflect on the interest their materials meet with other students.

Among the activities the students highly appreciated are seminars led by the in-service teachers. Personalities who actively use technology in teaching at elementary and high schools are invited to the lessons. During the workshops, specific technologies are presented that have been tried and tested in the classroom. Students have the opportunity to discuss with colleagues from practice experience in project implementation and practical questions on the use of technology in the classroom. These meetings are of great importance, especially for motivating students.

During their studies, the students also participate in excursions (into a virtual laboratory, the Centre for New Technologies, and the Centre for Robotics), as well as conferences (the Conference Učitel IN for those interested in the use of technology in education, and the conference of the Ministry of Education, Youth, and Sports, School for the future − a future for school). Attendance at the conference is for many students their first entry into the educational community, with discussions with experts and teachers from different corners of the Czech Republic. Within the framework of excursions and conferences, students have, of course, the chance to try out other technologies − interactive projectors, touchscreen tables, drones, robotic kits, robots for teaching robotics in elementary schools, various types of glasses for virtual reality, etc. Some examples of student work with technologies in Course Technology-Enhanced Learning are shown in Figure 2.

To support teaching, in the Technology-Enhanced Learning course, we use a Courseware system containing the basic organizational information system and LMS Moodle, in which study texts and links to other educational resources are presented.

Since 2015−2016, these systems have been supplemented by Google Documents. In the shared folder, students have available additional materials and information from teachers, especially in the area where

Figure 2.   Practical Activities Using Technologies. *Note*: Examples of practical student activities undertaken within the scope of Technology-Enhanced Learning (interactive projector, Arduino kits, flight simulator, drone).

they themselves contribute. Study materials for the subject are posted dynamically, constantly added to, and expanded. During the course, students work on shared tables, surrender records of completed practical activities, form the methodology sheets, and work with feedback questionnaires.

For student communication, sharing current links to interesting articles on the Internet, making contact with virtual communities, and promoting educational activities of students in the course, Facebook is actively used. Thanks to this, we have managed to motivate students to participate in workshops and conferences for teachers to enter the pedagogical communities (e.g. Google Edu Group), and in addition, the site provides the ability to draw public attention to the skills and accomplishments of our students, who also receive permanent job offers and casual work offers in the field.

Reflexions Based on Padagogy Wheel
During the course of 2015–2016, we noted that if the preservice teachers devise activities using ICT, it was usually based on the capabilities

of the technology or the application they wanted to use and not from the learning objectives. We sought a tool that would provide students with the necessary methodological support. After in-depth research of methodological tools to support preservice teachers, we chose the Padagogy Wheel concept from EDTECH Australian specialist Allan Carrington as the ideal solution. The Padagogy Wheel is based on Bloom's taxonomy, and lists action verbs, activities, and applications with respect to individual categories of educational objectives. The Taxonomy wheel, without the apps, was first discovered at Paul Hopkin's educational consultancy website mmiweb.org.uk. That wheel was produced by Sharon Artley and was an adaptation of Anderson and Krathwohl's (2001) adaptation of Bloom (1956). Allan Carrington, inspired by the Kathy Schrock's Bloomin' apps website, supplemented the taxonomic wheel with applications suitable for the iPad and later individual levels of the SAMR model (Puentedura, 2013).

Working with any methodological tool is easier in the mother tongue, therefore the Padagogy Wheel was translated into the Czech language by the team at UWB, with great support by Allan Carrington, and was titled the Kolo iPadagogiky (Rohlíková, Vejvodová, Rohlík, & Prade, 2016), tested, and put into practice within our Technology-Enhanced Learning subject. Students have tools available in an electronic form, as well as a printed poster (see Figure 3).

Since 2016–2017, we have therefore been able to supplement practical demonstrations of working with students' tablets with reflections on goals with the Padagogy Wheel. Before using the Padagogy Wheel in the creation of methodological papers, students received some training activities focused on reflection of cognitive goals. Examples of tasked activities are listed in Table 3.

School Project (Cooperation with an Elementary School)
The culmination of activities in the Technology-Enhanced Learning subject projects are implemented in cooperation with the science teacher in the elementary school. The topic and the technology used are different each year, but always innovative, usually using technologies that the students or the pupils of the elementary school have not worked with. The students are very actively involved in the planning, preparation, implementation, and even evaluation of the project.

In 2015–2016, students in pairs prepared several stations on which pupils fundamentally worked with Google Cardboard. Implementation of the project within the school was preceded by acquainting the students with Google Cardboard, research, and suitable applications. One

Figure 3.   Padagogy Wheel V4.1. *Note.* In the first year, we used V 4.1, which is available from bit.ly/PWposterCZEHD, we are currently working with the new, improved V 5.0 (available from http://bit.ly/AppleCZEV5Print in Czech, from http://bit.ly/AppleENGV5Print in English). The utility has been developed for iOS and Android.

Table 3.   Examples of Tasks Using the Padagogy Wheel.

Activity	Example of Student Task
Determining the category according to the formulation of educational objectives	**Think over the formulation of these educational goals and try to determine the appropriate category of revised taxonomy.**
	Pupils categorize words into two groups, according to whether the words are listed or not.
	Pupils in the group will perform sketches which typify good deeds. The sketch is recorded on video.
	Pupils solve 20 maths problems for subtraction in an application on a tablet.
Determining the category of educational	**Think over the following tasked activities and try to determine the appropriate category of revised taxonomy.**

Table 3. (*Continued*)

Activity	Example of Student Task
objectives according to tasked activities	Prepare a script for the creation of a fairy tale, which will later be animated with the tablet.
	Listen to the teacher explanations, supported by an electronic presentation, and write notes in the workbook.
	Prepare a hundred flashcards on the tablet, thanks to which the other students will be able to learn the flags of countries of Central Europe.
Use of one application to achieve different categories of cognitive objectives	**Think about the possibilities in group activities with the implementation of selected applications and enter your various activities to achieve the various categories of objectives of the revised taxonomy. For each activity, also consider the level of SAMR. Examples of applications used:** • Book Creator • Excel • Educreations • Bitsboard • Youtube

Note: For the duties listed in the table, students first work individually, then consult their solutions in pairs, and later in groups.

pair of students prepared an initial brief presentation on virtual reality, and another pair divided up which applications pupils would work with at their stations, thought up tasked activities for the stations, and created worksheets for the pupils. The actual teaching then took place at an elementary school in the science club. The children, divided into groups, passed from station to station and performed the tasks with the assistance of the students.

In 2016–2017, the theme of digital storytelling was chosen as the project. School teams were created, and each team was assigned a preservice teacher. Each team drew one point from the Decalogue of Internet Safety (e.g. Do not give anyone an address or phone number, as you don't know who is hiding behind the monitor.), and the team's task was to portray this point as a digital story, using Lego and Stop Motion applications on the tablet.

Figure 4 demonstrates the active learning of preservice teachers and elementary school pupils during joint projects.

Both projects were launched with a joint introduction and ended with a final evaluation. The final reflection and discussion on the experience acquired by the students were also very important. Examples of overall assessments of the projects are presented in Table 4.

The final evaluation of the project was in 2016–2017 also complemented by feedback from the participating elementary school students. Students could reflect not only their own observations and comments from classmates and teachers but also valuable insights as children. Examples of elementary school students' answers to a few selected questions are given in Table 5.

Formative Assessment
The practical skills acquired by students during the teaching of the Technology-Enhanced Learning subject are difficult to evaluate differently than on the basis of fulfilling a practical task. Therefore, treatment

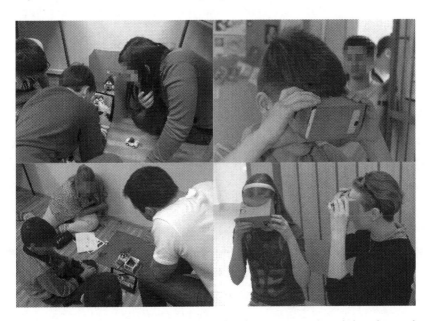

Figure 4. School Projects. *Note*: The images on the right show the project from Google Cardboard from 2015–2016, and the images on the left are from the Digital Storytelling project from 2016–2017.

Table 4. Examples of Students' Final Feedback Related to School Projects.

Feedback #7	*A very helpful event, where we could try working with children even before our official work experience, as a collective we put together a project, and we all depended on each other. Nobody slacked off during the creation of the project, everyone had a role they had to perform.*
Feedback #8	*I assess the project in the elementary school very positively. It greatly helped me in my subsequent start on my work experience.*
Feedback #9	*For myself, I have to evaluate the project positively. It would certainly be a good idea to try something like this during studies and to see pupil reactions with your own eyes, as well as gain additional experience. Practical knowledge and experience are more important to me personally than a "mere" understanding of the theory, and I think that it would be a good idea to implement similar projects. Of course, not all projects will appeal to pupils, and you may even come across schools that are not willing to cooperate.*
Feedback #10	*I really liked teaching in an elementary school. It was a good experience. Something completely different to classic work experience. I would certainly continue, it is worthwhile — for us as future teachers, as well as for the kids, who also learn something new.*

Note: Free expression of students in a questionnaire after completing the course.

Table 5. View of Elementary School Students on Preservice Teachers.

Question	Selection of Pupil Answers
What did you like about the UWB student involvement in your team?	*They listened to our ideas.* *When we did something wrong, they helped us.* *They helped us with ideas and implemented them.* *They explained everything to us.* *They showed us how it's done, and then we knew what to do.*

Table 5. (*Continued*)

Question	Selection of Pupil Answers
	I liked that they wanted everyone to join in, and came up with great ideas.
	They were kind and collaborated well (with us).
	They came up with ideas that we didn't come up with.
	It was fun with them.
What should the student work on to make them a better guide for pupils?	*I don't know, nothing.*
	I think nothing really.
	It was great.
	Nothing, it was all was good.
	Could show us how it's better.
	They seemed good to me, so I would not change anything.
	Nothing, they will definitely be a great teacher.
	I would not change anything, they were really great.
What advice would you give to the student before they start teaching?	*I don't know :D*
	Solid nerves and patience.
	None .... :)
	Not to have favorites, then when the student does something wrong, not to be sad from it.
	To stay just as they are.
	In order to have the patience with the children.
	To be themselves.

Note: Free expression of elementary school pupils in a questionnaire after the completion of a joint project.

methods and goals of teaching were also reflected in the adjustment of student assessments.

Original and current conditions for completing the course and student evaluations are presented in Table 6.

One major change is primarily the inclusion of work with the methodological sheet. The student first, within the framework of obtaining

Table 6. Conditions for Completion of the Course and Student Assessment.

	to 2014−2015	since 2015−2016
Credits	Part A − Student creates WebQuest. Part B − Student creates concept or mind map. Part C − Student creates a tutorial program. Bonus − A student may get extra points for activity in seminars and any accompanying events.	Part A − Student creates Webquest or concept or mind map (they can choose). Part B − Student prepares methodological work sheet with the application for the tablet of their choice, methodological document is presented at the seminar. Bonus − A student may get extra points for activity in seminars and any accompanying events.
Exam	Part A − Student fills in the test in Moodle. Part B − Student answers questions from the specified lines drawn from the theory lectures.	Part A − Student processes and presents methodological sheet activities (the teacher tasks the topic and technologies that are available). Part B − Student discusses the selected topics from the curriculum of lectures and answer the teacher's questions.

credits, creates, and according to comments of teachers and classmates, adapts the methodological sheet for the selected application. During the test, then prepares a methodological sheet again, but this time with slightly different tasking − he is not preparing an activity with a specific application, but an activity with the use of ICT, which is derived from a specified general topic, the number of pupils in the class, and given the technologies that are available.

In 2015−2016, an exam took place so that students approached the presentation of methodological sheets in pairs, and alongside their presentations and answers to questions, teachers should also evaluate the proposed activity of the classmate. In 2016−2017, a presentation took place with the participation of all students, so that students could reflect and comment on the ideas of classmates and also learn from all provided comments.

Table 7 lists examples of expressions of students on the form and during testing, which we gained from the quality assessment questionnaire.

Feedback from students tells us, among other things, that for 2017−2018 it would be appropriate to extend the time limit for preparing the methodological sheet for the test from 60 minutes to 90 or even 120 minutes, so that the test results do not affect students' stress levels, and so that they could think about the activity.

Table 7. Examples of Student Comments Regarding Evaluation Method Innovation.

Feedback #11	*Teaching skills need not be tested only in theory. This was practical. It suited me.*
Feedback #12	*Personally, I didn't like the time limit, I like to think things through more. In spite of that, the exam was interesting and beneficial.*
Feedback #13	*As I mentioned, I prefer the practical skills rather than theoretical, this type of test suited me. It was not a mindless learning concept, but I myself had to think about what and how the concept and subsequent discussion helped me to see where I make mistakes. Nevertheless, the discussion could have been a bit shorter.*
Feedback #14	*The test really suited me, because it directed us toward practical activities, and in a relatively short time. When one is in a hurry, he is forced to think something up, at least as a rough basis. It's very good to have long hours preparing for the materials cut down.*
Feedback #15	*The test was good, in that we were forced to think about how it's really done in practice. That to me is important, because I may be able to think of some great lesson plans, etc., but in reality it can go completely differently.*

Note: Free expression of students in a questionnaire after completing the course.

The discussion of teachers on the course and the test results also showed that for 2017–2018 this model will have completed trials of self-reflective evaluation of the student and meet the practical task of working with technology (e.g. completing a short specific task with the tablet, mobile phone, Google Cardboard, Internet applications, etc.). This will strengthen the practical nature of the tests and the ability pedagogical reflection even more among future teachers. Everything, however, will be continued on the basis of specific knowledge of the impact of the use of digital technologies in education, in line with current trends and scientific knowledge in this area.

Reflection and Evaluation of Teaching Quality

Within the scope of Technology-Enhanced Learning, students were taught various forms to reflect the different activities implemented, along with their benefits and pitfalls. This was a partial interim feedback on activities and a final evaluation of the course in the form of a questionnaire.

Examples of self-reflective activity may be the evaluation of a school project, which was carried out with the support of the shared table into which, in a short time limit within a lesson in the classroom, students supplement what is learned during the project in general, the teacher's work, about the children, about the technology. Examples of reflection of several students are given in Table 8.

Upon completing the table, the students discussed their experience acquired during the project, with the aid of an interactive whiteboard. They met with insights from classmates and mutually commented on other observations.

For future teachers, reflection of the active learning is very important, which they had the opportunity to experience first-hand. For this reason, the final subject interview is important, in which students come back to what they experienced during the semester, and a discussion of the results of this survey with the students. Table 9 shows examples of students' answers to the question "What do you think the difference is between the didactic subject form of the project and the usual way of teaching?"

Future Development

Active learning has given classes in the Technology-Enhanced Learning subject a new direction. Students gain practical experience and skills for

Table 8. Reflection of the Project Implemented at Elementary School.

What I Learned	Generally	About a Teacher's Work	About Children	About Technologies
Feedback #16	*How to lose the fear of standing in front of greater numbers of people, stay in control during presentation, and try to make as few mistakes as possible. Not be afraid to speak to pupils, give them interesting information, and not be afraid to communicate with them.*	*Approach, losing fear, trying to attract the children's interest so they are not bored. A great example was the class teacher who was active, and it was obvious that he really liked the pupils.*	*Not be afraid to communicate with them and give them suggestions, talk with them, so they don't just look and not talk (see when we were little ourselves). One must also learn from them to have some distance, not to get too close.*	*How Google Cardboard works, how to make computer science lessons more varied, and how to show pupils something new and current. Not to teach the same things all of the time which are from the last century. Try to lead them to learn about technologies themselves, to explore and develop.*
Feedback #17	*Even tasks that look simple to me can be difficult for others, and vice versa. It always depends on the situation and current knowledge of students.*	*It is necessary to be patient and to explain things more times, even if it seems that it should be perfectly clear to everyone.*	*If we tell them: stand right there, read this here, and do this exactly, then we can't expect any foresight (or even interest) from their side.*	*Most of the children did not know the technology, but had heard about it. I think that they really enjoyed it, unfortunately there are not more directly educational applications*

Table 8. (*Continued*)

What I Learned	Generally	About a Teacher's Work	About Children	About Technologies
				using VR, so I practically only used Google Street View.
Feedback #18	*If both parties are interested in something, the result will be great. We introduced the children to something new, they enjoyed it, we had fun.*	*It can also be fun for me.*	*Each one is different, is entertained by something else, and knows something else.*	*The technology can be fun for anyone if the topic is well presented.*
Feedback #19	*I liked the relationship of the teacher and pupil, his pleasant approach.*	*That if there are six teachers per class, so it can be quite easy :-)*	*The children were quite good, probably because they were interested in the topic.*	*The benefit of new technologies in teaching is that the students did not even know they were learning something.*
Feedback #20	*Simple tasks can be a big problem. Conversely, it may be surprising that even the*	*It takes patience, but so far I am really enjoying it.*	*Younger children are easier to work with. They are active and more enthusiastic.*	*You can find the correct usage in the classroom if the teacher wants to and*

	youngest of them know more than I do.	*I enjoy discovering new ones.*	*thinks out the work with them.*
Feedback #21	*The work of a teacher is mentally demanding and time-consuming (especially mentally).*	*In the beginning, it can be difficult to manage your speech and approach, but after a while it gets easier.*	*The students tried, the sixth grade pupils were "fired up," but of course with students from higher grades it was more complex work, school and lessons for them at their age are an inconvenience (we were no different).*	*Even a simple application that may at first glance seem only entertaining for a short time may serve well in the classroom.*
Feedback #22	*What seemed like a simple task for us when we created it took the children more time than expected.*	*I must speak slowly and ask questions.*	*Younger children are happier and easier to catch their interest.*	*They are fun for kids, but not to overdo it with them.*

Table 9. Examples of Student Comments Regarding Evaluation Method Innovation.

Feedback #23	*The classical method of teaching this subject is not entirely appropriate. After the experience of several lessons where we were inundated with just a lot of concepts, and where one sits and writes numbly, where one takes home a mark from a test mark, and forgets it all, is really useless. It is far more rewarding what we have received in this course, fieldwork, or direct experience on the devices. These are the things that we can really use, and I truly appreciate the efforts that the teachers make to liven up the lessons for us.*
Feedback #24	*I think that the subject in the form of projects is better. In the subject, we met with a lot of things that are usable in practice.*
Feedback #25	*Thanks to the usual method of teaching, in my opinion, one does not get as much practical experience and knowledge. Projects liven up the lessons, and it is also more exciting for our minds than usual lessons. However, there is a rule that nothing should be exaggerated.*
Feedback #26	*I liked this semester very much. The seminars were set up to prepare us for our work experience. As the biggest benefit, I see that I am now able, with the help of applications, to create lesson plans in another subject than my focus — for example in biology. Until then, I was really worried that I would be a substitute for a lesson and have no idea what I would do with the students. This subject opened my eyes in this direction.*
Feedback #27	*I definitely consider this course to be very beneficial. First of all, the teachers have a completely different approach to lesson management than the one I had — the opportunity to meet with other teachers during my previous studies. I consider all the activities that we had available as students very beneficial, especially the conference Teacher IN, organized by the Ministry of Education, Youth, and Sports, School for the future - a future for the school, visiting virtual labs, and finally the ability to work with students at an elementary school in Staňkov. I would appreciate such a possibility even with other teachers. Through them I improved my overview of the issues and have also gained valuable experience for future teaching practice.*

Note: Free expression of students in a questionnaire after completing the course.

meaningful use of technology in teaching and implementing projects, to develop their skills of teamwork and pedagogical reflection, and improve relationships amongst themselves, as well as their relationships with teachers.

Feedback from students and evaluation of academic performance, motivation, and practical skills of students by teachers shows that on the scope of Technology-Enhanced Learning toward greater use of active-learning techniques that we have implemented in the years 2015−2016 and 2016−2017 have the desired positive impact. Students are very actively involved in all activities of the subject and had near-perfect attendance at the seminars, even though it was not required.

The subject, in which students work on individual or group projects, requires a sufficient time allotment. In this respect, it proved effective primarily moving the 3-hour seminar to the same semester as the 2-hour lecture. This allowed an increasingly interlinked theoretical foundation with practical activities. Five hours of instruction in one semester proved to be a more profitable option than 6 hours spread over two semesters. Although 1 hour was saved in the subject, it was possible to realize a greater number of subactivities that were theoretically supported to the extent necessary.

Having enough time is very important for the practically-oriented exam. For the academic year 2017−2018, the time limit for the preparation of methodological sheet activities using ICT will be extended from 60 minutes to 120 minutes. The exam will not only include preparing a methodological sheet but also a practical example of working with technology during the planned activities.

In the academic year 2017−2018, the editing of content and methods of teaching will continue. Above all, we will put even more emphasis on reflection on practical activities with the Padagogy Wheel.

In the future, it will also be possible to inspect the Technology-Enhanced Learning subject in the broader context of teaching preservice teachers at the Faculty of Education. In the year 2017−2018, the subject of ICT in education in Bachelor studies will be innovated, which will be connected to the subject of Technology-Enhanced Learning in the future. For the subject of ICT in education, students from the academic year 2017−2018 will found digital portfolios and learn the basics of effective use of technology in teaching. For the Technology-Enhanced Learning subject implemented in connection with Master's studies will not need to address absolute basics, and this will leave enough time for more challenging projects and close links with practical experience.

Conclusion

In this chapter, the changes introduced at the Faculty of Education of the University of West Bohemia in Pilsen in Technology-Enhanced Learning were presented in detail. The changes concerned the inclusion of a whole range of active-learning techniques in subject teaching. Throughout their implementation, they have been consistently monitored and evaluated in the context of action research.

Research results have shown that active-learning techniques should be considered to be a very important part of preservice teacher education. Different types of activities and methods that preservice teachers have the opportunity to try and reflect together reduce the preservice teachers' fears of using technology in teaching. At the same time, they reinforce the motivation of preservice teachers to consider using technology in preparing their future teaching. School projects have the greatest practical impact, during which preservice teachers work in joint teams with primary school pupils. These projects are demanding in terms of both time and organization, but investments in their preparation, implementation, and evaluation pay off. Preservice teachers, through these projects, see the use of concrete technologies in practice and can reflect on the complexity of different types of activities, with respect to a specific age group of pupils.

Acknowledgments

The authors would like to thank the pupils of the elementary school in Staňkov, as their teacher, Miloslav Khas, for their rewarding, long-term cooperation within the framework of joint projects in the field of technology-enhanced learning.

References

Abbit, J., & Ophus, J. (2008). What we know about the Impacts of WebQuests: A review of research. *AACE Journal, 16*(4), 441−456.
Admiraal, W., van Vugt, F., Kranenburg, F., Koster, B., Smit, B., Weijers, S., & Lockhorst, D. (2017). Preparing pre-service teachers to integrate technology into

K-12 instruction: Evaluation of a technology-infused approach. *Technology, Pedagogy and Education, 26*, 105–120.

Agyei, D. D., & Voogt, J. M. (2011). Exploring the potential of the will, skill, tool model in Ghana: Predicting prospective and practicing teachers' use of technology. *Computers & Education, 56*, 91–100.

Albion, P. R., & Gibson, I. W. (2000). Problem-based learning as a multimedia design framework in teacher education. *Journal of Technology and Teacher Education, 8*(4), 315–326.

Anderson, L. W., & Krathwohl, D. R. (2001). *A taxonomy for learning, teaching, and assessing: A revision of Bloom's taxonomy of educational objectives.* New York, NY: Longman.

Angeli, C., & Valanides, N. (2009). Epistemological and methodological issues for the conceptualization, development, and assessment of ICT–TPCK: Advances in technological pedagogical content knowledge (TPCK). *Computers & Education, 52*, 154–168.

Barton, R., & Haydn, T. (2006). Trainee teachers' views on what helps them to use information and communication technology effectively in their subject teaching. *Journal of Computer Assisted Learning, 22*, 257–272.

Bean, J. C. (2011). *Engaging ideas: The professor's guide to integrating writing critical thinking and active-learning in the classroom* (2nd ed.). San Francisco, CA: Jossey-Bass.

Bloom, B. (1956). *Taxonomy of educational objectives, handbook 1: The cognitive domain.* New York, NY: David McKay & Company.

Bonwell, C. C., & Eison, J. A. (1991). *Active learning: Creating excitement in the classroom.* ASHE-ERIC Higher Education Report No. 1. George Washington University. School of Education and Human Development, Washington, DC.

Braxton, J. M., Milem, J. F., & Sullivan, A. S. (2000). The influence of active learning on the college student departure process: Toward a revision of Tinto's theory. *The Journal of Higher Education, 71*(5), 669–690.

Browne, N. M., & Freeman, K. (2000). Distinguishing features of critical thinking classrooms. *Teaching in Higher Education, 5*(3), 301–309. doi:10.1080/713699143

Brush, T., Glazewski, K., Rutowski, K., Berg, K., Stromfors, C., Van-Nest, M. H., et al. (2003). Integrating technology into a field-based teacher training program: The PT3@ASU project. *Educational Technology Research and Development, 51*, 57–72.

Crouch, C. H., & Mazur, E. (2001). Peer instruction: Ten years of experience and results. *American Journal of Physics, 69*, 970–976.

Crowder, N. A. (1959). Automatic tutoring by means of intrinsic programming. In *Automatic teaching: The state of the art* (pp. 109–116). New York, NY: Wiley.

Deslauriers, L., Schelew, E., & Wieman, C. (2011). Improved learning in a large-enrollment physics class. *Science, 332*, 862–864.

Dochy, F., Sergers, M., Van den Bossche, P., & Gijbels, D. (2003). Effects of problem-based learning: A meta analysis. *Learning and Instruction, 13*, 533–568.

Dodge, B. (2002). *WebQuest taskonomy: A taxonomy of tasks. [Website].* Retrieved from http://webquest.org/sdsu/taskonomy.html

Dougherty, R. C., Bower, C. W., Berger, T., Rees, W., Mellon, E. K., & Pulliam, E. (1995). Cooperative learning and enhanced communication: Effects on student performance, retention, and attitudes in general chemistry. *Journal of Chemical Education, 72,* 793–797.

Drent, M., & Meelissen, M. (2008). Which factors obstruct or stimulate teacher educators to use ICT innovatively? *Computers & Education, 51,* 187–199.

Goktas, Y., Yıldırım, Z., & Yıldırım, S. (2008). A review of ICT related courses in pre-service teacher education programs. *Asia Pacific Education Review, 9,* 168–179.

Goktas, Y., Yildirim, S., & Yildirim, Z. (2009). Main barriers and possible enablers of ICTs integration into pre-service teacher education programs. *Educational Technology & Society, 12*(1), 193–204.

Haak, D. C., Hillerislambers, J., Pitre, E., & Freeman, S. (2011). Increased structure and active learning reduce the achievement gap in introductory biology. *Science, 332,* 1213–1216.

Hake, R. R. (1998). *Interactive engagement methods in introductory physics mechanics courses.* Retrieved from http://www.physics.indiana.edu/~sdi/IEM-2b.pdf

Halonen, J. S., Brown-Anderson, F., & McKeachie, W. J. (2002). Teaching thinking. In W. J. McKeachie (Ed.), *McKeachie's teaching tips: Strategies, research, and theory for college and university teachers* (11th ed., pp. 284–290). Boston, MA: Houghton-Mifflin.

Hsieh, C. (2013). Active learning: Review of evidence and examples. In T. Y. Shiang, W. H. Ho, C. F. Huang, & C. L. Tsai (Eds.), *Scientific proceedings of the 31st international society of biomechanics in sports* (pp. 77–82). Taipei, Taiwan: National Taiwan Normal University.

Johnson, D. W., Johnson, R. T., & Smith, K. A. (1998). *Active learning: Cooperation in the college classroom* (2nd ed.). Edina, MN: Interaction Book Co.

Lavonen, J., Lattu, M., Juuti, K., & Meisalo, V. (2006). Strategy-based development of teacher educators' ICT competence through a co-operative staff development project. *European Journal of Teacher Education, 29*(2), 241–265.

Lumpe, A. T., & Staver, J. R. (1995). Peer collaboration and concept development: Learning about photosynthesis. *Journal of Research in Science Teaching, 3,* 71–98.

Meyers, C. (1986). *Teaching student to think critically: A guide for faculty in all disciplines.* San Francisco, CA: Jossey-Bass.

Meyers, C., & Jones, B. T. (1993). *Promoting active learning* (1st ed.). San Francisco, CA: Jossey-Bass.

Michael, J. (2006). Where's the evidence that active learning works? *Advances in Physiology Education, 30,* 159–167.

Naiz, M., Aguilera, D., Maza, A., & Liendo, G. (2002). Arguments, contradictions, resistances, and conceptual change in students' understanding of atomic structure. *Science Education, 86,* 505–525.

Nehm, R. H., & Reilly, L. (2007). Biology majors' knowledge and misconceptions of natural selection. *BioScience, 57,* 263–272.

Novak, J. D. (2010). *Learning, creating, and using knowledge: Concept maps as facilitative tools in schools and corporations* (2nd ed.). New York, NY: Routledge. ISBN 9780415991858.

O'Reilly, D. (2003). Making information and communications technology work. *Technology, Pedagogy and Education, 12*(3), 417−446.

Ottenbreit-Leftwich, A., Glazewski, K., Newby, T., & Ertmer, P. (2010). Teacher value beliefs associated with using technology: Addressing professional and student needs. *Computers & Education, 55,* 1321−1335.

Polly, D., Mims, C., Shepherd, C. E., & Inan, F. (2010). Evidence of impact: Transforming teacher education with preparing tomorrow's teachers to teach with technology (PT3) grants. *Teaching and Teacher Education, 26,* 863−870.

Prince, M. (2004). Does active learning work? A review of the research. *Journal of Engineering Education, 93*(3), 223−231.

Puentedura, R. R. (2013). *SAMR: Moving from enhancement to transformation [Web log post].* Retrieved from http://www.hippasus.com/rrpweblog/archives/000095.html

Rohlíková, L., Vejvodová, J., Rohlík, O., & Prade, M. (2016). *Kolo iPadagogiky V4.1.* [Czech translation of Carrington, A. Padagogy Wheel V4.1] (2015). Retrieved from bit.ly/PWposterCZEHD.

Roselli, R. J., & Brophy, S. P. (2006). Effectiveness of challenge-based instruction in biomechanics. *Journal of Engineering Education, 95*(4), 311−324.

Sahin, T. Y. (2003). Student teachers' perceptions of instructional technology: Developing materials based on a constructivist approach. *British Journal of Educational Technology, 34*(1), 67−74.

Sang, G., Valcke, M., van Braak, J., & Tondeur, J. (2010). Student teachers' thinking processes and ICT integration: Predictors of prospective teaching behaviors with educational technology. *Computers & Education, 54,* 103−112.

Silberman, M. L. (1996). *Active learning: 101 strategies to teach any subject.* Boston, MA: Allyn and Bacon.

So, H., & Kim, B. (2009). Learning about problem based learning: Student teachers integrating technology, pedagogy and content knowledge. *Australasian Journal of Educational Technology, 25*(1), 101−116.

Tearle, P., & Golder, G. (2008). The use of ICT in the teaching and learning of physical education in compulsory education: How do we prepare the workforce of the future? *European Journal of Teacher Education, 31*(1), 55−72.

Tondeur, J., van Braak, J., Sang, G., Voogt, J., Fisser, P., & Ottenbreit-Leftwich, A. (2011). Preparing pre-service teachers to integrate technology in education: A synthesis of qualitative evidence. *Computers & Education, 59,* 134−144.

Wiggins, G., & McTighe, J. (1998). *Understanding by design.* Alexandria, VA: Association for Supervision and Curriculum Development.

Wilke, R. R., & Straits, W. J. (2001). The effects of discovery learning in a lower-division biology course. *Advances in Physiology Education, 25,* 62−69.

Yoshida, H. (2016). Effects of active learning for curriculum management: With focus on the "Courses of Study" of Japan. *International Journal of Knowledge Engineering, 2*(2), 77−84.

Chapter 10

Intercultural Talent Management Model and its Application as an Active Teaching and Learning Strategy. Preservice Teachers in a New Time and Space Dimension: Virtuality

Eileen Sepúlveda-Valenzuela[★]*, Marcelo Careaga Butter and María Graciela Badilla-Quintana*

Abstract

To apply effective teaching and learning strategies, it is essential to understand the complexity of human groups, especially in educational contexts. To look for the relationship between the contributions that people make, it is critical to understand the singularities of cultures when developing innovations and to foster leadership in education. This chapter presents an experience developed in Higher Education in Chile focused on the ability of preservice teachers to enhance the development of individual talents as an active teaching and learning strategy to create a society made up of integrally developed people in educational contexts. In addition, we use virtual learning environments as a vehicle to connect students between physical and virtual boundaries. This strategy is based on the

[★]I (Eileen) dedicate this chapter to my special people whose voices I brought with me because they have shaped my life. Especially to my friend David Eduardo Vidal Iluffi who passed away very young, I will miss you always. Thank you forever.

**Active Learning Strategies in Higher Education: Teaching for Leadership,
Innovation, and Creativity, 247–272**
Copyright © 2018 by Emerald Publishing Limited
ISBN: 978-1-78714-488-0

Talent Management Model which was implemented in intercultural primary schools by professors and preservice teachers from the south of Chile. The *virtuality* dimension promoted the detection of individual traits of students and contributed to the development of a cultural identity. Additionally, it offered theoretical and practical knowledge that implied an innovation in the training of future teachers.

Keywords: Preservice teachers; virtuality; higher education; interculturalism; talent management; teaching and learning strategies

Introduction

Teaching and learning strategies have been researched in depth for an extended period in order to improve the educational system in different countries (Cousin, 2009; Davis, 1993; Díaz & Solar, 2011; Melrose & Bergeron, 2007; Winebrenner, 2001). Most of them are characterized by covering specific education areas and/or subjects. Other ones also consider different cognitive processes (Chi & Wylie, 2014; Gardner, 1995; Halpern, 1994; Huba & Freed, 2000; Jones, 1987; Riding & Rayner, 2012). However, current literature shows that there is little practical experience including cultural aspects as well as the cognitive aspects of teaching and learning strategies at different levels of education (Careaga, Sepúlveda, & Badilla, 2015; Ware, 2013). Thus, this chapter presents a novel experience that considers cognition, emotion, culture, and digital literacies in one model to enhance the preservice teacher experience in order to help students by developing their talents and awareness of their cultural identity.

When applying effective teaching and active-learning strategies, it is essential to understand the complexity of human groups to which they are applied. It is necessary to know the contribution of individuals for social identity creation. To look for the relationship between the influences that people make, it is essential to understand the singularities of culture to develop innovations and to foster leadership in education. This chapter analyses how preservice teachers can use the development of individual talents as an active-teaching strategy to create a society made up of integrally developed people in educational contexts, and how virtual learning environments are used as a vehicle to move students between physical and virtual boundaries.

This strategy is based on the Talent Management Model (Careaga et al., 2015) which was implemented in intercultural primary schools with the help of teachers and preservice teachers to detect individual traits of students and contribute to the development of the cultural identity of a human group. A network was created to foster the talents of primary students by using the Talent Management Model as the central teaching and active-learning strategy. Participants were university teachers and some of their Master's students taking the role of research assistants and virtual tutors, who belong to a university located in Chile.

Preservice teachers fulfilled the role of virtual tutors, supporting the students of intercultural schools, developing the functions of pedagogical, technological, social, and management support, which may allow future educators to visualize the extension of the traditional role of the teacher toward the diversity and complementarity of face-to-face and virtual roles that a two-dimensional (face + virtual) teacher should perform, prefiguring a more postmodern educational paradigm.

An advantage of this teaching and learning strategy is that it allows one to analyze the contribution and to understand the complexity of how human groups are formed. It is necessary to research in depth how individuals contribute to society at different schools' levels. A person is characterized by being unique and one of a kind. Vygotsky (1978) states that the human essence is not something abstract and inherent in everyone, it exists in her/his reality and is formed by the set of social relationships made by the person. Knowledge, values, customs, the sense of life, and traditions revolve around the social aspects and a person's human, spiritual, and professional development. This formation is achieved through her/his maximum expression when she/he interacts with another according to the sociocultural tendencies.

It is noteworthy that human talents are expressions conceived by society and culture and emotions that come with people's interactions in a sociocultural environment as Vygotsky (1978) proposed in the idea above. Talents are born from each individual with their values, customs, and traditions and then socialized when there is communication with other people. It is hard to identify a talent individually, and it is still not transferred without an audience or society with whom to share it. Jericó (2001) argues that talent should be based on skills, commitment, and action. It is not just innate because it is possibly developed. We understand that talent does not just come from the intellectual quotient, the quality of schools, and from a person's standard of living. Talent also comes with several other requirements, such as motivation, tools, knowledge, and the generation of new habits. It may be considered a concept closely related to the full development of individuals as unique and one of a kind and grows through contact with society.

In the same argumentative line, Sepúlveda and Careaga (2015) consider that talent is a higher emotional, intellectual, practical, and/or aesthetic capacity, which characterizes a person who can be identified for standing out above average as an individual and social value. Every talent needs a reciprocal action between two or more individuals. It is not surprising then that talented students need to set up teams to help them to define cultural interactions with others and consider that they contribute to the formation of the social identity of a human group. The way of helping students in this journey is the new teaching and an active-learning strategy that the Talent Management Model implies.

Theoretical Framework Regarding a New Time and Space Dimension: Virtuality

Since the early 1990s, the increased availability of digital technology in the world has profoundly influenced different areas of life, namely education. It has been influenced by a new epistemological paradigm in which information is presented in a faster and more dynamic way. The development of digital technologies has redesigned the relationships between individuals, organizations, and different groups (Careaga et al., 2015).

Access to the Internet has vastly increased. Students now have the information they want to obtain literally at their fingertips. At the same time, globalization, as a cause of cultural transformation, has exposed the unique identities of human groups to a highly dynamic phenomenon (Careaga et al., 2015). In addition, Barnes (2011) indicates "the introduction of new technological tools changes the conceptual understandings we have and the different ways in which we can work" (p. 274). The use of new digital tools has changed the understanding of many skills, which as a group are denominated digital literacies by some authors (Crotty & Farren, 2013; Malcolm, 2014). Thus, as this experience was conducted in physical and virtual space, it is essential to understand the complexities of some concepts linked to the development, improvement, and transference of students' talent. These concepts are *space, time, chronotope, and virtuality*.

The first is the Greek concept of *space*. Plato introduced geometry as the science of space, and Aristotle continued with a theory of space defining it as the sum of all places. The popular and current definition consists of the unlimited or incalculably great three-dimensional realm or expansion which all material objects are located and all events occur. Also, Grünbaum (1973) states that "absolute space, in its own nature, without relation to anything external, remains always similar and immovable, and our senses can determine it by its position to bodies" (p. 3). Now, for example, online spaces are not as similar and immovable as the aforementioned author suggested years ago. Therefore, the concept might be understood depending on the activity a person is performing and it can grow depending on the movement of people or objects.

The second concept is *time*, of which philosophers like Aristotle and Galileo were, of those, first interested. It is known as a measurement that indicates the duration of any aspect and/or action in the world. Nowadays, and thanks to Einstein's Theory of Relativity, it is considered that time is relative and dependent on other variables like space. Time can order the events on an axis that refers to the past, the present, and the future, also known as a timeline. Berkeley, an Irish philosopher of the 1700s, believed that time and space were illusions, an idea that the philosopher Johnson refuted. Then, Newton and Einstein "believed that the absolute time, that is, in the ability to measure unambiguously the intervals of time between events, and that these would match by being measured by someone, just if they used a good clock" (p. 34). Years later, Hawking (1988) defines space-time as "the four-dimensional space whose points are events" (p. 104).

The concepts of time and space can be very difficult to describe. Nowadays, time is still measured with the clock being the reference point of everyday activity. Besides, spatiality and temporality are related to actions or material processes. We experience space and time as we construct them (Timmis & Williams, 2016). These concepts are closely related to talent since they are developed in specific formal and informal educational space and time. So we consider, how teachers provoked and prepared these activities in specific classroom space-time to manage and promote students' talents in formal and informal educational contexts. Students develop skills or activities inside and outside of the school. So, space is spread everywhere and can be developed over time by different movements and transitions.

Another concept, related with the two defined before, is *chronotope*. In Greek, chronos means time, and topos mean space. According to Timmis and Williams (2016), they are characterized in learning across contexts, primarily as movements through both space and time. The Theory of Chronotope, developed by Bakhtin (1981), states that the spatial and temporal frames of a narrative are tightly integrated (space as a trace of time and time as a marker of space) and make up one unique *spatial-temporal* frame (chronotope) (Lorino, 2008). It was developed as a category to understand the world and is linked with matter and its movement (Bemong et al., 2010).

By exploring this concept, Timmis and Williams (2016) state "chronotopes, therefore, act as resources for mobilizing human agency. Digital learning environments afford distinct chronotopes that can both stabilize and reconfigure time and space" (p. 8). Since the introduction of this concept into education, the underlying assumptions are how to relate the concept of talent and to develop a better model to identify it. It is also possible to assume that the management and transfer of the talents of the students is essential for the conformation of their social and cultural identity. It is clear that chronotopes give clues about how to manage educational and social changes (Rajala, Hilppö, Lipponen, & Kumpulainen, 2013; Timmis & Williams, 2016; Eijck & Roth, 2010). However, the critical issue is how to fill the gap between the theoretical and practical aspects in applying the talent management model in promoting students' awareness of their actions and identities.

Another related element is *virtuality*, a concept that is involved in many spaces of everyday life (for example: in virtual libraries, virtual campus, virtual clouds, virtual radio, virtual friends, virtual games, etc.). However, virtuality's origin is much older. Centuries ago authors discussed that it was Aristotle who introduced the term *virtual* as a synonym for *potential* (Welsch, 2000). Virtual accentuated the potential's driving force to become actual; it was equivalent to emanating from the force of a thing, designating an active, not just a passive potentiality. This approximation means that the virtual is subordinate to the original feature of the real. The two main forms are immutable and separated from each other.

In addition, González (2005) argues that the definition of *virtual* is significant bases for understanding discourse about the communication technologies and the joints of time and space that they express as well as the forms of social organization as the community. The understanding of virtuality as a concept that constitutes a category to think about social and communicational areas helps us in the analysis of students' talents obtained by intercultural dialogue. The critical point is to argue that something virtual is real, and it is not the copy of something real. To solve this problem, it is vital to incorporate the chronotopes' movements to help with understanding.

Moreover, Castells (1997) considers communication relationships that occur in cyberspace as a possibility to incorporate the notion of bidimensional identity, referred to the space of places and the space of flows. Thus, the human performances occur in two spaces: the concrete world of objects and the digital world of virtuality which form a new category of knowledge (the fifth dimension of virtual epistemology). It is in this new dimension that human groups, from their unique cultural identity, are linked to the human-scale culture expressed in the global village (McLuhan, 1989).

The constant updating of technologies has implied that human intelligence needs to coexist and work with the artificial intelligence that comes from machines. For example, people can give orders to a computer (through a click); children can press a button to play video games, and pilots can control machines to fly a plane. Regarding these relationships, Careaga and Avendaño (2017) created a new concept that defines these people as the Homocybernetics. They argue that these people develop a cyber-intuitive consciousness. This means that they can interact easily with technology and virtual environments by having a cybernetic intelligence. However, it is also important that homocybernetics learn how to develop digital literacies.

Moreover, the development of smart cellphones enables people to develop all the aforementioned characteristics. These artefacts allow instant messaging to support both social and educational communications. Timmis (2011) states "instant messaging conversations offer a means of sustainable peer support for people and students by demonstrating how they emerge from everyday practices" (p. 1). The digital technology spread around the world by different machines causes a new representation of social relationships and new ways to manage the information that they offer. In the cultural transition that leads to postmodernism, access and representation of information have experienced profound changes that guide how to create and transfer new knowledge (Careaga & Avendaño, 2017).

This new epistemological phenomenon directly impacts students who are educated in conventional schools and universities. Every student at any level is challenged to develop new skills, abilities, and talents to meet the requirements of a society in which there are peculiarities of groups within a global culture. Virtual Epistemology guides the ways of teaching and learning, when traditional classrooms are complemented using ICT. In this context, the limitations of time and space are overcome by the exposure of teachers and students to the new dynamics of the Fifth postmodern dimension, virtuality. What is important is that new teachers learn to distinguish the existing epistemological boundary between information management and knowledge management.

Learning becomes more active when teachers and students can participate in networks of knowledge managers, using technologies as effective
means to transfer the result of their learning as a contribution to the
formation of knowledge understood as social capital, not only as an
opportunistic use of information that is reprocessed without contributing knowledge as added value.

Digital technologies have allowed and encouraged globalization and
ease of human relationships between people from nearby places and dis-
tant countries. The Theory of Six Degrees of Separation by Karinthy
(1929) declares what has been mentioned above. It states that all people
on the planet are connected to any other person through a chain of
acquaintances that has no more than six intermediaries (Careaga &
Avendaño, 2017). Social Networks such as Facebook, Twitter,
Instagram, YouTube, Myspace, among others enable the connection
between people and break geographical and time barriers. Social, educational, and cultural relationships may be based on the number of clicks
that a person makes.

Similarly, it is important to revise the concept of *social identity*.
Tajfel (1978) defines the term as "that part of the individual's self-
concept which derives from the knowledge of belonging to social
groups, link with the significant value given for that membership"
(p. 68). Social identity is formed by the image of an individual which
comes indirectly from the society to which she/he belongs. In the same
argumentative line, Timmis and Williams (2016) point out that "identities are constructed through our encounters with different figured
worlds and they can be either figurative or positional" (p. 3). Figured
worlds are related to the person's mental map of the world. Every person possesses their world according to their unique background, experiences, and contexts. It is formed by the social and cultural activities of
people.

Everyone lives and acts based on their convictions and their world.
People act according to their perceptions and beliefs of the world
because they create an internal representation of what they are living.
This representation can be observed through actions and language. The
task of preservice teachers and teachers is not only to didactically feed
the learning environment of their students but also to promote interaction with other environments and other remote students so that together
they manage information and their knowledge, forming mixed spaces of
learning, in which virtual learning complements face-to-face learning. It
is to broaden their view of the world, to help them make their dreams
reality, to provide new experiences and new contexts of learning, to

show a set of talents around the world, and to increase their ability to make thoughtful choices in life.

Talents are detectable and transferable. The former characteristic has great potential to contribute to an individual and to a social identity, whereas digital technologies in different time and spaces can help to promote the transmission and movements of information from one place to another.

Research Background

Taking into consideration the proposed framework about virtuality as a new time and space dimension, and reflecting on the implications in education, we considered essential that universities can prepare their students to be able to incorporate digital technologies into their practices and to understand the transcendence of the concepts of virtuality that were mentioned. Universities in theory and practice, especially in teacher training, might assume this challenge. On one hand, the training itineraries should be able to develop the acquisition of 21st-century digital skills, but also, they might be updated continually in their practices to fulfill the proposed standards (Fuentes & Badilla, 2017). In the same line, as mentioned by De Pablos (2010), incorporating technologies in the educational field demands changes in teacher training programs.

One example is the Chilean case study where the government has developed a set of strategies to promote these challenges, such as the creation of the Digital Agenda 2020, which defines the next steps to achieve an inclusive and sustainable development policy through Information and Communication Technologies (ICT) (Gobierno de Chile, 2017). In education, there are other initiatives on a similar path: (1) the definition of ICT Skills for Learning (HTPA in Spanish [Habilidades TIC para el Aprendizaje]), (2) the definition of ICT standards, and (3) the Performance Agreements. First, the HTPA is the ability to solve problems of information, communication, and knowledge as well as legal, social, and ethical dilemmas in a Digital environment (MINEDUC, 2012). Second, ICT standards imply the use of systems and tools to interact and improve or renew the curricula, generating instances for students' reflection as well as their teaching practice reflection (MINEDUC, 2010). Finally, Performance agreements are contracts between State and the higher education institutions to commit notable performances that imply significant improvement in their educational goals.

Most of these projects, or Institutional Improvement Plans, include an ICT orientation with goals to improve the training of teachers. The schools of Education work through landmarks or strategies including curriculum updates or renewal, provision of ICT infrastructure, upgrade and acquisition of software and technical advice, and others.

In addition, the Enlaces network – Education and Technology Center from the Ministry of Education – and the faculties of education from 16 universities in Chile have meetings each month (in the Initial Teacher Training Table) to support and to create initiatives of collaborative and cooperative work concerning how to incorporate digital technologies in the teachers' training (Enlaces, 2015). A good example is the ICT Observatory in Initial Teacher Training (ITT), a public and national reference on resources and experiences for the inclusion of technology in teacher training, used and nourished by all educational centers and faculties in the country (Observatorio TIC en FID, N/D). However, despite efforts that are achieved effectively through the implementation of public policies, Sancho (2012) emphasizes the existence of a significant difference between what is meant to be made concrete in the policy and what really happens in the classroom. Observing a policy implementation gap that needs to be solved.

More recently, the OECD (2015) published that less than 40% of teachers across the Teaching and Learning International Survey (TALIS) countries report using ICT as a regular part of their teaching practice, and they reveal that the use of technologies in initial teacher training is low (OECD, 2009). This is confirmed by Fuentes and Badilla (2017) who analyzed the ICT courses of the formative itineraries of the Initial Teacher Training programs by 21 universities in Chile. The analysis showed that on average there are four programs in each university that include ICTs in their curriculum. The mode is one course per program, which is taught during the first three years. This research reflects that the technology is present in Chilean universities' curriculum, because they have incorporated this topic as a subject but not as a transversal skill throughout the preparation of future teachers. It is vital to rethink this kind of integration because future teachers need to be prepared for teaching digital literacies to new generations. It is not just a matter of how to manage different software and programs; they have to be literate in the new digital world.

These antecedents may justify the lack of concrete experience of future teachers by how they use and replicate these strategies in their professional development and how they use the tools that today are habitual for contemporary students.

An Active Teaching and Learning Strategy through an Intercultural Model

The Model of Talent Management for Interculturalism (Sepúlveda & Careaga, 2015) is to be described in this chapter as a new strategy for learning and teaching oriented toward the development of talent in a face-to-face and in virtual context (see Figure 1). This model was informed by the theoretical framework described previously. It aims to allow the diagnosis and characterization of talent in intercultural contexts. With digital support, the model establishes the type of interactions between local intercultural contexts and remote links with other geographically distributed cultural backgrounds. The elements of the model consider a cyclical dynamic that repeats itself depending on the interest and communication capacity of cultural agents and their motivation to communicate their talents and search for convergence of common interests to build an intercultural dialogue. As Careaga et al. (2015) explicitly propose, it has six elements: the talent recognition from the cultural singularities, the talent identification, the talent selection, the talent stimulation, the control and monitoring in learning contexts, and the new

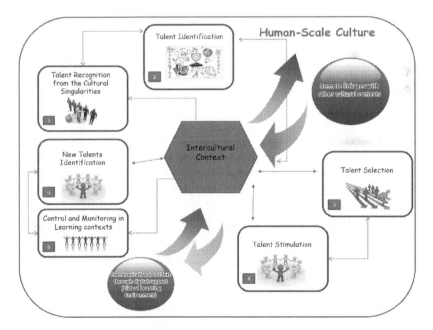

Figure 1.   Talent Management Model. *Source*: Authors' creation.

talents identification. Besides, this strategy contemplates the participation of primary students, preservice teachers as virtual tutors, as well as primary and university teachers to develop its phases.

The benefits that preservice teachers can obtain from the implementation of this strategy are varied. First, the strategy breaks the geographic barriers between rural schools that are located in remote geographic zones, and preservice teachers that can help primary students from the University's computer lab or their houses just by using their laptop, iPad, or cellphones. Second, a preservice teacher can help primary school teachers by the online monitoring of the interactions of students, which enables them to be in a real educational context. Third, this strategy stimulates undergraduate students' motivation to work with innovative digital tools and breaks the routine and the context of traditional face-to-face classrooms. Fourth, it allows students to recognize their mistakes as huge learning opportunities because through technology, they have the possibility to give feedback to primary students as many times as they can. Also, it is important to notice that preservice teachers did not receive credits or a grade for their interventions in this experience, so it was mostly viewed as an opportunity to learn and teach new strategies for their future as teachers. Fifth, it allows thinking about and reflecting on the importance of student diversity in a classroom and fosters intercultural dialogue to prepare primary students for the modern and diverse world. Sixth, it allows preservice teachers to be aware of the cultural phenomenon that is present in intercultural educational contexts, such as enculturation, acculturation, and transculturation, which are briefly described to understand the benefits of the Talent Model. Enculturation is understood as the transmission of cultural traits through generations of people (Careaga et al., 2015; Sepúlveda, 2015). Acculturation is the loss of cultural traits (Piñones & Valenzuela, 2016; Sepúlveda, 2015; Zagefka, González, & Brown, 2011). And transculturation is to receive, to adopt, and to transform cultural traits from other cultures (Careaga et al., 2015; Pozo, 2014; Sepúlveda, 2015).

The proposed Talent Management Model has six components. The first one is talent diagnosis which consists of detecting cultural agents who possess intellectual, practical, aesthetic, and/or emotional talents. The second one is the identification of talent for interculturalism which aims to identify talents that have the potential of intercultural dialogue. Third, talent selection for knowledge management which consists of choosing talents with potential for intercultural dialogue that can be systematized in the digital context and selected. Fourth, the talent stimulation that aims to recognize individual talent as a constituent element of cultural identity, understanding it as a unique contribution of the subject to the definition of group identity. Fifth, control and monitoring which are the actions that allow the detection of the communication development of the centers of interest formed around the management of talent. Sixth, the identification of new talents which consist of identifying talents that emerge because of the management of intercultural knowledge (Careaga et al., 2015).

This model is presented as a teaching and learning strategy to generate dialogue and knowledge using digital technologies and digital learning environments. In such relationships, globalization exposes the unique identities of human groups to be observed and analyzed. The loss of cultural traits occurs unconsciously many times as an automatic process (Sepúlveda & Careaga, 2015; Sobrevilla, 2001).

Deepening in cultural aspects, these processes are clearly present in the learning process associated with talent management of students in an intercultural context. However, they are not explicitly incorporated into the official curriculum reflected in the Chilean plans and programs, being evidenced as a real need to consider and educate teachers to be able to identify and manage them in favor of the country's culture.

The intercultural dialogue is born from the interactions in the virtual learning community based on the Talent Management Model and is very useful to identify, promote, and socialize the talents of students. In this sense, Jericó (2001) claims "one of the natural laws of talent is that this gets the best results through interaction. If the organisation facilitates interaction, it will act as a multiplier effect" (p. 32). Although the author talked in a company context, it is a fully replicable and favorable claim in education and allows for the realization of the dream of an integral education. In fact, teachers should teach not only the content included in the curricula but also prepare students for today's world and develop those talents that are the full expression of cognition, emotion, and culture that lay dormant in the students' minds.

Cultural singularities are unique expressions of a community; they are the manifestation of daily life and are made up of contributions from different cultural agents. The current educational demands in the context of globalisztion request talent management to guide teaching practices in intercultural contexts. Careaga and Avendaño (2017) suggest the urgency of moving from encyclopaedic and academic curricular approaches where teaching practices are based on mnemonics as the basis supporting the transfer of knowledge, toward more flexible and holistic approaches to the curriculum, developing pedagogical practices that promote the most divergent and heuristic aspects of human intelligence as our model does.

Talents are essential elements in the cognitive and personal development of students, which shape their cultural identity inside a social group providing differentiating features that give uniqueness to the human group to which they belong. The achievement of the transfer of their culture through their talents is as essential as the use of digital technologies to manage these talents. Thus, it allows them to socialize in order to make their talents transferable to show the current importance of maintaining their culture, feeling proud of their ancestors, creating awareness of their identity, and contributing positively to the process of enculturation.

Preservice Teachers' Teaching and Learning Experience

The experience of preservice teachers as virtual tutors was part of a project named "Virtual learning communities to promote interculturalism by applying teaching models of knowledge and Talent Management," funded by CIECII-MILLENIUM (Center of Education Research in an Indigenous and Intercultural Context) in Chile (see Figure 2). The purpose of this project was to create and implement a network of schools in an intercultural context to develop the students' talents. It was developed in two cities located in the south of Chile between 2013 and 2014.

Regarding technological aspects, a network was implemented in Moodle. This is an open source educational platform that helps teachers and preservice teachers to create and deliver effective online learning environments through the management of courses. To foster active-learning strategies and digital resources, in-service teachers and preservice teachers had access to different virtual settings inside of the platform. The first space was called "Let's go to the schools" which was characterized by having a subspace for each school where primary students were enrolled in and have a password to access it. Inside of this space, preservice teachers could support and foster the proposed activities directed by in-service teachers. They also can chat with students to support their learning overcoming the time and space barriers. In the platform, there was also a "resource centre" formed by pedagogical work spaces that were created to enable collaborative practices between teachers, preservice teachers, and primary students. As well as, to support students' homework through different resources such as learning

Figure 2. The Homepage of the Virtual Learning Environment.

web pages, education software, online games, didactic guides, learning guides, workshop results, laboratory results, homework results, among other learning resources. Another space in the platform was the "Talent management" where students worked around the Talent management model (described in Section 4). Students also posted their favorite leisure activities and cultural activities that they developed in their schools or at home. Those activities were shared with their classmates and students from others schools. Besides, there was also a space called "doubts zone" where participants could interact between them act to solve doubts and collaborate in their different activities. The platform also had chats, different forums, a calendar, and file stores (Careaga, Badilla, & Jimenez, 2014; Careaga et al., 2015).

One of the objectives of the network was to foster the talents of primary students by using the Talent Management Model as the central teaching and learning strategy. University teachers and some of their Master's students taking the role of research assistants and virtual tutors, who belong to a university located in Concepción in the Biobío Region, created this network. Participants of this network were: 6 preservice teachers from 2 universities from the south of Chile, and 8 primary school teachers of 6 schools in Temuco and Cañete and their students.

Participating schools were located in Temuco city ($n = 3$) and Cañete city ($n = 3$). These schools are rural schools, and they were purposely selected since their key features were having a high number of students belonging to the Mapuche[1] ethnic group and their educational curricula is focused, in some aspects, on rescuing and appreciating their culture. The census of the population carried out in 2012 reflects that 9.9% of the Chilean population is Mapuche. Most are located in the Araucanía region, Biobío region, Los Lagos region, and Metropolitan region (CASEN, 2013). González, Gerber, and Carvacho (2016) suggest that most Mapuche people are poor and have lower levels of education. Their culture and education are concentrated in their worldviews. Education is centered on the core elements of their Cosmo vision as spirituality and love for nature, which is transmitted from generation to generation. Quilaqueo, Quintriqueo, and Torres (2016) advise that education may consider the Mapuches' human, social, and cultural conceptions based on the relation between human−nature−spirituality.

As the central purpose of this chapter is to expose the experiences of undergraduate students in this new learning and teaching strategy, we are going to describe the virtual learning community and the students' role in it. Sepúlveda (2015) describes a virtual learning environment as a virtual place where regular curricula can be adapted to each student's needs and allow for the development of autonomy in the teaching-learning process.

These virtual environments were carefully planned following the pedagogical, curricular, management, and technological issues proposed by the Incremental Prototyping Model. Besides, the platform was created in a user-friendly format allowing students and teachers to navigate it easily. The Incremental Prototyping Model is based on an engineering methodology based on the design process which is based on four circuits: theoretical, pedagogical, technological, and management. The idea is to collect the contributions of users and experts about the design of a platform, which ensures the quality and usability of a platform for specific educational purposes (Careaga, Badilla, & Sepúlveda, 2014).

Preservice teachers were educated in a two-day workshop about the philosophical, practical, and ethical issues of the virtual learning environment and the application of the Talent Management Model in an intercultural context. That training was essential to know the different spaces of the platform, the understanding of the new dimension of virtuality that breaks the conventional notions of space and time, as well as the

---

[1]An ethnic Chilean group.

fundamental elements of the model and the school´s context, which was ethnically diverse. Then, they were educated about the role of being a virtual tutor in this context. Following the proposal of Garrison and Anderson (2005) and Salmon (2000), a good virtual tutor might develop coherence and understanding of four main areas: the pedagogical, the technological, the management, and the social. Thus, workshops were conducted to support preservice teachers in the understanding the four primary functions mentioned above. At the same time, it is important to consider the overlapping elements that this strategy encompassed and how preservice teachers were able to manage the presence of social, cognitive, teaching, and talents elements (Akyola, Garrison, & Ozdena, 2009).

Preservice teachers supported the schools' students and educators in a variety of additional tasks aiming to achieve the development of students' talents. Good examples are: the students' homework, the technological use of the platform and how they surf the Internet (e.g. how to log in and log out), as well as how they upload and share documents (Word files, photographs, and videos). Additionally, tasks included the kind of communication they had with students from different schools and the orthography, spelling, and punctuation of their messages. Additionally, tutors taught the schools' teachers how to supervise students, how to communicate with them through the forums and chats, and how to use the platform to support curricular contents.

Results of Talent Model's Application as an Active Teaching and Learning Strategy

During the project development, there were different stages of the data collection process. It includes a satisfaction survey, interview, and a register grid observation. These instruments were applied to preservice teachers, teachers, and primary students.

The activities developed in the virtual platform during 2012 and 2013 were classified per the type and number of comments. Reports show a total of 6,760 income from participating schools. The results indicate that 82% of the actions correspond to the category of access to information and access to relevant sources, while only 18% corresponds to actions related to knowledge management. The publications of the students are considered mostly as general and not necessarily cultural type since they identify comments related to talents (sports activities, music, cooking, drawing, and painting). There is a significant participation of the online community with similar interests, who make comments or contributions, what in words of Careaga and Avendaño (2017), is denominated like the representation of the information.

The satisfaction surveys applied at the end of the project revealed on one side that preservice teachers valued this new way of teaching and learning, which trains them to be teachers with a variety of tools and strategies for a new type of school combining two dimensions: time and space. On the other side, this experience allowed them to work in local and global cultures, enriching their personal and professional backgrounds. For example, preservice teachers work with the Mapuche legacy, as well as in a socioculturally diverse classroom (physical space) by using new communication strategies in generating an intercultural dialogue which prefigures a new educational paradigm based on physical and virtual spaces in different times. In this kind of experience, cultural singularities are linked to intercultural contexts and culture on a human scale by the using of ICT that enable students to transit between different spaces and time.

Regarding preservice teachers, Vergara and Careaga (2014) display the results of the in-service teachers' interviews which showed that it is good to include new technologies in this type of school because children do not have access to it in their homes, so the fact that the school offers them is good for them, as it can be seen in the following example:

> The children see that there are other students like them in other parts of the region and they knew it by the platform. They could never do it because they never leave this place or very few do it[2] (p. 101).

Interviews also showed that the main difficulty in fulfilling the activities is the problem related to the Internet connection, as can be seen in the following quote.

> We have help from the Chilean ministry but the companies do not have antennas ... we are very far from the urban centre[3] (p. 101).

---

[2] Authors' translation from the original in Spanish: Los niños ven que hay otros estudiantes como ellos en otras partes de la región y lo sabían por la plataforma. Nunca podrían hacerlo porque nunca salen de este lugar o muy pocos lo hacen.

[3] Authors' translation from the original in Spanish: "Tenemos ayuda del Ministerio (de Educación), pero las empresas no tienen antenas... estamos muy lejos del centro urbano"

Regarding primary students, Careaga et al. (2015) states that primary students like this learning strategy because it enables them to interact with people of other cultures and schools. Also, they learn more about customs and culture, they know more, it is fun, they make friends, and create new things. Besides, students are not confused when interacting with students from other cultures. They consider it as a learning opportunity and feel comfortable interacting and sharing talents with students from other cultures.

Also, the results reported by Bennasi and Careaga (2014) in interviews applied to primary students showed that students' focus was on the development of their activities and comments in the category of access to information, with little evidence of activity in the category of management knowledge. Besides, 100% of the students indicate that through the platform they can share their cultural values with others and that they notice that there is respect for the culture of other members (referring to children from all participating schools).

To sum up, preservice teachers developed all these skills as a benefit to the formal professional training at their universities. They acquired theoretical and practical knowledge of how to incorporate digital technologies into the educational curricula as well as how to develop students' talent in an intercultural context. They learned how to transform common spaces and time using the new dimension virtuality, which breaks geographical spaces and time. In addition, they learned how to support primary students from diverse contexts and most of them from rural geographic zones with a high indigenous population. Preservice teachers were essential in this project since they provided the forums with feedback to students who were enthusiastic about communicating with people from different places. Therefore, the practice of these four functions, designed for a pedagogy focused on students' talents in intercultural contexts, implied innovation in the training of future teachers, since the current curricula do not consider these kinds of teaching and learning strategies.

Conclusions

In recent years, there has been numerous research on how to implement the use of technology in educational contexts (Badilla, Vera, & Lytras, 2017; Christensen & Knezek, 2017; Prats, Simon, & Ojando, 2017; Schremm, Hed, Horne, & Roll, 2017). The initiatives are linked to the design, development, implementation, and evaluation of learning experiences enriched using digital devices and research projects. These activities emphasize using technology to think, create, and invent rather than just using them as productivity tools. A good example of these is the research conducted by Jacobsen and Lock (2004) who describe initiatives related to inquiry-based learning supported by technologies for education students. The purpose of these activities was to promote closer connections between university work and field research experiences by cultivating collaborative relationships with college professors, classroom teachers, and preservices students. In this context, these experiences are similar to the nature of the strategy presented in this chapter. The difference is related to the experiences in intercultural contexts because these actions enabled future educators to real pedagogical challenges linked to processes of transculturation (cultural transfer), acculturation (loss of Cultural identity), and enculturation (reaffirmation of one's identity), which are not explicit in the objectives or the methodological strategies of the formal curricula, neither in the university or K12 curricula.

In this vein, the Talent management model is a new educational strategy used to link individual contributions to the configuration of the collective identity of a human group. This strategy fosters teachers' and students' understanding and reinforces the idea that they are cultural and social agents, that through their talents, they can contribute to the development of culture and make the world better. Moreover, this model enables the development of a bidimensional identity that characterizes the postmodern cultural transition through the creation of distributed learning spaces such as the virtual learning environment that allows students to communicate with different geographical spaces and breaks time barriers.

Traditional educational contexts were established in physical spaces and preconfigured timetables that enabled students to learn and teachers to teach just in a specific room and in an exclusive time of the day. These dimensions have been reconfigured with the incorporation of digital tools in human life. Nowadays, we may talk about a new space and time dimension called virtuality that enables educational agents to interact in diverse geographical spaces and in different times. Therefore, teachers and students can participate in different kind of networks to manage knowledge crossing the boundaries of time and space. Learning becomes more active when students can use technologies as effective means to produce, represent, and transfer their knowledge. This knowledge can be considered as social capital constructed by students through their interactions.

Based on this experience, digital technologies are considered as a useful tool to develop and transfer unique characteristics of students through their talents and intercultural dialogue. When future educators favor the management of talents, they have the opportunity to learn how to teach by linking cultural singularities with culture on a human scale. In the students' case, they can learn from their cultural uniqueness and reaffirm their identity through the intercultural interaction with other cultural realities. This model enables the engagement of preservice teachers with the reality of their future jobs and gives them the opportunity to be present without being at the school (physical space) by allowing them to communicate with students at any time.

One of the main limitations evinced in schools was the lack of technological abilities of in-service teachers. In this sense, universities have the invaluable task to educate well-prepared students, who can acquire the digital literacies needed to teach future generations. Preservice teachers are the future teachers of our society, so it is urgent to incorporate new educational and sociocultural strategies for them to teach and learn in diversity including digital technologies. It is also essential to show the value of intercultural dialogue to support their teaching strategies and seed the change that Chilean society needs. As Timmis proposes "it may be possible to foster student agency and empowerment, and the development of knowledge building communities, and to resist the consumer-oriented, passive model of higher education that might otherwise take hold" (2011, p. 14).

Finally, it is relevant to consider more research on the practical and theoretical support of this teaching and learning strategy. In this chapter, an active and integrative point of view was adopted to contribute to the integral education of human beings. However, because it is an integrative approach that makes students become agents with digital and cultural wisdom, its consideration in the formal curricula of Chilean Higher Education is necessary.

Acknowledgments

This chapter has been written with support from the project called "International network of collaboration in research and academic and student mobility between CIECII-Chile and L-KIT, United Kingdom." Also thanks to the support of the National Commission for Scientific and Technological Research, CONICYT, Ministry of Education, Chile, through the Postdoctoral Scholarship Abroad [Becas de Postdoctorado en el Extranjero] Becas Chile, granted to Dr. María Graciela Badilla Quintana (File Number 74160087 at Arizona State University 2016−2018); and Doctorate Scholarship Abroad [Beca de Doctorado en el Extranjero] Becas Chile, granted to Eileen Sepúlveda Valenzuela (at University of Bristol).

References

Akyola, Z., Garrison, R., & Ozdena, Y. (2009). Development of a community of inquiry in online and blended learning contexts. *Procedia − Social and Behavioral Sciences, 1*(1), 1834−1838. doi:10.1016/j.sbspro.2009.01.324

Badilla, M. G., Vera, A., & Lytras, M. (2017). Pre-service teachers' skills and perceptions about the use of virtual learning environments to improve teaching and learning. *Behaviour & Information Technology, 36*(6), 575−588. doi:10.1080/0144929X.2016.1266388

Bakhtin, M. (1981). Forms of time and the chronotope in the novel. In M. Holquist (Ed.), *The dialogic imagination: Four essays* (pp. 84−258). Austin, TX: University of Texas Press, Slavic Series.

Barnes, S. (2011). The complexity of technology use in education: After thoughts. *Nordic Journal of Digital Literacy, 6*(4), 273−277. Retrieved from http://www.idunn.no/dk/2011/04/art05

Bemong, N., Borghart, P., De Dobbeleer, M., Demoen, K., De Temmerman, K., & Keunen, B. (Eds.), (2010). *Bakhtin's theory of the literary chronotope: Reflections, applications, perspectives.* Belgium: Academia Press.

Bennasi, C., & Careaga, M. (2014). Estudio acerca de la aplicación de un Modelo Pedagógico de Gestión del Conocimiento para caracterizar relaciones interculturales en estudiantes de educación básica en contextos mapuches. Unpublished Thesis of Master degree, Universidad Católica de la Santísima Concepción. Concepción, Chile.

Careaga, M., & Avendaño, A. (2017). Currículum Cibernético y Gestión del Conocimiento. *Fundamentos y Modelos de Referencia.* Chile: RIL Editores y Editorial UCSC.

Careaga, M., Badilla, M., & Jimenez, L. (2014). School networks to promote ICT competences among teachers. Case study in intercultural schools. *Computers in Human Behavior, 30*, 442–451. Retrieved from https://doi.org/10.1016/j.chb.2013.06.024

Careaga, M., Badilla, M., & Sepúlveda, E. (2014). Incremental prototyping model for the development of educational platforms: A process of design and quality standards. *Journal of Universal Computer Science, 20*(10), 1407−1417.

Careaga, M., Sepúlveda, E., & Badilla, M. (2015). Intercultural talent management model: Virtual communities to promote collaborative learning in indigenous contexts. Teachers' and students' perceptions. *Computers in Human Behavior, 51*, 1191−1197. doi:10.1016/j.chb.2015.01.030

CASEN. (2013). *Pueblos indígenas Contenidos: PUEBLOS INDÍGENAS.*

Castells, M. (1997). *La era de la Información* (Vol. I, II y III). Madrid: Alianza.

Chi, M. T., & Wylie, R. (2014). The ICAP framework: Linking cognitive engagement to active learning outcomes. *Educational Psychologist, 49*(4), 219–243.

Christensen, R., & Knezek, G. (2017). Readiness for integrating mobile learning in the classroom: Challenges, preferences and possibilities. *Computers in Human Behavior, 76,* 112–121. doi:10.1016/j.chb.2017.07.014

Cousin, G. (2009). *Researching learning in higher education: An introduction to contemporary methods and approaches.* New York, NY: Routledge.

Crotty, Y., & Farren, M. (Eds.). (2013). *Digital literacies in education: Creative, multimodal and innovative practices.* Switzerland: Peter Lang Publishing.

Davis, J. R. (1993). *Better teaching, more learning: Strategies for success in postsecondary settings. American Council on Education Series on Higher Education.* Phoenix: Oryx Press.

De Pablos, J. (2010). Políticas educativas y la integración de las TI, a través de buenas prácticas docentes [Educational policies and the integration of Information Technologies, through good teaching practices]. In J. de Pablos, M. Area, J. Valverde, & J. Correa (Eds.), *Políticas educativas y buenas prácticas con TIC [Educational policies and best practices with ICT]* (pp. 21–41). Barcelona: Graó.

Díaz, C., & Solar, M. (2011). La revelación de las creencias lingüístico-pedagógicas a partir del discurso del profesor de inglés universitario. *RLA. Revista de lingüística teórica y aplicada, 49*(2), 57–86.

Eijck, M., & Roth, W. (2010). Towards a chronotopic theory of 'place' in place-based education. *Cultural Studies of Science Education.* Retrieved from http://link.springer.com/article/10.1007/s11422-010-9278-2

Enlaces. (2015). *Conozca el trabajo de la Mesa de Formación Inicial Docente con TIC (FID-TIC)* [To know the work of the initial teacher training table with ICT]. Retrieved from http://historico.enlaces.cl/index.php?t=44&i=2&cc=1212.218&tm=3

Fuentes, C., & Badilla, M. G. (2017). ICT integration in initial teacher training in Chilean universities. A curricular comparative analysis. Paper presented to 11th annual International Technology, Education and Development Conference, INTED2017. Valencia, Spain.

Gardner, H. (1995). Reflections on multiple intelligences: Myths and messages. *Phi Delta Kappan, 77*(3), 200.

Garrison, D. R., & Anderson, T. (2005). *El e-learning en el siglo XXI: Investigación y práctica [E-learning in the 21st century: Research and practice].* Barcelona: Octaedro.

Gobierno de Chile. (2017). *Agenda Digital 2020.* Retrieved from http://www.agendadigital.gob.cl/#/agenda/que#top-page

González, I. (2005). Internet, virtualidad y comunidad [Internet, virtuality and community]. *Revista de Ciencias Sociales, 2*(108), 55–69.

González, R., Gerber, M., & Carvacho, H. (2016). Social identities and conflict in Chile: The role of historical. In S. McKeown, R. Haji, & N. Ferguson (Eds.), *Understanding peace and conflict through social identity theory.* Switzerland: Springer International Publishing.

Grünbaum, A. (1973). *Philosophical problems of space and time* (Vol. 12). Netherland: Springer Science & Business Media.

Halpern, D. F. (1994). *Changing college classrooms: New teaching and learning strategies for an increasingly complex world.* Jossey-Bass higher and adult education series. Jossey-Bass Inc., San Francisco, CA.

Hawking, S. (1988). *A brief history of time.* New York, NY: Bantam Books.

Huba, E., & Freed, J. E. (2000). *Learner-centered assessment on college campuses: Shifting the focus from teaching to learning.* Allyn and Bacon. Retrieved from https://doi.org/10.1080/713837537

Jacobsen, M., & Lock, J. (2004). Technology and teacher education for a knowledge era: Mentoring for student futures, not our past. *Journal of Technology and Teacher Education, 2*(1), 75–100.

Jericó, P. (2001). *Gestión del Talento [Talent management].* Madrid: Prentice Hall.

Jones, B. F. (1987). *Strategic teaching and learning: Cognitive instruction in the content areas.* Association for Supervision and Curriculum Development, Alexandria, VA.

Karinthy, F. (1929). *Chain-Links.* Retrieved from http://djjr-courses.wdfiles.com/local–files/soc180:karinthy-chain-links/Karinthy-Chain-Links_1929.pdf

Lorino, P. (2008). The Bakhtinian theory of chronotope (spatial-temporal frame) applied to the organizing process. *In conference paper at second international symposium on process organization studies.* Retrieved from http://www.alba.edu.gr/sites/pros/Papers/PROS-022.pdf

Malcolm, I. (2014). The future of digital working: Knowledge migration and learning. *Learning, Media and Technology, 39*(4), 449–467. doi:10.1080/17439884.2014.942667

McLuhan, M. (1989). *La aldea global.* Barcelona: Gedisa.

Melrose, S., & Bergeron, K. (2007). Instructor immediacy strategies to facilitate group work in online graduate study. *Australasian Journal of Educational Technology, 23*(1), 132–148. Retrieved from http://www.ascilite. org.au/ajet/ajet23/melrose.html

MINEDUC. (2010). *Actualización de Competencias y Estándares TIC en la Profesión Docente.* [Update of Competences and ICT Standards in the Teaching Profession]. Retrieved from www.enlaces.uda.cl/Anexos/lmc/libro_competencias_ticok.pdf

MINEDUC. (2012). *Matriz de habilidades TIC para el aprendizaje. Ministerio de Educación.* [Matrix of ICT skills for learning. Ministry of Education]. Retrieved from http://www.enlaces.cl/tp_enlaces/portales/tpe76eb4809f44/uploadImg/File/2015/documentos/HTPA/Matriz-Habilidades-TIC-para-el-Aprendizaje.pdf

Observatorio TIC en FID (n.d.). *Integración de las Tic en la Formación Inicial Docente. ¿Qué es el observatorio TIC en FID?* [Integration of ICT in initial teacher training. What is the ICT observatory in initial teacher trainning?]. Retrieved from http://ticenfid.org

OECD. (2009). *ICT and initial teacher training.* Paris: CERI.

OECD. (2015). Teaching with technology. *Teaching in Focus, 12,* 1–4. doi:10.1787/5jrxnhpp6p8v-en

Piñones, M., & Valenzuela, V. (2016). Being Mapuche today in Chile: Judgement criteria for ethnic identification among the new generation. *Journal of Ethnic and Migration Studies*, 1–17. doi:10.1080/1369183X.2016.1232159

Pozo, G. (2014). ¿Cómo descolonizar el saber? El problema del concepto de inter-culturalidad. Reflexiones para el caso Mapuche [How to decolonize knowledge? The problem of the concept of interculturality. Reflections for the Mapuche case]. *Revista Latinoamericana*, *13*(38), 205–223.

Prats, M., Simon, J., & Ojando, E. (2017). *Diseño y aplicación de la Flipped Classroom. Experiencias y orientaciones en educación primaria y en la formación inicial de maestros.* Barcelona: Grao.

Quilaqueo, D., Quintriqueo, S., & Torres, H. (2016). Características epistémicas de los métodos educativos mapuches [Epistemic characteristics of Mapuche educational methods]. *Revista Electrónica de Investigación Educativa*, *18*(1), 153–165.

Rajala, A., Hilppö, J., Lipponen, L., & Kumpulainen, K. (2013). Expanding the chronotopes of schooling for the promotion of students' agency. In O. Erstad & J. Sefton-Green (Eds.), *Identity, community and learning lives in the digital age* (pp. 107–125). New York, NY: Cambridge University Press.

Riding, R., & Rayner, S. (2012). *Cognitive styles and learning strategies: Understanding style differences in learning and behavior.* New York, NY: Routledge.

Salmon, G. (2000). *E-moderating. The key to teaching and learning online (First).* London: Kogan Pege.

Sancho, J. (2012). Las muchas decisiones y pasos de un proyecto. In J. Sancho & C. Alonso (Eds.), *La fugacidad de las políticas, la inercia de las prácticas. La educación y las tecnologías de la información y comunicación* (pp. 13–20). Barcelona: Octaedro.

Schremm, A., Hed, A., Horne, M., & Roll, M. (2017). Training predictive L2 processing with a digital game: Prototype promotes acquisition of anticipatory use of tone-suffix associations. *Computers & Education*, *114*, 206–221. doi:10.1016/j.compedu.2017.07.006

Sepúlveda, E. (2015). *Validación de un Modelo de Gestión del Talento aplicado para promover el diálogo intercultural y el desarrollo de los talentos en estudiantes de escuelas en contexto indígena* [Validation of a Talent Management Model applied to promote intercultural dialogue and the development of talents in students of indigenous context' schools]. Tesis de Magíster, Universidad Católica de la Santísima Concepción.

Sepúlveda, E., & Careaga, M. (2015). *Gestión del talento y TIC en contextos interculturales.* [Talent management and ICT in intercultural contexts]. Editorial Académica Española.

Sobrevilla, D. (2001). Transculturacion y heterogeneidad: Avatares de dos categorías literarias en América Latina. *Revista de Crítica Literaria Latinoamericana*, *54*, 21–33.

Tajfel, H. (1978). *Social categorization, social identity, and social comparisons. Differentiation between social groups.*

Timmis, S. (2011). Constantcompanions:Instantmessaging conversations as sustainable supportive study structures amongst undergraduate peers. *Computers & Education, 59*(1), 3–18.

Timmis, S., & Williams, J. (2016). Transitioning across networked, workplace and educational boundaries: Shifting identities and chronotopic movements. In T. Ryberg, C. Sinclair, S. Bayne, & M. deLaat. (Eds.), *Research, boundaries, and policy in networked learning.* Switzerland: Springer Link.

Vergara, J., & Careaga, M. (2014). Análisis de competencias interculturales docentes basadas en la aplicación de un modelo pedagógico de gestión del conocimiento en entornos virtuales dentro de contextos mapuches. *Estudio piloto para la formulación de nuevas propuestas en competencias interculturales docentes.* Unpublished Thesis of Master degree, Universidad Católica de la Santísima Concepción. Concepción, Chile.

Vygotsky, L. (1978). *Mind and society: The development of higher mental processes.* Cambridge, MA: Harvard University Press.

Ware, P. (2013). Teaching comments intercultural communication skills in the digital age. *Intercultural Education, 24*(4), 315–326.

Welsch, W. (2000). Virtual to begin with? *Subjektivität Und Öffentlichkeit, 25–61.* Retrieved from http://www.helsinki.fi/iiaa/io/welsch.pdf

Winebrenner, S. (2001). *Teaching gifted kids in the regular classroom: Strategies and techniques every teacher can use to meet the academic needs of the gifted and talented. Revised, expanded.* Minneapolis: Free Spirit Publishing Inc.

Zagefka, H., González, R., & Brown, R. (2011). How minority members' perceptions of majority members' acculturation preferences shape minority members' own acculturation preferences: Evidence from Chile. *British Journal of Social Psychology, 50,* 216–233. Retrieved from https://doi.org/10.1348/014466610X512211

Chapter 11

Active Learning in Practice: Techniques and Experiences in Information Systems Courses in Brazil

Ronney Moreira de Castro, Sean W. M. Siqueira, César Augusto R. Bastos and Maria Cristina Pfeiffer Fernandes

Abstract

The use of Active Learning (AL) techniques can significantly improve the teaching–learning process, as the content is explored in a more interactive, participative, and relaxed way. Although expositive classes are still broadly used in Brazil, in this chapter we present some AL techniques, as well as experiences of their application, used in Brazilian K-12, undergraduate, and graduate Information Systems courses. As a result, we have noticed learning has been more effective, and students have been motivated by the use of these AL techniques. Although used in the context of Information System courses, the techniques could be adapted to other scenarios.

Keywords: Active learning; computer science; education; teaching; maker movement; learning techniques

Introduction

An increasing number of strategies have gained visibility in getting students' attention by changing the traditional way of teaching and

Active Learning Strategies in Higher Education: Teaching for Leadership,
Innovation, and Creativity, 273–292
ISBN: 978-1-78714-488-0

assisting them in the learning process. Examples include flipped education, online learning, flexible learning, blended learning, and hybrid learning (Mitchell, Petter, & Harris, 2017). Active Learning (AL) is a strategy that became popular in the mid-1990s and proved to be a great aid to students' teaching–learning process (Meyers & Jones, 1993). In recent years, it has gained prominence and is perceived as a considerable change from the traditional teaching process. Teachers who seek alternatives to their classes look for AL techniques (Prince, 2004), which we are going to explore in this chapter in the context of Information Systems (IS) courses in Brazil.

The expositive class has been the most used method by teachers, even though it restricts learning (Bonwell & Eison, 1991; Fink, 2003; Gudigantala, 2013) and the students' attention span, which, according to Wankat (2002), lasts only 15 minutes. In an expositive class, the students are expected to follow facts and tasks, instead of thinking critically about what they are learning (Thomas & Brown, 2011).

On the other hand, due to the advances in Information and Communication Technologies (ICTs), nowadays people are facing a different reality. Recent research (Chi & Wylie, 2014) has demonstrated that students' engagement has changed from passive (read, watch) to active (participate), and from constructive (explain, generate) to interactive (discuss, debate, question). Retaining students' attention is not an easy task. It is up to the teachers to improve and adapt their classes to the students' different profiles in order to serve them as appropriately as possible (Chi & Wylie, 2014).

Jacoski (2015) discusses how Brazilian and American educators accept the use of innovative techniques in learning, such as AL. Moreover, Jacoski (2015) addresses the practice of AL in higher education. The results showed that the American educators have a positive opinion regarding the use of these approaches. However, the Brazilian educators do not share a common vision on the educational goals in the country, despite being aware of the advances.

This chapter describes some experiences of the use of AL techniques in K-12, undergraduate, and graduate IS courses in Brazil. We present some teaching practices and techniques that helped to improve Brazilian students' motivation.

The remainder of the chapter is organized as follows: the second section describes AL in the context of IS curricula from the point of view of specialized literature; the third section presents the Maker Movement and the Makerspaces; the fourth section describes some AL techniques used by the authors in IS Brazilian courses; and finally the last section presents some final remarks, drawing overall conclusions and also providing some limitations of this work and outlining some directions for future work.

Active Learning in Information System Courses

The work of Acharya, Manohar, Wu, Ansari, and Schilling (2015) showed that software companies expect undergraduates to be able to actually develop software by following strict quality standards. The authors used AL tools, such as class exercises, case studies, and videos, in partnership with software companies, in order to improve students' understanding of the concepts learned. The goal was to enable students to better understand software validation and verification topics, requirements engineering, configuration management, revisions, and inspections.

According to Massey, Brown, and Johnston (2005), many teachers feel frustrated about students preparing only for assessments undertaken. This can be attributed to the fact that students are not involved in classes that are mostly expositive, as those fail to promote discussion and critical thinking among them.

The authors used AL techniques to encourage students to engage more in classes and to review their materials. One of the techniques used was assigning crossword puzzles as homework. The objective was to complete them with answers to questions on a given subject. Another technique was the use of a web-based, question-and-answer game. The teacher created questions with various levels of difficulty, always taking into account the part of the content intended to be taught. In class, the students were divided into groups A and B and a coin was flipped to choose who would start. The teacher clicked on the question that was displayed for the first participant. If the participant responded correctly, points were accumulated and then the next question was presented to the next participant. If the answer was wrong, the question was passed to the next group according to the same procedure adopted before. Wrong answers took points from the team. The team who scored the most points won.

Ramiller (2002) showed the Virtual Interactive Project (VIP), which is an AL approach to text-based project interchange. Students were given a textual description of a business scenario, along with the preliminary details regarding the problem and information on the focus of the project to be developed. Acting in teams as if they were consulting firms, they began to interact with a "virtual client," who represented the company (in the authors' example, the role was assigned to the teacher, but it could have been either one of the students), to gather the necessary information for the project development. VIP engaged students in a story and profited from the narrative by promoting knowledge construction.

Maker Movement and Makerspaces

The technological evolution and the manufacture of both machinery and goods, which were fundamental for the industrialization and generation of wealth, relied on factories and companies for a long period. Then, access to knowledge was restricted, largely due to patenting and licensing, either nationally or internationally (Redlich et al., 2016). Therefore, many countries, especially the developing ones, were deprived of certain technologies (Pearce, 2012).

Nowadays, the number of individuals who want to design and manufacture their own physical objects is increasing. Formerly, the skills to perform these activities were restricted to some people, but this scenario has been changing due to the advance in three main technologies: manufacturing tools (laser cutters, milling machines, 3D printers, lathes, routers, among others), computer-aided design software programs, and systems of integrated control (Wilczynski, 2015). In addition, the ease of use of such tools has increased while their cost has decreased considerably.

The number of people who are interested in creating, designing, and manufacturing new objects evolved into the "Maker Movement." Using this designation, "Makers" are those who, besides building new devices and objects, share their experiences with others. The places, i.e., the physical spaces that "Makers" use to design and work on their projects, to hold their meetings, and to share information are known as "Makerspaces." These spaces are organized in general with the community and have a specific structure, function, programming, and financing (Moilanen, 2012; Wilczynski, 2015). The main idea is to bring together individuals of various social backgrounds and talents, providing access to technology, aiming to promote creativity.

The ease of access to Makerspaces technologies has spawned a considerable number of Makers and mainly gave underserved communities the opportunity to build their own objects. Beyers (2010) reports that people in these communities can be helped to solve local problems at low-cost, such as: building turbines to capture solar and wind power, long-range antennas, wireless data networks, tracking devices for sheep, among others.

The use of Makerspaces in schools, colleges, and universities has grown in recent years, allowing students to have an opportunity to become more involved in projects and develop a wide range of skills (Barrett, Pizzico, Levy, & Nagel, 2015).

This was a concern of Sigmund Papert: to change the way of teaching and to enable students to build knowledge. He brought the idea of bringing constructionism to schools, building laboratories for the creation of activities, toolkits, etc. (Blikstein, Martinez, & Pang, 2016). He stressed the importance of providing a pleasant environment to facilitate learning, i.e., the idea was that students could benefit from a relaxed environment to let their creativity flourish (Giannakos, Divitini, Iversen, & Koulouris, 2015).

Teaching children how to program, a matter that Papert stressed, has not yet been fully embraced in schools around the world, but a larger vision was created in which students could perform sophisticated tasks that were previously restricted to specialized practitioners such as robotics, use of diverse sensors, analysis of collected data, and engineering projects, for example. The Maker Movement and digital manufacturing are also important steps in the process of bringing new ideas to students, and much of their popularity is directly related to their attitudes (Blikstein & Krannich, 2013).

According to Giannakos et al. (2015), in the last decade there has been a significant increase in the number of Makerspaces. Those spaces facilitate young students' learning process through construction. Spaces such as Fab Labs, Makerspaces, TechShops, and Hackerspaces have enabled researchers to investigate the real benefits the Maker Movement has to offer in Learning.

Experiences with Active Learning Techniques

Mitchell et al. (2017) performed a systematic review of AL applied to IS curricula and classified the techniques that encourage this approach in five categories: (1) *visual presentations:* to encourage students to speak more in class and hence to participate more; (2) *collaborative projects:* getting students to work in groups to solve real problems and/or challenges, which increases collaboration and relationships between them, as well as it encourages critical thinking; (3) *technological interaction:* to encourage students' use of technology so they understand its benefits; (4) *evaluation:* to increase the students' ability to question and to test their performance; and (5) *games:* to encourage students' creativity, in order to increase their knowledge and improve their skills.

The authors of this chapter have been using AL techniques with their students. The experiences have been more effective compared to the traditional, expositive, classes. The authors extended the classification proposed by Mitchell et al. (2017), mainly using practices from the Maker Movement. Those techniques were used in K-12 education at *Ferreira Viana State Technical School* (*ETEFV*) in Rio de Janeiro, in an IS under graduate program at *Faculdade Metodista Granbery* in the city of Juiz de Fora in Minas Gerais, and also in the IS graduate program of the *Federal University of the State of Rio de Janeiro*; all of them in Brazil.

Makerspace and Robotics

In 2008, a Makerspace was built in ETEFV to support the Robotics course. The space is organized in three levels: beginner, intermediate, and advanced. It has the capacity for 20 students per semester, running with three donated computers and a computer acquired through funds provided by FAPERJ, the state government agency that funds research in Rio de Janeiro, for a research project. Recycled materials and computer scrap are also used for building robots and other artifacts. The space also has two Lego MindStorms NXT 2.0 kits, five Lego MindStorms EV3 kits, six Arduino Diecimila kits, and five Robotis Bioloid kits.

At the beginning of each year, a lecture is held for the school community in order to present the Makerspace team and some of its previous projects. Any student can apply for the Robotics extracurricular course by simply filling out a registration form explaining why they want to join it. A group of teachers selects 20 students joining the course each semester, whereas the other candidates are organized into a waiting list. The selection is made based on the candidate's personal statement, considering their interest in developing projects using the Makerspace. The assessment in the course is qualitative according to the student's participation and project development. Those who missed more than two classes are considered to have abandoned the course and, therefore, the next candidate on the waiting list is invited to join the class. So far, none of the selected students have left due to missed classes and all seem to be dedicated, which shows a high degree of motivation.

At the beginner level, students are familiarized with the tools and software available in Makerspace. Computer programming concepts are introduced for machine automation using Lego MindStorms kits and their respective graphical programming language. The aim is to encourage autonomy and creativity by challenging students to program a robot. After that, the Arduino board and its possibilities are presented to the students, so they can consider creating their own projects using free hardware. During the sessions, the teacher presents project ideas, motivating the students to participate in championships with their programmed robots. At the intermediate level, students become more autonomous and start to create their own projects using the material they'd prefer. At the advanced level, students learn how to use technology that requires C/C ++ languages to program. They use Bioloid, mainly to create humanoid robots capable of participating in robot competitions, such as racing or dancing. In addition, students actually exercise their authoring competencies.

Examples of previous projects developed by the students are Gduino, a gravity acceleration meter, and an intelligent house controlled by the cell phone robotic arms (manipulators) and a programmable marionette. The intelligent house is presented in Figure 1 and the robotic arms and the programmable marionette are presented in Figure 2.

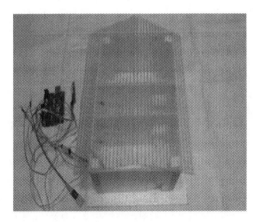

Figure 1.   Intelligent House.

Figure 2.   Robotic Arms and the Programmable Marionette.

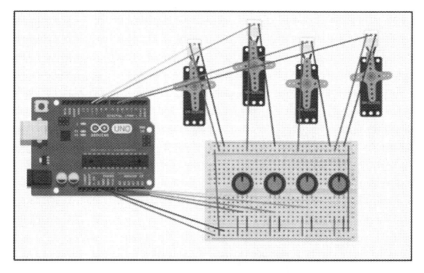

Figure 3.   Robotic Arm with a Simulator.

An activity that can be used in the IS curricula, more specifically in algorithms and programming courses, is the creation of an interactive object that uses sensors and other electronic components and uses an Autodesk Circuits simulator. The objective is to develop a manipulator with four degrees of freedom, also known as the robotic arm, for inter-action through buttons and later via cellular data. The activity is divided into four stages: (1) the creation of the circuit in the simulator; (2) the implementation of the program code; (3) testing the simulator's code, shown in Figure 3, and (4) the physical construction of the robotic arm, which can be assembled with low-cost material.

Figure 4.   Robotic Arm Built with Low-Cost Material.

The circuit has four slave-motors[1] and four linear potentiometers[2] of 100K ohms. An Arduino[3] UNO is used for programming and managing the movements of the slave-motors, according to the circuit built. Figure 4 shows the robotic arm built in this activity, using low-cost material.

The results show a high degree of students' satisfaction, which is confirmed by the great demand for joining the course each year, in addition to the high participation rate in classes in the Makerspace.

It is important to notice that the teacher must know how to improvise, as the material used in activities comes from scraps; thus, there is no control over its quality, not even of what will be made from it. With the use of the problem-solving methodology, the teachers are often challenged to assume a dynamic, questioning attitude and must also be committed to teaching and researching. The teachers' role in this process makes them partners of the students, engaging and leading them to develop their reasoning coherently with their learning objectives while working with different concepts from different areas.

---

[1]Electromechanical machines designed for use in motion control applications that require highly precise positioning.
[2]Electronic component that is capable of bounding the flow of electric current passing through it. This bounding can be adjusted manually and can be varied for more or less.
[3]Board used as low-cost electronic prototyping platform.

Quizzes

A question-and-answer game called "QuizES – A Game to Assist in Teaching Software Engineering" was developed using a web platform. It can be played individually or in groups.

The game consists of a virtual board with blue and orange squares. The blue squares contain questions related to software engineering and the orange squares contain pranks (e.g., "imitate teacher X," "sing a song," "imitate some animal," etc.). These pranks provide a more laid-back atmosphere to the game, and also add a challenging characteristic to it, as students are apprehensive if they will or not fall into an orange square. Each player or group is represented by a colored virtual pawn that walks on the board according to an automated draw of numbers (1, 2, or 3). The goal is to get students to absorb all the knowledge produced during the game, generating discussions on Software Engineering concepts.

The game was played in 2014, during a Software Quality course in the IS bachelor program of *Faculdade Metodista Granbery* – in Juiz de Fora. Thirty-two undergraduate students participated and answered a questionnaire (Castro & Santos, 2016) containing 25 questions and the scales: 1 (poor), 2 (reasonable), 3 (good), 4 (very good), and 5 (excellent). Most of the responses were in the range "4" and "5," which shows that the activity allowed a better understanding of the concepts and that different activities can, in fact, aid the teaching–learning process. Moreover, it was possible to perceive a greater involvement of the students through the observation of their actions during the game.

QRCodes

Other AL technique considers the use of QRCode[4] (*Quick Response Code*) in the Database (DB) course. QRCodes are used in many applications such as transport ticketing, product labeling, and commercial tracking. It is possible to use QRCodes for browsing, sending e-mails, watching videos, advertising products, getting coupons, accessing information, etc.

---

[4]Considered as an evolution of bar codes. The information is ordered in a matrix of two dimensions.

Figure 5. Example of a QRCode with Information of the Exercise.

The teacher prepared several sheets with information about a DB model exercise (consisting of a piece of text that explained it, tables with their respective attributes, relationships, and segments of SQL code) in QRCode format (Figure 5) and spread them around the computer lab at the task's running day. The teacher had asked the students in a previous class to download some software that could read QRCode on their smartphones. The goal was to make the students read the code and to do the DB creation script exercise.

When the students arrived, they saw the QRCodes on the classroom walls and got curious about what would happen. They were given instructions about the DB script exercise and were informed they were supposed to hand it in by the end of the class. They started reading the codes and putting the pieces together. Some of the codes contained "wild card" information, such as *"Wrong information. Go to another code,"* *"Search for the table's correct code,"* and others had information containing SQL code errors. These were obstacles the students had to overcome. The objective of the activity was not to have a winner, but that everyone had the chance to build a complete DB script to be generated in SQL.

The technique was applied in a class of 18 students during a Data Modeling course in the IS bachelor program of *Faculdade Metodista Granbery*, in the second semester of 2016. It was possible to notice the students' engagement, as they seemed anxious to find out the QRCodes content, and again when they realized the obstacles they had to overcome, such as codes with wrong information. The students did not tell each other codes were wrong, making the dynamics of the proposed exercise more challenging for everyone. Besides, the way students solved the exercise varied. Some read every code at first, then assembled the text and the database script; whereas others decided to read only part of the codes and build the text and script.

We used this technique in order to get the students engaged in class, in addition to reinforcing knowledge acquisition. It was possible to notice the SQL content (tables, primary key, foreign key, tables' attributes, attributes' types, and basic instructions regarding the DB creation such as Create Table, Alter Table, Drop Table, and Constraint) related to the course was successfully absorbed by the students. Although no formal questionnaire was used to collect results, all the students successfully solved the exercise and built the DB script.

Newspaper Doll

This technique consists in assembling a newspaper doll to illustrate the concept of process in Software Engineering (Castro & Souza, 2016). At first, the teacher divided the class into groups and placed them apart from each other. Then, cards with parts of the doll (head, neck, right arm, etc.), newspapers, and scissors were distributed. Next, it was explained that everyone should create the part designated on the card they got using the material they were handed. In that first moment, the teams couldn't communicate with each other. After 5 minutes, the teacher called the members of the groups, one by one, to assemble the doll on the board. The result was something completely disconnected, which demonstrated how important it is to have a project before building a product. The teacher made an analogy that if the software development process does not have a project plan, the final product will end up being problematic with poorly designed parts. Figure 6 shows an example of the result of the first turn of this activity.

A new turn followed, but in this second turn of executing the activity, the teacher asked each group to choose a person to be the project manager, and group managers could communicate. After five minutes, the members assembled the doll once more on the board, and it had improved considerably. A third turn was played in which a student was the modeler, making an analogy with the process of software documentation. Finally, there was a fourth turn which included quality and test analysts. The doll improved at each turn, and students could realize how important it is to plan the process in software development. The teacher asked students what changes they could suggest that could improve each step of the process. From the answers he could build up the process and continue the evolution of the doll. The dynamic depicted may have several variants; nonetheless, its main goal is to

Figure 6. Construction of a Doll in the First Turn.

make students realize that planning a process is not a static activity, but a dynamic one that must undergo continuing improvements.

The *newspaper doll* technique was applied in some classes of the Software Quality course in the IS bachelor program of *Faculdade Metodista Granbery* − (i) first time in the second semester of 2013, in a class of 32 undergraduate students; (ii) second time in the first semester of 2014 in a class of 35 students; (iii) third time in the first half of 2015 in a class of 25 students. As of 2016, the course name changed from "Software Quality" to "Advanced Topics in Software Engineering," but the technique being applied remained same. (iv) Fourth application was in the first semester of 2016 in a class of 28 students; and (v) the fifth, most recently, in the first semester of 2017 in a class of 15 students.

It was also applied in a graduate course on IS at the Federal University of the State of Rio de Janeiro (UNIRIO) in the first semester of 2015.

In the undergraduate classes, the same questionnaire was used to verify in QuizES (Castro & Santos, 2016) whether the content was better acquired with the use of AL techniques or with the traditional method (lectures), while also checking how the students were motivated using different artifacts. Ninety-five percent of the students marked 4 (very good) or 5 (excellent), which shows that they find traditional classes to be more monotonous and boring. It is interesting to highlight the results of Question 13 (*I learn better with dynamic experiences*), where about 91% of the participants rated "4" or "5." This shows that students prefer more interactive classes that allow a better understanding of the content. No questionnaire was applied to graduate students, but acceptance of the technique was noticed through their good participation.

Agility Scrum

Another recently created technique (Castro, Siqueira, Almeida, & Nascimento, 2017) is the Scrum methodology. The teacher organized the class into groups that could be compared to software development companies, and handed them a kit containing various electronic components (such as LEDs, batteries, battery holder, resistors, capacitors, wires, trigger buttons, and protoboards[5]). The teacher played the role of the product owner. It was further requested that the students of each group should pick someone to represent the Scrum Master. Sprint cards were then distributed and placed on a Kanban board, as shown in Figure 7. Sprints were sequential and incremental, as the circuit's complexity level increased to each of them (total of 5). The team that finished the whole circuit first was the winner.

In order to illustrate the problems and possible solutions that can occur in real companies' daily activities, there was a stack of cards containing penalties and benefits, such as, respectively, "Employee on a medical leave. A team member should be out for one turn" and "Capacitors don't need to be used in circuit assembly." Cards might be randomly drawn from the stack by the Scrum Masters in each Sprint.

Agility Scrum was not intended to show the Scrum methodology in detail, but to use a practical way to showcase the basic concepts of traditional teaching. Figure 8 illustrates the construction of Sprints.

This technique was applied in two classes of the Software Quality course in the IS bachelor program of *Faculdade Metodista Granbery* in

---

[5]Board used for testing on electronics stands. No need for solder to fix the components.

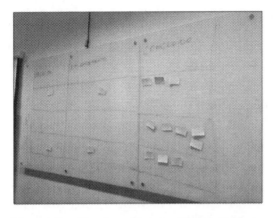

Figure 7.   Kanban Board with the Sprints.

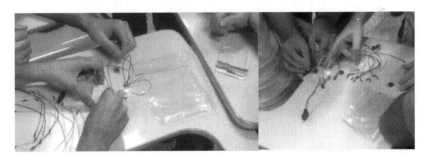

Figure 8.   Students Building the Sprints Using Electronic Components.

2016. One of the classes had 18 students and the other 8 students, reaching a total of 26 students. After the questionnaire application (Castro & Santos, 2016), 82% of the answers were on the 4 (very good) or 5 (excellent) ratings. Furthermore, the technique used Maker practices (along with the use of electronic components) and about 95% of the students did not have any previous knowledge on how to build a circuit. They learned how to use the components throughout their usage, that is, they learned from practice, a fundamental concept of the Maker Movement: Constructionism (Castro & Siqueira, 2017).

Performing Arts

One of the mandatory classes of the UNIRIO PhD Computer Science program is "Teaching Information Systems." The content is directly associated with the main didactic-pedagogical techniques that must be considered by a student who will become a faculty teacher after the course. The course proposes reflections on the role of teaching, on the roles of higher education, as it promotes analysis on the concept of didactics, on teaching models and planning, and on teaching and learning strategies (UNIRIO, 2017).

In one of the classes, scenic arts and tricks were used to demonstrate different teacher profiles. Some characters were interpreted with specialized material: lab coats, glasses, chalkboard, some chalk, a tablecloth, some miscellaneous books placed on the table, a briefcase, miscellaneous clothes for different characters, as well as some tricks, which meant to give a more relaxed atmosphere to every performance. The first character wore a lab coat and glasses, had a briefcase, and held a pointer and some chalk. This character represented the teachers of years past: energetic, holding all the knowledge, and keeping their students on their chairs as listeners. The second character no longer wore a coat. He had books and read their texts asking the students to copy what was being said. Then, tricks were used to illustrate that teaching should not be merely the reading of textbooks. The character ignited some fire on the book to illustrate that analogy. Figure 9 shows the first and second characters.

Some other characters were represented until the last one, who made use of AL methods for teaching. He then talked to the participants about everything that was done during the lesson. The students discussed the characters, sharing some problems they had experienced

Figure 9.   First and Second Characters – Technique Performing Arts.

throughout their academic lives. The character used a ball (randomly passed among the participants) to pick someone to ask which of the characters marked their lives, in terms of educational problems, besides grading them. Next, the teacher was called to the front of the room who had to bring a briefcase previously handed to him at the beginning of the class. The briefcase was opened, and the teacher wore a pair of gloves for the next act. The character asked the teacher to take his shoes off (that was the reason for wearing the gloves) and removed a paper that was already there. It was read out loud and its content was exactly what the students said about the teacher who most marked their lives and the grade attributed to him. Once again, tricks were used to unwind the class.

This technique was applied only in a PhD course at the *Federal University of the State of Rio de Janeiro* (UNIRIO). It was developed exclusively for the "*Teaching Information Systems*" course and no questionnaire was applied in the class. Observing the students, it was possible to perceive a greater engagement, participation, and learning. Moreover, in the end, everyone was able to contemplate the different teachers they met and to analyze different teaching–learning techniques they had adopted. The aim was to show students the different teacher profiles, from the knowledge-holder who kept students as listeners, to the most interactive one who builds knowledge together with the class and makes use of alternative education methods.

This technique involved careful assembling and preparing: from the material to be used to specific presentation skills, including performing tricks. Therefore, it required teacher training so that everything could be performed according to plan.

Conclusions

In recent years the search for new pedagogical practices has increased, and several educators have been questioning how education can be innovated to meet students' expectations. The use of new technologies and Active Learning is an alternative that has been more accepted by students than expositive lectures. Therefore, changing the traditional teaching scenario can motivate students and improve learning.

This work presented techniques and experiences of AL that can be used by teachers in IS courses, providing examples experienced in Brazil. The results of applying these techniques demonstrated the students' good acceptance of the method, which was verified through questionnaires and observation of their behavior. In addition, it was possible to notice more involvement, motivation, and engagement during classes. It shows how the use of AL techniques can support teachers to improve their skills and students' learning.

The use of these techniques is not the solution to every problem in the teaching–learning process, but can contribute significantly to improving the way of teaching, providing students innovative experiences.

While there are still limitations observed when adopting AL – such as the need for specific resources and knowing how to use them – AL techniques provide additional mechanisms for teachers and students to build new learning scenarios.

In order to analyze the results, benefits, and problems of using the proposed techniques, it is necessary to apply them to more classes in different learning scenarios. For instance: would the proposed techniques work the same way for older students? Would the students keep their motivation using the same techniques throughout several classes?

New AL techniques and exercises are being discussed and the authors are working on a teaching–learning methodology to support the planning, creation, structuring, development, application, and search of such methods, which can guide educators in the design of their teaching strategies.

Acknowledgments

We'd like to thank the students of the three institutions: *Faculdade Metodista Granbery* (undergraduate students of the Bachelor of Information Systems), *Ferreira Viana State Technical School* (ETEFV) (K-12 students), and *Federal University of the State of Rio de Janeiro* (graduate students of the Master and PhD on Informatics – Information Systems), for their participation in the activities described in this work.

References

Acharya, S., Manohar, P., Wu, P. Y., Ansari, A. A., & Schilling, W. W. (2015). Integrated active learning tools for enhanced pedagogy in a software engineering course. Paper presented at 2015 ASEE Annual Conference & Exposition, Seattle, Washington.

Barrett, T. W., Pizzico, M. C., Levy, B., & Nagel, R. L. (2015). A review of university maker spaces: Introduction. *122nd ASEE Annual Conference and Exposition* (pp. 1−16).

Beyers, R. N. (2010). Nurturing creativity and innovation through FabKids: A case study. *Journal of Science Education and Technology, 19*(5), 447−455.

Blikstein, P., & Krannich, D. (2013). The makers' movement and FabLabs in education: Experiences, technologies, and research. *Idc '13 (April)*, 613−616.

Blikstein, P., Martinez, S. L., & Pang, H. A. (2016). Meaningful making: Projects and inspirations for Fab Labs and Makerspaces.

Bonwell, C., & Eison, J. (1991). Active learning: Creating excitement in the classroom. *ASHE-ERIC Higher Education Report No. 1* (p. 2). Washington, DC: The George Washington University, School of Education and Human Development.

Castro, R. M., & Santos, G. (2016). *O Uso de Recursos Lúdicos Para o Ensino de Processos em Engenharia de Software.* In: Workshop sobre Educação em Computação, Porto Alegre, RS. 24º WEI.

Castro, R. M., & Siqueira, S. W. M. (2017). Aprendizagem Ativa em Sistemas de Informação: Novas Técnicas Propostas e Reflexões Sobre as Experiências. *13º SBSI − Simpósio Brasileiro de Sistemas de Informação, Lavras.*

Castro, R. M., Siqueira, S. W. M., Almeida, D. N., & Nascimento, F. C. (2017). AGILITY SCRUM − Um Jogo para Ensino da Metodologia SCRUM. *Accept for publication in 25º WEI − Workshop sobre Educação em Computação, XXXVII Congresso da Sociedade Brasileira de Computação, São Paulo.*

Castro, R. M., & Souza, G. S. (2016). O Uso de Recursos Lúdicos para o Ensino de Processos emEngenharia de Software. *24º WEI − Workshop sobre Educação em Computação, XXXVI Congresso da Sociedade Brasileira de Computação, Porto Alegre.*

Chi, M. T., & Wylie, R. (2014). The ICAP framework: Linking cognitive engagement to active learning outcomes. *Educational Psychologist, 49*(4), 219−243.

Fink, L. D. (2003). *Creating significant learning experiences.* San Francisco, CA: Jossey-Bass.

Giannakos, M. N., Divitini, M., Iversen, O. S., & Koulouris, P. (2015). Make2learn: Fostering engagement and creativity in learning through making. *CEUR Workshop Proceedings, 1450,* 1−6.

Gudigantala, N. (2013). An active learning approach to teaching undergraduate introduction to MIS course. Paper presented at the 19th Americas Conference on Information Systems, Chicago, IL.

Jacoski, C. A. (2015). Teaching methods and MOOCs: A vision specialist of Brazil and Usa. Conference: *XV Colóquio Internacional de Gestão Universitária − CIGU, At Mar del Plata − Argentina.*

Massey, A. P., Brown, S. A., & Johnston, J. D. (2005). It's all fun and games: Until students learn. *Journal of Information Systems Education, 16*(1).

Meyers, C., & Jones, T. (1993). *Promoting active learning: Strategies for the college classroom.* San Francisco, CA: Jossey-Bass.

Mitchell, A., Petter, S., & Harris, A. (2017). Learning by doing: Twenty successful active learning exercises for information systems courses. *Journal of Information Technology Education: Innovations in Practice, 16*(3), 21−46.

Moilanen, J. (2012). Emerging hackerspaces – Peer-production generation. *IFIP Advances in Information and Communication Technology, 378 AICT*, 94–111.

Pearce, J. M. (2012). The case for open source appropriate technology. *Environment, Development and Sustainability, 14*(3), 425–431.

Prince, M. (2004). Does active learning work? A review of the research. *Journal of Engineering Education, 93*(3), 223–231.

Ramiller, N. C. (2002). The Virtual Interactive Project: Teaching analysis and design through narrative and drama. *Communications of the Association for Information Systems, 9*(1), 1.

Redlich, T., Buxbaum-Conradi, S., Basmer-Birkenfeld, S. V., Moritz, M., Krenz, P., Osunyomi, B. D., & Heubischl, S. (2016). OpenLabs – Open source micro-factories enhancing the FabLab idea. In *System Sciences (HICSS), 2016 49th Hawaii International Conference* (pp. 707–715). IEEE.

Thomas, D., & Brown, J. S. (2011). *A new culture of learning: Cultivating the imagination for a world of constant change* (Vol. 219). Lexington, KY: CreateSpace.

UNIRIO. (2017). Docência em Sistemas de Informação. Retrieved from http://www2.uniriotec.br/ppgi/informacoes-sobre-o-programa/curso-de-doutorado-em-informatica/disciplinas/basicas/copy_of_estagio-em-docencia.

Wankat, P. (2002). *The effective efficient professor: Teaching, scholarship and service.* Boston, MA: Allyn & Bacon.

Wilczynski, V. (2015). Academic maker spaces and engineering design. *American Society for Engineering Education, 26*, 1.

Chapter 12

Using Socrative App for Accounting Students in Higher Education

Inés González-González, Cristina Alcaide-Muñoz and Ana Isabel Jimenez-Zarco

Abstract

Accounting education in universities is always a hard subject for the students, who find it boring and little stimulating. So, even though students increasingly demand the integration of varied technologies and mobile devices into learning environment (Wash & Freeman 2013), educational systems of the public universities continue to be traditional. The role of students is totally passive, so the main responsibility of class development lies on the shoulders of professors, but this situation can change with the use of Socrative App in a learning environment, since it encourages students to play an active part in class.

That is why professors have to find new ways to capture the students' attention, facilitating their learning, and at the same time, making it fun and entertaining. In this work, a teaching innovation case to first-year students in a university is presented using Socrative App. This study aims to investigate how the university can combine ICT close to traditional methodologies of learning, in order to increase interest in the subject, awakening in them passion and vocation for the accounting area.

Keywords: Socrative App; teaching innovation; accounting; higher education; ublic university

Active Learning Strategies in Higher Education: Teaching for Leadership,
Innovation, and Creativity, 293–313
Copyright © 2018 by Emerald Publishing Limited
ISBN: 978-1-78714-488-0

Introduction

Teaching innovation is a constant concern in the university. It must be able to respond to the needs of a changing society, in which a wide variety of potential students coexist. Therefore, it is necessary to use new training models and tools that make it possible for the students to be trained in a continuous way, with programs adapted to their work and personal needs, and making use of resources that are accessible and facilitate learning.

The constructivist theory establishes the basis for the development of new formative models, which gives students an active role and is the one who sets the time of their learning (Duffy & Jonassen, 1992). Together with this, technological development makes it possible for students and academics to have a wide variety of resources and teaching tools that facilitate, streamline, and make the learning process playful, increasing student engagement with the subject and the educational institution.

Among them, it is important to note the Socrative App. It is an online student response system that facilitates teachers' question-giving and answers-receiving tasks. Teachers can generate quizzes and other educational exercises for their students and obtain their response in real time. Its main advantage is that it is not necessary to use any software or any extra electronic device; users only need a smartphone or laptop with connection to the Internet. Moreover, the excellent results obtained in terms of satisfaction and improving student participation and performance have made it a highly popular tool in higher education in different types of subjects (Méndez & Slisko, 2013).

With these thoughts in mind, the present work describes and implements a teaching innovation project developed in a traditional university, such as the Public University of Navarre (UPNA). This study aims at glimpsing the impact of the use of ICT resources in the learning process in accounting, in particular, the Degree of Human Resources Management and Labor Relations. For this, a methodology based on the use of the Socrative App is adopted. The study carried out is of an exploratory nature. The information was obtained through an electronic questionnaire to a total of 60 students of the subject of Accounting, of which only 40 participated actively in the process. Due to the small sample size, nonparametric statistical techniques were used, namely, the Mann–Whitney U-statistical analysis.

This chapter adopts the following structure. First, we proceed to define the determinants and implications of university teaching innovation, noting its importance in the field of business, and identifying some of the teaching practices that favor learning by students. Then, we are going to contextualize the teaching innovating project that we have defined in order to develop a methodology for the development and measurement of the level of learning of the subject matter being studied. We will finally present our conclusions and the main limitations.

Theoretical Framework

Teaching innovation is a constant in the current university model. Prendes (2011) and Salinas (2004) point out the existence of at least three factors that endorse teaching innovation, the first being promoted by the social, political, and legislative environment. Meanwhile, the last two, with internal origin, are directly related to the level of adoption of technology and new teaching methodologies by academics and Higher Education Institutions.

Determinants of Teaching Innovation

The adoption of the European Higher Education Area (EHEA) offers an opportunity for renovation and improvement of the university education system. Although it is undoubtedly the first factor that promotes teaching innovation, this process requires a deep reflection and a continuous monitoring and common effort of cooperation on the part of all the agents involved. In fact, its implications affect the university institution itself, with the consequent rethinking of its concept, functions, and role as creator and transmitter of knowledge. It is proposed that the university adapts to the knowledge society (González, 2008). And so it provides an education oriented to the permanent formation of student along their lifes, using teaching models centered in the work and learning of the student − in the development of competences for an autonomous and continuous learning throughout life and an adaptation to the cultural diversity.

Academic institutions establish models and educational resources appropriate to the current context. That is why some of the main changes that the university undertakes internally include the introduction of training models based on constructivist theory, as well as the intensive use of ICT as a teaching resource and a tool for communication and collaboration.

Constructivism considers that the learning process has the following characteristics (Duffy & Cunningham, 1996):

- It is a complex process of analysis, understanding, and interpretation, and, later, it is a construction of a series of concepts and explanations that allow us to "function" effectively in a given context, taking into account the circumstances presented to us (Boethel & Dimock, 1999).
- It is conditioned by the circumstances in which it is developed and used (Von Glasersfeld, 1995).
- It is constructed by the individual (Perkins, 1992).
- Experience and previous mastery play a key role in the learning process (DeVries & Kohlber, 1990).
- There is resistance to change on the part of individuals (Duit, 1995).
- Social interaction plays a fundamental role in the learning process.

With regard to the use of ICT, the labor market today requires professionals capable of using ICT, both in the development of their activity and in the development of information searching and decision-making (Cerderblom & Paulsen, 2005; Ennis, 1996; Huit, 1998). That is why universities are beginning to implement educational models based on the use of ICT. However, in universities, the level of ICT use is very variable, as with the agents involved: students and professors. Thus, Roberts, Romm, and Jones (2000) identify up to four different models, depending on the level of incorporation of ICT in the normal activity of the institution. These range from a level of initiation to the most advanced, or radical, where students, professors, and educational resources interact in a virtual space. In them, students divide into groups and learn by interacting with each other, in addition to a large number of existing web resources, while the professor acts as a guide, adviser, facilitator, etc.

Implications of Teaching Innovation

The universities are committed to designing new teaching models, based on constructive learning and intensive use of ICT (Adell-Segura & Castañeda-Quintero, 2010; Hannafin & Hill, 2002). The radical nature of this teaching innovation is largely determined not only by the way learning is understood as a constructive process (Sandholtz, Ringstaff, & Dwyer, 1997), but also, by the use of a new teaching approach, oriented toward practical training and the use of technological resources.

It is too early to know the level of success achieved by teaching innovation undertaken. For the moment, only some evidence regarding the level of satisfaction and performance of students is available. However, it is possible to begin to take stock and to point out the strong implications that its application has on the university institution, its mission and management model, as well as the role played by the different agents involved in the teaching process and the relationships established among them.

The incorporation of ICTs in the teaching—learning processes has led universities to lose the monopoly over the production and transmission of knowledge. This allows the emergence of new players who use ICT intensively and respond professionally to a continuous demand for specialized knowledge and acquisition of certain professional skills (Salinas, 2002). Likewise, there is a substantial change in the role of professor and student. The changes produced in the institution modify the role that the professor plays in the teaching—learning process. They go from being the transmitter of knowledge to students, to being a mediator in the construction of own knowledge (Pérez, 2002).

In this new context, the professor acts first as a person and then as an expert on the subject. He/she promotes the personal growth of students and facilitates learning rather than transmission of information. Therefore, the university and the professor cease to be the source of all knowledge, and professors become the guide for students, facilitating the use of resources and tools they need to explore and develop new knowledge and skills (Salinas, 2002). For their part, the student takes an active role in the learning process. From simple receiver and "storekeeper" of information, he/she becomes a constructor of knowledge. He/she decides the pace of learning and the resources it will use to acquire them. In a personal way, he will take on the problem and explore in depth the different solutions or possible alternatives (Nanjappa & Grant, 2003).

With all this, there is also a change in the relationships established between the professor, the student, and the institution itself. If it is a unidirectional and unilateral relationship, it is transformed to a collaborative relationship. It will no longer be the educational center that defines the curricular itinerary of the student, nor the professor who sets the pace of learning and establishes the contents, and the way in which the student has to acquire them. Now it will be the student who stands at the center of the process and defines and designs the learning process. Meanwhile, the educational center and the professor develop a work of accompaniment for the students, and they put at their disposal a wide range of resources so that they acquire the knowledge and competences that are considered necessary for his/her labor and personal training.

Another of the main implications is the use of resources and technological tools that make possible the construction of knowledge, through collaborative learning processes, as a means to promote dialogue and reflective exchange (Duffy & Cunningham, 1996), as well as the application of the learning by doing methodology, based on an inductive learning procedure. In this sense, Bagley and Hunter (1992) point out how the use of this type of tools allows students to have a greater degree of autonomy and resources in the process of learning construction (Knuth & Cunningham, 1993). As a counterpart, they must dedicate a greater effort and time, specifically in the development of collaboration processes with other students (Kulkarni et al., 2015).

The New University Student Profiles

To a large extent, teacher innovation is determined by the emergence of new student profiles: those known as digital natives and digital immigrants. The international academic community is faced with the need to determine who they are and respond to the needs of students in the 21st century. The nature and profile of the university student has changed. And this change is not a voluntary act; on the contrary, it has been promoted by the labor needs and technological development that they face.

Currently, the common profile of the university student is a modern, connected, and dynamic young person who is accustomed to experimentation, online socialization, and immediacy (Tymon, 2013). Known as "digital natives" (Prensky, 2001) or "Net Generation" (Tapscott, 1998), they are individuals born in the 1990s and who have grown up in the digital era. Their relation with technology is direct and intense, a fact that influences the way in which they learn and create knowledge (Beasley & Smyth, 2004; Bennett, Maton, & Kervin, 2008; Collins, 1990; Pea & Collins, 2008).

As students, they prefer images to text, need to change activity frequently, and feel the need to master the process, developing several tasks (Prensky, 2001). There is no consensus as to the role of enhancer or inhibitor of technology in the cognitive process (Ertmer & Ottenbreit-Leftwich, 2010). However, reality evidences how the effects of technology on the outcome of the learning process will be determined by the intensity of its use and the level of sophistication of the tools used (Prendes, 2011).

On the other hand, we find another generation of students called *digital immigrants*, a student who, due to his age, has work and family responsibilities (Ariño, 2008). The interest of these students in resuming their studies is based on their intention to improve their work situation; they are usually highly motivated students (Gibbs, Morgan, & Taylor, 1984), and they have sophisticated learning resources based on their work or personal experience, and can use it effectively (Devlin, 1996; Van Rossum & Taylor, 1987). Moreover, they have well-developed time planning and self-management skills (Trueman & Hartley, 1996).

Your decision to go back to class means coping with several circumstances, which to some extent may be counterproductive (Adiego, Asensio, & Serrano, 2004) such as the need to reconcile studies with their professional and family life and acquire the habit of studying again, in a context where the models, resources, and even the educational environment are totally different. Unlike digital natives, adult learners have had to adapt to the digital society. These students must learn, on the one hand, to use the technologies, and on the other, to integrate them as a resource in their learning process.

Using Mobile Apps

Despite the differences between the two student profiles, it is clear that the intensive use of technology is a common factor in both groups. In addition, the possibility of using, in the learning process, the same technological devices that are used in our daily lives, leading to mobile learning, begins to reach high rates of diffusion among university students.

The use of mobile devices constitutes a true revolution in the classroom (West, 2013). Mobile learning refers to the use of mobile or wireless devices for the purpose of learning while on the move. Typical examples of the devices used for mobile learning include cell phones, smartphones, palmtops, and handheld computers; tablet PCs, laptops, and personal media players can also fall within this scope (Kukulska-Hulme & Traxler, 2005). The first generation of truly portable information has been integrated with many functions in small, portable electronic devices (Peters, 2007). Recent innovations in program applications and social software using Web 2.0 technologies (e.g., blogs, wikis, Twitter, YouTube) or social networking sites (such as Facebook and MySpace) have made mobile devices more dynamic and pervasive and also promise more educational potential.

In particular, mobile technologies perfectly fit new student profiles, increasing their levels of involvement in the process, and improving knowledge acquisition and soft skills development (Park, 2011). In this sense, Goel et al. (2015) highlight that mobile devices have gained lot of popularity in recent years. The student community is a major user of smartphones, tablets, and other mobile devices. Students are using mobile devices for learning, entertainment, shopping, bill payment, information exchange, social networking, etc. An App on the mobile devices brings useful information directly to pockets of the students and provides an engaging user experience.

In particular, some Apps, such as Socrative, are widely used in education (Awedh, Mueen, Zafar, & Manzoor, 2015). The reason for this is simple: it is a free and easy-to-use App, which allows you to answer quizzes in a very attractive way for the student. It contributes dynamism to the class, which makes it very attractive to the student.

The Research Design

The design of our teaching innovation is presented below.

Phase 1: Define and Implement the Methodology

In order to improve accounting learning, the Socrative App has been used during the second semester of 2015–2016 in the accounting course required in Human Resources Management and Labor Relations Degree at Public University of Navarre (Spain). Because of the high use of mobile phones in the classroom, we decided to adopt this app in order to make it more enjoyable and facilitate students' acquisition of theoretical concepts at once. Additionally, it helps us encourage discussion as well as teamwork skills; to do this, a team competition took place in the last class.

Based on our previous experiences in the use of ICT as learning tools, we adopted it, pursuing two main objectives:

1. To help students understand and assimilate course material in an entertaining way.
2. To encourage discussion and exchange of views among students.

Before using it, because our students were unfamiliar with Socrative App, we were to carry out a simulation explaining how it works. Having said that, first, we explained the lesson (or lessons involved in Socrative) as always. Then we encouraged students to take their mobile phone and use the app. To use the app, we first created a "teacher account" and facilitated the room number of a virtual classroom where students were able to see and answer different questions related to the lessons explained previously. The students had to write their names, so we could know the answers of each one, which were sent to our email. Each question was tabled individually; they could not see the following question until every student had answered it, so they could share their point of view and argue their choices, resulting in an interesting feedback. Finally, we clarified any doubts before moving on to the next question.

In the last class, a competition took place. Ten teams, nine of them formed by four students and one of them formed by three students, had to answer seven questions related to the subject in a short period of time. It led to a discussion and created a competitive environment.

Phase 2: Create Questions Database

To make available tests, we created a database with various questions, based on different practical and theoretical concepts concerning this subject and similar to the final test. Each test had four response options, with only one correct.

Phase 3: Monitoring the Learning Process of Students

To evaluate the students' work, they must be able not only to answer questions properly linked to theory presented during the course but also to participate in the class discussion. Participants carried out individually the test, except in the last test that – as we have pointed out – was conducted in teams. We could observe that our students normally fail tests because they do not read questions carefully. So, according to Frederick (2005), people are inclined to check the fastest response in a test, initially. However, those who adopt a more reflexive and methodical attitude will respond in the right way, overcoming the "barrier" of the first reaction. Our aim was to help students be aware of this problem before the final test, in addition to facilitating the acquisition of practical and theoretical concepts.

Phase 4: Evaluate the Perception of Students

In this phase, we wanted to evaluate students' perceptions, reactions, and suggestions about the implementation and use of this methodology. In order to do this, we prepared a questionnaire that contains 30 questions with multiple answers and an open-ended question.

To distribute this questionnaire, we used Google forms and university virtual platform, which eliminated associated errors with the transcription of data and automatically estimated the time spent by each student on completing the questionnaire. The assessment has been designed to evaluate the work done during the whole course. That is why the questionnaire is distributed at the end of the semester.

Initial Evidence

Methodology and Variables

As noted above, this is an exploratory study. This is why to test the effects of Socrative App over the assimilation of theoretical concepts and the development of practical skills in a learning environment (theoretical model) it was performed on a small sample of students, particularly, in the accounting course (Degree of Human Resources Management and Labor Relations), using a simple random sampling. Table 1 shows the study specifications.

With regard to the variables, in our study, the dependent variable is "perception of Socrative use." It is a dichotomous variable where 0 indicates a negative valuation and 1 is a positive valuation. Furthermore, the variables that are shown in Table 2 and which are part of the theoretical model are considered as independent variables. In specific terms, to analyze if the use of Socrative App facilitates the assimilation of

Table 1. Study Specifications.

Sampling universe	60 enrolled students
Sample	40 students
Interview	Electronic
Margin of error	$\pm$ 7.6 ($p = q$) at the 95% confidence level
Fieldwork dates	Second semester (from February to June) 2016

Table 2. Study Variables.

Dimension	Variable	Type	Definition
Student Profile	Perception of the uses of Socrative	Categorical	Positive or negative perception of the use of Socrative; 1 = strongly disagree to 4 = strongly agree
	Age	Categorical	1 = 18–25 years; 2 = 25–35 years; 3 = older 35
	Gender	Dichotomous	0 = male, 1 = female
	Professional experience	Categorical	1 = no experience; 2 = experience less than 1 year; 3 = 1–3 years; 4 = more than 3 years' work experience
Perceived Utility	Students can identify the problem	Categorical	After using the app, the student can understand the problem raised and answer properly; 1 = strongly disagree to 4 = strongly agree
	Students can understand the problem	Categorical	The use of Socrative App in class made it easier to understand the subject; 1 = strongly disagree to 4 = strongly agree
	Students finds Ideal solution	Categorical	The contents studied in the subject allowed students to find an ideal solution to the raised problem; 1 = strongly disagree to 4 = strongly agree
	Student participation	Categorical	While using the app, students were actively involved in class discussion, which helped them achieve a greater understanding about the subject; 1 = Strongly disagree to 4 = strongly agree

Table 2. (*Continued*)

Dimension	Variable	Type	Definition
Perceived Ease of Use	Students assimilate information	Categorical	The use of Socrative App allows students to assimilate much information, with less time and effort; 1 = strongly disagree to 4 = strongly agree.
	Student devote attention	Categorical	Students attend to the information over the short duration; 1 = strongly disagree to 4 = strongly agree
	Funny work	Categorical	Work with Socrative App seemed more funny and stimulating than using other types of resources; 1 = strongly disagree to 4 = strongly agree
Tool Adaptation to Learning Environment	Appropriate time	Categorical	The time for the activity was sufficient; 1 = strongly disagree to 4 = strongly agree
	Activity design	Categorical	The activity was designed and planned correctly; 1 = strongly disagree to 4 = strongly agree
	Adjustment model UPNA	Categorical	Socrative App fits UPNA's educational model; 1 = strongly disagree to 4 = strongly agree

Source: Own formulation.

theoretical concepts and the development of practical skills in a learning environment, we have chosen the following variables as a reference point to the activity design using Socrative App: time available, course content, and university educational model.

Regarding the effects of the use of Socrative App, students indicated their ability to understand the material, identify the problems, and offer adequate solution. We also asked whether they perceived that the material made learning fun and whether it helped them get involved in class discussion (see Table 2). All of them are based on one-to-four Likert scale, ranging from 1 "strongly disagree" to 4 "strongly agree."

On the other hand, demographic variables were also included, such as age, work, experience, and gender. Regarding demographic variables, we considered it necessary to modify the age and work experience variables as dichotomous variables in order to discern their influence on students' responses. So, the age variable appears with three categories and the work experience variable with four. Therefore, if the student did not show in the particular category, the value will be equal to 0 and 1 otherwise.

Data Analysis

Considering this is an exploratory analysis, we applied Mann–Whitney *U* test, which is a nonparametric statistical technique. This method appears the most appropriate for a small sample. It is equivalent to analysis of variance for small samples, fewer than 30 or 40 individuals.

In our study, we focus on analyzing students profile and how it can affect the perceptions of students in respect with the adoption of Socrative App and its effects on academic activities. With respect to age and gender, our sample reveals that 60% are woman, with 90% of them in the age range of 18–25 and only 2.5% of them more than 35 years old (see Table 3).

Regarding work experience, see Table 4, most students do not have experience (37.5%) or have less than one year (30%); it certainly makes sense, given that students are young, as shown above. However, there seems to be no significant differences among these categorizations in terms of students' perceptions on the use of Socrative App, as 99.95% of students had positive perceptions of Socrative App use during the course.

On the other hand, from our sample, we extracted that 97.5% have positive perceptions on academic activities. Most students claimed that

Table 3. Age and Gender.

	Student Profile			
	Age 18–25	**Age 25–35**	**Age more than 35**	**Gender**
Mann–Whitney U	53,000	46,000	10,000	182,500
Wilcoxon W	719,000	749,000	790,000	482,500
Z	−.971	−.553	−.933	−.297
Asymp. Sig. (2-tailed)	.332	.580	.351	.766

Table 4. Work Experience.

	Student Profile			
	Not professional experience	**Experience less than 1 year**	**Experience 1–3 years**	**Experience >than 3 years**
Mann–Whitney U	168,500	168,000	92,500	64,000
Wilcoxon W	288,500	574,000	113,500	659,000
Z	−.601	.000	−.408	−1.631
Asymp. Sig. (2-tailed)	.548	1.000	.683	.103

Socrative App facilitates the understanding of the subject (95%) in addition to finding proper solutions in order to answer questions raised (90%). Further, 90% of them indicated that the use of this methodology allowed them to take part in a class discussion. As a consequence, they prefer this format of material over others, at the 99% or 97% confidence levels (see Table 5).

In fact, in the open question, some students strengthen these results with their statements, such as "the tests helped me better understand the content of the course and shared my point of view with my colleagues," "the activity (the use of Socrative App) encouraged us to get involved in the classroom and also interact with the rest of students, creating a

Table 5. Perceived Utility.

	Perceived Utility			
	Student can identify the problem	**Student can understand the problem**	**Student finds ideal solution**	**Student participation**
Mann–Whitney *U*	73,000	9,500	34,000	53,000
Wilcoxon *W*	118,000	12,500	44,000	63,000
Z	−2.441	−2.004	−1.941	−.971
Asymp. Sig. (2-tailed)	.015	.045	.052	.332

Table 6. Perceived Ease of Use.

	Perceived Ease of Use		
	Students assimilate information	**Students devote attention**	**Funny work**
Mann–Whitney *U*	19,000	78,000	19,000
Wilcoxon *W*	22,000	93,000	22,500
Z	−1.336	−.440	−1.336
Asymp. Sig. (2-tailed)	.182	.660	.182

good learning environment," or "I liked the use of Socrative App, because it helped me train for final test."

Next, we assessed if this app was perceived as easy to use, namely, if students obtain information, devote attention, and find this format fun. The findings, just as shown in Table 6, show that 90% of students prefer these cases to others, because it helped them assimilate information due to the increasing participation. In addition, students highlight that this app makes learning more fun.

Table 7 shows the tool adaptation to learning environment at UPNA. And 45% of students consider that time designated to this

Table 7. Tool-Adaptation to e-Learning.

	Tool Adaptation to Learning Environment		
	Appropriate time	Activity design	Adjustment model UPNA
Mann–Whitney U	169,500	54,500	10,000
Wilcoxon W	422,500	75,500	11,000
Z	−.878	−2.039	−.933
Asymp. Sig. (2-tailed)	.380	.041	.351

activity is appropriate; besides, they believe that this methodology can get adjusted to UPNA's educational model. In sum, the findings show that the design of this activity has significant positive effects on students' perceptions.

The analysis shows that students are capable enough to properly apply theoretical concepts in order to answer different questions raised. Furthermore, they perceived that this kind of software is a fun way to learn, and, accordingly, students demand its use in the learning environment, as it mostly helped them understand the material course in addition to developing discussion skills.

Conclusions, Limitations, and Future Research

Today, it is widely acknowledged that the university has a third mission: Transfer of knowledge. This characteristic is key for the future and the sustainability of the university, as well as for the economic and social development of the territory. However, there are doubts about its relationship and degree of involvement with other activities of the university. It is clear that teaching and research are complementary activities. But in addition to this, the university has promoted transfer of knowledge, not only limited to the field of research but also affecting the teaching activity.

The EHEA provides the basis of this process, recognizing the importance of the university as a social agent. But additionally, economic crisis and the change in the profile of the student show the strong social and economic implications of the university's activity.

In this way, the university not only has to know what society needs, but must train qualified and competent professionals. Professionals who must have the combination of knowledge (knowledge, skills, and attitudes) necessary to perform a task and achieve a purpose within a specific context and in accordance with established norms or conditions. To this end, the EHEA establishes the so-called competency-based training system, where:

- The student is the central axis of the model, playing an active role in the process.
- Cocreation of knowledge is key. Therefore, teaching models must be designed on the basis of different learning models used by the student.

We move toward a new model where the knowledge and the way of acquiring them are determined by the needs of the students. And this adjustment, the academic offer and the market demand, cause the university to pursue educational models characterized as: dynamic, flexible, and cooperative as well as personalized and interactive. ICT-intensive models are also carried out according to a student who can be defined as digital, native, or immigrant.

With this in mind, today, in an environment with a hypertechnologized society, it is vital that professors introduce this methodology in their teaching. In addition, students are increasingly demanding the integration of ICT use in the classroom, since they belong to a digital generation. In this context, the educational system of UPNA remains very traditional with master classes. The role of students is totally passive, so the entire responsibility of class development lies on the shoulders of teachers, but this situation can change with the use of Socrative App in a learning environment, since it encourages students to play an active part in class.

In fact, it seems that most students have positive perceptions of Socrative App as a teaching tool and prefer it to other traditional systems. They consider Socrative App a useful tool to understand and assimilate concepts, as it helped them to be aware of their knowledge in an entertaining way. Further, the use of tools such as Socrative App increased classroom participation and interaction, leading to increasing engagement in class. Moreover, it provided instant feedback on what students know, which is really useful for teachers, because the teachers can then adapt the future classes to strengthen some concepts. Therefore, Socrative App supports learning, increases motivation, and

helps to create an environment where students may share their point of view.
This study was developed using a small sample, so future research should test the use of Socrative App using a larger sample in order to determine whether the results can be generalized, since this app not only facilitates the assimilation of theoretical concepts but also helps to develop competences such as teamwork, participation, and interaction.

References

Adell-Segura, J., & Linda Castañeda-Quintero, L. (2010). Los entornos personales de aprendizaje (PLEs): Una nueva manera de entender el aprendizaje. In R. Vila & M. Fiorucci (Eds.). Retrieved from http://hdl.handle.net/10201/17247

Adiego, V., Asensio, S., & Serrano, M. A. (2004). Transformando espacios: el aprendizaje de estudiantes no tradicionales en la educación superior. In *VIII Congreso Español de Sociología de la Federación Española de Sociología*. Alicante, Spain.

Ariño, A. (2008). *El oficio de estudiar en la Universidad: Compromisos flexibles, Valencia*. Valencia: Publicacions de la Universitat de València.

Awedh, M., Mueen, A., Zafar, B., & Manzoor, U. (2015). Using Socrative and Smartphones for the support of collaborative learning. *arXiv preprint arXiv:1501.01276*.

Bagley, C., & Hunter, B. (1992). Restructuring constructivism and technology: Forging a new relationship. *Educational Technology, 32*(7), 22–27.

Beasley, N., & Smyth, K. (2004). Expected and actual student use of an online learning environment: A critical analysis. *CiteSeerX. Electronic Journal on e-Learning, 2*(1), 43–50.

Bennett, K., Maton, K., & Kervin, L. (2008). The "digital natives" debate: A critical review of the evidence. *British Journal of Educational Technology, 39*(5), 775–786.

Boethel, M., & Dimock, V. (1999). *Constructing knowledge with technology: A review of the literature*. Austin, TX: Southwest Educational Development Laboratory.

Cerderblom, J., & Paulsen, D. (2005). *Critical reasoning*. Belmont, CA: Wadsworth Publishing Company.

Collins, A., Brown, J. S., & Newman, S. E. (1990). Cognitive apprenticeship: Teaching the crafts of reading, writing, and mathematics. In L. Resnick (Ed.), *Knowing, learning, and instruction: Essays in honor of Robert Glaser* (pp. 453–494). Hillsdale, NJ: Erlbaum.

Devlin, A. (1996). Criminal classes: Are there links between failure at school and future offending? *Support for Learning, 11*(1), 13–16.

DeVries, R., & Kohlberg, L. (1990). *Constructivist early education: Overview and comparison with other programs.* Washington, DC: National Association for the Education of Young Children.

Duffy, T. M., & Cunningham, D. J. (1996). Constructivism: Implications for the design and delivery of instruction. In D. H. Jonassen (Ed.), *Handbook of research for educational communications and technology* (pp. 51, 170–198). New York, NY: Simon & Schuster.

Duffy, T. M., & Jonassen, D. H., (Eds.). (1992). Constructivism: New implications for instructional technology. *Constructivism and the technology of instruction: A conversation* (pp. 1–16).

Duit, R. (1995). The constructivist view: A Fashionable and fruitful paradigm for science education research and practice. In L. P. Steffe & J. Gale (Eds.), *Constructivism in education.* Hillsdale, NJ: Lawrence Erlbaum Associates.

Ennis, R. H. (1996). Critical thinking dispositions: Their nature and assessability. *Informal Logic, 18*(2 & 3), 165–182.

Ertmer, P. A., & Ottenbreit-Leftwich, A. T. (2010). Teacher technology change: How knowledge, confidence, beliefs, and culture intersect. *Journal of Research on Technology in Education, 42*(3), 255–284.

Frederick, S. (2005). Cognitive reflection and decision making. *The Journal of Economic Perspectives, 19*(4), 25–42.

Gibbs, G., Morgan, A., & Taylor, E. (1984). The world of the learner. In F. Marton, D. Hounsell, & Entwistle, N. (Eds.), *The experience of learning.* Edinburgh: Scottish Academic Press.

Goel, A., Taneja, S., Singh, A. P., Bakshi, I. S., Gupta, S. C., Bajaj, D., ... Kumar, M. (2015). DUIT: A Mobile App developed using interdisciplinary approach. *DU Journal of Undergraduate Research and Innovation, 1,* 2395–2334.

González, J. C. (2008). TIC y la transformación de la práctica educativa en el contexto de las sociedades del conocimiento. *Revista Universidad y Sociedad de Conocimiento, 5*(2), 1–8.

Hannafin, M. J., & Hill, J. R. (2002). Epistemology and the design of learning environments. In R. A. Reiser & J. V. Dempsey (Eds.), *Trends and issues in instructional design and technology.* Upper Saddle River, NJ: Merrill Prentice Hall.

Huitt, W. (1998). Critical thinking: An overview. *Educational Psychology Interactive.* Valdosta, GA: Barnesville.

Knuth, R., & Cunningham, D. J. (1993). Tools for constructivism. In T. Duffy, J. Lowyck, & D. Jonassen (Eds.), *Designing environments for constructive learning* (pp. 163–188). Berlin: Springer-Verlag.

Kukulska-Hulme, A., & Traxler, J. (2005). *Mobile learning: A handbook for educators and trainers.* London: Routledge.

Kulkarni, S. S., Klassner, F., Gehlot, V., Dougherty, I. I. I., Metzger, S. M., & Wagner, W. P. (2015). Mobile App development: A cross-discipline team-based approach to student and faculty learning. *The Journal of Engineering Entrepreneurship, 6*(2), 69–82.

Méndez, D., & Slisko, J. (2013). Software Socrative and smartphones as tools for implementation of basic processes of active physics learning in classroom: An initial feasibility study with prospective teachers. *European Journal of Physics Education, 4*(2).

Nanjappa, A., & Grant, M. M. (2003). Constructing on constructivism: The role of technology. *Electronic Journal for the Integration of Technology in Education, 2*(1), 38−56.

Park, Y. (2011). A pedagogical framework for mobile learning: Categorizing educational applications of mobile technologies into four types. *The International Review of Research in Open and Distributed Learning, 12*(2), 78−102.

Pea, R. D., & Collins, A. (2008). Learning how to do science education: Four waves of reform. In Y. Kali, M. Linn, & E. Roseman (Eds.) *Designing coherent science education: Implications for curriculum, instruction, and policy* (pp. 3−12). New York, NY: Teachers College Press.

Pérez, A. (2002). Elementos para el análisis de la interacción educativa en los nuevos entornos de aprendizaje. Píxel-Bit. *Revista de Medios y Educación, 19*, 49−61.

Perkins, D. N. (1992). *Smart schools: From training memories to educating minds.* New York, NY: Free Press.

Peters, K. (2007). m-Learning: Positioning educators for a mobile, connected future. *The International Review of Research in Open and Distributed Learning, 8*(2). 1−17.

Prendes, M. P. (2011). Innovación con TIC en enseñanza superior: Descripción y resultados de experiencias en la Universidad de Murcia. *REIFOP, 14*(1), 267−280.

Prensky, M. (2001). Digital Natives, digital immigrants: Do they really think differently? *On the Horizon, 9*(6), 1−9.

Roberts, T., Romm, C., & Jones, D. (2000). *Current practice in web-based delivery of IT courses.* APWeb2000.

Salinas, J. (2002). Modelos flexibles como respuesta de las universidades a la sociedad de la información. *Acción Pedagógica, 11*, 4−13.

Salinas, J. (2004). Innovación docente y uso de las TIC en la enseñanza universitaria. *Revista Universidad y Sociedad del Conocimiento, 1*(1), 1−16.

Sandholtz, J. H., Ringstaff, C., & Dwyer, D. C. (1997). *Teaching with technology: Creating student-centered classrooms.* New York, NY: Teachers College Press.

Tapscott, D. (1998). *Growing up digital: The rise of the net generation.* New York, NY: McGraw-Hill.

Trueman, M., & Hartley, M. (1996). A comparison between the time-management skills and academic performance of mature and traditional-entry university students. *Higher Education, 32*(2), 199−215.

Tymon, A. (2013). The student perspective on employability. *Studies in Higher Education, 38*(6), 841−856.

Van Rossum, E., & Taylor, I. P. (1987). The relationship between conceptions of learning and good teaching: A scheme of cognitive development. Paper presented at the Annual Meeting of the American Educational Research Association, Washington DC.

Von Glasersfeld, E. (1995). *Radical constructivism: A way of knowing and learning.* London: Falmer Press.

West, D. M. (2013). *Mobile learning: Transforming education, engaging students, and improving outcomes.* Brookings Institution Policy Report (pp. 1−7).

Chapter 13

Enhancing Learner Autonomy and Active Learning Using Digital Portfolio

Linda Pospisilova

Abstract

In recent years there has been a constant growth in digital portfolio use in tertiary education. Portfolios are used by educational institutions for assessment, as a showcase of both student and institution work, and with an increasing trend also as a tool for higher employability of graduates and support of lifelong learning. This chapter introduces concepts of portfolio, digital portfolio, language portfolio, autonomy, and self-assessment. It approaches both positivist and constructivist paradigms of digital portfolio and presents examples of ePortfolio implementation at the University of Pardubice. Selected examples of good practice with respect to autonomous learning, experiential learning, and international cooperation are also given.

Keywords: Digital portfolio; ePortfolio; Mahara; language portfolio; self-assessment; autonomy

Introduction

The e-portfolio is the central and common point for the student experience ... It is a reflection of the student as a

Active Learning Strategies in Higher Education: Teaching for Leadership, Innovation, and Creativity, 315–335
ISBN: 978-1-78714-488-0

person undergoing continuous personal development, not just a store of evidence.

Geoff Rebbeck, e-Learning Coordinator,
Thanet College, JISC (2008)

There are many definitions of ePortfolio, but they all seem to be very similar. I have selected a definition from the sphere of higher education published on university webpages and it reads that "an ePortfolio is a digital collection of work that documents and showcases knowledge, skills, and abilities, and their growth over time" (California State University, 2015). Numerous researchers consider an ePortfolio student-centered approach to be key, including collecting work, selecting key work samples, and reflecting upon the work. There are two main theoretical approaches to portfolio assessment and thus to ePortfolio introduction to the institutions (Paulson & Paulson, 1994): Positivist and Constructivist paradigms as defined below.

> Positivist Portfolios: The purpose of the portfolio is to assess learning outcomes and those outcomes are, generally, defined externally. Positivism assumes that meaning is constant across users, contexts, and purposes ... The portfolio is a receptacle for examples of student work used to infer what and how much learning has occurred. (Paulson & Paulson, 1994, p. 36)

> Constructivist Portfolios: The portfolio is a learning environment in which the learner constructs meaning. It assumes that meaning varies across individuals, over time, and with purpose. The portfolio presents process, a record of the processes associated with learning itself; a summation of individual portfolios would be too complex for normative description. (Paulson & Paulson, 1994, p. 36)

A digital portfolio was first introduced to the Language Centre of the University of Pardubice as a positivist portfolio. Students of technical fields who were learning specific foreign languages were assigned selected tasks to be completed and displayed within their ePortfolio, and these assignments were subsequently assessed according to the given criteria. The constructivist portfolios were introduced by a team of experienced ePortfolio teachers to their students with the aim to promote self-assessment techniques, goal setting, and autonomous learning in university students. These two phenomena will be further discussed in the following section and selected examples of ePortfolio use in language courses portraying both approaches will be given.

Theoretical Background and State-of-the-Art in Digital Portfolio Use

Portfolios in Language Learning

European Language Portfolio (ELP) came to the attention of experts in the year 2001. It was released together with the Common European Framework of Reference (CEFR) during the same year. The earliest idea of the ELP was first introduced at the symposium in Rüschlikon in 1991 by the experts Little, Gouillier, and Hughes of Council of Europe (1992). Fifteen European states participated on the ELP and CEFR development. The outcomes of numerous pilot projects were published in a form of paper portfolio comprising three parts: The Language Passport, The Language Biography, and The Dossier. Several language versions were made available in the course of time, including the Czech version published by Bohuslavová (2007). The paper version of the language portfolio was later, through the development of Internet and new media, transferred into a digital form and is still available online in six language mutations Aplikace EJP (2014). The original Dossier section of the language portfolio corresponds with the current concept of digital portfolios. The Dossier available online can function as a folder for storage of learning outcomes; however, this original section does not significantly differ from folders we all create in our personal computers or cloud storages. Such a storage tool available for portfolio creation can be considered outdated, as there is non-existent space for feedback, reflection, and comments, and very limited possibility for sharing selected artifacts with target audience. In addition, current content presentation tools and digital content curation tools have advanced significantly and such a storage format cannot compete with current needs and requirements of modern institutions and their students. In the past decade, several electronic tools for portfolio design have been designed, also called digital portfolios or ePortfolios which reflect the needs of current teachers and students and the reality of Internet and social networks, including a plethora of application plugins as well as answering the needs for responsive design on various mobile devices. The key word in the area of work with portfolios, as in language portfolios, has become "a digital portfolio."

Digital Portfolios

Digital portfolios can be found at numerous higher education institutions, especially in the Anglo-Saxon academic world, where they frequently form an integral part of university learning and teaching. The parties benefiting from digital portfolio implementation can be university students, university graduates, alumni, academics, and also educational institutions themselves. Portfolio work can contribute to knowledge and competence consolidation and collection; nevertheless, portfolios can also function as potential tools for 21st-century skill development, namely, information literacy, initiative, and self-direction. Further some institutions set a strategic aim when implementing and developing digital portfolios to increase competition and employability of future university graduates. In such cases, digital portfolio acts as a showcase of a student's personal and professional profile. Speaking of language portfolio, the digital tool is implemented with the aim to develop language and ICT competence in students, to assist in critical thinking development, self-reflection, creativity, communication, and collaboration. Consistent work with the tool can also assist in the development of character features, such as curiosity, initiative, and persistence.

A concept of digital portfolio as a collection of artifacts created with the aspiration to document knowledge, competence, skills, and abilities of a student in time has been applied and researched at several educational levels. The authors who have mapped digital portfolio theory and practice are Barrett (2007) and Benson (2007, 2011), to name a few. There were also several initiatives and projects launched, for instance, EPAC in California (2002) which has since become a leading resource on electronic portfolios, MOSEP in Europe (2006), and eFolio in Great Britain. In the Czech Republic the digital portfolio implementation is still in its initial phase and has been primarily used in teacher training. In contrast with the situation in Great Britain, Australia, the United States, or New Zealand, portfolios are very often employed only on the faculty level and not university wide. So far there have been very few Czech publications mentioning digital portfolios and mostly on informative levels. The ePortfolio tool was described as a tool for personalized learning by Zounek and Sudický (2012) and Zounek, Juhaňák, Staudková, and Poláček (2016) who characterize ePortfolio as an environment directed and codirected by students, thus touching the concept of autonomous learning.

The implementation process and actual work with ePortfolios has been supported by user communities on both national and international levels through its community of users, teachers, trainers, and administrators of the open-source LMS Moodle. There are several tools available which can be used on individual or institutional levels. Google Sites, Evernote, Wordpress, or Mahara ePortfolio can be considered as the most frequently used open-source solutions. Recently, an application called SeeSaw has been accessible at most major platforms: iOS, Android, Kindle, Chrome, and Firefox.

Numerous educational institutions utilize open-source solutions and accessible applications; on the contrary, there are many universities which provide their students with commercial or tailored online environments for creation of student portfolios. One of the worldwide openly accessible ePortfolio systems with consistent support and a lively user and developer community is Mahara ePortfolio system. It has been in existence for more than 10 years and the phase of implementation, research on the system feasibility, and student attitude studies, pilot studies, and case studies have been conducted in the early phase of the system life cycle. There are studies on development of an ePortfolio success model by Balaban, Mu, and Divjak (2013), on integration of ePortfolios in Learning Management System by Queiriós, Oliveira, Leal, and Moreira (2011), and a study providing an evaluation tool for a suitable ePortfolio system selection by Balaban and Bubas (2009). In this study, two ePortfolio systems were compared: Mahara and ELGG. The study concludes that Mahara ePortfolio system dominated in all assessed categories. The studies focusing on the technology acceptance and student attitudes and the level of students' adaptation to a digital portfolio, which may assist potentially interested institutions in the successful introduction and implantation of ePortfolio system, are Lopez-Fernandez and Rodriguez-Illera (2009), Miller and Morgaine (2009), Balaban and Bubas (2010), and Tzeng (2011). Another perspective on ePortfolio implementation can be obtained from the findings of Scottish researchers conducting a qualitative study on tutor response to ePortfolio implementation potentials and barriers by Peacock, Gordon, Murray, Morss, and Dunlop (2010).

Autonomous Learning and ePortfolios

A documented history of the concept of autonomous language learning dates back to 1971. Yves Châlon is considered to be the father of the idea of autonomy in foreign language learning. Unfortunately, he died shortly after the foundation of the Centre de Recherches et d'Applications en Langues (CRAPEL). The key researchers in the area of autonomous language learners are Holec, Benson, Little, and Littlewood. David Little was also one of the founders of the ELP. Based on the literature review, we can assume that there is a tight link between portfolio and autonomy in the field of language learning.

Well-known experts in the research of autonomy and autonomous learning, such as David Little and Phil Benson, date the beginnings of the concept of autonomy in language learning back to the 1960s. The key document is considered to be a report for the Council of Europe in which Holec (1981) puts autonomy into a social and ideological context, shifting the definition of social progress from so-called wealth assurance to the quality of life assurance. Along with this development, higher emphasis is put on lifelong learning and related acceptance of responsibility for one's own learning. This self-directed learning approach was defined as learning containing setting of learning goals, learning processes, and assessment of learning all performed by the students themselves. According to Holec (1981) and his currently most-cited definition, autonomy is the "ability to take charge of one's own learning," in a sense of acquired ability to take the responsibility of all aspects of one's own learning.

David Little in Schwabrick (2002, chapter 9) defines autonomy in the form of a negative definition, explaining what is not an autonomy: it is not strictly only learning without teacher's guidance; in the classroom context not necessarily all responsibility is shifted from a teacher to a student who would be left to one's own fate; autonomy is not a teaching method; it is not single, easily defined type of behavior; autonomy is not a certain point students would be supposed to reach. Who is an autonomous learner then? According to Holec (1981) an autonomous learner should be prepared to take over an initiative in the learning process and be responsible for partial steps in learning as mentioned above: goal setting, progress definition, selections of methods which will lead to fulfilling the goals, self-management and monitoring of one's own learning process, leading to assessment of one's own accomplishments.

Benson (2007) points out that David Little made an extension to the Holec's definition of autonomy in foreign language learning.

"Autonomy in foreign language learning depends on development and capacity for detachment, critical reflection, and independent action Little (1991). Autonomous learners accept responsibility for determining the objectives, content, pace, and methods of their learning; they control their learning process and assess their outcomes Holec (1981)."

Benson (2013) also mentions an importance of portfolio work, self-direction, and self-assessment. He adds that there should not be mere self-assessment in progress, emphasizing learner capabilities, but formative assessment should be present and a cyclic approach to goal setting and planning is preferred. Several of these ideas were projected in the suggested learning model which will be further elaborated on in the section "Constructivist Approach – Autonomous Learning Cycle."

Formal, Non-Formal, and Informal Learning

In the context of autonomous learning and digital portfolio utilization, a shift from formal to non-formal and informal learning can be observed. According to Arnseth, Erstad, Juhaňák, and Zounek (2016), "We are still facing lack of information … about how and why [young learners] use digital technologies … alternatively, why they do not use them in certain situations (in learning processes)."

What is the difference between the terms formal, non-formal, and informal education? Higher education as we know it today can be considered to belong to formal education since education is provided by educational institutions regulated by law, standardized, and providing certification for achieved education. Non-formal education is provided by other institutions such as private educational institutions, non-governmental institutions, through free time educational activities, which are usually not certified. Non-formal education plays a complementary role to formal education. On the contrary, Palán (2002) defines informal learning as unorganized, unsystematic, and uncoordinated. Informal learning is defined as acquisition of knowledge, skills, and competences in everyday situations; in some cases it can even be an unconscious process. Both active learning and ePortfolio enhanced learning, especially those following the constructivist approach, enter the territory of informal learning. The future findings of the study presented in the section "Constructivist Approach – Autonomous Learning Cycle" may contribute to the search for answers to the questions asked by Arnseth et al. (2016) at the beginning of this section.

Examples of Active Learning with ePortfolio

Positivist Approach – International Projects

In all levels of education, international projects providing students with priceless opportunities of international experience are encouraged and run. During such projects and exchanges, if prepared purposefully, students are given space and situations which can help to develop necessary 21st-century skills, including life skills (agility, flexibility, and adaptability), workforce skills (collaboration, leadership initiative, and responsibility), applied skills (accessing and analyzing information, effective communication, and problem solving), personal skills (curiosity, imagination, and critical thinking), and last but not least interpersonal (cooperation and teamwork) and non-cognitive (managing) skills, further elaborated on in Saavedra and Opfer (2012). These international exchange projects can become even more valuable assets in foreign language learning, providing participating students with added value in the areas of communicative skill development and intercultural experience.

In such cases when both institutions participating in an international exchange program use the ePortfolio tool, ideally the same system, the exchange experience can result in collaborative creation, publication, and feedback collection on one common portfolio, mapping and reflecting experience of both hosting and visiting students and their teachers (Figure 1).

An example presented in this section is taken from a publically available portfolio collection which is an outcome of international exchange organized within a subject: SP02-Moduls Tschechisch (Czech language module) between University of Pardubice, Czech Republic and Leipzig University, Germany. The participating students were, respectively, learning the German and Czech languages. They created a portfolio before the actual exchange stay, during the stay – in a form of reflective diary, and after the stay providing mutual feedback to the participants (Figure 2).

Positivist Approach – Mahoodle Project

Mahoodle as a term is still quite infrequently used both in the academic community and the communities of educators. What does the word Mahoodle mean? It represents an integration of the open-source online learning platform Moodle (LMS) and Mahara, an open-source

Figure 1. An Example of a Portfolio Collection Created Collaboratively by Students of the University of Pardubice and the Leipzig University as a Result of an Exchange Stay Which Took Place in 2013, Studienreise SoSe 2013. *Source*: Wanner and Nesswetha (2015). *Note*: The *screenshot* is taken from the Mahara instance at the Leipzig University. "Mahara" is a trademark registered to Catalyst IT, and the logo is used with permission here.

ePortfolio system. The easiest and most straightforward way to integrate the systems is the so-called SSO (Single-Sign-On) when the users log on to the systems with the same login details; thus, the sign-up experience for the new users is dramatically improved. In our case the SSO method was not utilized because the ePortfolio system was maintained outside the integrated university systems. This ensured that students have lifelong access to their portfolios at the expense of abandoning the integrated sign-on and its obvious advantages. This technical solution does not stop the teachers from pursuing the Mahoodle project content wise. The students involved in the Mahoodle project are provided with a content rich course in LMS Moodle designed by their teachers and they are invited to build upon this course by developing their own reviews and extended views of the course themes in a form of a portfolio page. This page is then presented in the class and consequently added to the content of the course by a hyperlink; thus, it is integrated into the

324   *Linda Pospisilova*

Figure 2.   Sandra schreibt: Der Gegenbesuch: Studienreise nach Leipzig
von Studienreise nach Pardubice SoSe 2013. *Note*: Evidence of Language
Learning Experience as a Part of ePortfolio Created by the Students of
the University of Pardubice and the Leipzig University.

course content. The students become initially critical reviewers and subsequently co-creators of the course content. In addition, their contributions stay in their portfolio for later use and reflection. The shared and
published course pages created by the students are also used in the follow-up course to reflect upon further students work on the subject. The
course is enriched by the results of the Mahoodle student projects every
year, thus contributing to the quality of the course itself and to the
increasing standard of student work built upon the work of previous
cohorts.

Positivist Approach − Reflective Diaries

A beautiful quote by Anne Frank introduces an article on reflective
diary methodology by Travers (2011): "When I write, I can shake off all
my cares." Travers defines a diary as "a frequently kept, often daily,
record of personal experiences and observations in which ongoing
thoughts, feelings, and ideas can be expressed." She also mentions an
increasing trend in diary use in academic and educational settings.
Diaries have been used as a part of portfolio creation in two different
contexts. The exchange students are asked to keep their diaries in the

Figure 3. An Example of a Fragment of a Reflective Diary from a Student Exchange Stay of the University of Pardubice and the University of Leipzig SoSe 2014. *Note*: The *screenshot* is taken from the Mahara instance at the University of Pardubice. "Mahara" is a trademark registered to Catalyst IT, and the logo is used with permission here.

target language during their international stays, and our nursing students are encouraged to keep reflective diaries in the second language during their hospital trainings. Students reflect on their hospital trainings from several aspects — communication, multicultural experience, SWOT analysis, reflective evaluation of their experience in the target language. They also provide feedback to fellow students in the form of comments (Figure 3).

Constructivist Approach — Autonomous Learning Cycle

As presented in the introduction to this chapter, there are two different paradigms of portfolios. The second paradigm outlined by Paulson and Paulson (1994) is called a constructivist approach. Unlike in the previous examples when the outcomes of the portfolio and learning are defined externally and collected to meet assessment requirements, in case of constructivist approach, students create a portfolio as a process and result of their learning, the outcomes of learning are defined internally, by the students themselves, and the assessment is made by both the teacher and the students. While Barrett (2007) sees and discusses a tension between the two mentioned approaches or paradigms, the differences do not necessarily need to result in a conflict but rather in a mutual coexistence of both approaches at a given institution. For the sake of the creation of a meaningful and sustainable portfolio for our students, both positivist and constructivist approaches can be utilized in a process of scaffolding and learning about the work with ePortfolio and about its role in lifelong learning.

As a part of the pilot study, a learning model was created. The model consists of the following phases: introductory ePlacement language testing diagnosing students' current level of the second language according to which the students enroll in the subject. Within the subject, students undergo initial self-assessment based on the ePlacement test results and self-reflection using can-do statements describing each language skill: Reading Comprehension, Listening Comprehension, Spoken Production, Spoken Interaction, and Writing as stated by CEFR. For instance, a student diagnosed to be at B1+ or B2 level according to CEFR performs self-assessment using B2 level descriptors for each skill. During this phase, descriptors published by· European Council in the document called *Common European Framework of Reference for Languages: Learning, Teaching, Assessment* (Council of Europe, 2001) as a part of the ELP are used. Both the CEFR framework and its descriptors are being revised in the course of 2017. Based on the self-assessment, the students set their own goals or more specifically micro goals for each assessed language skill. This phase seems to be crucial and requires a lot of attention from both the student's and the teacher's side. The goal-setting phase is closely followed and further facilitated by the third phase in which the students are given a standardized yet shorter version of a language test. The test comprises of Listening, Reading, and Use of English parts. In our case, B2 students are tested with an FCE mock test. Further, the tests are evaluated skill wise and as a whole, and both the results and mistakes are analyzed with students. In the next phase, students are invited to revisit their goals with regards to the results of the mock test and they are encouraged to restate their own goals if necessary. The two previous phases play a key role in the overall success of the learning cycle implementation and represent the concept of guided autonomy. The second to last phase, called Evidence Collection, is the most extensive phase of all and represents a switch from guided autonomy to full autonomy of students. Their work can be assisted with optional consultations offered to the students. This is also the phase during which the ePortfolio creation is in progress.

The phase called Evidence Collection is the key phase during which the students fulfill their own goals, monitor their own learning processes, record their learning outcomes, and create learning diaries, thus collecting evidence of goal fulfillment in the form of digital portfolio. This phase is supposed to be fully autonomous, assuming that students have undergone the previous facilitative phases which could be categorized rather as steps representing guided autonomy. Autonomy is founded in the free format of the portfolio within the given framework, choice of learning processes and outcomes, and evidence presentation. The last phase of the learning cycle is called Final Self-assessment, Assessment, and Feedback. This phase concludes the whole cycle and culminates in a final exam which consists of a presentation of a portfolio consisting of self-assessment, goals, and evidence proving the goal fulfillment covering all the above-mentioned language skills. The self-assessment and assessment phase is concluded with critical evaluation of the learning processes and outline of prospects for future learning, thus opening space for the cycle repetition either with the teacher or fully autonomously without any further guidance from the teacher. Students are left with a powerful tool and a set of skills transferrable into other fields of learning and future working life. The scheme in Figure 4 illustrates a complete learning cycle which was suggested as a part of a pilot study.

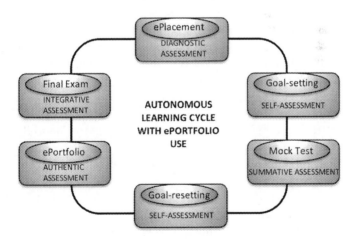

Figure 4. A Learning Cycle Model Enhancing Autonomous Learning Using Digital Portfolio as a Tool for Self-Assessment, Goal Setting, and Evidence Collection and Presentation. *Source*: Linda Pospisilova.

Autonomous Learning Cycle – A Pilot Study

A pilot study was conducted within subjects English for Chemistry and English for Economists at the University of Pardubice in the spring term of the academic year 2015/16. There were 3 experienced teachers and 48 students involved in the study. The students were both undergraduate and postgraduate university students. The pilot study was designed for a length of one term, starting at the end of February 2016 and ending in July 2016. It covered a period of five months including the examination period.

All three participating teachers had previous two-year experience with digital portfolio use in education, including a skill for student portfolio user training. The students were selected according to the following criteria: a choice of smaller groups of students which could be justified with implementation of new methods, time-consuming teaching and learning method, reinforcement of higher individualization of the learning process and offering more space for intensive consultations if necessary. The aim to include all three levels of tertiary education was also accomplished in order to obtain comparative data concerning students' prerequisites for autonomous learning. Another criterion was the language level of the students diagnosed by the entrance ePlacement test. According to assessment and self-assessment criteria given by the European Council and used in the ELP and CEFR descriptor characterization, a student becomes an independent language user when the B1 level is reached. The CEFR defines levels B1 and B2 as Independent levels and the students diagnosed as B1 level users can "describe experiences and events, dreams, hopes and ambitions and briefly give reasons and explanations for opinions and plans, they can narrate a story or relate the plot of a book or film and describe their reactions" (Council of Europe, 2001). This description meets the lowest necessary bar required for the self-assessment, self-reflection, goal-fulfillment, and evidence gathering, all in the target language. Based on these assumptions, only the groups of students with B1 + and higher target level were selected for the study.

Students were given an overview of can-do statements in single language skills and assigned to perform self-assessment and goal-setting steps as shown in Figure 5.

The goal-setting phase was assessed by both students and teachers as the hardest of all above-described phases. The goals are frequently worded in a very general manner, regardless of the time limit of one term and without consideration of the weakness or even the skill in question. Consultations with teachers were essential to complete the task successfully. Table 1 provides examples of goals set by students before and after consultations.

TASKS:

1. Make your own Mahara Page self-assessing your strong and weak points based on the description below and set your own partial, achievable objectives for the following term leading to your language competence growth in each category (Listening, Reading, etc.).

2. Collect artefacts in Mahara portfolio tool to evidence your individual progress.

B2 Listening Comprehension	B2 Reading Comprehension	B2 Spoken Interaction
• I can understand standard spoken language on both familiar and unfamiliar topics in everyday situations even in a noisy environment. • I can with some effort catch much of what is said around me, but may find it difficult to understand a discussion between several native speakers who do not modify	• I can quickly scan through long and complex texts on a variety of topics in my field to locate relevant details. • I can read correspondence relating to my field of interest and readily grasp the essential meaning. • I can obtain information, ideas and opinions from highly specialised sources within my	• I can participate fully in conversations on general topics with a degree of fluency and naturalness, and appropriate use of register. • I can participate effectively in extended discussions and debates on subjects of personal, academic or professional interest, marking clearly the relationship between ideas.

Figure 5. Autonomous Cycle Task Assignment in the ePortfolio tool. *Source*: Linda Pospisilova. *Note*: The *screenshot* is taken from the Mahara instance at the University of Pardubice. "Mahara" is a trademark registered to Catalyst IT, and the logo is used with permission here.

Table 1. Goal-Setting Phase.

Examples of Goals Set by Students Before and After a Consultation	
Goal 1	**Goal 2 (consulted and rewritten)**
I want to be better in listening.	*I want to watch one video per week.*
I need to improve my grammar.	*I will write sometimes a text and that will help me in terminology and grammar.*

In the final de-briefing session with involved teachers, which took place at the end of the pilot study time period, the teachers agreed on several adjustments to the Autonomous Learning Cycle for the future period. One of them was regarding the goal-setting phase and its efficiency. Teachers agreed on introducing the SMART method by Lawler and Hornyak (2012) to their students right before and during the goal-setting phase, thus bringing attention of students to five descriptors of SMART goals. They were first described by George T. Doran (1981) in his article "There's a S.M.A.R.T. Way to Write Management Goals and Objectives" where he shares advice on how to write effective objectives using the acronym SMART and suggests that objectives should be:

Specific − target a specific area for improvement

Measurable − quantify or at least suggest an indicator of progress

Assignable − specify who will do it

Realistic − state what results can realistically be achieved, given available resources

Time-related − specify when the result(s) can be achieved.

A slight adaptation to the original version, with the term "Assignable" replaced with "Attainable," has been found in Williams (2012) − asking whether the goal can be achieved and perfectly meets the needs of this particular self-assessment process culminating in setting one's own goals. This slight refinement of the learning cycle may qualitatively improve the key step in the self-assessment cycle and enhance autonomy of involved students. In addition, introducing SMART method to students can assist in their competence development and help to increase their employability and success in future job positions. The goal-setting phase also functions as a trigger for the autonomous creation of the student portfolio which is shared at the goal-setting point with the teacher and he or she can be helpful during the portfolio creation process, if necessary, in being able to see the changes to the page in real time.

During the Evidence Collection phase, a swap session can be organized to allow participating students to exchange tips and tricks on the learning processes and goal fulfillment. This session can help some students find inspiration, increase motivation, and stay on the track during the autonomous phase.

In the final phase called "Final Evaluation, Feedback, and Self-evaluation," students present their digital portfolio consisting of evidence showing their autonomous learning processes and outcomes from formal, non-formal, and informal learning environments. The final consultation has a given structure during which the students first assess themselves in writing and also outline their prospects for future learning. This form of self-assessment is then complemented by the actual portfolio analysis, resulting in a set of recommendations for future improvements and possible new goals. The questionnaire students use to assess themselves was adopted from the questionnaires published in Cheng and Chau (2013) and in Benson (2011), who are Hong Kong University researchers. The last question from a short list can be considered as a key one to reinforcement of the cyclic nature of learning as it asks about the future plans for further learning. Frequently, the portfolios consist of several pages and artifacts (video links, book covers, video and audio files recorded by the students themselves, scans of vocabulary lists, and PDF documents with students' writing of their choice); very often all the above-mentioned examples of artifacts make a single portfolio.

The organic nature of the portfolio itself can be considered a disadvantage for a teacher. Since the students choose their own learning goals and learning processes, the outcome of their work can be varied and in some cases rather complex. It is very helpful and important to ask students to submit a portfolio in a consolidated form in order to make the final collection clearly arranged. The portfolio software (in this case Mahara) allows for creating several pages and organizing them into collections of pages or using a hyperlink to link several pages to one page. Possible ways of portfolio assessment are presented in the next section.

Approaches to ePortfolio Assessment

As Strivens et al. (2009) defines, assessment can be considered as "an act of making a judgment about the value of someone's product or performance." It is also mentioned that the person who performs the assessment does not need to be only a person with responsibility for teaching, but this role can be taken by peers (peer-assessment) or even by the learners themselves (self-assessment). When working with ePortfolios both assessment and self-assessment should be involved since both types contribute to students' further development and learning. Implementation and use of ePortfolios in higher education inevitably brings a question of suitable tools or criteria for ePortfolio assessment. However, Chen and Light (2010) emphasize a role of an ePortfolio itself functioning as an assessment tool:

> As an assessment tool, the student portfolio is unique insofar as it captures evidence of student learning over

time – in multiple formats and contexts – documents practice, and includes a student's own reflection on his or her learning. Portfolios also encourage students to represent and integrate their formal and informal learning experiences.

Allowing for this possibility, along with the two approaches to portfolio creation that have already been discussed in this chapter, namely Positivist and Constructivist Approach, the following two approaches to portfolio assessment should also be considered: summative and formative assessment, also called assessment for learning. Summative assessment is designed to evaluate students' learning against certain criteria or benchmark. On the other hand, formative assessment is focused on providing student with ongoing feedback and recommendations for improvement, with a focus on identifying strengths and weaknesses of individual students. Both approaches to ePortfolio implementation are applied at the University of Pardubice, together with the use of summative and formative assessments to fulfill their purposes. Only summative assessment is used when positivist approach is applied. In the case of the autonomous learning cycle, both approaches to assessment are employed in order to provide assessment on individual task performance and provide feedback formatively on student progress. A combination of both self-assessment and two forms of teacher assessment seems to allow students to benefit from the complexity of the evaluation process.

Conclusion

This chapter has outlined two possible approaches to ePortfolio implementation in language learning at the University of Pardubice, which has been illustrated by selected examples of case and pilot studies demonstrating both positivist and constructivist approach. It is believed that most of the above-mentioned examples of ePortfolio use are transferrable into other fields of studies by extracting the main ideas behind every single instance and adapting them.

How does ePortfolio use enhance active learning? Following the definition of active learning as a method which actively involves students in the learning process, work with ePortfolio can fulfill the definition in several ways. According to works published on active learning, e.g., Bonwell and Eison (1991), active learning needs to reach beyond listening which is considered to be passive learning. Active learning should involve reading, writing, discussions, and engaging in problem-solving activities. There is a need for engaging high-order thinking tasks such as analysis, synthesis, and evaluation. Most of the above-mentioned activities defining active learning can be found in individual examples presented in this chapter. Thus, it can be concluded that both positivist and constructivist approaches to ePortfolio use enhance active learning in slightly different ways, involving also different methods of assessment or their combination. I believe that formative assessment, which is not coincidentally also called assessment for learning, is more suitable for facilitating autonomy and active learning in our students.

References

Aplikace, E. J. P. (2014). Evropské jazykové portfolio: Registered model number 2014. ESP project CZ.1.07/1.1. 00/08.0014. Retrieved from https://ejp.rvp.cz

Arnseth, H. C., Erstad, O., Juhaňák, L., & Zounek, J. (2016). Pedagogika a nové výzvy výzkumu ICT: Role digitálních technologií v každodenním životě a učení mládeže. *Studia Paedagogika*, 87−110.

Balaban, I., & Bubas, G. (2009, January). Evaluating an ePortfolio system: The case of a hybrid university course. In *Proceedings of the ICL 2009 conference: The Challenges of Life Long Learning*, Villach, Austria (pp. 638−643).

Balaban, I., & Bubas, G. (2010, June). Educational potentials of ePortfolio systems: Student evaluations of Mahara and Elgg. In *Information Technology Interfaces (ITI), 32nd International Conference* (pp. 329−336).

Balaban, I., Mu, E., & Divjak, B. (2013). Development of an electronic Portfolio system success model: An information systems approach. *Computers & Education, 60* (1), 396−411.

Barrett, H. C. (2007). Researching electronic portfolios and learner engagement: The REFLECT initiative. *Journal of Adolescent & Adult Literacy, 50* (6), 436−449.

Benson, P. (2007). Autonomy in language teaching and learning. *Language teaching, 40*(01), 21−40.

Benson, P. (2011). *Teaching and researching autonomy* (2nd ed.). London: Pearson.

Benson, P. (2013). *Teaching and researching autonomy* (pp. 170−172). New York, NY: Routledge.

Bohuslavová, L. (2007). *Evropské jazykové portfolio: Klett.* ISBN: 978-80-86906-84-3.

Bonwell, C. C., & Eison, J. A. (1991). *Active learning: Creating excitement in the classroom.* ASHEERIC Higher Education Report No. 1. Washington, DC: George Washington University.

California State University webpage: ePortfolios Academics. (2015). Retrieved from www.fresnostate.edu/academics/eportfolio/definition.Last.edited:2015-01-30

Chen, H. L., & Light, T. P. (2010). *Electronic portfolios and student success: Effectiveness, efficiency, and learning* (p. 1). Washington, DC: Association of American Colleges & Universities.

Cheng, G., & Chau, J. (2013). Exploring the relationship between students' self-regulated learning ability and their ePortfolio achievement. *Internet and Higher Education, 17,* 9−15.

Council of Europe. (1992). Ruschlikon symposium. Retrieved from www.coe.int/t/ dg4/linguistic/Ruschlikon1991_en.pdf

Council of Europe. (2001). *Common European framework of reference for languages: Learning, teaching, assessment.* Cambridge, U.K: Press Syndicate of the University of Cambridge.

Doran, G. T. (1981). There's a S.M.A.R.T. way to write management's goals and objectives. *Management Review, 70*(11), 35−36.

EPAC. (2002). Electronic portfolio action & communication. Retrieved from http:// epac.pbworks.com

Holec, H. (1981). *Autonomy and foreign language learning.* Oxford: Pergamon (First published 1979, Strasbourg: Council of Europe).

Jisc (2008). Effective practice with e-Portfolios, 9. Retrieved from http://www. ssphplus.info/files/effective_practice_e-portfolios.pdf

Lawler, K. B., & Hornyak, M. J. (2012). SMART goals: How the application of SMART goals can contribute to achievement of student learning outcomes. *Developments in Business Simulations and Experiential Learning, 39*(12), 259−267.

Little, D. (1991) *Learner autonomy: Definitions, issues and problems.* Dublin: Authentic Language Learning Resources Limited.

Lopez-Fernandez, O., & Rodriguez-Illera, J. L. (2009). Investigating university students' adaptation to a digital learner course portfolio. *Computers & Education, 52*(3), 608−616.

Miller, R., & Morgaine, W. (2009). The benefits of e-portfolios for students and faculty in their own words. *Peer Review, 11*(1), 8−12.

MOSEP (2006). More self-esteem with my ePortfolio. Retrieved from http://electronicportfolios.com/mosep/index.html

Palán, Z. (2002). *Lidské zdroje − výkladový slovník.* Praha: Academia. ISBN: 80−200-0950-7.

Paulson, F. L., & Paulson, P. R. (1994). Assessing portfolios using the constructivist paradigm. In R. Fogarty (Ed.), *Student portfolios* (pp. 8−9). Palatine: IRI Skylight Training & Publishing.

Peacock, S., Gordon, L., Murray, S., Morss, K., & Dunlop, G. (2010). Tutor response to implementing an ePortfolio to support learning and personal development in further and higher education institutions in Scotland. *British Journal of Educational Technology, 41*(5), 827−851.

Queirós, R., Oliveira, L., Leal, J. P., & Moreira, F. (2011, June). Integration of eportfolios in learning management systems. In *International Conference on Computational Science and Its Applications* (pp. 500−510). Berlin: Springer.

Saavedra, A. R., & Opfer, V. D. (2012). *Teaching and learning 21st century skills: Lessons from the learning sciences* (pp. 4−5). Santa Monica: RAND Corporation.

Strivens, J., Baume, D., Grant, S., Owen, C., Ward, R., & Nicol, D. (2009). The role of e-portfolios in formative and summative assessment: Report of the JISC-funded study. Unpublished study. Centre for Recording Achievement for JISC. Retrieved from http://www.jisc.ac.uk/media/documents/programmes/elearning/eportfinalreport.doc

Swarbrick, A. (2002). *Teaching modern languages* (p. 81). New York, NY: Routledge. ISBN: 9780415102551.

Travers, C. (2011). Unveiling a reflective diary methodology for exploring the lived experiences of stress and coping. *Journal of Vocational Behavior, 79*, 204–216. doi:10.1016/j.jvb.2010.11.007

Tzeng, J. Y. (2011). Perceived values and prospective users' acceptance of prospective technology: The case of a career eportfolio system. *Computers & Education, 56*(1), 157–165.

Wanner, I., & Nesswetha, J. (2015). Mit Mahara nach Pardubice und Leipzig. Warum ePortfolios auch bei Studienreisen mit in den Koffer müssen und wie sie zur Internationalisierung beitragen. In A. Hettiger (Ed.), Vorsprung durch Sprachen. Fremdsprachenausbildung an den Hochschulen. Dokumentation der 28. Arbeitstagung 2014 an der Technischen Universität Braunschweig (pp. 301–317).

Williams, C. (2012). *MGMT* (5th ed.). Florence, SC: Cengage Learning, Inc.

Zounek, J., Juhaňák, L., Staudková, H., & Poláček, J. (2016). *E-learning: učení (se) s digitálními technologiemi: kniha s online podporou.* Praha: Wolters Kluwer.

Zounek, J., & Sudický, P. (2012). *E-learning učení (se) s online technologiemi.* Praha: Wolters Kluwer Česká Republika.

SECTION III
A VISION FOR HUMANITY
THROUGH HIGHER EDUCATION

Chapter 14

The Pedagogical Legacy of Dorothy Lee and Paulo Freire

Azril Bacal Roij

· **Abstract**

In the face of the erosion of democracy and the reemergence of authoritarian styles of rule and leadership in the contemporary world scene, the author reintroduces the anthropological and pedagogical insights of Dorothy Lee and Paulo Freire in the ongoing debate on active learning and higher education. In the case of Dorothy Lee, these insights refer to "valuing the self" of the student, and to the value of learning (values) from "remote cultures" and, last but not least, on the meaning of freedom and autonomy bounded by culture and structure in the teaching–learning process. In the case of Freire, the author selectively points to: (1) the value of community as a sociocultural anchor of identity, freedom, and autonomy, (2) the view of education as a tool for raising awareness, critical thinking, inspiration, hope, empowerment, cultural action, and social transformation, and (3) the view on citizenship education. The author discusses, in this regard, the significant role assigned by Dorothy Lee and Paulo Freire to the neglected notions of dialogue, freedom, culture, self, autonomy, and structure. Lastly, the author argues in favor of reincorporating the pedagogical insights of Dorothy Lee and Paulo Freire in the curricula and structure of higher education and also reminds those concerned with

Active Learning Strategies in Higher Education: Teaching for Leadership, Innovation, and Creativity, 339–359
Copyright © 2018 by Emerald Publishing Limited
ISBN: 978-1-78714-488-0

upholding democracy that these formative values and concepts were acknowledged in the early conception and development of active learning.

Keywords: Freedom; self; autonomy; culture; structure; world crisis; active learning; democracy; citizen education

Challenges of Active Learning in the 21st Century

Humanity faces today a complex set of global environmental, climate, social, cultural, ethnic, and political challenges, intertwined with each other. Beck (1999) defined these challenges in terms of a "global risk" and a "world crisis," indicated by new inequalities, environmental damage, climate warming, and other related problems. These problematic conditions are complicated nowadays by other features, such as the growth of international migration, a dramatic (and poorly managed) refugee catastrophe, xenophobia, cultural intolerance, the proliferation of authoritarian governments and leadership style, the rise of white national populism, fundamentalism, far-right parties, global militarization, global crime, war and violent conflicts, nuclear threat, terrorism, human insecurity, and the erosion of liberal democracy. Informed by the sociology of education, we understand that learned beliefs and values are reflected in human behavior and social action, and also why education and media play a key strategic role in helping to worsen or to improve on the alluded problems. We also understand in that light, the reasons why education and mass media are hotly contested spaces, between the public and private agencies of social control – and the social forces striving today on behalf of freedom and democracy. In short, educational institutions and mass media exert much influence on the minds of students, as well as on their individual and collective behavior.[1]

The creation of the United Nations and UNESCO were efforts of the international community to overcome the traumas resulting from the horrors of war in the past century, the most violent era in human history. These efforts were based on a shared vision to rebuild a new world, based on principles of democracy, peace, the rule of law, and the 1948 Universal Declaration of Human Rights. The role of science,

---

[1]Significantly, the first office of education in the modern German nation-state was located in the Ministry of Interior.

education, and culture were key features in the efforts to rebuild a world left in ashes, after the war and during the postcolonial era.

Since the root causes of the scourge of war and violence were traced to the human mind, much hope and resources were invested to advance the educational conditions for democracy, justice, peace, and develop-ment – in the world at large. Once again, the civilized world resorts today to education, science, and culture to support the efforts to iden-tify, help to solve, and overcome the severe problems that threaten human survival in this day and age.

The above initial material and conceptual considerations frame the present work on active-learning strategies in higher education. A ques-tion is raised in this respect: How do the existing strategies of active teaching fare in fostering the kind of democratic leadership needed today, to address the social, economic, environment, and climate chal-lenges of the 21st century? If education would have worked as required in the past, we might not be forced to witness the precarious quality of global leadership and governance which lie behind the world crisis and the perilous state of humanity, who finds itself today near the brink of disaster. These troublesome features cannot be wholly blamed on mod-ern education, yet one knows that something has gone wrong with the educational venture of modernity and postmodernity. That "something" that went wrong alludes to some identifiable distortions associated with the human capital approach to education, actively promoted by the global forces of market fundamentalism.

Against this background, the author seeks to reincorporate the peren-nial insights of Dorothy Lee and Paulo Freire into the frame of active learning, notions of freedom, self, culture, institutional structure and autonomy in the formative axis of the curricula, design, and educational strategies of active learning, as a way to effectively respond to the press-ing problems of the 21st century. These educators emphasized the important role played by these values and notions, from a concern with the formative dimension of learning in higher education.[2] Next follows

---

[2]This article is written in deference to the kind invitation by a Greek colleague and friend, whom I hold in high academic regard and personal esteem. The enclosed reflections draw from my life-long path and engagement in the world of higher edu-cation, as a nomadic university teacher and researcher in several countries: Perú, México, USA, Spain, and Sweden, from my work as a consultant at UNESCO's educational office in Latin America (OREALC) and, last but not least, teaching tea-chers in Mexico and partaking in the World Education Forum and the network "Universidad y Compromiso Social" in Seville, Spain.

an overview of active learning, including a reference to recent changes brought about by the forces of market globalism, at the expense of its humanist and formative vocation.

Active Learning under the Siege of Global Marketism

> Active learning has received considerable attention over the past several years...is generally defined as any instructional method that engages students in the learning process. In short, active learning requires students to do meaningful learning activities...
>
> (Michael Price, 2004, p. 1)

What is known as "active learning" is a well-established educational trade mark, owing much to the valuable inputs from: philosophers, psychologists, pedagogues, researchers, and practitioners, as well as a wide and diverse range of disciplines and study fields. A few authors associated with active learning are selectively named in this regard: Paulo Freire (1970), Vygotsky (1978), Revans (1982), Barnes (1989), Glenda (1996), Bandura (2001), Prince (2004), Brookfield (2005), Weltman (2007), Bonwell and Eison (1991), Michael (2006), McKeachie and Svinicki (2008), and Martyn (2007).[3] Beyond the teaching views and intentions of these authors, it is highly probable that active-learning strategies have been modified in the past decades, due to the forces and implications of globalization. What we have in mind refers to the increasing reliance of active learning and higher education on market mechanisms, privatization, competition, technological development, and an instructional style of education.

From another angle, active-learning strategies are often modified in response to the demands of the emerging network, information, knowledge, and increasingly complex societies (Castells, 1998); in addition to the global and regional efforts to standardize the curricula and praxis of higher education. Under the increasing pressures exerted by these new global demands, the focus of active-teaching strategies seemingly lies today reduced to searching for more effective methods and instructional techniques to motivate and awaken students from

---

[3]There were 26,000 items in a first run for citations on active education via google.

their assumed slumber. A brief review of the pertinent literature reveals no shortage of theories, methods, and techniques, irrespective of their formulation in terms of "action" and/or "active" orientations to teaching and learning. On the contrary, a perusal of the literature reveals the existence of a large and varied array of theories and research with documented evidence, on how different disciplines and institutions of higher education today adhere to the key premises of active education.

By the same token, one also finds a large battery of methods and techniques readily available to support active teaching in most centers of higher learning located in the industrialized world. In sum, theory, research, methods, and techniques of active learning are no scarce commodities. Research additionally tells us, that to a large extent, active-learning methods and techniques work rather well. Thus, if theories and research data on active learning tell us that most of everything is working pretty well and under control, what can we constructively add to the active-learning venture? A preliminary answer to this question might lie not in the reliance on the latest technological educational gadget, nor in the scientific approach to the learning process, but somewhere in the insights and lessons on formative education provided by the humanistic and critical Western traditions.

Another aim of this article is to raise a number of issues and questions, from a democratic normative perspective and concern about: citizen education, diversity, social inclusion, and "educational justice," beyond the conventional liberal approach to "equal educational opportunities." In other words, we have in mind an alternative educational project, which supports equal access to quality higher education for qualified students, irrespective of their nationality, class, gender, race, ethnicity, sexual preference, and any other criteria of social exclusion.

A well-known sociological tenet on self-fulfilled prophecies tells us that: What is defined as real is bound to have real consequences. Accordingly, if we believe that students lack self-motivation to learn, our educational efforts would likely seek to motivate them via external methods and techniques. If we consider, on the other hand, that students are intrinsically motivated to actively learn, our efforts to improve their learning would focus on the active attention that we (ourselves) *cum* teachers provide them, as well as on our responsibility to redesign the existing institutions of higher education to effectively support the eagerness held by students to learn.

A Value Perspective on Self, Autonomy, and Self-Determination

> Science can only be rational if you have explicit value pre-
> mises. One needs value premises to ascertain facts. There
> are no questions except to questions. No questions except
> from viewpoints.[4]

Against the above background, we address in this section, the strategic role played by values in the process of active learning, concerning equal access to quality higher education that were advocated by Dorothy Lee and Paulo Freire and further elaborated by the author.[5] I view Dorothy Lee (1959, 1976, 1986, 1987) and Paulo Freire (www.paulofreire.org) among the great educationalists of the Twentieth Century, whom I met and befriended.

While Dorothy Lee and Paulo Freire valued dialogue in their pedagogical praxis, as well as held great respect for the autonomy and freedom of each unique individual student, they also differed in some respects. Dorothy Lee tried, through her unique and engaged style of teaching, to open and expand the cultural and perceptual windows of her students, inviting them to learn values from "remote cultures." From his educational corner, Freire emphasized "conscientization," namely, a way of teaching–learning intended to raise the awareness of students. This task was carried by means of various strategies, such as the "pedagogy of the question" and also by using the combined methods of dialectics and dialogue in his political-pedagogical approach to trans-formative education and cultural action. The use of dialectics is a way to induce students to reflect on their own thinking, and also to help them understand the dynamics and contradictions inherent in the opera-tion of nature and society. Dialogue alludes to actively listen to each

---

[4]Gunnar Myrdal, at a lecture at Campbell Hall, University of California at Santa Barbara, November 2, 1973.

[5]Bacal, Azril (1996). From Organism to Identity: The Road from Psychology to Social-Psychology (Towards an Epistemology of Self-Determination." University of Karlstad, Department of Social Sciences, Section of Communication. Working Paper 94:1. This work conveys a vision of a socio-educational space of freedom, as we move from the biological notion of organism in psychology to the social-psychological concept of identity. When psychology outgrows its views on externally conditioned ("taught") organisms and moves toward social-psychology, individual persons *cum* students are seen as endowed with peculiar human attributes and skills: self-reflection, freedom, free will, autonomy and self-determination, to respond, and not merely to react to external stimuli.

other, as a way to foster empathy by inviting students to "wear the shoes of the other" — a manner of speech referring to the effort to better understand the views of "the other." Since we don't know everything, and neither does the other, we can learn from each other. In this view, we are all colearners and coresearchers in the educational game.

How to convey the sense of urgency today required by the need to incorporate back the original formative dimension of active learning in contemporary higher education? To address this question, my thoughts on the matter are framed within a time and existential frame perspective as next described. And this task is approached with reference to a 3-minute Ted Talks presentation by Rich Elias about things he learned while his plane was about to crash.[6] In short, he learned at the moment of confronting imminent death that all can change at once. This abrupt realization let Elias to raise the following question, here paraphrased by the author in terms of educational change: How can we overcome some problematic features of active education in the 21st century? In this respect, we briefly narrate later in this article how Dorothy Lee approached such existential and pedagogical task, from an active and meaningful perspective on higher education. To sum up the previous thoughts, my argument in this respect contends that active education should not merely be reduced to abstract theory, applied research, and the development of participatory methods and motivational techniques. And furthermore, it suggests that the contemporary strategies of active learning should incorporate a variety of educational spaces and opportunities, taking into account the values and notions of freedom, self, and autonomy of the students, in the frame of their particular culture and social structure.

The Educational Context: An Invitation to "Read" and to Transform the World

According to Mészáros (2004) and Bacal (2011, p. 69), the teaching—learning contexts frame a dynamic process, which is simultaneously facilitated and/or blocked by the key players in the educational game. The teacher's role is dual in nature, namely, it actively facilitates and/or

---

[6]Let us start this dialogue on perspectives, by placing us in a time and change perspective via a three minutes presentation of Rich Elias (www.ted/talks.Rich.Elias) entitled "3 Things I learned while my plane crashed," based in a recent dramatic experience, when Elias survived the US Airways Flight 1549 forced to land in the Hudson River.

creates obstacles in the learning process. Moreover, the context of active learning implies more than a spatial *locus*. The educational context is also framed by time, and active learning occurs within constructed spatial–temporal boundaries. These constructed socioeducational spaces and times are often modified by new waves of educational reform, one way or another. These contextual institutional boundaries also change via the intervention of the educational actors, who actively partake in the teaching–learning process.

It follows from the above considerations that we are key influential agents in the educational context and process, given our multiple roles and engagement, as individual persons, teachers, researchers, educational decision makers, planners, and administrators. In other words, we are no onlookers looking dispassionately at the educational scene. We are rather key active players, much too often with an upper hand in defining the rules and routines of the educational game. In this respect, how much are we ready and willing to examine the implications of our own actions? I close the previous reflections on the teaching–learning context with a normative value-laden question: Should the institutions of higher education actively offer their students a formative contextual opportunity, intended to develop their capacity of critical thinking, and further invite them to partake as students-citizens in the democratic decision-making process to design, and to partake in the cogovernment of their centers of higher learning, as well as in their societies, cultures, and communities as active cultural agents? This question leads next to briefly introduce Dorothy Lee, an outstanding anthropologist who also was an engaged educator, along the steps of the humanist and existential traditions in anthropology and education.

Dorothy Lee

I met Dorothy (Thora) Demetracapoulou Lee, as a graduate student in sociology and anthropology in the mid-1960s, and remained in touch with her until her death in 1975. Dorothy Lee was born the last of nine children in a Greek evangelical family, in an environment mostly Greek orthodox in Muslim Istanbul (earlier Constantinople) in 1905. The reader who is interested in the biography and work of this remarkable woman and anthropologist is well-advised to refer to the works of Jeffrey Ehrenreich. This anthropologist, Ehrenreich discovered Dorothy Lee late in graduate school from Edmund Carpenter, who was a close friend and colleague. And deeply touched by his late discovery, Ehrenreich

(1986, pp. v—xii) interviewed close friends, colleagues, and relatives and sketched a biography of Dorothy Lee. He also reviewed the main contributions made by Dorothy Lee to humanistic anthropology.[7]

Dorothy Lee was a cultural anthropologist actively engaged in the debate and the praxis of education — an engagement shared with Margaret Mead and other anthropologists at that time. It is best to convey the meaning of Dorothy Lee's work in her own words:

> ...The original impetus to inquire into the philosophical dimension of culture came from my husband, Otis Lee (a philosopher), for whom all experience and behavior has its philosophical content, and all reality held value. My search into the cultural codification of experienced reality, and into the conceptual and value implications of language and other aspects of culture, came through an attempt to find answers for his disturbing questions. In recent years, I have been concerned with questions revolving around freedom, individual autonomy, responsibility, creativity, the self...

According to Ehrenreich (1986, p. 176), Dorothy Lee was deeply concerned with the question of: "How does an individual's *autonomy* and *freedom* connect with community and society?" In contrast to the neo-liberal view of freedom, both Dorothy Lee and Paulo Freire shared a view of freedom and autonomy as socially grounded in community. To illustrate this point, Dorothy Lee taught at the educational sit-ins at University of California at Berkeley in the 1960s and gave her speaker's fees to the Free Speech Movement. The reader will have to reflect on whether, and to what extent, the prevailing culture in the context where one works actively values and supports (or not) the *self* and autonomy of the student, as members of their learning community. Ehrenreich (1986, pp. v—vi) wrote on Dorothy Lee's views on autonomy as follows:

> ... Through comparative analysis of numerous cultures both Western and primitive, Lee suggested that in order for the individual to achieve *autonomy* ('being in charge of myself') it was essential that the community ('people around me') truly value the *self*...

---

[7]First published in 1976, and also in the epilogue written in 1988 and added to her collection of essays on freedom and culture (1959), reprinted in 1987 (pp. 76—180).

According to Dorothy Lee, different cultures vary in their value orientation toward the freedom and integrity of the young person *cum* student, within their cultural boundaries. From a comparative perspective, one finds some cultures "valuing the self" (Lee, 1986), as well as the "autonomy" of students (Freire, 1997).

One also finds "cultures against man," in the sense attributed by Jules Henry (1963), who studied cultures which value and enforce obedience, discipline, social control, conformity, and even to the extent of the "soul murder" of children and young students maybe as epitomized, but not restricted to Nazi-like pedagogy (Schatzman,1973).

In the student-learner-shared space envisioned by Dorothy Lee, students are regarded and treated as being innately curious and actively engaged in exploring, learning about, and in intimate relation with their relevant universe. In other words, students would not need external motivation in terms of reward and/or punishment as advocated by educators with a behaviorist orientation. Lee was extremely critical of B.F. Skinner, her colleague at Harvard University, for his manifested lack of respect toward his students, who were often treated as research pigeons. The misgivings concerning the ill-defined problem of student passivity are likely to have been extended by Dorothy Lee to the corresponding remedial measures, also built on faulty assumptions on the "need" of motivational techniques and external reinforcement. This would be the case, even if such corrective measures are well-intended by the educational decision makers, wishing to turn apathetic students into active ones. In short, the educational context in our view is comprised by the institutions of higher education and, in particular the educational "spatial—temporal room," mediated by the quality of the dyadic teacher—learner relationship.

The dramatic episode and lessons drawn from Rich Elias, earlier transcribed, brings to mind what Dorothy Lee told us when we met at our first lesson: She invited us to imagine and to make a choice about who would still be willing to stay in that classroom, were the world suddenly to end? Similarly to Rich Elias, Dorothy Lee suddenly confronted us with an existential choice: either to stay with her in the classroom or to go elsewhere. My clear decision was to stay, even if the world were to end in no time. In our days, plagued by an existential crisis, lack of meaning and hope, the provocative question made by Dorothy Lee, already in the first class, infused my life thereafter with the "meaning of meaning," and transformed my personal life and teaching style, with lasting consequences to this very day.

The issue of lack of meaning in education was discussed by Dorothy Lee in terms of an existential crisis reflected, for instance, in massive consumerism and the drug culture of our times. This existential crisis was attributed by Dorothy Lee to the noticeable demise of community in the contemporary world. This author is not alone in finding organic links between the educational project of modernity, capitalism, alienation, and anomie in contemporary society. Dorothy Lee's view on the urgent need to rebuild community was also central to the intellectual work of Martin Buber (Marin, 2010, p. 56), as well as a recent subject of research by epidemiologists like Wilkinson and Prickett (2009). With the above considerations in mind: can we conceive of contemporary institutions of active learning in higher education as learning communities, which acknowledge, respect, and support the freedom, self, autonomy, personal development, and citizen formative education of their students? One partial answer to this question is found in the educational vision and praxis envisioned by Paulo Freire.

Paulo Freire

This section briefly introduces Paulo Freire and his contributions to active learning, from a perspective of a humanist and critical pedagogy, based on freedom, autonomy, dialogue, dialectics, and a transformative education leading to cultural action and social change. I trace my encounter with the seminal work of Paulo Freire, to his work on "Extension or Communication" (1973), alluding to the issue of "conscientization" in the rural areas. In this work, Freire defines agricultural extension as a kind of "monological" (persuasive and oppressive) communication, which is contrasted with a "dialogical" and liberating kind of interpersonal communication. This discovery took place in the late 1960s, when teaching a Master's course on extension, at the National Agricultural University La Molina (UNALM) in Perú. Shortly after, we were invited to apply Freire's transformative educational approach to the realm of popular education, peasant-training, and radio-forum in the context of the Peruvian Agrarian Reform (1969–1976).

As mentioned earlier, Paulo Freire was influenced by the Socratic (dialogic) approach to the teaching–learning process. Freire borrowed in the intellectual development building up to his pedagogical approach from various sources, among which stand out the views on dialogue in human communication elaborated by Martin Buber (1955). Buber was a social and political philosopher, who made a theoretical distinction between two opposite modes of interaction and communication. If applied to the field of higher education, these two modes would look something like the following two paths of teaching–learning: (1) The "I-It" path of teaching–learning, where the "other" (the teacher) views the student as an "It," an object to be taught and molded as wished and (2) the "I-Thou" path of teaching–learning, this time, based on respect, care, and mutual appreciation, when teaching is intertwined with learning through dialogue, and where the roles of teacher and students mesh, enabling them to learn from each other as coteachers/learners. My contention about the pertinence of dialogue in higher education reads as follows: under learning settings with primacy of the I-It mode of teaching active-learning suffers and *vice versa: under conditions of the I-Thou mode of teaching active learning flourishes.*

Even though Paulo Freire is acknowledged as an early pioneer of active-learning theory, some of the humanist and critical tenets of education associated with his work are currently lost or neglected in the rush and noise resulting from the fast pace of a globalized world. In this frame of mind, how valid is the assumption that students are passive and thus in need of external motivation and reinforcement, a view commonly widely spread in behaviorist quarters. An alternative view is argued in this regard, contending that the early curiosity and eagerness of freshmen to learn, and to follow what interest them most, is often neglected in our conventional routines and ways to organize and manage the learning process. This latter view, above, reminds us of a story about a man sitting on someone's shoulders saying: I would do everything for you, except to step out of your shoulders. As earlier mentioned, a perspective concerned with the freedom, autonomy, and self-determination of the students in higher education is brought to bear in this paper on the interpersonal "educational locus," a way to refer to the teacher–student interaction, within the conceptual frame of active learning.

Gadotti (2000, p. 82), a prominent pedagogue of our time, whose life-work is closely related to Paulo Freire, helps us briefly to recall in this respect the teachers' triad envisioned by Rousseau: The "I" (active learner), "other persons" ("teachers") and "things" (the surrounding natural elements and man-made artifacts). The role of "significant (educational) others" *cum* teachers and educational administrators entails their dual power to facilitate and/or to create obstacles in the innately active and exploratory learning process of students. "Things" in turn acquire their instrumental and existential meanings through human interaction, mediated through the student's interaction with "significant other persons," both actors framed by the learning game of growing up in a community. In other words, we have in mind "the" meaningful persons in our daily environment, who transmit the cultural meanings and names attached to the world of natural things and also human artifacts. This interpersonal process of transfer of knowledge and meaningful information is filtered at all times by the particular cultural values, language, and personal teaching styles of "significant others" *cum* teachers.

The teaching—learning context, the world, the classroom, and/or the educational spatial—temporal locus were regarded by Dorothy Lee as a "relevant (educational) universe." In other words, students experience their educational journey framed by the boundaries of a meaningful environment, populated by a community made of significant people, in meaningful places and times. It follows from this view, that if the concrete learning context is experienced as irrelevant, the active-learning process suffers and further higher education is likely to be deemed as irrelevant by the students (Majfud, 2017).

For Freire, the context was viewed as problematic, exploitative, oppressive, alienated, and alienating – and therefore in need to be critically "read" by learner—student. Raising the awareness of the learners—students *cum* citizens was expected to empower them and engage them in cultural action to change its problematic features.

From their respective anthropological and educational windows, Dorothy Lee and Paulo Freire regarded the whole of human life as a learning context and therefore as a fertile ground for students to engage in active learning. The conventional view of student apathy was in their eyes a misguided diagnosis, in turn based on a faulty premise on student *passivism*.

Dorothy Lee was furthermore critical of the fashionable view asserting that students are in need of external motivation, and regarded the grading system as a sign of disrespect, as well as "degrading" the value of the student's personal integrity. Dorothy Lee regarded students as intrinsically self-motivated and self-driven by values and interests. Their apparent apathy or passivity of students resulted, in her eyes, from a meaningless or irrelevant educational environments and curricula. The view on educational banality entertained above was insightfully captured by Paul Goodman in "Growing Up Absurd" (1960).[8]

For readers interested in deepening their understanding of Freire's seminal contribution to active learning, two sources are highly

---

[8]Goodman, Paul (1960). Growing up Absurd.

recommended: "Uma Biobliografía" by Moacir Gadotti (1996), and "Paulo Freire" (1921–97) by Heinz-Peter Gerhardt (1993). One finds all available references covering the life and work of Paulo Freire in the following website: www.paulofreire.org. The transformative influence of Paulo Freire in my own life-long teaching, both at the higher educational level and elsewhere, is shortly illustrated in the next section with a few number of case studies and at more length in the notes at the end of this article.[9]

This section ends with a question: Can we envision an alternative active learning in the contemporary institutions of higher learning, in multi-inter-trans-cultural communities, under the guidelines of an "I-Thou" mode of teaching–learning? One way to illustrate how this alternative way of active learning could work, in contrast to the fast pace of modern life, is slow reading and a slower pace of active learning, next introduced.

A Slow-Reading Approach to Active Learning

By way of illustration, such an I-Thou perspective on intercultural dialogue and social inclusion, depicted in previous lines, was applied in a case study of cultural diversity and institutional development at

---

[9]A partial account of my teaching experience inspired by Paulo Freire is transcribed in the chapter "Permeando muitos Projetos" in Gadotti (op.cit, 1996, pp. 232–234). The alluded teaching–learning experience covers a long time span, scope, and a varied range of activities, which can be traced to: the tasks associated with Peasant training and Radio-Forums contextualized by the Peruvian Agrarian Reform (1969–1976). This approach of aware-raising pedagogics was later applied at an experimental course on "Overcoming the personal consequences of Racism," at the University of California, Santa Barbara (1979) – later elaborated in terms of "decolonizing ethnic identity" with Mexican Americans (1994). This perspective was also applied to the realm of self-management, with a work on "A Participatory Organizational and Training Strategy for the Self-Management Sector: A Case Study of Action-Research in Perú" (1991:121–135). "La Universidad Iberoamericana en el Contexto de la Globalización" (2000, pp. 161–218), "Socioanálisis y Concientización en las Ciencias Sociales" (2002), "Espacios de Intervención Socio-Educativa en el Mundo Actual" (2004). "Movimientos Sociales y Educación Transformadora." My views on "transformative education" inspired by Freire were summarized in Bacal (2011, pp. 65–84)). Last but not least, the recent experience of teaching teachers in various doctoral educational programs in México enabled me to explore and actively engage my teachers-students in a group effort to recreate the basis of an active learning in higher education geared to the construction of other different worlds, oriented to the common good.

Uppsala University (Bacal, 1998). The findings of this study tell us that multiculturalism does not go hand-in-hand with egalitarian lines of social inclusion, in the institutional developmental process of this highly reputed university. The pedagogical views and teaching styles of Dorothy Lee and Paulo Freire were also applied in "Culture and Ethnicity," a course designed *ad hoc* when invited to teach as a Visiting Humanities Scholar at Otterbein College, Ohio (Autumn 1995), whose main features are next transcribed.

> This course is designed to provide a theoretical, methodo-
> logical and experiential approach to the study of culture,
> ethnicity and ethnic identity. The methodology of this
> course is based on participation and dialogue, combining
> individual, small-group projects and classroom levels of
> work and discussion. Daily personal reading and writing
> is combined with study circles, which also function as
> support peer groups. The lecture format will be comple-
> mented with seminars and panel discussions .... Films and
> field projects will also enrich our collective learning experi-
> ence ... the attempt is made to relate the dynamics of
> this course to the activities of the 'integrative studies
> festival' ... focused on 'Culture, Conflict and Community'
> ... and to the 'Human Rights Conference' in October...

The kind and pace of individual reading adopted in this course fol-
lowed Dorothy Lee's admonition was to be very, very slow (!), to enable enough time to walk so to speak in the pages, to imagine oneself walk-
ing in the landscape, smelling the smells of nature, "meeting" the places, "listening" to, and even "relating" to the persons introduced by the authors in the books, meant to be slowly read. Students were invited then to reflect and to write about their deep reactions and reflections, including gut feelings and/or intellectual analysis. These deeply personal responses were later shared and discussed in the context of group dialogue in the classroom space. The following discussion was usually enriched by the cultural plurality and perspectives of its members, mostly teachers from all corners of the world. In this way, the individual aha (!) sense of personal discovery was coupled with the analytical dimension in an active-learning space and process.

Among the list of obligatory readings, we included books by authors from different cultures, such as Chinua Achebe *Things Fall Apart* (2008), Deavere Smith's *Fires in the Mirror* (1993), Ricardo Pozas's

Juan the Chamula (1962), and Richard Rodriguez' *Hunger of Memory* (1982). The course assignments included, from a perspective on active learning, writing a personal diary with individual comments about the student's reactions and reflections to their "personal encounters" with the characters and places the students "met" in the pages of the books assigned in the course. These notes were regularly discussed weekly with the teacher, which added to the group reports on the readings and other activities related to the course. A similar approach was taken in a 1998 course on "Learning from Remote Cultures," this time taught at the institution of Culture and Library Studies at Uppsala University, where a text by Ricardo Pozas (*Juan the Chamula*) was used to actively learn from, and intimately understand, the world of the Chamula (Maya) Indigenous People in Chiapas, Mexico.[10]

Concluding Notes

As a way to conclude the enclosed reflections on active learning in higher education, final questions are raised about the fashionable notions of quality education and teachers' competence built in the Bologna guidelines of higher education, against the background of the return of authoritarianism, extreme right-ism and white nationalist-populism in the Western privileged region of the world. This question is posited in the following terms: Can we envision and help to construct an alternative approach to active education in the contemporary institutions of higher education, where the individual learning *tempo* of each and all students is recognized and supported by teachers and school administrators in learning communities? Could the alternative view of active learning outlined above actually replace the currently individualistic, competitive, and stress-filled approach, associated with the fast pace and *commoditized* higher education of our times? Taking into account the heavy demand of time and work commitment required by this kind of engaged I-Thou approach to the teaching–learning process,

---

[10]My Mexican graduate students in a similar course had the privilege to personally meet and converse with Ricardo Pozas, a distinguished anthropologist at "Universidad de las Américas, Puebla" (UDLAP), Mexico, in the 1980s. This pedagogical approach had also been tested earlier in Perú, where my students met with the writer-anthropologist José María Argüedas to discuss "Todas las Sangres," a seminal book on his envisioned project of a plurinational and multicultural country.

one understands why it is rarely found and implemented today in most institutions of higher education.

Nonetheless, it might be worthwhile to ponder like *Prometheus*, against all odds, on the value of building an alternative educational approach to active learning, which values and supports the freedom, self, and the "autonomy" of the students – bounded and conditioned by their particular cultures and societies. Admittedly, such an approach to active learning sounds unrealistic in our age of fast-food, fast reading, one-week courses, and lack of concern with critical thinking and citizenship education, which nowadays prevails in most Western institutions of higher education. To make this point to my Mexican teacher-students at the doctoral level, I show them a video film interview with a student who just graduated from high school in Finland, the country with the highest PISA high score in the world. The question goes as follows: Now that you graduated from school, what do you wish to do, which job interests you most? His answer was: I want be the manager of Coca-Cola (sic!). Is this the best product of what today is known as quality education? Let us not forget that the term "quality" was imported, as an adjective in the language of contemporary education, from the original meaning attached to the quality of products in the commodity market. In such a reduced meaning of quality education, something valuable is lost concerning the formative and ethical dimensions of active learning and higher education. From another angle, my argument about the quest raised by the so-called "vulnerable" segments of the population, increasingly claiming equal access to quality education, reads as follows:

> Under prevalent world and socio-educational conditions, currently threatened by the erosion of democracy as indicated, for example, by the compliance of millions of persons with the so-called "alternative facts" (fed by the hate media), and by the recent return of white native-populism to the world political, media and educational arenas;[11] the notions of *self,* autonomy, self-determination, dialogue, multi/inter-trans-cultural education, and citizen (civic) education, are needed nowadays to occupy a central place in the formative axis of the curriculum, and also in the institutional design and daily praxis of higher education.

---

[11]Snyder (2017).

In the above lines lies a promise of an alternative view on active learning in higher education based on dialogue, a key feature of active learning framed by the interpersonal educational *locus*. As earlier mentioned, the enclosed views on the role of dialogue in education draw from the "I-Thou" approach to interpersonal communication developed by Martin Buber (1955) — whose writings influenced Paulo Freire and his approach to the realms of extension and education. My reflections and suggestions to improve on active learning are envisioned not only as a critique but also as a complement or a supplement to all the ongoing efforts to bring excitement to actual learning in the classroom,[12] to search for better alternatives and replace with them traditional ways of (passive) teaching,[13] and lastly, to learn from top performing education systems about competence and quality learning in reading, mathematics, and science.[14]

In the end, quality active learning is also about formative citizen education. If democracy worth its name is to have a viable future in the 21st century, the values of freedom, self, autonomy, dialogue, intercultural understanding and appreciation, as well as democracy need to be acknowledged, nourished, and incorporated in the curricula and daily praxis of active learning, by the key planners and players in the institutions of higher education.

Dorothy Lee and Paulo Freire continue to be a lighthouse in the troubled waters of higher education in this day and age, best described in terms of techno-barbarism.[15] If they were alive today, they would watch in dismay how the *freedom, self and autonomy of students* are neglected terms in the standardized vocabulary and daily praxis of contemporary higher education. What can we do in this respect? An inclusive perspective on active learning which values the freedom, self, autonomy, and self-determination of students *cum* citizens, as well as the implications of their cultures and societies would incorporate all the key players engaged in the institutions and processes of higher education: educational planers, policy makers, teachers, administrators, and students.

---

[12]Bonwell, Eison, and James (1991).

[13]Prince (2004).

[14]Crehan (2014).

[15]It is interesting to point out to the unusual fact that Dorothy Lee and Paulo Freire resigned or reduced their appointment time as professors at Harvard University. This decision might suggest something about their sense of freedom and autonomy to pursue their own educational values and praxis.

Paulo Freire shared with Dorothy Lee a "communitarian" and socio-cultural educational approach to the teaching–learning process. And even further, Freire regarded education as a social movement, namely, as a collective way to intervene in the socioeducational arena, a view which even includes the human imagination. These authors understood the intimate nexus established between the freedom, self, autonomy of the students, within the constructed boundaries of their cultures and social structures. The above remarks lead us back to our own stance as teachers and administrators in the educational game and raise the following questions: Are we ready to critically reflect about our own ways to help reproduce and/or to change the educational problems we seek to solve? In this respect, how much are we willing to personally change, when required by the present situation? And last but not least, to what extent are we ready to question and to engage in the task to transform the institutions of higher education, where we work and which pay our salaries? Admittedly, such existential questions and dilemmas depicted above are plausibly more troublesome, demanding, and painful to deal with, than to merely look for participatory methodologies and techniques to activate the learning skills of students. These considerations point to a final question: Are we willing (or not) to engage with ourselves (as self-reflecting persons) in the thrust to encounter and engage in dialogue with students (in-and-out of the classroom) as unique individual persons?

References

Achebe, Ch. (2008). *Things fall apart.* New York, NY: Bantam Doubleday Dell Publishing Group Inc.

Bacal, A. (1996). Permeando Muitos Projetos, Cap.5, Parte II. In M. Gadotti (Ed.), *Paulo Freire: Uma Bibliografia*, Cortes Editora (pp. 232–234). São Paulo, Brasil: UNESCO, Instituto Paulo Freire (IPF).

Bacal, Azril. (1998). Reflections on cultural diversity and institutional human development, in red. Karin Apelgren och Ann Blückert, Universitetet som kulturell mötesplats: Verkligheten – utmaning – möjlighet!, Uppsala Universitet. *Rapportserie från Enheten för utveckling och utvärdering.* Rapport nr 15, pp. 51–64.

Bandura, A. (2001). Social cognitive theory: An agentic perspective. *Annual Review of Psychology, 52*:1 (February).

Barnes, D. (1989). *Active learning.* Leeds University TVEI Support Project, p. 19.

Beck, U. (1999). *World risk society.* Cambridge, MA: Polity Press.

Bonwell, C. C., and J. A. Eison (1991). *Active learning: Creating excitement in the classrrom,* ASHEERIC Higher Education Report No. 1. George Washington University, Washington, DC.

Brookfield, S. D. (2005). *Discussion as the way of teaching: Tools and techniques for democratic classrooms* (2nd ed.). San Francisco, CA: Jossey-Bass.

Buber, M. (1955). *Between man and man.* Boston: Beacon Press.

Bonwell, C. C., Eison, J. A., & James, A. (1991). *Active learning: Creating excitement in the classrrom,* ASHEERIC Higher Education Report No. 1. George Washington University, Washington, DC.

Castells, M. (1998). *The rise of network society.* Oxford: Blackwell.

Crehan, L. (2014). Teacher-led professional development in Singapore, blog post, Inside classrooms project, 6 June 2014. Department for Business, Innovation and Skills [BIS] (2015).

Elias, R. (2014). Retrieved from www.ted/talks.Rich.Elias. Accessed on July 10, 2014.

Freire, P. (1970). *Pedagogy of the oppressed.* New York, NY: Herder & Herder.

Freire, P. (1973). *Extensión or Comunicación: La Concientización en el Medio Rural.* México: Ed. Siglo XXI y Tierra Nueva.

Freire, P. (1997). *Pedagogia da Autonomia.* São Paulo: Editora Paz e Terra.

Gadotti, M. (2000). *Pedagogia da terra: Ecopedagogia e Educacao Sustentável. CLACSO.*

Gerhardt, H. (1993). *Paulo Freire (1921-97), in Prospects:* The quarterly review of comparative education. Paris: UNESCO: International Bureau of Education, vol. XXIII, no. 3/4.

Glenda, A. (1996). Active learning in a constructivist framework. *JSTOR, 31*(4), 3482969. Retrieved from https://www.jstor.org/stable/3482969

Goodman, P. (1960). *Growing up absurd: Problems of youth in organized society.* New York, NY: A Vintage Books.

Henry, J. (1963). *Culture against man.* New York, NY: Vintage Books. A Division of Random House.

Lee, D. (1986, 1976). *Valuing the self. Epilogue by Jeffrey Ehrenreich.* Prospect Heights, IL: Waveland Press, Inc.

Lee, D. (1987, 1959). *Freedom and culture. Prologue by Jeffrey Ehrenreich.* Prospect Heights, IL: Waveland Press, Inc.

Majduf, J. (2017). *Educación. Hacia donde Vamos? Rebelión* (01 Junio).

Marin, L. (2010). *Can we save true dialogue in an Age of Mistrust* Uppsala: Dag Hammarskjöld Foundation. *Critical Currents* no. 8 (January).

Martyn, M. (2007). Clickers in the classroom: An active learning approach. *Educause Quarterly (EQ), 30*(2).

McKeachie & Svinicki. (2008). Teaching and learning in higher education. *Academy of Management Learning & Education, 7*(1) (March), 139–142.

Mészáros, I. (2004). *Education beyond capital.* III Foro Mundial de Educación. Porto Alegre, RGS, Brasil, in Bacal (2011, op.cit, p. 69).

Michael, J. (2006). Where's the evidence that active learning works? *Advances in Physiology Education, 30*(4), 223–231.

Myrdal, G. (1973). *At a lecture at Campbell Hall* (p. 2), University of California at Santa Barbara. November.

Pozas Arciniegas, R. (1962). *Juan the Chamula.* Berkeley, CA: Berkeley University Press.

Prince, M. (2004). *Does active learning work?* A review of the research. *Journal of Engineering Education, 93*(3), 223–231.

Revans, R. W. (1982). *The origins and growth of action learning.* Bromley: Chartwell-Bratt Ltd.

Rodriguez, R. (1982). *Hunger of memory. New York, NY: Bantham Dell, A Division of Random House, Inc.*

Schatzman, M. (1973). *Soul murder.* New York. NY: Random House.

Smith, D. (1993). Fires in the mirror: Crown heights. *Brooklyn and Other Identities.* New York, NY: Pinguin Random House Inc.

Snyder, T. (2017). *On tyranny: Twenty Lessons from the twentieth century.* London: The Bodley Head.

Vygotsky, L. (1978). *Interaction between learning and development. From mind and society* (pp. 79–91). Cambridge, MA: Harvard University Press.

Weltman, D. (2007). *A comparison of traditional and active learning methods: An empirical investigation utilizing a linear mixed model,* PhD Thesis, Arlington: The University of Texas.

Wilkinson, R., & Pickett, K. (2009). *The spirit level: Why equality is better for everyone.* London: Penguin Books.

Chapter 15

A New Vision for Higher Education: Lessons from Education for the Environment and Sustainability

Christina Marouli, Anastasia Misseyanni,
Paraskevi Papadopoulou and Miltiadis D. Lytras

Abstract

Contemporary globalized societies face important environmental and social problems that require urgent action and citizen engagement. Active learning in contemporary societies is being reemphasized in order to prepare active learners, capable of critical thinking and innovative problem solving and able to become responsible citizens. Environmental Education (EE) and its descendant Education for Sustainability (EFS), or Education for Sustainable Development (ESD), have been a very important first effort for introducing active learning in contemporary education at all educational levels. They constitute an important variant of active learning. EE and EFS by definition propose and adopt active learning and experiential methods, as they seek to prepare people that will work for a healthy environment and better societies. And this is where the difference lies between EE/EFS and the generic active-learning approaches. EE or EFS are committed active-learning approaches; they have an explicit goal to work for social and environmental change.

The transition from learners to active learners is addressed by active learning, which however assumes that active learners will also become responsible and active citizens. EE and EFS have however demonstrated that this is not an obvious development.

Active Learning Strategies in Higher Education: Teaching for Leadership,
Innovation, and Creativity, 361−387
Copyright © 2018 by Emerald Publishing Limited
ISBN: 978-1-78714-488-0

Education should be clear about its purpose – individual change, empowerment, integration, or social transformation – and peda-gogical methods and tools should be selected appropriately.

This chapter first discusses the main characteristics of EE/EFS. Then, it explores what facilitates the transition from active learners to active citizens, based on lessons from EE and EFS. Finally, it reflects on the implications of these lessons for Higher Education and, as a result, a new vision for Higher Education and a brief guide for educators and Higher Educational managers are proposed.

Keywords: Higher education; environmental education; education for sustainability; action research; empowering education; transformative education

Introduction

Contemporary societies face serious environmental problems that chal-lenge the sustainability of present human communities with their culture and socioeconomic practices. This has been recognized since the 1960s. With the globalization of the Western economic system and culture of consumerism and materialism, these problems have expanded globally too. Along with the serious environmental challenges, societies today contend with significant socioeconomic issues – like the expanding gap between poor and rich, increasing number of people living in poverty and social exclusion, and increasing violence – that beg attention. Contemporary problems require urgent action and effective problem solving, while they challenge us to rethink the organization of our socie-ties and our relationship with nature and the environment. The exten-sive introduction of Information and Communication Technologies (ICT) has also altered human interactions and citizens' perceptions of the civic sphere. The present reality – with the unquestionable need to transition to a new society that cultivates a balance with nature and the environment and more equitable relationships among humans – requires citizens that are capable of critical and creative thinking, with a diversity of technical and interpersonal skills, as well as ready-to-be active citizens, among other things.

Education has always played a significant role in human societies, making individuals literate, promoting self-fulfillment, controlling parts of the population, dividing power, and promoting innovations and new ways of thinking. The purpose of education remains an unresolved issue although an extensively discussed one; education has been viewed as a tool for social reproduction or for social transformation depending on the authors/promoters' views of society (Jickling & Wals, 2008). As Dewey (1934) indicated, education reflects the society that has generated it and its needs.

> Any education is, in its forms and methods, an outgrowth
> of the needs of the society in which it exists.

Consequently, it is no surprise that active learning has become a common, much-discussed theme in education in the recent decades. The traditional teaching and learning approach of knowledge transmission from the knowledgeable educator to the "ignorant" students is not sufficient for the challenges of today. Traditional teaching creates passive learners, ready to absorb past — generally accepted — knowledge, but unprepared of critical thinking or of solving problems on their own. Active learning was introduced in education in the recent decades to change this trend, engage students in the learning process, and cultivate critical thinking and problem-solving skills. (Huba & Freed, 2000; Meyer & Jones, 1993; Smith, Sheppard, Johnson, & Johnson, 2005). Innovative teaching approaches with focus on various active-learning methods and assessment have been explored by the authors of this chapter (Lytras, Misseyanni, Marouli, & Papadopoulou, 2016; Lytras, Papadopoulou, Marouli, & Misseyanni, 2018; Marouli, Lytras, & Papadopoulou, 2016; Marouli, Misseyanni, Papadopoulou, & Lytras, 2016a, 2016b, 2017; Misseyanni & Gastardo, 2017; Misseyanni, Daniela, Lytras, Papadopoulou, & Marouli, 2017a; Misseyanni, Marouli, Papadopoulou, & Lytras, 2017b; Misseyanni, Marouli, Papadopoulou, Lytras, & Gastardo, 2016; Papadopoulou, Lytras, & Marouli, 2016; Papadopoulou, Lytras, Misseyanni, & Marouli, 2017; Shor, 1992).

Although active learning aims to prepare active learners and responsible citizens, the transition from active learners to active and responsible citizens is not at all obvious (Račinska, Barratt, & Marouli, 2015; Lange, 2004), but this is what we need today. Thus, the main questions this chapter aims to address are: What are the characteristics of EE, EFS that make them a very dynamic active-learning approach? What insights can one extract from the EE/EFS theory and practice for effective active learning that can cultivate active and socially as well as environmentally responsible citizens? What should the goals and characteristics of Higher Education be in the 21st century?

In order to address these questions, we will first briefly discuss the main characteristics of EE/EFS that we consider relevant for our discussion. Then, we will explore what facilitates the transition from active learners to active citizens, based on lessons from EE and EFS. Finally, we will reflect on the implications of these lessons for Higher Education, and we will propose a new vision for Higher Education.

Environmental Education and Education for Sustainability

Environmental Education arose in the 1970s as a response to the increasing social awareness of the significance of environmental issues and the recognition that modern environmental problems are a consequence of social practices and the organization of human communities. Solutions to them require knowledge of the ecosystems and the interrelations of human societies with the environment, as well as willingness to do something about environmental protection (United Nations, 1975, 1977). Environmental Education was proposed as a significant "tool" for the required social change that would lead to societies that live in harmony with the environment. At the same time that EE practices proliferated and environmental thinking matured, the concept of sustainable development (United Nations World Commission on Environment & Development, 1987) arose – a concept that highlighted that as the environment is made up of inextricably interwoven webs of life, integrative approaches connecting environmental, social, economic, and cultural aspects are needed. An even more significant change is required in human societies, their organization, culture, and practices for a transition to sustainable communities and economies. Education is fundamental in this transition. Environmental Education (EE) was thus transformed to or replaced by Education for Sustainable Development (ESD), or Education for Sustainability (EFS).[1]

---

[1]ESD and EFS sometimes are used interchangeably. However, they have a different emphasis and some prefer to use one or the other depending on their worldview. ESD has a more direct connection with economic development. As economic development is most often considered the same as economic growth, people that question the possibility of economic growth to promote sustainable communities and a healthy environment may prefer to use the term EFS. We also prefer to use the term EFS.

Much has been written about EE and ESD/EFS; some have positively hailed the transition from EE to EFS, while others have considered this development as a "watering down" effect of the transformative potential of EE (Jickling & Wals, 2008; Kopnina, 2014). Indeed, as sustainable development has been vaguely defined, it has since been interpreted in many diverse ways, allowing for cooptation and systemic adjustments and often compromising the needed radical changes in worldviews and practices. In the same way, ESD/EFS has expanded the domain (topics, methods of coverage, etc.) of EE sometimes to a degree that it has become a token approach to environmental issues, leading to even further deterioration of the environment and ecosystems. As our intention is not to indulge further in this debate but rather to extract the useful lessons from EE and EFS for the future of Higher Education in the context of contemporary environmental and social–economic–political challenges, we will now critically discuss some important and useful elements of EE and EFS.

EE and EFS: Goals and Main Characteristics[2]

Environmental Education from its very conception has been explicitly committed to protect the environment and lead to societies that can live in balance with nature. Environmental Education arose after ecology had sufficiently progressed as a science, so that it could provide a sound knowledge base for EE, and ecological movements were strong enough to lobby for changes in industrial and economic practices for the protection of the environment. In this context, EE aimed to raise people's awareness, especially in Western human societies, supported by sound scientific knowledge regarding the then-prevalent environmental problems and their human causes, as well as to lead to the adoption of environmentally friendly practices. EE is committed education.

Initially, EE wished to share scientific knowledge on how ecosystems work and on the natural laws and limits that no human society can ignore or avoid. Toward this aim, interdisciplinary collaboration – at

---

[2]For more information on Environmental Education and Education for Sustainable Development or Education for Sustainability, please refer to Flogaiti (1998), Kalaitzidis and Ouzounis (2000), Flogaiti and Liarikou (2009), Tilbury (2004), UNESCO (2005), Goncalves (2012). For some more recent developments in the field, see the following references: Eco-justice pedagogy, Bowers (2002), Multicultural Environmental Education, Marouli (2002).

first, in the natural sciences — has been characteristic of EE initiatives. Environmental Education efforts also tried to mobilize feelings of caring for and interest in nature and its creatures. One of the first forms of EE was "outdoors education," where students were exposed to nature (e.g. tree hugging, games in nature, etc.) with the aim to get familiarized with nature and develop feelings of compassion toward its creatures. The underlying belief that guided/guides this type of education is that emotion is a fundamental stimulus of learning — something that has been forgotten and even exorcized in modern education, and especially Higher Education. The assumption behind both of these approaches was that knowledge about the environment and feelings for the environment would mobilize environmentally friendly behaviors; this was the ultimate aim of EE.

ESD, or EFS, built on EE and underlined the need for interdisciplinary–multidisciplinary approaches that connect environmental, social, and economic aspects toward the understanding of a selected topic and the design of effective, viable, and durable solutions. ESD/EFS redefined the purpose of education as helping societies and people transition toward sustainable development or toward sustainable communities. As integrative approaches constitute a main characteristic of ESD/EFS, such educational initiatives can start from any problem as long as they work at the intersection of environment–society–economy–culture. Such multidisciplinary and integrative approaches presuppose collaboration not only among experts of different disciplines but also between experts and lay people and other entities interested in or with stakes in the same topic. ESD/EFS inevitably looks for "compromise" solutions as they seek to integrate a great diversity of parameters and views. Furthermore, given its emphasis on the integration of environmental–social–economic aspects, ESD/EFS retains a human-centered viewpoint, easily leading to the undervaluing of environmental issues when social or economic aspects are considered significant or urgent (Kopnina, 2014).

Based on the aforementioned trajectory of EE, it elaborated a very useful in our view classification of EE — one that highlights the significance of the purpose of any environmental (and not only) educational effort and its clarification. Environmental Education can be *on, in,* or *for* the environment. Education *on* the environment refers to learning processes that focus on knowledge acquisition regarding the environment. Education *in* the environment places learning about the environment inside the environment itself, via experiential approaches to learning (like outdoors education). Education in the environment explicitly seeks to touch and mobilize feelings (emotive learning) related to the environment in order to mobilize interest and make learners ready to learn and potentially act for the environment. Education *for* the environment seeks learning and knowledge creation that aims to action: environmental protection and adoption of environmentally friendly behaviors. It explicitly aims to mobilize action and cultivate active and caring citizens. Education for the environment proposes an eco-centric approach to environmental education, which is a challenge to the existing and widely adopted anthropocentric worldview (which often leads to compromised solutions to environmental problems). ESD/EFS is committed education just like EE for the environment, although it more readily supports an anthropocentric worldview.

EE and EFS: Pedagogy

The distinction of education into *on, in, or* for the environment is useful for any learning process. Consciously reflecting on the purpose, any form of education helps making the learning process a creative, critical, and forward-looking enterprise by making the assumptions behind the teaching and learning process more transparent. Furthermore, making the purpose of education clear opens the way for the selection of appropriate didactic methods. And indeed EE and EFS have constituted an alternative pedagogical proposition from their inception.

a. *Experiential learning, building, on students' knowledge*
   Given their commitment to social change, EE and EFS challenged the then (and still) traditional didactics that treated students as empty slates and/or ignorant beings and viewed the instructor as the vehicle that passed knowledge to students. They proposed that instruction should be *experiential, building on students' knowledge* and involving them in an active-learning process. Hands-on education has always characterized EE and EFS.

b. *Project-based learning*
   Projects have been a favored teaching method in EE and EFS efforts (Flogaiti, 1998; Kalaitzidis & Ouzounis, 2000). Project-based learning is built around projects that involve students in research, problem solving, and synthesizing diverse bodies of knowledge; projects in which students experience the environment and nature and also have hands-on experience on research and formulating and assessing solutions. Projects − with their relative long duration − can

provide time for holistic investigation, collaboration, reflection, and even time for consideration and actual adjustment of personal behaviors. Other engaging teaching methods — like games, role playing activities, field work, in-nature experiences, interviews of local people, theater plays, etc. — are also used. All of them are used in the context of a larger design — the project — which serves and respects the *procedural nature of learning*. Learning is not an outcome; it is a process. As such, not only the pedagogy is adjusted but also *assessments* are reconceived, as traditional forms of assessment which measure output or at best outcome are not considered sufficient.

c. *Problem solving and action research*
   Problem solving of real — usually local — problems is paramount in EE and EFS. Probably in one of its more radical forms, EE/EFS does not promote only problem solving but also *problem posing*, i.e. formulating a challenging question for research based on a critical understanding of the local environment, reality, and needs. In this context, action research has been frequently adopted in EE/EFS as a pedagogical approach. *Action research* (Carson & Sumara, 1997) implies that learning should investigate a real — usually local — problem in the effort to solve it effectively, learners systematically collect information from diverse sources. In action research, learners and community work closely together to address the selected local real problem. This approach to learning creates a learning context that is closely related with the local reality; it is a place-based learning, involving investigation for knowledge creation, activities that mobilize feelings, and leads to a better balance in the environment. As the stimulus for learning is an issue related with local reality, knowledge becomes more evidently relevant to students/learners.

d. *Individual issues and social problems: The power connection*
   As it has been repeatedly discussed in literature that focuses on the connection between education and behavioral change, learning that is relevant to the learners' reality and that builds on their prior knowledge and experiences more effectively mobilizes feelings and behavioral changes (Dobson, 2007; Marouli & Duroy, 2014; Račinska et al., 2015). Furthermore, in a learning context that uncovers the relevance of the learning process, learners also gain experience on recognizing the *connection between individual issues and social problems*. Feminist literature explicitly argued that "personal is political"; individual problems and power relations in society are intricately interrelated, the one influencing the other.

This connection should constitute the basis of all learning that aims to generate active and responsible citizens (Dewey, 1966; Jickling & Wals, 2008).

e. *Integrative and systemic thinking*

Finally, EFS has emphasized the need for *integrative and systemic thinking*. This emphasis on integration and systemic thinking calls for the dissolution of boundaries among disciplines, between the educational institutions (i.e. educational institutions as Ivory Towers) and the community, between expert and lay knowledge, and even the reconsideration of the divide between operations and academics inside the universities themselves (for more information, see the movement for sustainable universities, e.g. the Association for the Advancement of Sustainability in Higher Education (AASHE)[3]. Thus, such integrative and systemic approaches can also lead to the questioning of relevant hierarchies (e.g. in the classroom, among sources of information, among bodies of knowledge, in an institution or a community, etc.) implicit or explicit, delineating spaces for more creative and more dynamic learning processes.

From Learners to Engaged Learners to Active and Responsible Citizens: Lessons Learnt

Given that EE and ESD/EFS have always aimed to cultivate engaged learners and active and responsible citizens, their 70-year-long experience is a rich source of lessons for active learning and modern Higher Education that aspire to similar goals.

An important lesson is that both pedagogy (i.e. curriculum and course design, implementation, evaluation, and redesign) and educational-institutional context are important parameters that contribute to (or inhibit) the "making" of engaged learners and active and responsible citizens. This is in line with Vygotsky's (1978) understanding of learning as a dialectic interaction of humans with others and a social context, mediated by tools and cultural objects.

Pedagogy − i.e. the teaching and learning methods used in the context of a class/course − indeed has a pivotal role in creating engaged

---

[3]For more information on the Association for the Advancement of Sustainability in Higher Education, you can visit www.aashe.org

and creative learners. For such a goal, some ideas are significant as premises of pedagogical design:

- Learning is a process and not an outcome. A *spiral methodology*, (Papadopoulou et al., 2016) around a theme, with steps building one on the other and with increasing degrees of difficulty, is very useful. *Project-based learning* is thus a useful approach to learning as it provides opportunities for development of higher level skills and reflection time.
- Learning is developed in the process of relations and interaction with others and the environment. Meaning arises in relation to a context. Thus, *collaborative learning* methods are very useful and in addition, teach significant transformative social skills that also impact on an individual's theory of learning (which happens throughout life).
- Example teaches better than words. Thus, the instructor's behavior demonstrates his/her theory of learning (and teaching), which inadvertently influences learners. The class organization − i.e. instructor as the decision maker or decision-making is shared among instructor and students − predisposes students to certain learning roles (e.g. passive or active, accepting, or critical learners). In this context, democratic "classroom" settings and *collaborative teaching* is significant as an example of cocreation of knowledge, collaborative learning and their benefits. (Marouli et al., 2017).
- *Emotion* is a great (if not the only) motivational force for learning. Emotive learning is engaged learning. The pedagogical choices we make (e.g. games, role playing, etc.) should aim to mobilize especially positive feelings − like fun, love, caring etc. − as these constitute a constructive force for the sustenance of the effort and perseverance that is required in the learning process.
- Connection between the learning space and object, on the one hand, and the local reality on the other, reveals the *relevance of knowledge* to real life, which in turn renders learning interesting and useful. This characteristic of learning excites students, especially when the learning process starts from their already acquired knowledge, validates it, and builds on it. This connection can also mobilize interest for creative thinking in the context of real problem solving. Thus, engaging pedagogy often involves *real-world problem solving,* with an emphasis on local problems. Furthermore, *action research* − usually an effort to study and address a local problem; a process during which studying, researching, collaborating, and some form of political action are required − is a very useful pedagogical approach.

- Given the procedural nature of learning, it should be assessed as such too. *Assessment* itself passes a very strong message regarding the specific learning space and the assumed character of learning.
- The learning environment of a classroom should explicitly and consistently pass the message that instructors do not aim to transmit knowledge but to facilitate students' learning process. A *democratic "classroom"* invites creative thinking and contributes to student empowerment.
- The learning process should be *integrative,* and instructional design should "consciously disrupt the integrity of taken-for-granted assumptions and interpretations of experience to bring to light contradictions and thereby facilitate the move toward inclusive, permeable, integrated-meaning perspectives" (Mezirow, 1991). It should cultivate *systemic (not fragmented) thinking* – i.e. understanding how systems (social and ecological) work, their dynamics beyond the addition of their parts and their implications for individual lives. The learning process should promote an in-depth understanding of how personal issues are related with social problems.
- The learning process should also provide *technological (especially Information and Communication Technologies) skills,* accompanied with the ability to critically assess their usefulness and appropriateness in different occasions, beyond the excitement of the novice (which we still have as societies in front of such new technologies, like virtual reality, augmented reality, haptic technologies, etc.). (Lytras & Papadopoulou, 2017; Lytras et al., 2017; Marouli et al., 2016).

EE and EFS efforts address real problems of the environment and the world. Thus, EE and EFS emphasize the significance of place-based learning, which renders learning relevant and makes students' empowerment as citizens more feasible. This emphasis highlights the *significance of the context*: the community (context external to the university) and the university itself. Working for community issues (e.g. pollution of a local river, organic waste management in the local community) makes learning socially and individually relevant and thus more stimulating. Furthermore, learning related to community-based issues may mobilize learners' desire for action. Working on a university-related issue (e.g. energy consumption on campus, promotion of campus initiatives for respect of diversity) reveals the connection of academic reality with university operations and even scholarship opportunities. In addition, campus-based learning opportunities teach students transferable (e.g. communication, collaboration, political, interviewing, etc.) skills and can make them aware of real-life complexity and the challenges that are significant to consider in the organization of one's own actions. Innovative, engaging, collaborative, and challenging pedagogies may stimulate learners' thinking but alone, they can leave learners feeling powerless in terms of their ability to impact their social environment (Marouli & Duroy, 2014). A democratic learning space, the campus as a "living laboratory" and addressing real community challenges, can contribute to the development of organizational skills needed to active citizens. According to Ada (2007) and as stated in Marouli (2016), learning environments should be guided by the following principles:

- "... we learn better in an environment that offers love and respect, and allows us to experience and honor the truth of our thoughts, emotions and feelings."
- "... we learn better in an environment that allows us to learn at our own pace and in our own way, that honors what we care about, and that builds on what we have already learned from our life experience."
- " Racism, as well as other forms of prejudice and oppression ... are pervasive in our world and influence all of us in unconscious ways. Therefore we need to begin by recognizing prejudice and oppression in order to unlearn them."
- "... we learn better in an interactive, supportive and noncompetitive environment. As we live in a competitive society, it takes intention and effort to establish a cocreative atmosphere."

As Potter (2010) indicated, the desired outcome of education for the environment and sustainability has been "educated citizens who take an interested and active part in their communities and in their country." However, the transition from creative, critical, and active learners to active and responsible citizens is not at all obvious. As Marouli (2016) indicated, numerous efforts have been made to educate the public on waste generation and management and the associated problems in the last 6–7 decades; however, waste management continues being a major challenge of modern societies. Empowerment is needed too. Paulo Freire (2006) was a pioneer in *empowering education*. The *critical pedagogy* that he proposed starts from the harsh life of his students (personal issues) and helps them analyze and understand their sociopolitical underpinnings (social problems) and simultaneously learn, create, and apply knowledge to their lives. Critical pedagogy aims to liberate participants via praxis, "a process of reflection as a preparation of action, followed by reflecting on the results of our action, which leads us to new insights and therefore to new action, in an ongoing cycle of growth and learning. An essential part of that learning is a critical analysis of our own culture" (Ada, 2007). In this view, active citizens can critically reflect on their and other experiences and synthesize the findings into new knowledge, which they then apply to real-life problems; they can pose challenging questions and perform integrated and scientific research to solve community problems, with a sense of social responsibility and the understanding that individual action and social structures are intricately connected. Interest, knowledge, desire to act for change, empowerment, and social commitment seem to be important elements of the required mix that can lead to action and change.

A New Vision for Higher Education in the 21st Century

Higher Education in the 21st century needs to be engaged with real social concerns. As Lytras et al. (2018) indicate, "The entire process in HE [Higher Education] should be considered as a holistic contribution to creativity and innovation with commitment to the benefit of society." We live at times where changes are not only obvious but also needed. We need an education that is socially and individually relevant and empowering, and we need universities that consciously and actively strive to be virtuous as described by Jon Nixon (2008) in his book *Towards the Virtuous University*. We need Higher Education that prepares for change (Junyent & Geli de Ciurana, 2008) that moves beyond the pretense of objectivity and into social and environmental commitment and responsibility (not biased or indoctrination-oriented though), while retaining the scientific approach that it has developed in the last decades but also reconnecting with emotion and morality. Time for self- and group-reflection should be planned within our educational processes in order to move beyond the pervasive mechanistic thinking of today's societies and toward the required critical and morally based assessment of change.

Furthermore, in today's world, literacy in ICTs is an important asset and skill that can facilitate action. ICTs provide enormous capabilities for the democratic collection and sharing of information, as well as a powerful tool for connections across space and time. Powerful as these technologies are, they require an ethical background that guides their uses. Dobson's (2007) concept of "environmental citizenship" — i.e., a sense of stewardship for the environment and responsibility to work for the public good — delineates this ethical background. In addition, ICTs enormous power to collect huge amounts of data from diverse sources makes them vulnerable to violations and uses for private purposes; thus, in-depth technical knowledge is also required in order to avert social control and diversion in the course of the transition toward environmentally sustainable and caring societies.

Lange (2004) talks about the dialectic of transformative and restorative learning. Transformative learning processes prepare students for change as active agents in society; restorative learning is more akin to social reproduction or transmission of traditional and accepted knowledge. She highlights the need for a dialectic relation between these two, so that education and learning can lead to better and sustainable societies. Jickling and Wals (2008) go a step further and propose a heuristic in which transformative learning is counterposed to transmissive learning, where knowledge is prescribed and transmitted to the learners, which is akin to the "restorative learning" of Lange. Jickling's and Wals' heuristic is built around two dimensions: one that extends from transmissive to socioconstructivist or transformative dimension — a dimension that highlights the purpose of education and another one from authoritative to participatory learning — an aspect that relates more to the pedagogical method. This useful heuristic was proposed as a tool for "the evaluation of education initiatives concerning poverty, health, social justice, development, and other global agendas" (Jickling & Wals, 2008) for the support of "nonconformism" and social change.

In our view, the new basis for the Higher Education for a better and sustainable (environmentally sound, socially just, economically viable, happy, and fulfilling) future comprises the following characteristics and goals:

- A (re)new(ed) sense of *connection and responsibility for the collective well-being*, based on the understanding that "I can thrive only when others, nature and other species around me are also well." This implies:
  • Pedagogy should become more *collaborative*, involving both collaborative learning (Smith & McGregor, 1992; Johnson, Johnson, & Smith, 2014) and collaborative teaching (Ferguson & Wilson, 2011) methods. The development of collaborative skills and practices that consider all living beings (including other

humans) as brothers and sisters sharing the same Earth-home should be a main objective of Higher Education. (Marouli & Misseyanni, 2017; Marouli et al., 2017; Misseyanni et al., 2017a).

- *Universities* are institutions that have traditionally been organized on the logic of "silos" – fragmented spaces; they should be reorganized in ways that reveal *connections and encourage respectful collaborations* between its different parts: different disciplines; academics and operations; students, faculty, and staff (Marouli & Misseyanni, 2017; Misseyanni et al., 2017a, 2017b).

− A good understanding and respect of natural laws – how ecosystems/nature works along with a (re)new(ed) commitment to moral values. This should promote a *new humanistic morality that is based on an eco-centric worldview* (i.e. aiming to the health and wellness of the environment and all species, including present and future human generations, but not primarily humans or of humans over other species as this is an impossible and false premise). Consequently:

- Contemporary environmental problems, with their long-term and far-reaching implications for all forms of life – including humans – call us to develop skills and ways of being that favor the collective good, over the individual (inevitably short-term) profit. We need an education that facilitates a new worldview and promotes the required "shift towards 'systems and citizenship' rather than 'me and consumerism'" (Webster, 2013).

- Modern education should assist learners in acquiring knowledge, motivation, and skills that promote balance in nature as human societies cannot exist without a healthy environment or living beyond natural limits. What is in danger is not nature but humanity.

− A deep understanding that *personal troubles are public problems* (Mills, 1959); an understanding that our personal woes or benefits are reflections of the social system in which we live, its strengths and weaknesses. Systemic thinking and a sense of agency (Cassell, 1993) are both important elements of empowerment of creative learners and active and responsible citizens.

− The cultivation of critical-thinking skills that allow the new generation to *distinguish and boldly select* what of modern and traditional cultures, socioeconomic practices, and technological and social innovations can lead us to effective and durable solutions to contemporary problems and new visions for human societies.

− The cultivation of the ability to critically understand and use (or not use) *modern technologies, where and if appropriate.* Young generations should be technologically literate, deeply knowledgeable of diverse traditions and cultures, and unwaveringly committed to the creation of a new sustainable, caring, and healthy world – a vision that remains to be constructed. They should be capable of daringly selecting more "traditional" over technocratic approaches, new over already widely accepted worldviews and practices when this is an equally or a more effective way of transitioning to this new vision-in-creation.

– Its *(re)connection with real communities* – social and ecological – for interfertilization and exchange of ideas, for proposition of relevant, socially responsible and appropriate solutions, for selection of appropriate methods and technologies, for a *relevant education* that can motivate, inspire, and challenge all involved to moral and sustainable societies. And finally,

– The *empowerment* of learners (and teachers) not only as agents of learning (and teaching), moving beyond the already accepted knowledge to the creation of knowledge, but also as active, responsible, and caring members of human societies and socioecosystems that can think and act creatively, constructively, daringly, morally, respectfully, and with social and environmental responsibility.

As Marouli (2016) indicates, the education that we need in order to support the required transition toward more sustainable and caring societies should involve learning for individual change, learning for (individual) empowerment, learning for integration (and the collective good), and learning for social transformation. Furthermore, we need educational settings that (re)make knowledge creation a combination and the product of thinking and acting, with an explicit moral ground. Education today (and always) should be open to change, inviting new ideas and conceptions, and rigorously checking for their validity. Below, we present our vision for the Higher Education of the 21st century in a tabular form, building on Vygotsky's (1978) view of learning and enriching and adjusting the table of Marouli (2016). The proposed vision falls primarily in quadrants II (transmissive and participatory), III (authoritative and transformative/socioconstructivist), and IV (transformative/socioconstructivist and participatory) of Jickling's and Wals' (2008) heuristic as we believe that our times require, on the one hand, out-of-the-box thinking while critically using traditional and currently accepted bodies of knowledge, and on the other, respectful collaborations bringing all our mental and ethical energies together toward better societies.

The proposed vision for educational praxis presented in Figure 1 builds on the following heuristic, which we consider complementary to one of Jickling and Wals (Figure 1).

Generally, education works to enhance individuals. However, we need education for the collective good, for the good of the community. And this need is very prevalent today, especially in Western societies with intense emphasis on individualism. Furthermore, the active learning we need in contemporary societies may aim to the cultivation of critical and creative thinking or to develop active and socially responsible citizens. These two trends are reflected in Figure 1 on the two axes of the diagram, creating a space where different active-learning initiatives can be placed.

On the space delineated by these two axes, we reflect the different possible purposes of active learning. Active learning can aim for critical learners that can critically assess knowledge presented to them; or for empowered learners that can create knowledge; or for learners able to integrate knowledge for solutions to social concerns; or for active citizens that not only can but actively use and create knowledge for effective solutions. We envision that each of these aims presupposes the previous ones (Table 1).

Table 1 builds on this heuristic model and offers suggestions for pedagogical methods and instructional tools.

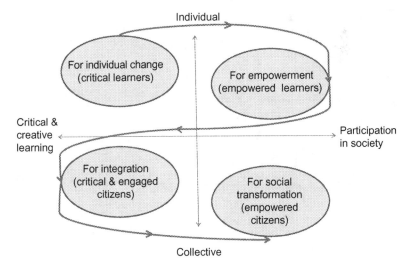

Figure 1. Positioning the Educational Praxis Within Two Force Fields.

Table 1. A New Vision for Higher Education for the Transition to Environmentally Sustainable and Caring Societies: Connections between Educational Purpose, Characteristics, Methods, Tools, Desired Outcomes and Institutional Context.

Educational Purpose	Characteristics/ Skills Targeted	Learning Context – Teaching Methods	Instructional Tools	Key Outcomes	Institutional Context
For individual change→ Critical learners	– Critical thinking – Creativity & innovation – Knowledge creation – Relevant knowledge	– Case study analysis – Dialogic classes – Problem analysis – Instructor as facilitator – Building on students' prior knowledge	– Case studies – Audio visual materials – Role-playing – Laboratory activities (guided) – Basic use of ICTs	– Critical knowledge – Analytic ability – Synthetic ability	– Technical support for laboratories and ICTs – Flexible classroom arrangements
For empowerment→ empowered (and critical) learners	– Real-life problem solving (connection of education with society/ community) – Desire to act – Sense that you can cause	– Real-life problem solving – Investigating connection of personal troubles & public problems ('personal is political')	– Projects on problems/ questions seeking answers – Group activities in class & outside – Experiments – Field work	– Problem solving – Systems thinking – Research ability – Team working skills – Emotive learning – Constructive self-reflection	– Flexible learning environments – University policies supporting/ facilitating out-of-classroom activities – University policies

For integration→ critical & engaged citizens (and critical & empowered learners)	– Integration of different bodies of knowledge – Integration of experience & knowledge; of diverse sources of knowledge – Circular logic – Local and global connections	individual and social change – Political literacy – Systems thinking	– Mobilizing emotions – Self-reflection activities – Service learning (offer your services & learn) – Experiential learning (learning concepts by doing) – Class as a "think tank"	– Integrative projects, requiring diverse sources – Collaborative learning & collaborative teaching – Multicultural exchanges – Investigation of end-of-life uses	– Work in a NGO – Internet searches – use of knowledge databases – Journals/self-reflection activities	– Group projects & in-class group activities – Different groups on different aspects of a multifaceted problem – including ethics	– Holistic – circular – transdisciplinary thinking – Collaborative skills – Identifying connections & relations – Knowledge cocreation	acknowledging and supporting instructors that adopt this approach – Flexible learning environments with access to various sources of knowledge – Universities actively promoting collaborations, inside (across disciplines and between

Table 1. (*Continued*)

Educational Purpose	Characteristics/Skills Targeted	Learning Context – Teaching Methods	Instructional Tools	Key Outcomes	Institutional Context
		– Multiscalar analysis (local, regional, national, global) – Class as a "research group"	– Local/international problems – Social media/web-based tools – Use of synchronous & asynchronous Internet-based tools	– ICT skills for communication	operations and academics) – Spaces/"Agoras" for laid-back interactions in universities
For social transformation→ empowered citizens (& critical citizens, critical & empowered learners)	– Understanding sociopolitical, economic, and cultural context/dynamics – Sense of social responsibility & significance of common/public good	– Action research (local problem, investigation, collaboration with community, problem solving, policy implications, action) – Connection with society	– Group work – Working on a local problem/issue – Collaboration with local community & experts from different disciplines	– Embracing change as positive – Social responsibility – Sociopolitical, savvy, & relational power – Action research capabilities	– Virtuous university (Nixon, 2008) vision, policies & practices – Active university feedback mechanisms – University collaborations

– Collective action & participation in community affairs	– Democratic decision- making in class – Self- and group-reflection activities	– People research – On line tools (ICTs) for connectivity – Group-reflection time	– Constructive self- & group-reflection	with local community and other bodies for socially responsible and scientific real-life problem solving

Note: Enriched and adjusted from Marouli (2016).

Table 1 is a very compact representation of the pedagogy and educational—institutional settings we propose (which we intend to analyze further in our future published works). It reveals the connections between educational purpose, instructional methods, tools, desired outcomes, and institutional setting depending on the educational purpose, different methods, tools, desired outcomes (with implications for the assessment methods that should be adopted) and institutional settings are appropriate or needed. Table 1 starts with the educational purpose, as we believe that this is a fundamental and even determining element of education which guides the design, evaluation, and success of curriculum and instructional choices. However, this element − educational purpose − is usually taken for granted and not discussed, often leading to misguided evaluations (of curriculum, instructors, and even students) and subsequent decisions. The sequence of educational purposes (from "for individual change" to "for social transformation") has been intentionally selected as it moves from the easiest and more familiar one to present educators and moves to the more encompassing and systems-oriented one, which we advocate is needed in our times. The educational practice that has been designed to serve an "advanced" educational purpose builds on the previous one(s) too. Thus, this gradation is also aligned with the spiral methodology that we propose in curriculum and course design (Lytras & Papadopoulou, 2017; Lytras et al., 2016; Papadopoulou et al., 2016). It reveals the connections between educational purpose, instructional methods, tools, desired outcomes, and institutional setting; depending on the educational purpose, different methods, tools, desired outcomes (with implications for the assessment methods that should be adopted), and institutional settings are appropriate or needed. The table connects different aspects of educational praxis, it intends to be useful for instructors and administrators in the design process.

If we aim for individual change and for the development of critical learners, then some basic skills that should be cultivated are acquisition of relevant knowledge, critical thinking, creativity, and innovation. Active-learning methods such as case study analysis, problem solving, interactive and dialogic classes, role-playing, experiential learning through lab activities as well as basic use of ICTs would help toward the acquisition of critical knowledge, analytic ability, and synthetic ability. Technical support (e.g. labs, ICTs) and flexible classroom arrangements should be provided from the part of the institution.

If we aim for the development of empowered and critical leaners, then learners should become capable of real-life problem solving, sometimes in connection with society and/or community; they should develop a sense that they can cause individual and social change and a desire to act. Political literacy and a systems-thinking approach would be important skills targeted as well. Active-learning methods such as problem-based learning, collaborative learning, experiential learning (lab and field work), work in NGOs, use of knowledge databases, exposure to original research, and self-reflection activities would be important instructional methods and tools leading to the desired outcomes: problem solving, systems thinking, ability for research, for collaborative work and for constructive self-reflection. Institutions, on the other hand, should be able to provide flexible learning environments and establish policies facilitating out-of-class activities and supporting instructors in their efforts.

If we aim for integration and for the development of not only critical and empowered learners but also of engaged citizens, then learners should be able to integrate different bodies of knowledge and experiences. They should develop a circular logic and transdisciplinary thinking, be able to make local and global connections, develop good collaborative skills and ability for cocreation of knowledge. Teaching methods that promote integration of knowledge from different sources such as integrative projects, collaborative learning and teaching, multicultural exchanges, multiscalar analysis, using the class as a "research group" would help toward the acquisition of the above skills. Group projects, projects in which students examine different aspects of multifaceted problems, analysis of local/international problems, and use of ICTs such as social media, synchronous and asynchronous web-based tools would be important instructional tools. To achieve this educational purpose, academic institutions should provide appropriate flexible learning environments and should actively promote collaborations across disciplines and between operations and academics.

Finally, for developing empowered citizens that are capable of social transformation, learners should acquire an understanding of the sociopolitical, economic, and cultural context/dynamics; they should develop a sense of social responsibility and of the significance of common/public good and an ability for collective action and participation in community affairs. Teaching approaches based on action research (problem solving, collaboration with community, etc.), promoting connection with society, democratic decision-making in class as well as self and group reflection would contribute to the development of empowered learners and citizens. Group work on local problems/issues, collaboration with community and/or experts on a topic, people research, ICTs for connectivity, and group reflection time would be important instructional tools toward this purpose. In this way, learners will learn to embrace change as positive and will develop an ability for action research as well as for constructive self- and group-reflection. Academic institutions should adjust their vision, policies, and practices to support this direction they should develop feedback mechanisms and promote collaborations with local community and other bodies for socially responsible and scientific real-life problem solving.

We hope that the thoughts shared in this table, this chapter, and the whole book will stimulate further research and daring novel propositions for the new vision and practices needed for Higher Education in the 21st century so that it systematically acts as a leading agent in the transition we need toward more sustainable and caring societies.

References

Ada, A. F. (2007). A lifetime of learning to teach. *Journal of Latinos and Education*, *6*(2), 103–118.

Bowers, C. A. (2002). Toward an eco-justice pedagogy. *Environmental Education Research*, *8*(1), 21–34.

Carson, T., & Sumara, D. (eds.) (1997). *Action research as living practice*. New York, NY: Peter Lang.

Cassell, P. (ed.) (1993). *The Giddens Reader*. London: The MacMillan Press.

Dewey, J. (1934). Individual psychology and education. *The Philosopher*, 12. Retrieved from http://www.the-philosopher.co.uk/2016/08/individual-psychology-and-education-1934.html

Dewey, J. (1966). *Democracy and education: An introduction to the philosophy education*. New York, NY: Free Press.

Dobson, A. (2007). Environmental citizenship: Towards sustainable development. *Sustainable Development*, *15*(5), 276–285.

Ferguson, J., & Wilson, J. (2011). The co-teaching professorship: Power and expertise in the co-taught higher education classroom. *Scholar-Practitioner Quarterly*, *5*(1), 52–68.

Flogaiti, E. (1998). *Environmental education. Athens: Ellinika Grammata* (in Greek).

Flogaiti, E., & Liarakou, G. (2009). *Education for sustainable development: From theory to practice*. Arhanes: Arhanes Center of Environmental Education (in Greek).

Freire, P. (2006). *Pedagogy of the oppressed: 30th Anniversary Edition*. New York, NY: Continuum.

Goncalves, F. (2012). *Contributions to the UN decade of education for sustainable development*. Frankfurt am Main: Peter Lang AG. Retrieved from http://web.a.ebscohost.com.acg.idm.oclc.org/ehost/ebookviewer/ebook/bmxlYmtfXzQ4ODAwOV9fQU41?sid=51f8c226-1e86-4cd4-a3b8-da861526442e@sessionmgr4003&vid=6&format=EB&rid=2

Huba, M. E., & Freed, J. E. (2000). *Learner-centered assessment on college campuses: Shifting the focus from teaching to learning* (p. 35). Boston, MA: Allyn and Bacon.

Jickling, B., & Wals, A. E. J. (2008). Globalization and environmental education: looking beyond sustainable development. *Journal of Curriculum Studies, 40*(1), 1–21.

Johnson, D. W., Johnson, R. T., & Smith, K. A. (2014). Cooperative learning: Improving university instruction by basing practice on validated theory. *Journal on Excellence in University Teaching, 25*(3&4), 1–26.

Junyent, M., & Geli de Ciuran, A. M. (2008). Education for sustainability in university studies: A model for reorienting the curriculum. *British Educational Research Journal, 34*(6), 763–782.

Kalaitzidis, D., & Ouzounis, K. (2000). *Environmental education: Theory and practice*. Xanthi: Spanidi Publications (in Greek).

Kopnina, H. (2014). Revisiting education for sustainable development (ESD): Examining anthropocentric bias through the transition of environmental education to ESD. *Sustainable Development, 22*, 73–83.

Lange, E. A., (2004). Transformative and restorative learning: A vital dialectic for sustainable societies. *Adult Education Quarterly, 54*(2), 121–139.

Lytras, M., Misseyanni, A., Marouli, C., & Papadopoulou, P. (2016). Integrating research to teaching in higher education: A value chain model for academic excellence and student development, *ICERI2016 Proceedings*, pp. 5332–5342. doi:10.21125/iceri.2016.2296

Lytras, M., & Papadopoulou, P. (2017).Virtual reality systems for introductory biology labs: An integrated survey of industry solutions, *12th International Conference, Open education towards a knowledge-based society*, DisCo 2017, Prague, Czech Republic.

Lytras, M., Papadopoulou, P., Misseyanni, A., Marouli, C., Alhalabi, W., & Daniela, L. (2017). Moving virtual and augmented reality in the learning cloud: Design principles for an agora of active visual learning services in STEM education, *EDULEARN17 Proceedings*, pp. 7673–7678. doi: 10.21125/edulearn. 2017.0395

Lytras, M. D., Papadopoulou, P., Marouli, C., & Misseyanni, A. (2018). Higher education out-of-the-box: Technology-driven learning innovation in higher education. In: S. Burton (Ed.), *Engaged scholarship and civic responsibility in higher education* (pp. 67–100). Hershey, PA: IGI Global. doi:10.4018/978-1-5225-3649-9.ch004

Marouli, C. (2002). Multicultural environmental education: Theory and practice. *Canadian Journal of Environmental Education, 7*(1), 26–42.

Marouli, C. (2016). Moving towards a circular economy: The need to educate – Why and how? *4th International Conference on Sustainable Solid Waste Management*, 23–25 June 2016, Limassol, Cyprus (e-proceedings).

Marouli, C., & Duroy, Q. (2014). The nexus between climate change and social practices: Theoretical and empirical reflections for policymaking. *Journal of Diplomacy and International Relations, XVI* (1), 131–146.

Marouli, C., Lytras, M., & Papadopoulou, P. (2016). Design guidelines for massive open online courses (MOOCS) in STEM: Methodological considerations towards active participatory teaching and learning, *EDULEARN16 Proceedings*, 5686–5693. doi:10.21125/edulearn.2016.2359

Marouli, C., Misseyanni, A. Papadopoulou, P., & Lytras, M. (2016a). ICT in education for sustainability: Contributions and challenges. In *Proceedings of the International Conference The Future of Education, 6th edition*, pp. 189–193.

Marouli, C., Misseyanni, A., Papadopoulou, P., & Lytras, M. (2016b). Game based learning and gamification: Towards the development of a how-to-guide in STEM education, *ICERI2016 Proceedings*, pp. 5343–5352. doi:10.21125/iceri.2016.2299

Marouli, C., & Misseyanni, A. (2017). Sharing knowledge in higher education: Collaborative teaching, collaborative learning and ICTs, *Proceedings of the 12th International Conference, Open education towards a knowledge-based society*, DisCo 2017, Prague, Czech Republic.

Marouli, C. Misseyanni, A., Papadopoulou, P., & Lytras, M. (2017). Co-teaching in higher education: Teaching collaboration "by example" – lessons learnt from selected case studies, *EDULEARN17 Proceedings*, pp. 4817–4824. doi:10.21125/edulearn.2017.2069

Meyer, C., & Jones, T. B. (1993). *Promoting active learning: Strategies for the college classroom*. San Francisco: Jossey-Bass.

Mezirow, J. (1991). *Transformative dimensions of adult learning*. San Francisco: Jossey-Bass.

Mills, C. W. (1959). *The sociological imagination*. New York, NY: Oxford University Press.

Misseyanni, A., Daniela, L., Lytras, M., Papadopoulou, P., & Marouli, C. (2017a). Analyzing active learning strategies in Greece and Latvia: Lessons learned and the way ahead. *INTED2017 Proceedings*, pp. 10117–10124. doi:10.21125/inted.2017.0940

Misseyanni, A., & Gastardo, M. T. (2017). Active learning in the sciences: The case of an undergraduate environmental science class. *Academic Journal of Science, 07*(02), 207–216.

Misseyanni, A., Marouli, C., Papadopoulou, P., & Lytras, M. (2017b). Exploring Collaborative learning as an active learning approach in higher education. *EDULEARN17 Proceedings*, pp. 8041–8050. doi:10.21125/edulearn.2017.0479

Misseyanni, A., Marouli, C., Papadopoulou, P., Lytras, M., & Gastardo, M. T. (2016). Stories of active learning in STEM: Lessons for STEM education. In *Proceedings of the International Conference The Future of Education, 6th edition*, pp. 232–236.

Papadopoulou, P., Lytras, M., & Marouli, C. (2016). Capstone projects in STEM education: Novel teaching approaches, mentoring and knowledge management for empowering students, *EDULEARN16 Proceedings*, pp. 5675–5685. doi:10.21125/edulearn.2016.2358

Papadopoulou, P., Lytras, M., Misseyanni, A., & Marouli, C. (2017). Revisiting evaluation and assessment in STEM education: A multidimensional model of student active engagement, *EDULEARN17 Proceedings*, pp. 8025–8033. doi:10.21125/edulearn.2017.0477

Potter, G. (2010). Environmental education for the 21st century: Where do we go now? *The Journal of Environmental Education, 41*(1), 22–33.

Račinska, I., Barratt, L., & Marouli, C. (2015). *LIFE and land stewardship*. Report to the European Commission.

Shor, I. (1992). *Empowering education: Critical teaching for social change*. Chicago, IL: The University of Chicago Press.

Smith, K. A., Sheppard, S. D., Johnson, D. W., & Johnson, R. T. (2005). Pedagogies of engagement: Classroom-based practices. *Journal of Engineering Education, 94*, 87–101.

Tilbury, D. (2004). Environmental education for sustainability: A force for change in higher education. In: P. Blaze Corcoran & A. E. J. Wals (Eds.) *Higher education and the challenge of sustainability* (pp. 97–112). Dordrecht: Kluwer.

UNESCO (2005). *United Nations decade of education for sustainable development 2005–2014*. Retrieved from http://unesdoc.unesco.org/images/0013/001399/139937e.pdf

United Nations (1975). *The Belgrade Charter*. Retrieved from http://www.gdrc.org/uem/ee/belgrade.html

United Nations (1977). *Tbilisi declaration*. Retrieved from http://www.gdrc.org/uem/ee/tbilisi.html

United Nations World Commission on Environment and Development (1987). *Our Common future. United Nations*. Retrieved from http://www.un-documents.net/wced-ocf.htm

Vygotsky, L. S. (1978). *Mind in society*. Cambridge, MA: Harvard University Press.

Webster, K. (2013). A Practitioner's perspective – Missing the wood for the trees: Systemic defects and the future of education for sustainable development. *The Curriculum Journal, 23*(2), 295–315.

Index

Printed in the United States
By Bookmasters